VOID

Library of
Davidson College

Militant Professionalism

 SOCIOLOGY SERIES

John F. Cuber, *Editor*

Alfred C. Clarke, *Associate Editor*

The research reported herein was performed pursuant to a contract with the United States Office of Education, Department of Health, Education, and Welfare under the provisions of the Cooperative Research Program.

Ronald G. Corwin
The Ohio State University

Militant professionalism
a study of organizational conflict in high schools

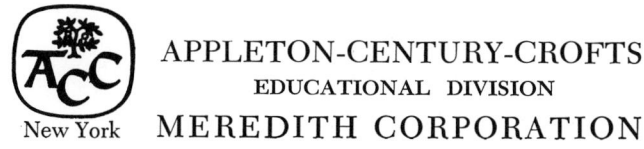

APPLETON-CENTURY-CROFTS
EDUCATIONAL DIVISION
MEREDITH CORPORATION

Copyright © 1970 by

MEREDITH CORPORATION

All rights reserved

This book, or parts thereof, must not be used or reproduced in any manner without written permission. For information address the publisher, Appleton-Century-Crofts, Educational Division, Meredith Corporation, 440 Park Avenue South, New York, N. Y. 10016. Reproduction in whole or in part is permitted for any purpose of the United States Government.

689-1

Library of Congress Card Number: 75-98400
PRINTED IN THE UNITED STATES OF AMERICA
390-21168-0

To

Blair, Cheryl, and Marcia

Preface

This is a revised version of two final reports funded by the United States Office of Education, Bureau of Research: *Staff Conflicts in the Public Schools, Phases I and II* (USOE Cooperative Research Projects No. 1934 and 5-2637). Some of the tabular material in the present version has been condensed from more detailed tables reported in the above sources, especially in 5-2637. Anyone who wishes to review the full reports may do so in microfiche at nominal cost, by writing to ERIC, Bureau of Research, U.S. Office of Education, 400 Maryland Avenue, S.W., Washington, D.C.

However, every effort has been made to keep to a minimum the omissions from the original reports insofar as it could be done without sacrificing readability. In order not to overburden the casual reader, while at the same time providing the information that is likely to be useful for a more technical reading, each chapter has been organized into distinct sections, as follows: an overview of the major findings; a presentation of the findings, including tabular materials; a statement of implications; and an extended technical notes section. The casual reader can survey the principal findings by reading Chapter 1 and the Overview of Findings and Implications sections of each chapter; he also may be interested in our speculations about some of the broader issues and practical implications considered in Chapter 10. The professional social science researcher, interested layman, and professional educator also may wish to read the presentation of findings and, in some cases, the Technical Notes sections.

This book, then, is designed to communicate with a wide range of audiences. It should be of interest to practicing teachers and to educational administrators. Since the study both draws upon, and feeds back into, a general organizational theory and framework, the study also should be of relevance to administrators in a large number of related settings, who face the dual problems of professional militancy and organizational complexity. The book also might be useful as a supplement for teachers' education programs—that is, as an example of an empirical study of educational settings and as a source of insight it may provide into the problems which teachers confront in different types of schools.

The first four chapters, which comprise Part I, outline the theoretical background and describe the methodological tools used in measuring and analyzing the data. The dual concern in this study with the theory of organizations and professionalization are reflected in the titles of Chapters 2 and 3. From time to time the reader may find it necessary to refer back to Chapter 4 to review the procedures used to measure concepts which are alluded to throughout the report.

Part II deals with the problems of teacher militancy from an individualistic point of view. Chapter 4 relates some anecdotes and personal comments abstracted from interviews with teachers and administrators, which should serve to introduce at least a flavor of the substance of both the typical and some of the more extreme cases of staff conflict. Chapter 6 deals more systematically with the social identities and other personal characteristics of the more militant professional teachers in the sample, as they compare with the rank-and-file teachers and their adversaries.

The burden of the report is contained in Part III, where evidence is presented concerning the organizational and professional factors related to various types of conflict. An empirical description of the school as an organization is provided in Chapter 7, based on a general profile of organizational patterns. Then, the various characteristics of organizations and of the professional role are examined in relation to conflict incidence, individually in Chapter 8 and collectively in Chapter 9. Although we lay no claim to having developed a "theory" of organizational conflict, efforts have been made to introduce and test sets of related hypotheses insofar as feasible; the hypotheses center around patterns of organization, professionalism and patterns of conflict, and their interrelations.

In the last chapters (Chapters 10 and 11), the data are used as stepping stones to more speculative horizons, encompassing the probable sources and likely consequences of teachers' militancy, and including guidelines to various alternative courses of action implied as well as the pitfalls of such action.

I am indebted to a number of persons whose cooperation and efforts on behalf of this project were instrumental for its successful completion. I am especially grateful to the U.S. Office of Education-Bureau of Research for making funds available for this research and for the considerate assistance and consultation provided by numerous members of that agency, especially the assistance of Dr. Glenn Boesigter and Dr. Alice Scates. Also, the assistance of Mr. Louis Higgs of The Ohio State University Research Foundation has been very helpful.

I deeply appreciate the valuable consultation of Professors John Cuber and Alfred Clarke, in their capacity as editors, colleagues, and friends. And I am especially grateful to Professor Russell R. Dynes, who had the patience to persevere through a painstaking reading of the manuscript as well as to provide invaluable administrative assistance at critical points of the research; his sagacious advice and his friendship over the past few years have been most valuable. Of course (since I have been unable to find other alternatives), the shortcomings of the research are entirely my own responsibility.

The research staff of this study is, of course, especially indebted to the more than 1,500 high school teachers and administrators who graciously participated in the study despite their busy schedules. Although they must remain anonymous, those of us on the project will long remem-

Preface

ber many of them for their confidence in us, and, in a few cases, for their thought-provoking criticisms. Hopefully, their cooperation in this and similar projects eventually will provide better information about the public schools.

The competent and conscientious efforts of several students and colleagues have been instrumental to the project's completion. Dr. Lewis Walker's assistance, in supervising the development of the instruments in the earlier phase, was invaluable for the successful completion of the present study. The patient and responsible fieldwork of Mr. Fredrick Brechler, Mrs. Sandra Sletto Swisher, and especially of Mr. Layton Thomas has contributed much to the progress and success of the project. The persistence of Mrs. Swisher and Mr. Thomas, in the laborious task of coding 900 interviews, is greatly appreciated; their diligence and firsthand knowledge of the schools involved has been extremely helpful. Mrs. Swisher's work on teaching professions and unions also provided an especially important contribution. Special thanks are due to Mr. Dennis Kitts, whose intimate friendship with the computers on campus made it all possible. Most of the programs used in the analysis were specifically designed for this project by Mr. Kitts.

For their assistance at an earlier stage of the project, I am also grateful to Dr. David Clark, Dr. Lewis E. Harris, President of the Ohio School Board Association, Dr. John Ramseyer, Dr. Gerald Smith, Dr. Willavene Wolf, and to The Ohio State University high school faculty and administration.

Finally, for their clerical, editorial and technical assistance, appreciation is gratefully extended to Mrs. Vicki Lankamer, Mrs. Judith Layman, and Miss Susan Israel. Special acknowledgment is due to Mrs. Anna Schwartz, who has so dutifully supervised the painstaking details of manuscript completion, and to Mrs. Joan Rosenfield for editing.

R. G. C.

Contents

Preface   vii

Part I. Background of the study

1. Teacher militancy in the United States: An overview   3
    Guides for the Study   6
       The individual versus the organization   6
       Professional versus employee principles of organization   7
       Professionalization as a militant process   8
       Identity of the militant teachers   9
       Issues   9
       Organization characteristics and conflict   10
       Causes of organization   12
    Implications   13
    References   15

2. Perspectives on organizations   17
    Overview: Organization Theory and Public Education   17
       Organization theory and education   17
       Schools of thought   19
    Toward a Model of Complex Organization   24
       A definition of complex organization   24
       Elements of a model   25
       Implications: The relationship of conflict to stability   28
    Implications   29
    Notes   33
    References   38

3. The professional-employee quandary   41
    Overview   42
    Professionalization as a Militant Process   43
       What is a profession?   43
       Profession as process   44
       The profession of teaching   44
       Militancy in teaching   46
       Professionalism in bureaucracies   48
    Previous Related Research in Education   49
       Role conceptions of teachers   52
       Role conflict among administrators   53
       Empirical approaches to overt conflict   54

Implications 55
Notes 57
References 61

4. Procedures 65
The People and the Places 65
The State of the Art 66
   Sampling the fieldwork problems 66
   Problems in the field 69
Measurement 73
A Typology of Measurement 74
   Personal orientations 75
   Demographic characteristics 81
   Relational measures 81
   Distributional measures 83
   Properties of the formal structure 85
Implications 88
Notes 90
References 101

Part II. The pugilistic pedagogues

5. Confrontations 105
Overview 105
Authority Problems 109
   Lack of authority 109
   Lack of administrative backing 117
   Conflict over students 120
   Participation in formulating school policy and control over the classroom 125
   Competence 131
   Supervision problems 134
   Red tape and rules 136
Scheduling and Distribution Problems 139
   Allocation of students 139
   Assignment of teacher's work 155
   Scheduling of facilities 158
   Competition for status 162
Personality Clashes 167
Lack of Conflict 168
Implications 169
Notes 171
References 171

6. Who are the belligerent professionals? 173
- Overview of the Findings 173
  - Rank-and-file militants 174
  - The leadership 176
  - The adversaries 178
  - Work satisfaction 178
- Characteristics of the Rank-and-File Belligerents 179
  - Professional orientation and behavior 179
  - Employee orientation and behavior 183
  - Role organization 183
  - Identities of the professional militants 184
- Work Satisfaction 186
- Identity of the Militant Professional Leaders 186
  - Social relations 187
  - Social backgrounds 189
  - Selected types of conflict 191
  - Comparison with officers of teacher organizations 192
- The Adversaries 195
  - Professional orientation 196
  - Client orientation 196
- Implications 196
- Notes 198
- References 200

Part III. Schools and their discontents

7. The organization of work 203
- Models of Bureaucracy 203
  - The reinforcement model 204
  - The independence model 205
  - The compensatory model 205
- Overview of Findings 206
  - Control mechanisms 208
  - Disruptive elements of organization 208
  - Controls compared to disruptive characteristics 209
- Standardization 211
  - Emphasis on rules 211
  - Standardization 213
- The Official and Informal Status Systems 214
  - Informal status 214
  - Centralization of power and authority 216
- Supervision 221
  - Teacher-administrator relations 221
  - Teacher-administrator ratio 221

Remote supervision	222
Close supervision	222
Evaluation	223
Professional and employee norms	223
Professionalism and bureaucratization	225
Specialization	227
Division of labor	228
Recruitment	231
Heterogeneity	231
Staff additions	231
Implications	232
Notes	235
References	240

8. The organizational roots of discord 243

Overview of the Findings	245
Official Position and Conflict	248
Departmental position	252
Structural Subdivisions and Linkages	256
Number of levels of authority	257
Organizational complexity	259
Specialization	261
Participation in the Authority System	262
Routine decision making	264
Centralization of policy decisions	264
Regulating Procedures	264
Standardization	265
Emphasis on rules	267
Close supervision	268
Reference Group Climates	268
Role consensus between principal and faculty	269
Facilitating Channels	269
Lunching patterns	270
Social occasions	270
Membership in employee associations	271
Vulnerability and Stability	272
Staff additions	274
Local and cosmopolitan principals	274
Longevity	276
Goals	276
Some Consequences	277
Job satisfaction and work satisfaction	277
Quality of product	278
Summary	278
Notes	280
References	285

9. Profession and bureaucracy in process — 289
- Concepts and Procedures — 291
  - Total bureaucratization — 291
  - Structural crystallization — 292
  - The bureaucratic pattern — 292
  - Professionalism — 292
- Assumptions and Hypotheses — 293
  - Corollaries — 294
- Overview of Findings — 295
- Analysis — 298
  - Professional orientation — 298
  - Professional behavior — 302
  - Employee orientation — 302
  - Employee behavior — 303
  - Comparison between the extremes — 303
  - Role organization — 305
  - Patterns of bureaucracy — 312
- Implications — 313
- Notes — 316
- References — 319

Part IV. Aftermath

10. The anatomy of militant professionalism — 323
- Institutional Developments — 323
  - National relevance of education — 323
  - Affluence — 324
  - Involvement in politics — 324
- Changes in School Systems — 324
  - The climate of innovation — 324
  - Teacher power — 325
  - Erosion of traditional modes of administration — 326
- Some Qualifications — 327
- Theoretical Perspectives — 332
- Conclusion — 336
- References — 338

11. Teacher militancy: Reflections — 339
- Characteristics of Militancy — 339
  - Is professionalization a militant process? — 339
  - How militant are teachers? — 341
  - Who are the militants? — 342
  - What are the issues? — 342
  - What motivates professional militancy? — 344
  - What is the effect of conflict on morale? — 345
  - Do schools have characteristic patterns of organization? — 345

Are organizational characteristics associated with conflict?	346
Do schools form characteristic organizational patterns?	348
Approaches to Minimizing Conflict	348
Recruitment	349
Informal structure	350
Structural change	350
Institutionalizing Conflict	354
Routinizing procedures	354
Coping mechanisms	355
Research and dissemination	356
Conclusions	357
References	359

Appendix   363

part I. Background of the study

FROM TALKS WITH TEACHERS on subordination

IT IS *very difficult when you have a group of people who are trying to be professional and trying to do a job, and who are not particularly prone to be "company people." If you try to be an individual at all, you are the first to have difficulty in this hierarchy that we have.—a teacher*

I THINK *that the faculty members in this community, as in many communities, are very passive. They have a tendency to respond to authoritarian leadership without much attempt to think through the problems, and they don't have the tendency to get into things and participate and take part in it.—a teacher*

SHE IS *particularly outspoken in the area of academic freedom . . . in a very lovely way. She has teachers' support. . . . She is not afraid to go all the way up to the superintendent, and she says it if she feels something should be said. She is a responsible speaker. An excellent teacher, liked by students, but very outspoken.—a teacher*

I WAS *not a "company man," and some of the things that come out of the office are just "one-two-three," and "you do it or else!" Consequently, being young and eager, I made the mistake of contradicting them [the administration] two or three times. Once would have been sufficient. I heard that once something happens, it is never forgotten. I found out this is true. My problem was that I was called in and he felt I wasn't coming to school on time. Well, I was three or four minutes late in the morning.—a counselor*

FOR THE *most part, there are females who are satisfied. In many cases it is a second income and generally the case with teaching, and they are indifferent to what is taking place. But among the males, there is the feeling that we should be more militant in the procedures and ethics used.—a teacher*

OLD TIMERS *around here each have their own way of operating. Some of the old timers think they can get their own way by two methods. One is asking for it. And, then, if they don't get it, they just go ahead and do it anyway because nobody knows what they are doing. This is one way of solving their problems. . . . If they aren't told they shouldn't do it, then it's all right.—a counselor*

1. Teacher militancy in the United States: An overview

Twenty years ago, it seemed easy to account for organizational conflict by blaming the problem behavior of individuals. But the simple formula, trouble is due to troublemakers, is unfortunately inadequate in the light of our present knowledge of the social process. Troublemakers, we now see, are usually troubled people, and their difficulties may be attributed in large part to the situation in which they live or work.—Sanford, 1964, p. 95.

April 11, 1962, was the day of the New York City teachers' strike. Some people thought it a "glorious day"; for many others it was a "tragedy." One New York City high school teacher wryly observed: 'If you win, you're right; if you lose, you're wrong" (Buder, 1962, p. 376). But regardless of the right and wrong of it, that day marked a turning point in the relationship between this country's teachers and the educational establishment. For with this walkout teachers dramatized their determination to lash out against the system which they held responsible for poor working conditions, obstacles to effective teaching, the feeling that they were being treated as cogs in a great impersonal machine. In short, they were striking to improve their status.

Of course the New York strike was not the nation's first. Between 1940 and 1962, there had been more than 100 work stoppages involving teachers. April 11, 1962, was a turning point. After that date strikes would occur with accelerating frequency, eventually affecting nearly every major city in the country. In 1966, there were thirty, nearly as many as during the preceding decade (Glass, 1967). National Education Association (NEA) affiliates, which had not been involved in a single work stoppage between 1952 and 1963, participated in one third of the 1966 stoppages; 80 percent of the year's teacher-strikers were NEA members. And in 1967, there were 42 strikes with the American Federation of Teachers (AFT) alone accounting for thirty.

In February, 1968, teacher militancy entered still another phase. For the first time an entire state was affected: half of Florida's public school teachers failed to report for work. The teachers essentially scored the equivalent of industry-wide bargaining with the state legislature. Significantly, this massive work stoppage was organized by a local affiliate of the traditionally less militant National Education Association. For the first time many people, including many NEA members, were beginning to realize the full implications of what it meant to be one of the largest professional organizations in the world. Indeed, Sam Lambert, NEA national secretary general, predicted that the Florida walkout might prove to be "granddaddy of them all."

It seems safe to conclude that the long-range implications of the teachers' demands go far beyond increased wages. Rarely, if ever, has salary been the exclusive concern. The Florida teachers, for example, refused to accept a state-proposed settlement that provided substantial salary increases but left conditions of education virtually untouched. Teachers seem to be demanding a massive reorganization of public education in the United States.

Pressure exerted by teachers for public school reorganization is being duplicated by militant civil rights groups in the big cities, most visibly in New York City, which demand more control over educational policy, including curriculum and staffing. The fact that teachers and civil rights groups are at loggerheads about how education should be reformed and who should do it is immaterial; what is important is that both groups have begun to focus on the system of organization itself.

These events represent an important change in perspective on the part of educators and the public. Until recently, the learner, and not the system, was the primary target of educational reform. As Fantini and Weinstein (1967) have noted, the emphasis was on giving the child concentrated doses of the same thing—more teachers, more guidance services, more trips. Within the last few years however, educators have begun to go beyond the individual child. This new approach was first reflected in proposals to improve the quality of teachers, which was found by the Coleman study (1966) to be one of the few school-controlled characteristics that affects the achievement of minority group children. Now educators are demanding that the system itself be reevaluated. And the system is the key, for unless it is changed, experimental ideas injected into it will continue to be rejected like foreign bodies.

It is significant that in its report (1968) to the mayor of New York, an advisory committee, which was headed by McGeorge Bundy of the Ford Foundation, proposed a basic reorganization of the city's massive public school system. The Bundy plan would divide the city's 900 schools, representing over a million students, into 30 to 60 autonomous districts, each run by an eleven-man board, six members elected by local parents and five appointed by the mayor. Teachers have reacted negatively to the plan; they consider it a basic threat to their professional authority. But the report's implications for the immediate status of teachers are less important than its very clear implications for the future of public education. It marks the demise of an efficiency-conscious generation of educators engrossed in grand-scale planning and signals the beginning of a total reassessment of how forms of organization affect the kind and quality of education. It demonstrates the willingness of the American public, for the first time on a concerted basis, to tackle the formidable school system that has evolved in the United States. It means that the organization of public schools is no longer immune to planned change.

It can be concluded, therefore, that the problems of teacher militancy and of school organization are integrally related to one another. Public school organization not only is worthy of detailed study in its own right, but also is relevant to the understanding of teacher militancy. And, given the saliency of organization, it would be indeed surprising if forms of organization, especially the changing roles of teachers, did not also play a prominent role in much of the conflict surrounding public education. A great deal of conflict is probably a product of particular modes of organization, and new and varied forms of organization, in turn, may emerge from conflict.

Of course, both militancy and school organization have taken shape in a broader social context. Two factors seem especially significant: the bureaucratization of society and the professionalization of work. While each of these developments, taken separately, is responsible for major advances in man's ability to control his social environment, they are not entirely compatible, and as concurrent forces they have created serious dilemmas which probably lie behind teacher militancy. Bureaucratization consists of a set of practices for controlling work and supervising employees. However, both professionalization and the complexity of modern organizations are at least partially incompatible with such control. Complexity creates alternatives which demand employees to use initiative and to exercise discretion in making decisions; and professionalization raises their aspirations for, and legitimates their right to, such discretion. Consequently, it can be expected that bureaucratization, professionalization, and organizational complexity are each associated with organizational conflict in general, and with teacher militancy in particular.

Militancy refers to group-based challenges to authority; it is an ideologically couched confrontation between groups. Militancy can take many forms, some minor and some major in scope. Oftentimes the minor, routine incidents have been overshadowed by the more visible and well-publicized large-scale conflicts. However, it would be a mistake to assume that these major incidents can be understood apart from the day-to-day disputes which are the primary ingredients of militancy. In other words, the turmoil in public education today has been distilled from thousands of inauspicious daily episodes of conflict which have taken place as a routine part of the public school scene across the country for many years and which have finally risen to the surface.

Therefore this study will be concerned with the day-to-day interpersonal problems of teachers and school administrators, not only because their disputes are important from a purely compassionate, humane standpoint, but also because the understanding of such conflicts will illuminate the broader issues—in particular, the character of professionalism, the principles on which schools are organized, and some of the tensions within the teaching profession.

The fieldwork was conducted between the years 1963 and 1965, which proved to be the dawn of the new day of teacher militancy. The subjects of the study are nearly 2,000 teachers and administrators in more than two dozen midwestern public high schools. In many ways, of course, these particular people, in these particular locations, are unique, but they probably have problems in common not only with other teachers but also with professional employees in a wide variety of occupational settings, such as factories, hospitals, commercial organizations, and universities.

In short, the study set out to empirically identify various forms which bureaucracy takes in public schools and to see whether these forms are relevant to routine conflicts. Friction incidents described in interviews and role conflicts evident from teachers' responses to the questionnaire were taken into consideration. Propositions were tested about how certain types of organizational conflict are related to bureaucratic characteristics, informal and formal status of organization's members, and a faculty's professional and employee role conceptions.

GUIDES FOR THE STUDY

The Individual Versus the Organization

Perhaps it is appropriate that this study should start with one of the perennial questions posed by philosophers and social scientists alike, and which in one way or another concerns the conflict between the individual and society. Hobbes stated the question bluntly in terms of individuals versus other individuals: "How is society possible in a state of war of all against all?" Since such frightful issues were first raised, social scientists have become sophisticated enough to realize that man is basically a group-centered creature and hardly in a constant state of warfare with his fellows. On the contrary, critics complain of an "organization man" with little independent will. With this prospect of conformity in view, contemporary scholars have posed the issue in a slightly different form—the individual versus the organization.

Social critics are aware of the apparent problems that the organization poses for the individual. Social scientists also are aware of the issue. Some maintain that there is a conflict between the needs of "mature" individuals for independence, variety, and challenge and the demands of organizations for dependent and submissive employees. Such statements of the problem pit the individual against the organization. There are, however, serious disadvantages in this way of formulating the problem. One stems from the component of "the individual" in the equation; it prompts analysts to explain what are essentially organizational problems in individualistic terms. This approach deflects the focus of attention from the central problem of organization to philosophical speculation on the nature of individuals, which is a residual problem from the standpoint of understanding organizational principles. Given this formulation, the person in trouble is defined either as hero or maladjusted personality, depending upon one's point of view. But personality merely seems to be significant, and only because a given way of organizing is taken for granted; for if a specific form of organization is assumed to be natural and legitimate, then nonconformity will, by definition, appear as personal "maladjustment."

There is a related tendency to take for granted the legitimacy of a presumed set of overriding organizational goals. Any behavior that does not conform to the organizational logic—that is, the logical means for fulfilling the organization's official objectives—is difficult to explain except in terms of "problems" and personal deviations. Consequently, all forms of behavior that do not "fit" the assumed logical structure are often grouped into a residual category—that is, a category consisting of elements that have little in common except the fact that they do not correspond to the logic. Whenever behavior cannot be explained in organizational terms, it is explained in such residual categories as accident, circumstance, personality, or, amorphous creature bred for the purpose, "informal organization."

To summarize, when the logic of organization is taken for granted, behavior unsuitable to the organization in question tends to be explained in individualistic rather than organizational terms. The problem is that organizational tension, despite its prevalence, cannot be incorporated into existing models of organization in other than a residual way.

Professional Versus Employee Principles of Organization

There is another alternative, however. Using a different line of reasoning, behavior that is deviant in one form of organization may be seen as conformity in another.

On the one hand, the bureaucratization of American society is one of the fundamental developments of this century, and that bureaucracy presently represents a dominant form of organization. A bureaucratic society is also an "employee" society. The employee status of teachers has been reinforced, first by a strong tradition of local, lay control over educators, and then by the subsequent control of complex school systems, which have required more administrative control to maintain coordination.

However, on the other hand, it is equally true that the social forces that have produced this bureaucratic society also have created alternative forms of organization, among which are professional principles which constitute a prominent but competing way of organizing an employee society. The growth of systematic knowledge in teaching and a firm sense of responsibility for students' welfare supports teachers' claims to an exclusive monopoly over certain aspects of teaching, which is the basis of a professional image that points teaching in quite another direction. In a professional-employee society the fundamental tension is not between the individual and the system but between parts of the system—between professional and bureaucratic principles of organization.

In teaching, the immediate issues concern the amount of autonomy teachers should have over selection of textbooks, methods, and curriculum development. But the underlying issues are not peculiar to teaching. One issue concerns the appropriate role of professional employees in complex organizations. A second involves the place of experts in a democracy. In a sense this conflict between expertise and democratic principles has already been waged by administrators of public organizations. In these struggles, on the one hand, the growth of knowledge has almost forced laymen to forego their right to make many technical decisions; but on the other hand, many people feel that ultimately only public control will safeguard public interests. Militant professionalism, then, is intended to compromise both the control that administrators have gained over public education and the control traditionally exercised by the lay public.

Despite the efforts of many occupations to professionalize, the characteristics of complex organizations do not uniformly support professional behavior. The professional person's self-conception as an individual capable of critical ability and capacity for original thought can be only superficially followed in any large-scale organization. Standardization of positions and superordination-subordination by rank are incongruent with the need for creative thinking and peer relations which prevails among professionals. The principle of delegating authority seems inconsistent, especially with the idea that professional authority is independent of the sanctions applied by a particular organization.

Professionalization as a Militant Process

Professionalization, then, is a drive for status. It represents the efforts of some members of a vocation to control and to monopolize their work. They will seek to wrest power from those groups that traditionally have controlled the vocation. Professional associations were, of course, originally formed in order to free vocations from lay control; and the efforts of teachers to professionalize are no exception. The process of professionalizing publicly supported vocations, then, is likely to be militant, representing a challenge to the traditional ideologies of control by laymen and their administrative representatives.

In addition to "boundary" disputes with laymen and public administrators, professions also are infected with internal struggles among segments or coalitions which compete among themselves: one, a small but active militant leadership group, spearheads the movement, while other coalitions constitute small groups of supporters and the opposition. Each segment then attempts to control the conditions of work in terms of its own definitions.

Identity of the Militant Teachers

The first, but not necessarily the most important, question, is: Who are the militant teachers? Are men more militant than women, as is often maintained? Are younger teachers more militant than middle-aged or older teachers? And how do the officers of the AFT compare with their counterparts in the NEA? These questions also stimulate speculation about the opposite side of the coin: Who is the "organization man" in public education? And what about the stereotype of the teacher as being passive and obedient to authority? Just how obedient and loyal are teachers?

These questions point to the broader issue of the teacher's authority in society today. The current militancy in teaching would indicate that they are not content with their present level of authority and that at least many teachers believe that they deserve to play a larger role in finding the answers to educational problems.

Perhaps, as already indicated, the key to these issues lies in the extent to which teachers define their roles professionally. But just how many teachers are professionally oriented, and are they in fact militant? Also, behind the façade of unification among militant teachers there undoubtedly is a great deal of turmoil among teachers themselves. How much do teachers dispute among themselves about their roles and about the appropriateness of professional orientation, and what is the composition of these coalitions?

Issues

These questions raise still other closely related questions. Which parties become involved in disputes? Over what issues? What form do the conflicts take? If professionally oriented teachers are militant, does this mean that they are involved with equal frequency in the most intense conflicts as well as the less intense ones, or are they selective about the types of conflicts in which they engage? And do the majority of conflicts in public schools in fact involve issues of authority between teachers and administrators; or are teachers more likely to dispute among themselves, perhaps about the students, discipline procedures, extracurricular activities, and so forth?

And what about the concern of teachers for students? Is there any reason to believe that the militant teachers are more concerned about the students' welfare than their less militant colleagues? Indeed, is there any evidence that conflict is detrimental either to the outcome for students or to the morale of the faculty?

Organizational Characteristics and Conflict

This line of questioning has very quickly gotten us away from questions about the characteristics of the people involved in conflict and into considerations about teachers' roles, their relationships in the system, and the content and form of the issues themselves. The direction of this line of thought can be explained by the assumption, as already asserted, that the problem of teacher militancy has had more to do with the structure of school systems than with the particular individuals who happen to be operating within that structure and cannot be explained entirely by personality differences. Consequently, it would be advisable to examine the system of public school organization itself in terms of more general principles upon which that system rests.

One of the first tasks is simply to describe this system. What patterns of organization are found in public schools and what difference do these patterns produce? For example, one might expect that the decision-making process would be different in a large, centralized system than in a smaller decentralized one. Do teachers have less decision-making authority in more bureaucratized schools, or do size, complexity, and scale give teachers more room to maneuver? Looking at the patterns of association among the components of organizations, one wonders whether standardization is associated with other bureaucratic characteristics such as centralization, close supervision, and specialization. Or does the pattern of control in a school depend upon other conditions, such as its size and complexity? For example, standardization and close supervision probably would not be used with equal frequency in both large and small schools. A related question concerns the patterns of organization most commonly associated with organizational tension. For example, perhaps schools that place a different amount of emphasis on rules or on centralization also have different patterns of conflict.

Social organization itself is built on a dilemma. On the one hand, principles of organization may help to reduce conflict by clarifying the structure and promoting regularity; but on the other hand, it is equally clear that organizations promote cleavages that otherwise provide reasons for conflict. One of the primary sources of tension is created by the need for coordination and the equally pressing need to have flexibility and to recognize the autonomy of groups within the organization. The critical task, then, is to identify the conditions that help this latent conflict to materialize. Perhaps the most complex organizations, those with the highest rates of staff turnover and those having a heterogeneous membership, are also the most conflict prone. But what role do organizational controls play in reducing conflict? Presumably, chain of command, centralized authority, standardized procedures, rules, and close supervision are all ways of clarifying the system and maintaining control so that conflict either will not have to occur or cannot occur. Yet, under some conditions, might not the same controls provoke conflict, or at least help to maintain existing levels of conflict?

In light of what already has been said about the conflicting requirements of bureaucratic and professional roles, it might be anticipated that any attempt to apply bureaucratic principles to more professionally oriented faculties would only serve to aggravate and provoke conflict rather than reduce it. Therefore, it would be important to determine whether professionally oriented teachers are disproportionately concentrated in certain types of schools where they might become an especially potent force. It would be equally important to know whether professionalization is making some inroads on public school bureaucratization—that is, whether bureaucratization is accommodating to professional requirements.

There are other equally fundamental questions about the role that school organization might play as a facilitator of conflict. For example, is there less conflict in schools where teachers have more decision-making authority? This question is part of a more fundamental issue in sociological theory concerning the effect that open and closed channels of participation in the decision-making process might have no conflict rates. It can be argued that if channels are closed, people will become frustrated, their discontent accumulating until it erupts into violent conflict. But on the other hand, it also can be argued that if people have the opportunity to participate in decisions, they will also have more opportunity to express whatever differences of opinion may exist among them, and hence conflict would occur more frequently than had they not had the opportunity to participate.

Related questions can be raised about the influence of close supervision on minimizing or provoking conflict. Closely supervising subordinates may simply provoke interpersonal tensions; but it is also possible that close contacts between administrators and employees provide a channel of contact that can help to minimize disruption.

There is also the related dimension involving the rate of informal interaction among faculty members, such as the frequency with which they associate over lunch. Close informal relationships may help create a congenial atmosphere which minimizes conflict, but it is also possible that such relationships act as a facilitating mechanism, simply providing more opportunity for the expression of interpersonal conflict. In each of these cases, answers may differ for the more professional and for the less professional faculties.

Causes of Organization

The answers to these questions will help provide some clues to even more fundamental questions about the basic nature of public school systems and the origin of bureaucratic organization. For example, in contrast to the picture of red tape and control so often evoked by the term "bureaucracy," it will become apparent in the course of the following pages that autonomy, tension, and conflict are at least as characteristic of modern bureaucratic organizations as rules and supervision. The paradox is that even as society becomes more highly organized, conflict appears to be increasing, or, as Wilbert Moore (1967, p. 222) has observed, as the indices of organization increase, so do the indices of disorganization. One way of explaining this anomaly is that organization itself represents a response to forces already existing in the environment that threaten to create disorder in the organization. In other words, organization evolves in reaction to conflict; the greater the external and internal threat to the organization, the more highly organized the system will become. Bureaucratization is the product of this race between disorganization and control. Particular patterns of organization as well as the total amount of organization might very well reflect the nature and extent of disorder within the organization's environment.

Bureaucratic controls might be visualized as a set of emergency measures, used only sparingly under normal conditions, with several forms of control evolving simultaneously only under extremely disruptive conditions.

These themes and the related possibilities which they suggest will guide the discussions in the following chapters. Of course, the data to be reported will not be conclusive by any means, but they will shed some light on the issues, and hopefully, therefore, will provide a better grasp not only of militancy and the organization of public schools, but ultimately of the relationship between bureaucratization and professionalization in modern society.

IMPLICATIONS

Behind the study about to be reported is the thesis that an emerging profession such as teaching must, by the very nature of professionalization, achieve more authority over the policies that govern its work. But school systems are bureaucracies designed to control and standardize work and otherwise constrain the authority of employees. Militancy is the expected outcome of this clash between what are essentially competing principles of organization integral to organizations themselves.

But this bureaucratic-professional role conflict which confronts professional employees is only one of many sources of organizational tension and must be understood within this broader context of conflict. Since social institutions in complex societies generally seem to be infected with conflicts, it is crucial today for people in all walks of life to attempt to understand the conflict process, for undoubtedly conflict shapes our personal lives and ultimately our national life. Indeed, conflict is so much a part of complex societies that it is safe to say that understanding conflict is essential for understanding social life. The problem of conflict touches upon one of the imposing riddles of life—the problem of the "social glue," that is, what holds organizations together? How do organizations function in the face of apathy, organized resistance to official objectives, internal friction, intrinsic competition, and, sometimes, radical cleavages within them?

Just as the study of disease and medicine has advanced knowledge about the healthy organism, much of both practical and theoretical importance can be learned about schools by examining their pathologies. For the normal functioning of a system is sometimes most discernible at those points that are experiencing the greatest tension.

Studies of conflict are providing challenging new evidence about the wisdom of traditional assumptions about the importance of consensus and harmony. Indeed, conflict may be considered to be as "normal" as stability. Many of what we like to call organization "problems" are problematic only because it is assumed that organizations should be stable and harmonious. The issues that people fight about also reveal the sore points of which people need to be aware; they reflect the inconsistencies that account for life's little dilemmas, and they dramatize what has been left undone in the way of organizing. Through conflict analysis we can learn that the method of allocating students to classes may be detrimental to their welfare, that the division of labor is ambiguous, that the organization is already in the process of reorganizing itself, or that the authority system does not function in practice as job descriptions and legal theories describe it. But above all, the study of conflict should help us all to understand a little better the social and organizational forces that bear upon our own actions.

REFERENCES: Chapter 1

Buder, Leonard. The teachers revolt. *Phi Delta Kappa,* June, 1962, **43**, 370–376.

Coleman, James, *et. al. Equality of educational opportunity.* Washington, D.C.: U.S. Government Printing Office, 1966.

Fantini, Mario, and Weinstein, Eugene. Taking advantage of the disadvantaged. *The Record,* November, 1967.

Glass, Ronald W. Work stoppages and teachers: History and prospect. *Monthly Labor Review,* August, 1967, 43–46.

Moore, Wilbert. *Order and change: Essays in comparative sociology.* New York: Wiley, 1967. P. 222.

Sanford, R. Nevitt. Individual conflict and organizational interaction. In Robert L. Kahn and Elise Boulding (Eds.), New York: Basic Books, 1964. P. 95.

FROM TALKS WITH TEACHERS *more on subordination*

THERE IS *a feeling that the interest of our former superintendent was not in education. He considered administrator-teacher relationships as employer-employee relationships. It was more than being impersonal; it was a tyrannical approach. He gave us the feeling that we weren't important at all. It was reported a couple of times that he was pleased with losing experienced teachers because it was cheaper to have inexperienced ones. He was in favor of education for as little money as possible. He bragged about this several times. We reportedly had one of the lowest costs per student in the state. . . . It was probably true, but we also had some of the poorest education.—a teacher*

I FEEL *that there are things which go on in the front office that can't be discussed with the faculty. You can't sit down and go over the entire case. I think it is a problem in administration today to know how to relate the goings-on in the front office to the faculty and the students; there is a lot of information they can't know about.—an assistant principal*

LAST YEAR, *one of our most chronic problems was the "checking-in" of the teachers before they reported to their class. The school had gotten so big that it was difficult to tell who was present and who wasn't. We don't like the idea of making teachers check in and ringing a time clock. We instituted a checking system for the purpose of determining as soon as possible whether anyone was absent so that if there was, we could get a substitute for them. After the teachers check in and the first bell rings, they are expected to go to their individual rooms for a 15-minute period before their classes begin. This is probably the worst period of the day, and therefore we expect teachers to be there. Of course, instead of being there, they would come into the office and check in and then remain for a social hour. I got on the public address system and instructed the teachers to please go where they belong. Of course, this was bad, but sometimes this is the only type of procedure that has any results, unless you get a club and just bat them over the head. . . . Well, the social studies teacher came to me and said: "Isn't there a code of ethics that a profession has to follow that would preclude an administrator from making an announcement of this type?" And I said to him: "Yes, there is, I admit I have violated it; but there is also a code of ethics that says that people with four years of college ought to have the sense to be where they belong without having to be told about it." We settled the thing amicably. He and I are on exceptionally good terms today.—an assistant principal*

IT WOULDN'T *be a very healthy situation if no one disagreed. I am glad we do have the type of administration that if you do have a disagreement, you are fairly free to say so within reason. I have always been perfectly free to go to any of the administrators, including Dr. ——— and gripe or complain if it is a reasonable complaint. . . . The attitude or general feeling is that when you have a disagreement about an educational matter, it is impersonal and can be handled in a fairly civilized way; you are free to go to an administrator and sit down and discuss it.—a teacher*

2. Perspectives on organizations

All the good advice, from ethics to economics, that wise men give their fellows is meant to change behavior and not explain it; but our business is with explanation.—Homans, 1961, p. 81.

OVERVIEW: ORGANIZATION THEORY AND PUBLIC EDUCATION

Nearly every day during at least ten months out of each year, Mr. Sears has climbed the two flights of stairs to his classroom in Central High where he has taught for the past four years. Before coming to Central, he taught in North High across the city, and before that in the city of Excelsior located in another part of the state. Now thirty-seven years old and married, in 1965 he was earning $7,000 per year; he believed that he should be earning more for his five years of formal education and eight years of teaching experience. But he is interested in his work, subscribes to several professional journals, and is active in the local teachers' association. This study is about Mr. Sears.

Organization Theory and Education

But more important, the study is about Mr. Sears' colleagues and about the kinds of schools in which they work. The impetus behind it grows from a newly formed convergence between the public's interest in education and the sociologist's renewed enthusiasm for his traditional appreciation of the vital role played by all types of complex organizations and occupations in modern society. Schools will be viewed as complex organizations, operating on their own organizational principles and apart from the psychological and cultural factors already known to influence the educational process. Traditionally, this branch of knowledge has not been an important source of perspectives on education because, as Floud and Halsey have complained, social scientists have customarily concerned themselves with either limited facets of teacher-student relations in the classroom or with broader historical and philosophical developments that have shaped education as a social institution.[1] The underlying structure of schools as social organizations, by comparison, has been largely taken for granted—treated either as a merely convenient means capable of serving any ends desired by educators, or as a stubborn fact of life to be accepted and worked around. Even most educational administrators, who as managers must confront organizational problems daily, seem to have been less concerned about the underlying organizational principles than about improving morale, school-community relations, computing basic-foundation formulas, planning for building schools, or improving efficiency.

But there is a growing awareness that organizational analysis, which has contributed to our understanding of businesses, hospitals, and other types of organizations, can be of similar use to education. The recent interdisciplinary interest in organizational theory, signified for example by the founding of the *Administrative Science Quarterly* in 1956, had its counterpart during the 1950s in the writings of Halpin, Griffiths, Campbell, and others. Within the past few years, the U.S. Office of Education has funded at least three research and development centers wholly or in large part concerned with schools as social organizations and the effects of organizational principles upon learning and teaching. With the first issue of the *Educational Administration Quarterly* in 1965, the study of educational organization became a fully assimilated part of the swelling interdisciplinary attack on the intellectual problems presented by complex organizations.

The timeliness of this refocus on traditional interests, the application of organizational theory to educational problems, and the embracement of this theoretical approach by scholars in education was fated in the far-reaching evolution that educational organizations have achieved in recent years. Educational organizations have become one of the most prominent parts of our organizational society.[2] They are in fact so much a part of the social fabric that it can be said that one cannot fully understand society without understanding them. The large-scale growth and recent innovations within educational organizations are of considerable sociological consequence, providing a natural setting for the study of such world-wide institutional, tension-producing situations as bureaucratization, professionalization, the formation of semiautonomous and interdependent groups, and subordination and domination of groups within large-scale systems.

What is unique about contemporary education is precisely the variety of organizational forms it has assumed in mass urban settings. And, as a consequence, the well-established ideologies and dogmas that served traditional education so well are being challenged by new alternatives now emerging. Traditional psychological approaches to education, which emphasize how individuals assimilate their culture, are not up to the task of explaining these complex and unstable situations. While the psychological approach assumes that what is problematic about learning is the ability of people to assimilate their culture, it is the social structure itself that has become problematic. Bureaucratic relationships alter and sometimes impede learning, and educational systems have assumed many additional burdens—of science, technology, and vocational training. The system itself, consequently, has become a determining factor in the way people learn. As Floud and Halsey (1958) have stated it, the problem of public education cannot be understood solely in terms of educational process—that is, what is done to people; they must be understood in terms of the wider context of the structure that shapes educational functions.

These developments have rendered public education more susceptible to the perspectives of organizational theory. While there is perhaps much that is unique about the objectives and processes of public high schools, their typical organizational forms and the variability among them so closely resemble those of churches and military, political, and other complex organizations that it seems likely that a broad-gauge theory, applicable to a variety of organizational types, can be applied to the analysis of schools as well. Hughes has said (1963): "While the purposes for which an organization is established may have some effect on its form and functioning, they do not make an organization so peculiar that it can be fruitfully compared only with others devoted to the same purpose and studied only by people devoted to that purpose."

On the hunch, then, that the system of organization is probably responsible for at least some of the problems now aborting certain educational objectives—this study examines how what are apparently technical methods of running public organizations can affect the lives of the people working in them. In particular, we shall inquire about how methods of organization can promote or suppress the human capacity of high school teachers to disagree among themselves, and how, in turn, teachers as total persons bring their human concerns and emotions to bear in defending both their professional roles and their personal interests from the constraints imposed by organization. Most important, the study will reveal the beginnings of uniform patterns among what apear to be discrete, personal, minor dramas that take place daily in the nation's schools. The uniformities in these conflicts can tell us something about the nature of complex social organization.

But organizational theory is still in its infancy. Indeed, there is not one theory, but a confusing variety of incomplete viewpoints based on different concepts and assumptions. So before proceeding, it will be necessary to review the state of the art and locate this study within its broader context.

Schools of Thought

Everyone has, at least unconsciously, collected some information about organizations and has evolved his own implicit way of looking at them. Organization theories are outgrowths of this "street knowledge." The body of knowledge has advanced beyond common sense, although there is not yet available a ready-made, tested model which can readily explain conflict. But the ingredients are there; the intellectual soil is rich with fragments of potent ideas from several streams of thought that now may be converging into a coherent model; with a little ingenuity they can be modified and assembled into a facsimile at least sufficient to serve as a reasonably adequate guide to a rudimentary theory of organizational conflict.

Functionalism

Modern organizational theory is of mixed lineage. There are at least four basic schools of thought. One, which Martindale (1966) calls positivistic organicism, baptized a conception of social organization as an organic whole, with each part dependent on every other one; a change in one element of the system alters its entirety, including the individual members in it. One must understand the social system in order to understand the people in it.

The most popular version of this perspective today is called functionalism. However, many functionalists, while accepting the premise that the system is the appropriate unit of analysis, also recognize that the total system can be understood only in terms of its component parts. Subunits of the system are to be considered products of the system of which they are a part. Functionalists analyze how segments of society are related to one another and try to understand how a system maintains a state of equilibrium through constant readjustments to social change. This organic conception of organization in terms of its mutually interdependent parts, however rudimentary and fragmentary in its present state, has become a permanent foundation of modern organization theory.

Recent developments in functional theory have wrought two special cases: equilibration and exchange models. The notion of balance among parts is central to both models. But in the case of equilibration, balance is achieved through the equalization of the similar parts; while in the exchange model, balance is symbiotic and based on often unequal transactions between dissimilar parts. In the equilibration model, tension arises when parts are inconsistent and is supposedly automatically reduced by a "strain for consistency" among the various parts; presumably, this strain is generated in the ambiguities created by inconsistent expectations. For example, a person in a position of great prestige but low income and little influence will seek to make income and power correspond with prestige; he will do so partly to clarify possible confusions about the amount of deference due to him and about the limits of his authority, and partly because his prestige, though favorable, will be in jeopardy so long as it is not reinforced by other positions (Lenski, 1954). At the organizational level, for similar reasons, there are parallel pressures to bring various organizational forms of control into line to mutually reinforce one another.

In the exchange model one element of the system serves as a substitute (that is, is exchanged for) another. Hence, some elements become accentuated in the process of compensating for the absence of other elements. In this model the system does not act to reduce tension; rather, the system itself is held together by various kinds of internal tensions and external pressures. For example, a person may accept a high income in lieu of lack of prestige or influence; we say that he is "bought off." Or, he may be willing to sacrifice prestige in order to gain influence exemplified in the case of a corrupt politician. At the organizational level a parallel example can be found in the substitution of rules and other remote controls in situations where every employee cannot be closely supervised by his employer.

Role theory

However, the functional model does not provide a convenient method for making fine discriminations among different relational forms, and, more important, it does not explain the seemingly voluntary efforts of the members of an organization to maintain regularity in their behavior, and their ability to do so without great confusion. It is clear that in addition to the behavioral structure there is a normative system prescribing how people in different positions ought to act. The norms are most clearly revealed in the mutual expectations of the members. Role theory has evolved as a means of identifying common expectations that people have concerning how people in an organization ought to conduct themselves.

Briefly, from this second perspective, a social position (such as that of "teacher") is viewed as a set of roles, each role defining how a person in the position should relate toward people in other relevant positions (such as parents or students). A role, in turn, is a set of standardized norms associated with related activities; a norm specifies the rights and obligations of persons in a relationship (for example, "don't spank children"). The role model, in other words, provides a way of analyzing the normative system in terms of expectations commonly attached to the different positions that make up the organizational structure.

While the concept "role" has social-psychological roots, its advantage is that both individual and group properties can be taken simultaneously into account. More important, members' role conceptions of their organizations can be divorced from their other personal values and analyzed separately as distinct properties of an organization.[3] A role, in other words, can be viewed as an organizational property to the extent it is understood to refer to commonly held expectations.

Formal theory

Formal theory provides a third perspective. From this perspective the essence of organization resides in the forms of social action, abstracted from the specific content, objectives, or personalities involved (Martindale, 1966). This school of thought, more than any other, brings into focus the importance of formal relations (structures) within the total system. It provides a set of concepts which can be applied universally and which place all organizations under a single rubric, despite the seemingly incomparable variety of distinct goals, values, histories, interests, and tasks separating them. Among the intellectual legacy of this school are the concepts of domination-subordination, division of labor, and clique structure and the theoretical importance of group size.

Conflict theory

Finally, there is still a fourth perspective, sometimes referred to as conflict theory, which supplements and cuts across all of these perspectives. Like functionalism, this approach focuses on the structural interdependence of society, and as a type of formal theory it concentrates particularly on the structural subdivisions. But conflict theory stresses the tension inherent in the very fact of differentiation within social structures. Conflicts arise between persons and groups located in different parts of the system because of their competing positions. Whereas functionalists treat conflict as a special case of equilibrium, in conflict theory harmony is a special case, an accommodation to social tensions.

It is Dahrendorf's (1958a) contention that the task of a distinctively sociological theory is to produce proof that conflict is based on certain structural arrangements and, hence, arises when these arrangements are present.[4] Sociological conflict is produced by differences between social positions; it arises between persons only insofar as they occupy or are products of certain positions. Theories premised on the assumption that conflict arises primarily because people do not fully understand one another or because people have hurt feelings or personal ambitions, and theories that ignore the impersonal issues on which much conflict is based, are inadequate for sociological purposes (Sheppard, 1954). Much more must be learned about the structural sources of conflict before the joint effects of personality factors and organizational problems can be examined with any sophistication.

Key concepts

These theories are woven from a few key concepts. The most important of them are rationality, value (normative) consensus, functional interdependence (either equilibration or exchange), and social power. Distinct combinations of these terms form three implicit models of society in terms of which the various theories can be classified. The first three terms are central to the rational, or the integration model of organization; the last two form the foundation of the coercion, or natural systems, model.[5] Dahrendorf (1959) proposes a model which, in direct contradiction to the integration model, uses the following premises: (1) every organization is at every point subject to the processes of ubiquitous change; (2) every organization displays at every point dissension and ubiquitous conflict; (3) every element in an organization renders a contribution to its disintegration and change; (4) every organization is based on the coercion of its members by others. Contrasting the integration and coercion models, he concludes (1959):[6]

It is evidently virtually impossible to think of society in terms of either model without positing its opposite number at the same time. There can be no conflict unless this conflict occurs within a context of meaning, i.e., some kind of coherent "system." No conflict is conceivable between French housewives and Chilean chess players, because these groups are not united by, or perhaps "integrated into," a common frame of reference. Analogously, the notion of integration makes little sense unless it presupposes the existence of different elements that integrated.

In looking at social organizations, not in terms of their integration and coherence but from the point of view of their structure of coercion and constraint, we regard them as [imperatively coordinated] associations rather than as social systems. Because social organizations are also associations, they generate conflicts of interest and become the birthplace of conflict groups.

Implications

The fundamental question about these models at this point is not whether the integration or the natural systems model is more "true to life," but which model raises the more significant questions.[7] In the conflict model organization is problematic. By calling for an investigation of the question "What causes organization?" this model challenges usual assumptions and for that reason, if for no other, promises to be more fruitful. The study of routine conflicts in organizations may help answer the question. The task of sociology, in particular, is to identify the specific structural arrangements that are produced by conflict, and that in turn, generate other conflicts.

Each perspective has contributed to our knowledge about social organizations.[8] But none of them provides a sufficient basis for a complete picture of modern organizations. The challenge is how to synthesize the most promising contributions of each perspective into a coherent framework without unduly compromising the utility of each perspective taken by itself. Martindale (1966) warns that "monstrosities are created by the patch-and-paste procedure of attempting to put together the acceptable [from some points of view] features of a variety of theories. . . ." But there is little choice: The potential inherent in any eventual synthesis cannot be easily dismissed.

TOWARD A MODEL OF COMPLEX ORGANIZATION

What is needed is a model that incorporates the principles of both stability and conflict; one that places priority on the interdependence of formal components of the system, but one in which conflict plays a central rather than a residual role. The model should take into account both formal structures and the way personal attributes are distributed among positions and organizations, and it should provide for individual and group initiative as well as compliance; finally, it should simultaneously take into account the social context and the values and norms endorsed by the system. In the following discussion a position will be taken toward some of the issues already explored. During the course of the discussion a working definition will be provided, key variables and an appropriate unit of analysis will be identified, some of the conditions conducive to conflict will be specified, and the issue of the relationship of change to stability in the system will be considered.

A Definition of Complex Organization

The term "complex organization" should be defined in such a way as to identify the components that are primarily responsible for both the stability of an organization and conflict within it. Accordingly, an organization can be defined as: *(1) stable patterns of interaction (2) among coalitions of groups having a collective identity (for example, a name and a location) and (3) pursuing interests and accomplishing given tasks, and (4) coordinated through a system of authority.*[9] Patterns of interaction are largely determined by the positions of the people involved. These patterns form an organization's power and authority structures, by which tasks are coordinated. As mentioned, a "position" consists of roles, or families of norms, maintained in part by common expectations and in part by sanctions imposed for conformity and deviation. The major responsibilities are allocated via these roles.

Probably the most crucial set of relationships are those in which one party exercises control over another. The control system, in turn, includes three components: the official status system, by which authority to issue commands is delegated through a hierarchy of positions; rules and procedures to provide guidelines for coordinating the organization's parts and regulating the conduct of its members; and a division of labor, partially produced by and supplementing the first two elements. The status system refers to hierarchies of power and authority. By comparison, the division of labor fixes responsibilities laterally among the distinct units or positions at the same level of authority. It establishes "who does what." (In the process, prestige and power also become identified with positions, often in a way somewhat different from that dictated solely by the status hierarchy.)

Subparts often develop a certain amount of autonomy and distinct and competing subgoals and activities. As a result, organizations must be viewed as configurations of their subparts rather than as coherent wholes. Supervision, rules, standard procedures, administrative staffs, and other elements of a coordination system are used as means of integrating the subdivisions; some coordination is also accomplished informally through personal contacts and bargains. The objectives of the organization as a whole are shaped by the bargains made among its members and between its members and outside groups (Cyert and March, 1959). Thus, organizations are continuously in process, simultaneously expanding through delegation and bargaining, and then contracting as authority is retracted by centralized controls, close supervision, and standardization. As a result, the component parts of an organization will not necessarily be consistently associated with one another.[10]

Elements of a Model

With this definition, and drawing upon some of the features of existing theories, we advocate a model constructed along the following lines.

Key variables

First, these four variables must certainly be taken into account: rationality, personal sentiments, power, and cultural values.[11] Of these, a conflict model must assign priority to power. Tension is likely when power is distributed differently among segments of the organization and when there are disparities between the systems of power and prestige. Overt conflict evolves from the efforts of groups to shift the balance of power in particular instances.

However, the occasions for using power and the way it is applied are determined largely (but not exclusively) by the moral system and, more specifically, by contradictions among alternative moral systems. Hence, morality also plays a prominent role in provoking and regulating conflict.[12] Role theory provides a means of objectively analyzing the moral dimension, since a role is a normative standard prescribing the way in which parties ought to conduct themselves as members of their positions.

Premises of a conflict model

Some of the premises at the foundation of this model can be stated explicitly as follows:

 1. *Group nature of conflict.* Conflict is an intergroup activity which has sources beyond the subjective attitudes of individual members. Conflict, like cooperation, is as likely to arise from a person's interest in solving organizational problems as it is out of his own selfishness or emotional instability. Just as a thousand loves between soldiers and enemy women is not equal to peace, says Barnard (1950), so a dozen disputes between American tourists and French cab drivers is not equivalent to a French-American conflict.[13]

 2. *Cultural relativism.* Historically, the "good" people have fought the "good." The good man is generally the supporter of his own group's values while the "bad" man is on the opposing side. Thus, neighbors who dispute their property lines can both be equally "good citizens." The problem is not to determine which side is "good," but what the fight is all about.[14]

 3. *Organization as a balance of power.* What has come to be generally acepted as the right way of doing things usually has had a long history of struggle for acceptance. Christianity, for example, was at one time the religion of a downcast minority. As it exists, an organization represents the outcome of historic power struggles and exists under the shadows of remaining animosities. Since the defeat of an idea or a group seldom implies complete annihilation, history leaves scars and cleavage. Smoldering beneath the present balance of power are undercurrents of animosity which can be easily rekindled. Therefore, complete understanding of this situation requires historical review.

 4. *Conflict requires cooperation.* Sociologists realized early that cooperation and conflict are not polar opposites. Rather, conflict between groups promotes cooperation within them. Groups need to cooperate in order to wage conflict. Even groups that are usually in competition may work together when their mutual interests are jeopardized by outsiders.

This alternating current of conflict and cooperation, as people shift identifications, contributes to the flux in organizational structures.

5. *Groups must be visible to wage conflict.* Conflicts cannot occur between groups that are otherwise unidentifiable by means of physical or symbolic identity. Conversely, as groups in conflict lose their identity, the conflict between them declines. Probably, most conflicts disappear without being resolved, as groups change identity. The ideology a group uses to justify its position is probably the highest expression of its identity. The ideology of local control over schools bolsters the resistance of laymen to the growing influence of the teaching professions and the federal government, while government and the professions justify themselves on the basis of protecting the standards of education.

6. *Conflict influences goals.* People disagree over organizational objectives. Tension contributes to the diversity of goals and unplanned compromises with the original goals. The operating goals are, consequently, forged out of the conflict process.

7. *The primary unit of analysis.* Given this conceptual framework, what is to be studied with it? The primary units of analysis should be the component parts of a system. Focusing on components perhaps makes it difficult to arrive at a picture of the whole (which is the advantage of holistic concepts such as *verstehen* and *gestalt* over analytical methods), but the way the elements are related to one another is what gives the whole its meaning (Tiryakian, 1965). Therefore, in practice most social scientists cannot for long avoid making refined analyses of the elements.[15]

8. *Structural arrangements influence conflict.* In particular, the structural elements of an organization should be given close attention. The way the organization has been formed—that is, its structural arrangement—will determine whether the conflict predicated in the above postulates will materialize. Some of the critical variables are:

(a) Specialization and functional interdependence promote tension. White (1961) found that the drive for autonomy was greatest in those areas where hostility among departments was greatest and the interrelation of tasks was highest.
(b) Centralization is equally decisive to the extent that separate echelons develop autonomy.
(c) Uncertainty is instrumental in conflict (March and Simon, 1958; Crozier, 1960; White, 1961). White found that every department is unable to tolerate certain kinds of uncertainty and is willing to trade less uncertainty in that aspect, for certainty in others. Crozier (1960) found that

each unit of an organization struggles to prevent rationalization and control of its own activities while attempting to further the certainty and control of other parts of the organization.

(d) Competing principles of organization, especially between bureaucratic-employee principles and professional principles, are responsible for contradictory norms being incorporated within the same organization, which can lead to conflict.

(e) Interorganizational relations are influenced by the internal autonomy of subparts, and the tension that develops among these subparts is in turn influenced by the organization's connection with other organizations in the environment.

(f) Limited and "free-floating" resources are the subject of competition and conflict to the extent that the allocation system has not been completely routinized and legitimatized (Eisenstadt, 1958).

(g) The system of interaction and participation facilitates or prevents conflict by establishing channels for the expression of existing conflict.

(h) Mobility patterns alter conflict by influencing the opportunity of malcontent subordinates to advance and hence to be siphoned off and coopted; organizations in which mobility is uniformly blocked will be tension ridden, especially if the expectations of subordinates are rising (March and Simon, 1958).

(i) The recruiting system determines the amount of turnover and disruption in the organization and is responsible for interruptions in the system. It accounts for heterogeneity of its latent culture, all of which influence the amount of tension.

Implications: The Relationship of Conflict to Stability

In studying an organization from this viewpoint, the competitive relations are as important as cooperative ones. Although organizations differ in the specific balance between cooperation and competition, whenever power is exercised in a free society, subcultures are likely to arise that oppose the source of power (Dahrendorf, 1958a). Opposition, in turn, helps to regulate and compromise the functions of the various parts. The way in which the total system functions, therefore, depends less upon the amount of cooperation among the parts than upon the amount of opposition among them.

Since the parts are linked by competition and the boundaries of their functions are defined by tension, the distribution of tension throughout an organization is as responsible for coordination and stability as it is for disruption. Reductions (or increases) of tension can bring about corresponding modifications in the way activities are performed, which in turn can create new tensions in other parts of the system. Recurrent outbreaks of minor conflicts, accordingly, can help to maintain the system as it exists when they develop in defense of established procedures; they also can be responsible for change when current procedure is successfully challenged.

Inconsistent principles of organization are responsible for much tension. Coalitions evolve around equally legitimate but conflicting principles, and, in that sense, conflict is produced by the organization itself and involves one aspect of the organization against another. It is in the daily round of routine friction that principles are defended and sometimes eventually defeated. When competing principles are supported by different segments of an organization, legitimate alternatives can be supported and one part of the organization can be prevented from overcoming the others. Thus, inconsistency among organizational principles predetermines the spheres in which conflict is likely to occur and some of the forms it is likely to take. The situation creates a system of checks and balances by which the separate parts of an organization can expand but are kept within bounds.[16]

IMPLICATIONS

Some people will naturally question the utility of taking a theoretical approach to educational problems, such as the one taken in this chapter and throughout the study. Some will point to the widely discussed findings of the Department of Defense's "Project Hindsight," which found that theoretical research over the past two decades, by comparison to more narrowly focused applied research, has made little discernible contribution to the development of certain military weapons. Understandably, teachers, administrators, congressmen, and funding agencies would like educational research to provide some practical information that could be of use in solving immediate problems. And social scientists are easily flattered by the public's faith in their research as a cure for social ills.

Nevertheless, it is our contention that the lure of practical findings should not be permitted to take precedence over longer range contributions the theoretical side can produce. Project Hindsight is not very convincing on this point; certainly, the full sweep of the effects of scientific theory on modern science could not be detected in a project that examined only a limited number of very recent inventions. Recent changes in the practices of public schools will support the opposite conclusion; for example, revisions in preschool programs and curriculum approaches can be attributed largely to theoretical research on early childhood education and cognitive structures.

Research must be viewed as a total system. It needs a foundation.

Just as banks must be stocked with capital before short-term loans can be made and interest paid, so there must be a fund of theoretical knowledge available to social scientists to draw upon in working with applied problems. There is another analogy, perhaps closer to home. Everyone in a school system is not in the classroom forty hours a week. Administrators are never in the classroom, and teachers take at least some time out for preparation. But presumably they make a contribution. Similarly, the fact that all scientists do not work on practical problems should not be taken to mean that nothing useful will come of their work. Of course, on the other side of the coin, all practical solutions certainly do not come from research either. The work of educational practitioners in designing the great cities' projects demonstrates that social scientists have no monopoly on creative approaches to educational problems.

The distinctive contribution of sociologists, qua sociologists, lies in whatever middle-range theories they are able to evolve to provide educators with some perspectives on the social contexts that consciously or unconsciously influence them and are sources of the anomalies that face them. Theory is, after all, merely a sophisticated form of common sense. It seeks to answer many of the same questions practitioners must answer for themselves. Therefore, theory can provide the practitioners with one of their most useful tools: perspective and insight into their own problems. In fact, the practitioner needs a good theory of organization more than the social scientists do, for by the very fact that he faces practical problems in organizations every day of his life, he is forced to make certain assumptions and to take some viewpoint toward organizations. If it is not a sophisticated viewpoint, with roots in empirical research and theory, it will be an incomplete and largely implicit one, not well thought out and devoid of either the power of systematic integration or the sense of "tentativeness" that comes from an awareness of alternative explanations. There is no other choice. One must pay close attention to theory if he is to avoid repeating traditional mistakes and find new perspectives through which he can improve schools.

If nothing else, approaching conflict through organizational theory should help to correct a common tendency to explain problems in schools in terms of the characteristics of particular individuals in them and instead focus attention on finding remedies in reorganization in the system itself. For a theory of organization need not, and perhaps cannot, be derived from an aggregation of the principles of individual behavior; on the contrary, the latter set of principles are assumed to be mediated by and to reflect principles of organization. Organizational properties are assumed to represent an independent form of social life having a uniquely characteristic dynamic and logic. An organization represents a single unit in the total population of organizations. This does not mean that individuals are unimportant or can be ignored. Organizational principles are reflected through the behavior of people; much tension between persons arises from inconsistent principles of organization; and personal conflict is as responsible for linking parts together as it is for disruption, because opposition helps to regulate and compromise the functions of the various parts and to keep them within bounds.

Whether it is fruitful to search for the causes of conflict depends upon whether peace is assumed to be the normal state of affairs. If conflict is assumed to be normal, then it is more important to ask, with Burns, "what causes peace, hence organization?" (Burns, 1953; 1958). Burns proposes that, far from being a natural element of organization, "routine" is a substitute for the more normal process of change. What is recognized as "social change" and "conflict" is actually the failure of routine substitutes. Structure may be viewed as a temporary curtailment of the more fluid, viable processes. What does account for the stability of organizations, and why does not tension normally completely disrupt them? One answer is that most members are unlikely to become directly involved in any single issue because the parts of the organization are segmented. The division of labor discourages people from uniting because they are likely to face different problems at any one moment. Another answer lies in the interdependence among the parts. Each part depends on the others for assistance, recognition, and its own power. For example, advanced algebra teachers depend upon teachers of elementary algebra, and coaches depend upon English teachers to excuse the boys from class for other events. In this sense, the organization is a bargain, a series of bargains really, between the parts. Sometimes it is a "live and let live" policy; sometimes it is, "You scratch my back and I'll scratch yours"; sometimes it is "Let's all pull together." Hence, despite their tensions, groups are kept within bounds by the mutual realization that the work and the status of each will be jeopardized if others are alienated. While some groups may wish to increase their bargaining position, once the bargains have been worked out, most members will find advantages in the existing system and would be threatened by sudden or extreme change.

Most conflict, then, does not seriously impair an organization. Certainly, the possibility that conflict may be discomforting to the individuals involved does not mean that it is necessarily detrimental to either the organization or to the over-all morale of its members; in fact, conflict provides one way of upholding valued principles and for that reason can be both useful and personally satisfying.

One's impression of the nature of organizations is likely to affect his attitudes toward his own responsibilities and his performance in the organization. For example, an administrator who subscribes to the integration model will probably evaluate his own success and failure by the standards implied in that model. He is likely to reward conformity and promote consensus with administrative policy. He will seek to maintain tight control over all facets of the system, becoming upset when employees intentionally deviate from established standards. One who accepts the natural systems model, on the other hand, will be more willing to live with conflict and inconsistency and to accept and encourage disputes and compromise; he probably will be more willing to take risks and to tolerate open disagreement and honest mistakes from subordinates; and he is likely to rely less on the official chain of command and to have more appreciation of informal strategies of working with people. Many problems are probably created by people themselves because they try to live up to an inappropriate model which is unreasonable in the existing situation.

In sum, it has been the thesis of this chapter that we should beware of reducing sociological problems of organization and structure to the problems of individual psychology; this does not mean that personal problems are unimportant, but that they should be seen within a broader context. And we should be prepared to challenge traditional assumptions, especially assumptions that conflict is abnormal and entirely disruptive, period; there is a growing awareness that it is as important to explain the absence of conflict as its presence. We said that before we can arrive at any conclusions we need a model of organization in which power and conflict between groups occupies a place that is at least as important as consensus; a model in which conflict is produced by the system itself and can provide a basis of cohesiveness as well as flexibility. One was proposed. Studies of schools can contribute to better formulation of such models and, in the process, increase our understanding of organizations of all types.

NOTES: Chapter 2

¹ The important role that organization plays in education was implicit in some of Dewey's writings, but his followers became more involved with implementing the practical facets of his theories than in tracing out the principles of organization about which Dewey had written.

² Public education is a forty-billion-dollar enterprise, one of the nation's largest and, according to some estimates, one of its most productive capital investments (Schultz, 1961). During one third of its waking hours, one fourth of the nation's population is involved in educational organizations in one capacity or another; schools are the first organizations outside of the home with which children have extensive contact. And concentration in education is as real as it is in industry: only 25 percent of the public schools educate about 80 percent of the public school children.

³ The idea that roles can be identified by asking people to state their beliefs about the conduct that is appropriate when dealing with other people does not alter the fact that these beliefs apply to anyone occupying the positions; they do not define unique situations for specific individuals, even though beliefs are held by individuals. A person can hardly avoid taking into account the known beliefs and pressures of others when stating his own beliefs about their roles. It should be emphasized, also, that roles pertain to a relationship between positions rather than to a single individual or position. The standards that people in an organization prescribe for a position, then, are objective facts to be reckoned with, even though they are based upon a system of beliefs.

⁴ Challenging the traditional assumption that stability and harmony are inherent in organizations, Dahrendorf asks: "If . . . Utopia . . . is a product of poetic imagination divorced from commonplaces of reality, how is it that so much of recent (empirical) theory has been based on exactly these assumptions . . . ?" (Dahrendorf, 1958, p. 118). Within recent years conflict has begun to receive more of the attention that it deserves, but it is still treated, as Coser (1956) charged, as "disruptive," having primarily "dissociating and dysfunctional consequences." Indeed, charges Wrong, the question originally posed by Hobbes—"How is society possible in a state of war of all against all?"—has been transformed by many modern scholars into its opposite, "How is it that selfishness and conflict exist at all?" (Wrong, 1961, p. 186). Much of the current interest in conflict, too, centers upon unique, large-scale events, such as war and strikes (Barnard, 1950), or on well-publicized incidents which reach the newspaper. Systematic, empirical study of conflict in the daily routine of organized life is still largely ignored. By contrast, conflict theorists have insisted that conflict is integral to social life itself, peace being little more than a change in the form of conflict (Weber, 1947). Simmel proposed that conflict is essential to both the structure and process of group life, and that groups require disharmony as well as consensus to function effectively: conflict creates groups, provides a bond between opposing groups, provides a safety valve which prevents complete disruption within social structures, and reestablishes unity (Simmel, 1955; Coser, 1956). Simmel attributed conflict to group characteristics rather than to personal hostility, which he believed was the product of conflict rather than its cause. Small, Park, Ross, and others also viewed conflict as a central and integrating process. More recently, Dalton (1959), among others, has suggested that it is inherent to leadership positions, and Coser (1957) has emphasized the role of conflict as a source of flexibility and creativity within organizations.

⁵ Gouldner (1959) calls it the "rational" model; Dahrendorf (1959) refers to it as the "integration" model. It is a compound of functionalism and role theory, with strong emphasis on the concept *rationality,* found in Weber's writing, and the con-

cepts *value consensus* and *functional interdependence* which characterize Parsons'. In this model social structure is seen to consist of a functionally integrated system of parts whose equilibrium is maintained by rational applications of authority (that is, legitimate and acceptable uses of power), norms, and recurrent patterns of interaction. The "natural systems model" (Gouldner, 1959) or the "coercion model," as it is called by Dahrendorf (1958a), is an amalgamation of some of the elements of role theory and functionalism, but, more importantly, formal theory and conflict theory. Social structure is seen as being differentiated into autonomous parts having competing objectives and held together by domination, mutual opposition, and constraint. The structure produces forces within itself that maintain both stability and conflict —stability because of the control one group exercises over another and the mutual dependence of the segments of the organization upon one another; conflict because the incumbents of positions have differing degrees of power and subscribe to different objectives as dictated by their positions.

6 There is also a "behavioristic model" which capitalizes on the personal meanings that arise from interpersonal relations. The actions of individuals take priority over the system and, as a result, values are viewed from the standpoint of the individuals who subscribe to them rather than from the standpoint of the culture. Social structure is a derivative of meanings implicit in interaction which is determined by personal attitudes and sentiments and value consensus between role partners.

7 Functionalism and behaviorism are idealistic. In the case of functionalism, abstract systems are treated as holistic entities, and in both theories values are assumed to be causative—cultural values presumably are prior to and responsible for integrating social systems. By contrast, both formalists and conflict theorists have argued that there is much more to modern society than is suggested in the notion of values and personal attitudes. Conflict theorists, in particular, maintain that the collective interests of groups are not equivalent to a collective of individual interest. Some have taken the extreme position that individuals are mere reflections of social categories.

More important, conflict theorists have faulted the inability of notions such as value consensus and system integration in functional theory to account adequately for the ferment of tension, conflict, compromise, and change within modern society; these processes are the products of power as much as values. They maintain that society and social organization itself represent the present compromises to past conflicts; that inherent within existing social arrangements are the seeds of future conflicts; that social organizations, even relatively stable ones, represent coalitions of groups having some basic conflicts of interest as well as common purposes; and that conflicting principles of organization, scarce resources, the distribution of power, authority and subordination, and social rank are keys to explaining organizational behavior.

8 Historically, the study of large-scale organization was almost synonymous with the study of "bureaucracy," a rational and integrated form of organization. Although Weber was not strictly a functionalist himself, his ideal bureaucratic type characterized the rational integration of bureaucratic components. For a long while after Weber social scientists treated the inconsistencies within organization only parenthetically; they primarily were concerned about the convergence between the way organizations actually function and the ideal characteristics of bureaucracy. Through repeated misemployment, the "ideal type" contributed to a number of misconceptions about organizations—that is, that large-scale organizations are monolithic, that they are rationally controlled through infallible rules and an informal authority system, and that organizations have a single purpose (Lane, Corwin, Monahan, 1967).

The notions of rational impersonal control in the integration model were well adapted to the purposes of industrial management, which concerns methods of impersonally controlling workers from the top. This approach left a permanent impression on educational administration through its emphasis on the mechanics of efficient school management—that is, record keeping, schoolhouse construction, and transportation and accounting procedures. Then, during the 1930s, a series of well-known experiments by Harvard sociologists in a Chicago factory turned social scientists' attention from the rational structure itself to the way employees conform to that structure. The behavioristic model is more appropriate than the functional one if one is interested in explaining the behavior of the workers. The emphasis on impersonal relations became the hallmark of the human relations approach, which in fact was a strategy for capturing workers' loyalties. Explanations of organizational problems understandably shifted to a search for characteristics of deviant individuals. The human relations approach to educational administration is apparent in the writings of Campbell and Gregg, Mason, Dressel and Bain, and Halpin, who concern themselves respectively with problems of morale, job satisfaction, and styles of leadership and supervision.

Many social scientists have become disenchanted with industrial management and human relations perspectives. For one reason, these approaches painfully neglected the problems of power. As Eisenstadt points out: "If one believes that a perfect equation between satisfaction and productivity can be achieved under permissive leadership, one does not have to study power; one has only to fight to accelerate its withering away." On the other hand: "If one believes that coordination, conformity to orders, and the will to produce can be brought about with only economic and financial incentives—i.e., if the world of human relations is ignored altogether—then power problems need not be taken seriously" (Eisenstadt, 1958, p. 149). So a third movement evolved which filled the vacuum by paying more respect to problems of power, bargaining, and deviance. Page (1946), among others, found bureaucracy's "other face"—that is, the personal relationships and deviance that exist beneath the façade of impersonal settings.

But the informal organization approach was merely a modification and extension of the rational model. Some social scientists believed it did not go far enough and eventually became so disillusioned with the entire model that they discarded it and substituted in its place the natural systems model. Currently, behavioral scientists are primarily concerned with the way organizations actually function. The "ideal type" has become the subject of criticism, and it is now unfashionable to conclude an investigation of large-scale organization without some reproach to Weber and proposing some refinement of his model. The emerging models do not draw upon the concept of bureaucracy in the traditional sense so much as the concept of complex organization, a term that connotes the diversity of form, irrationality, and power conflicts typical of large-scale social systems. In this model organizations are considered to be run by power in a context of power. Subordinates in these organizations can function as relatively free agents who not only submit to the power structure but also participate in that structure (Eisenstadt, 1958). There can be, Eisenstadt maintains, no purely rational bureaucratic organization free from the personal interests of power blocks, because all organizations need to manipulate their environments.

[9] This definition follows some of the suggestions by Bakke (1959). See also Cyert and March (1959). The basic model of bureaucracy was formulated by Max Weber. In his terms, bureaucracy refers to a certain kind of formal organization characterized by (a) an administrative hierarchy, (b) a specialized work force, (c) prescribed rules for organizational members (with responsibilities for different task areas), (d) impersonal relations between the organization's officials and with the organization's clients, (e) separation of control and ownership, and (f) recruitment and career advancement based on individual competence.

[10] In order to maintain itself and perform its tasks, an organization must necessarily perform certain functions: (a) coordinate its division of labor, (b) allocate its authority and power in a generally stable way and devise procedures for regulating conflicts, (c) replace its members and procure other resources, (d) regulate its output and direction by constant readjustments in policies, and (e) establish and maintain its boundaries against outside control. However, if organization must maintain these processes at some minimum level, that level presently is not precisely known. While one can maintain that if organizations do fail or lose effectiveness, it is probably be-

cause any one of several of these processes has not been sufficiently maintained, it is certain that most successful organizations do not function at the optimum level in all of these respects. In fact, it seems plausible that an overemphasis on any one process can be as detrimental as failure to perform at all, and that during certain periods a degree of conflict, ambiguity, scarcity of supply, and floundering are normal (Corwin, 1967). Perhaps, as suggested, the ineffective performance of some functions can be compensated for by emphasizing others. For example, abstract goals (such as citizenship training) and inconsistencies between an organization's practices and its stated goals can be made up for by an exceptionally clear authority structure or effective defenses against outsiders.

[11] Rationality and power are not necessarily contradictory, however. Rationality is the limited case where (a) there is complete consensus on the priority of objectives, (b) each central office and subunit has effective power and knowledge to achieve its commitments, and (c) there is extensive organizationalized planning, involving consideration of several alternatives over a period of time. Unless there is complete consensus, the amount of effective planning that can be done is inversely related to the power of the subunits. Extensive planning cannot be put into effect as long as subunits are autonomous enough to pursue their separate objectives. Unless the unlikely assumptions are made that consensus is completely probable and power is usually distributed in accordance with the authority system, rationality must be considered to be a limited case and highly improbable in large-scale systems. It is for this reason that focusing on power relationships promises to be a more fruitful approach to the study of organizations than analyzing the logic behind administrative decisions.

But power is not sufficient. The concepts of values and goals must be given some priority because men are bound by a moral tradition which regulates the amount and forms of coercion that are appropriate. When personal attitudes are viewed as personal reflections of cultural values, they deserve to have some priority in the model too.

[12] The role of morality in social behavior raises the free-will issue. Models of social behavior have tended to portray man either as a volitional individualist or as a passive receptor responding automatically to social pressures. From the first perspective, man has a moral sense of purpose and the free will to exercise choice, which makes him responsible for his actions. On the other hand, from the second, more mechanistic view, a person cannot be expected to resist the social pressures on him.

But such simple statements of the issue sidestep the complex structural arrangements between individuals and their groups. A person can choose between inconsistent but legitimate moral principles supported by different groups. Hence, a man can choose between some alternatives and still conform to certain other social pressures. Conformity to one set of principles permits, and indeed, often requires, deviation from other legitimate standards. Hence, individuals are simultaneously moral and immoral; they both conform and deviate at the same time. The problem is not exclusively a conflict between individualistic interests versus social standards; rather, the problem develops from inconsistency among existing standards themselves. Therefore, freedom of choice increases with the number of alternative moral systems available. From this point of view, the problem of first importance is not to identify the specific individuals who may or may not uphold certain moral values, but to ascertain the number of competing value systems and the degree of inconsistency among them.

[13] Parties in conflict may even display affection toward one another, as in the case of conflict between the sexes or age groups and the numerous wars fought by "peaceloving" people (Barnard, 1950). Barnard suggests that improving interpersonal relations by "getting people together" will not necessarily reduce conflict in cases where enemies have something to fight about, in which case getting them together may simply expose their basic differences. Coser (1965) points out that Marx, in fact, felt that self-interest is detrimental to collective interests and that combination always has

the double aim of putting an end to personal competition while enabling a group to compete as a whole. The level of cohesiveness and discipline within a group reflects upon the disputes going on between it and outsiders. As new conflicts occur, new forms of cooperation emerge.

14 I am indebted to the late Professor George Vold for part of this discussion.

15 Most methods of measurement involve subdividing a concept and somehow recombining the specific indicators. Organizations are no exception. Their character depends upon the balance between autonomy and the interdependence among their subdivisions, and the degree of consistency among the status, power, and value systems. One cannot describe a "school's" relationship to its community without taking into consideration the specific parties involved and their positions within the organization and community. It makes considerable difference whether a relationship involves influential superintendents of a powerful big city system or a kindergarten teacher, and whether the community member represents a political machine or an uninfluential minority group.

16 The widely quoted and picturesque phrase "dynamic equilibrium" does not in itself clarify how the dynamism is generated, nor how equilibrium is maintained in the face of dynamic pressures. The dynamic element arises internally from disproportionate power among autonomous groups subscribing to different moral standards and having different interests. (This discussion will ignore the outside pressures to change, which arise from differences in power between outside groups and groups within the organization.) As long as there is consensus that power differences are legitimate (or authorized), little pressure for change will be generated. However, three types of disruption can take place, depending upon the relationships between power, values, other rewards, and activities. First, a change in activity made necessary by structural change may alter the distributions of rewards in relation to power. For example, either unanticipated increases in enrollment or the inability of schools to replace teachers who leave may increase the teaching load. If their rewards remain at the previous level while they are assigned disproportionately more work, they will resent the change, but will be able only to resist passively (for example, by quitting) until they have increased their power. It seems unlikely that a major change in activity will not alter the distributions of rewards and that changes of reward in turn will lead to renewed efforts to adjust the balance of power.

Second, a change in activity may be logically required because of changing values. Changes in values can arise because an initial inconsistency becomes more prominent, or because new values are brought into the organization. For example, as newer, better trained teachers enter the profession, they may agitate for new teaching methods. Teachers whose status depends upon the existing procedures are likely to resist. In this case, the status difference between new and old teachers is no longer justified by the new value system, and older teachers continue to resist in terms of the older value system. The outcome again depends on their relative power.

Third, a change can occur in power distributions while the prestige and value systems remain similar. For example, a coach may obtain disproportionate influence in a school because of the backing of a newly formed booster club. Teachers may be reluctant to grant him more prestige despite his influence, and so mobilize their influence against him. It seems plausible that inconsistencies between power and rewards are major sources of conflicts among peers, while between subordinates and superiors the major conflicts arise from discrepancies between power and values.

REFERENCES: Chapter 2

Bakke, E. Wright. Concept of the social organization. In Mason Haire (Ed.), *Modern organization theory.* New York: Wiley, 1959. Pp. 16–75.
Barnard, Jessie. Where is the modern sociology of conflict? *American Journal of Sociology*, 1950, **56**, 11–16.
Burns, Tom. Friends, enemies and the polite friction. *American Sociological Review*, 1953, **18**, 654–662.
Burns, Tom. The forms of conduct. *American Journal of Sociology*, 1958, **64**, 137–151.
Corwin, Ronald G. The school as a complex organization. In Don Hansen and Joe Gerstl (Eds.), *Education and sociology: Essays with integrated readings.* New York: Wiley, in press.
Coser, Lewis A. *The functions of social conflict.* New York: Free Press, 1956.
Coser, Lewis A. Social conflict and the theory of social change. *The British Journal of Sociology*, September, 1957, **8**, 197–207.
Coser, Lewis A. Karl Marx and contemporary sociology. *Clearing house for sociological literature.* Washington, D.C.: Microcard Editions, Inc., 1965.
Crozier, Michel. Human relations at the management level in a bureaucratic system of organization. *Human Organization*, 1960, **19**, 51–64.
Cyert, R. M., and March, J. G. A behavioral theory of organizational objectives. In Mason Haire (Ed.), *Modern organizational theory. Op. cit.* Pp. 76–90.
Dahrendorf, Ralf. *Class and class conflict in industrial society.* Stanford, Cal.: Stanford University Press, 1959.
Dahrendorf, Ralf. Out of Utopia: Toward a reorientation of sociological analysis. *American Journal of Sociology*, September, 1958, 115–127.
Dalton, Melville. *Men who manage.* New York: Wiley, 1959.
Eisenstadt, E. Bureaucracy and bureaucratization: A trend report and bibliography. *Current Sociology*, 1958, **7**, 99–163.
Floud, Jean, and Halsey, A. H. The sociology of education. *Current Sociology*, 1958, **7**, 186.
Gouldner, Alvin W. Organizational tensions. In Robert K. Merton, Leonard Broom, and Leonard S. Cottrell, Jr. (Eds.), *Sociology Today.* New York: Basic Books, 1959. Pp. 400–428.
Homans, George. *Social behavior.* New York: Harcourt, Brace & World, 1961.
Hughes, Everett C. Is education a discipline? In John Walton and James Kuethe (Eds.), *The discipline of education.* Madison: University of Wisconsin Press, 1963. Pp. 154–155.
Lane, Willard, Corwin, Ronald G., and Monahan, William. *Foundations of educational administration: Behavioral contexts.* New York: Macmillan, 1967.
Lenski, Gerhard. Status crystallization: A non-vertical dimension of social status. *American Sociological Review*, 1954.
March, James, and Simon, Herbert. *Organizations.* New York: Wiley, 1958.

Martindale, Don. *Institutions, organizations, and mass society.* Boston: Houghton Mifflin, 1966.

Page, Charles Hunt. Bureaucracy's other face. *Social Forces,* October, 1946, **25**, 88–94.

Schultz, Theodore W. Education and economic growth. In Nelson B. Henry (Ed.), *Social forces influencing American education.* Sixtieth Yearbook of the National Society for the Study of Education. Chicago: The University of Chicago Press, 1961. Pp. 46–48.

Sheppard, Harold L. Approaches to conflict in American industrial sociology. *British Journal of Sociology,* 1954, **5**, 423–434.

Simmel, George. *Conflict and the web of group-affiliations.* (Trans. by Kurt H. Wolff and Reinhard Bendix.) New York: Free Press, 1955.

Tiryakian, Edward A. Existential phenomenology and the sociological tradition. *American Sociological Review,* October, 1965, **30**, 674–688.

Weber, Max. *The theory of social and economic organization.* (Trans. by A. M. Henderson and Talcott Parsons.) Fair Lawn, N.J.: Oxford University Press, 1947.

White, Harrison. Management conflict and sociometric structure. *American Journal of Sociology,* September, 1961, **67**, 185–199.

Wrong, Dennis H. "The over-socialized conception of man." *American Sociological Review,* April, 1961, **26**, 183–193.

FROM TALKS WITH TEACHERS on *everyday irritations*

I FOUND *out by going into the teachers' room that they were nice people, but they were people who hadn't anything good to say about anyone else. I found myself getting so burdened down and upset over what everyone was saying that I made up my mind that I was going to stop eating lunch because all they did was gossip. The superintendent told me: "I want to give you a bit of advice to remember as long as you teach. Keep out of the teachers' room and don't hear anything."—a teacher*

IT IS *a kind of pettiness that exists here. One librarian will put a bulletin on the board, and the other two will take it down. I think basically that the difficulty is that one teacher would like to be head librarian; and the administration will not appoint a head librarian.—a teacher*

I THINK *everyone complains [about the Junior-Senior Prom]. I think it has been pretty much the case every year. Most people do not like the idea that the students who are preparing for it are given a day or two of school time before and after the dance in order to put it on. They are automatically excused from school in order to get ready and clean it up after it is over. I've noticed that there is always a lot of discussion among ourselves about the fact that they should not be allowed to do this.—a teacher*

THE PROBLEM *is, when they [the students] came up from junior high, they have had several different teachers, and then everybody is in a different place. You have a problem putting them all together. It's hard to teach. Either they haven't had it, or they have forgotten it.—a teacher*

3. The professional-employee quandary

> As work becomes professionalized—specialized around esoteric knowledge and technique—the organization of work must create room for expert judgment, and autonomy of decision-making and practice becomes a hallmark of the advanced profession.—Clark, 1966, p. 286.

Contemporary novels portray bureaucracy as a cruel, dehumanizing and overbearing system, limiting the individual's autonomy and compromising his integrity (Friedsam, 1954). In the romantic solution the hero may rebel, but it is the threat that man will succumb, will become an "organization man" or a "bureaucratic personality," that has alarmed the public.

Similarly, in the humorous best-seller *Up the Down Staircase*, Bel Kaufman sympathetically portrays the anguish of teacher Sylvia Barrett as she valiantly muddles through the bureaucratic hurdles of the New York City school system in a vain effort to reach a few of her students. She is surrounded by inept colleagues—the "Desk Despots, Blackboard Barons, Classroom Caesars, and Lords of the Looseleaf"; and she is overwhelmed by seating plans, attendance sheets, requisitions, and the library blacklist. Hers is a universe of time-clocks and mandatory meetings, purportedly called for superficial discussions of democracy amidst a sea of tyranny; it is a world run by the J. J. McHabe's and the Sadie Finches—the administrators and clerks—who at every turn spew out new memos bearing old directives: "Teachers who line up in front of the time-clocks waiting to punch out in the afternoon create a crowded condition in the doorway" (Kaufman, 1966, p. 198). There is undoubtedly some truth behind this image of teachers, these puny beings waiting huddled before the door, this pettiness and this despotism. Yet, this is only part of the picture.

There is little resemblance between this spector of oppression and monolithic organization, and the loosely integrated, tension-ridden systems portrayed in the preceding chapter. We need only recall that teachers' strikes have taken place almost annually for the past six years in the same system which Kaufman is describing. During an impending teachers' strike in New York City in 1964, *The New York Times* reported (1964):

A resurgence of militancy among the nation's public school teachers marked the year of 1963. There was mounting evidence that teachers are no longer content to rule only the classroom to which they are assigned. They want a hand in the assignment and a voice in the policy that controls their professional lives. They are not asking to run the schools, but they want their view heard and heeded.

The irony is, then, that though traditionally not noted for their militancy, teachers, under our very noses, are making a substantial dent in the chain of command. And they appear to be most successful in precisely the most bureaucratic places. Perhaps bureaucracy provides alternatives which expand the range of choice open to teachers.

OVERVIEW

One set of alternatives inherent to modern organizations are provided by the professional roles and employee roles that define the teacher's job. These alternatives, however, are not entirely compatible. For there is a fundamental contradiction between the subordinate status of teachers in the system and their rights and obligations as professional persons responsible for improving the quality of education. Their professional responsibilities require a great deal of latitude for coping with the students' problems and room to exercise discretion and initiative in interpreting and altering school policy. The professional person is primarily responsible to his colleagues, who evaluate him and determine the standards for his conduct. And his professional reputation depends upon his special knowledge which must be constantly demonstrated, no matter what other official recognition he may have achieved.

These principles are inconsistent with the fact that teachers are hired and evaluated by administrators to do a specific job; they also are inconsistent with many of the standardized requirements, a centralized decision-making system, close supervision, and task-oriented rules under which schools operate.

The teacher, therefore, inherits with the job inconsistent expectations about his proper role in education. The fact that he is an employee establishes one set of obligations; the fact that he is a professional employee compounds the situation by establishing competing expectations and standards. If he attempts to straddle both roles simultaneously, he can expect to experience some turbulence during his career.

What is involved here, then, is not an entirely personal reaction, nor even a question of individual needs opposed to those of the organization. But rather, what is in conflict is one against another aspect of an organization. Kornhauser states the problem well (1962, p. 8):

The problems posed by the interaction between professions and work establishments are to be viewed from the standpoint of relations between two *institutions*, not merely between organizations and individuals. The situation of professional employees is misconstrued if they are viewed only as isolated individuals pitted against the crushing force of a powerful bureaucracy.

Incompatibilities between bureaucratic and professional principles produce tensions which trap particular individuals and which become the source of conflict between people who disagree on the priority of the two types of roles. In particular, some teachers and most administrators are likely to place more emphasis on the subordinate employee roles, whereas at least some other teachers will probably wish to emphasize their professional rights and responsibilities. Hence, the incompatibilities between these roles are likely to produce conflict between teachers and administrators and among groups of teachers who place different priorities on the different expectations associated with each role. Professionalization reflects a change in priorities and a shift in the balance of power. In the sense that professionalization sharpens the conflict between advocates of professional and employee roles, it is a militant process.

PROFESSIONALIZATION AS A MILITANT PROCESS

What Is a Profession?

There are many definitions of the term "profession." Generally speaking, a mature profession is an organized work group that has a legal monopoly to establish procedures for recruiting and policing members and for maximizing control over a body of theoretical knowledge and applying it to the solution of social problems. Greenwood (1957) points out that although some nonprofessionals are more "skilled" than professionals, the latter are distinguished by the fact that their skill is based upon theoretical knowledge and research. The "clients" of professionals can be distinguished from mere "customers" by the fact that they must rely upon the professionals' judgment about their needs. Professions have more legal control over their membership than other occupations, too, through accrediting and licensing procedures and a code of ethics enforceable by law; the code renounces members' self-interest and affirms their intention to serve people in need, while at the same time protecting members of the profession from extreme competition among themselves. This whole system is sustained by a distinct culture and by networks of formal organizations, training and research centers, and communication channels.

Kornhauser (1962) identifies four criteria of a profession: specialized competence having an intellectual component; extensive autonomy in exercising this special competence; strong commitment to a career based on a special competence; and influence and responsibility in the use of special competence. Goode (1961) reduces the term even further to two dimensions: (1) training in a body of abstract knowledge which is prolonged and specialized enough that a monopoly can be obtained, and (2) a collectivity with a service orientation.

Profession as Process

These definitions, however, are limited to the structure of mature professions and neglect the dynamics of transitions in occupational status. A vocation's drive to professionalize is as revealing of its character as its actual accomplishments. Commenting on the problems of identifying professions, Hughes has said in an earlier study of real estate agents (1958):

I started this study with the idea of finding out an answer to this familiar question, "Are these men professionals?". It is a false question, for the concept of "professional" in all societies is not so much a descriptive term as one of value and prestige. . . . The movement to "professionalize" an occupation is thus collective mobility of some, among the people in an occupation. One aim of the movement is to rid the occupation of people who are not mobile enough to go along with the changes.

Typically, only a small minority of an occupation spearheads the movement, but the presence of a few determined leaders who are not reluctant to confront administrators and laymen has changed the complexion of entire vocations (Bucher and Strauss, 1961). Professional status is seldom easily won, however; the laymen and authorities in control are not likely to relinquish their hold without provocation, criticism, defiance, and even legal action on the part of aspiring occupational groups. Professionalization, in this sense, is frequently a militant process.[1]

The Profession of Teaching

This thrust of the skilled occupations toward professionalization, with its attendant militancy and status anxiety, is reflected in the occupation of teaching. Like many occupations of its kind trying to make an uneasy transition between past and future, teaching has developed a "split personality" as it attempts to accommodate simultaneously to the demands of bureaucratization and professionalization.

Bureaucratization

Dimmock (1965) defines bureaucracy as a way of life in which institutions overshadow individuals. From the tradition of local control over education has emerged an image of the teacher as a "public servant" of the community, and more specifically a salaried employee of the school board and administration which control his advancement. This image continues to be reinforced by a "community school" ideology which posits schools as service centers for local taxpayers, by some advocates in colleges of education anxious to train people whom school boards will hire, and by standardized controls of large-scale, complex educational bureaucracies.

Many of the educational issues of the day—such as educational television, the growth of required courses, and large-size classes—concern the presumed effects of standardization and centralization on education. The specific issues surrounding standardization include the importance of course guides, the appropriateness of required courses, the proper number and specificity of rules, and job descriptions governing classroom routines and teachers' authority within the school. There are salient pressures to justify standardization, the ideologies of individual attention notwithstanding: a high student mobility, teacher turnover rates, and a promotion system which requires uniformity in order to articulate grade levels. Conant's (1961) proposal to require a standard curriculum compulsory for all "talented youth" reflects the times.

Bureaucracy was once a revolutionary social institution. Standardization increased with urbanization, partly because impersonal rules provided some protection against the patronage aspects of corrupt city governments. Centralization often has accompanied recent increases in both the scope and size of the system. The increasing scope of government raises a number of questions. What is the proper authority and influence of state departments of education? How do state and federal legislation affect the curriculum and school policies? And which governmental level is ultimately responsible for educational leadership? Besides the population growth, the Cold War and resulting public pressures to raise educational standards have given further impetus to these centralizing tendencies. The vastness of the educational system has also created considerable concentration. Currently, 20 percent of the school systems educate 80 percent of the children. The number of the smallest school districts decreased by one half between 1947 and 1959, and despite the many small schools that persist, the trend is toward mass centers, metropolitan-wide school districts, and educational parks as the population explosion concentrates in metropolitan areas.

With growth, the problems of internal control increase and are "solved" by more standardization of work, centralization of the major decisions, and the proliferation of regulations over work. As a result, administrators need more education and technical skill to manage the operation, but the educational gap between administrators and teachers, officially at the lower echelons, appears to be closing.

Professionalization

Thus, the traditional viewpoint is being challenged by the progressively vocal claims of teachers that they have special competence and hence deserve more control over their own work. This professional image propels teaching in quite another direction. Behind it is this same "drive for status" that characterizes other emerging professions. School systems are beginning to adapt to some of these demands; it is the belief of some that modern teaching technologies—such as computer-assisted instruction, teaching machines and team teaching—will permit more flexibility in the curriculum and encourage more decisions to be made at the classroom level. However, teachers as a group are ambivalent as to how far they should go in attempting to increase their authority. They resent "outside" influence from laymen and administrative controls, but they feel some obligation to their communities and to their administrators.

The ideological conflict can be expected to grow as school systems become more bureaucratized, as pressures for more efficient decision making increase, and as the gap between pedagogical and lay wisdom increases. Solomon's protest illustrates some of the general problems that have developed. His encouragement to teachers in 1961 to defy bureaucratization anticipates a movement that has increased in momentum since that time (B. Solomon, 1961):

> Perhaps the most crucial fact to be reckoned with in public education organization is the contradiction between the teacher's role as a subordinate employee and his role as a professional person. . . . [p. 289].
> . . . Teacher organizations must focus on developing unified groups in local schools . . . [pp. 295–296].

Militancy in Teaching

Under provocation from the problems such as those Solomon describes, the center of gravity between the bureaucratic and professional components of teaching has been shifting. The grim picture of laconic teachers subordinated to inept administrators, painted by Solomon in 1961 and by Kaufman in 1966, is out of focus. Teacher organizations have shown renewed signs of life—so much so that an educational writer for the *American School Board Journal* could warn in 1963:

> The great challenge to public education as we know it today is not in the curricular areas; it is not the increasing demands for the tax dollar; it is not frills in building or the nature of professional courses for teachers. Rather, the challenge is in the rapidly developing conflict between the National Education Association and the American Federation of Teachers [Jordan, 1963, p. 38].

Through their organizations today's teachers are increasingly active in such matters as civil rights, academic freedom, manpower needs, and international affairs. They have become vitally concerned about their rights and responsibilities in the development of the policies and regulations that affect their work conditions (Steffensen, 1964).

During the 1966–67 school year the AFT alone sponsored 22 strikes across the country, and in September, 1967, teacher militancy reached a new high; teachers stayed out in 36 communities in Michigan alone. Teacher-initiated strikes, boycotts, or walkouts in the past few years in New York City, Gary, St. Louis, Indianapolis, and Louisville are only the more visible signs of collective action. Several of these episodes achieved special prominence—for example, the one-day strike by the teachers of New York City during the summer of 1962, the 2½-week strike there in 1967, a two-day walkout by the teachers of the state of Utah in the spring of 1964, and major strikes in the Detroit area. That militancy has been increasing is implicit in the fact that between 1960 and 1966 there were 36 strikes; nearly half of them occurred in 1966. These are the more dramatic events, the ones that reach the news headlines, but they are not the only forms of militancy. It is safe to assume that more subtle, less dramatic, but persistent tensions exist in the day-to-day routine of many systems.

The apparently widespread idea that defiance is stirred up entirely, or even primarily, by unions is not accurate. Twelve of the 36 strikes between 1960 and 1966 were called by affiliates of the NEA. The NEA Affiliated Overseas Education, for example, exerted a great deal of pressure on the United States government to prove the alleged unsatisfactory conditions in the operation of overseas school systems. Indeed, although the NEA precludes the use of strikes by teachers, it has used an almost identical practice, the "sanction"; the Utah and Tulsa walkouts were backed by the NEA, and the local NEA affiliate collaborated with the AFT local in the Jersey City walkout.

Nor is it accurate to assume that teachers' unions are concerned exclusively with bread-and-butter salary and fringe-benefit issues. Unions have bargained over the amount of community support of schools, class size, standards of employment of professional personnel, and other personnel policies, including transfer policies, in-service training, teacher turnover, educational programs, and curriculum development. Regarding the union in New York City, the New York City superintendent of schools was quoted in connection with a potential teacher strike in September, 1963, as follows:

I'm convinced that the teachers don't want to strike anymore than I or anyone else in the city does. Money is only part of what the teachers want. Frankly, I think that what the United Federation of Teachers wants basically is more control of the school system. I mean that they would like to be able to have more say in every school and in every phase of the administration of the school system, a little more say-so in what goes on [Superintendent of Schools of New York City, quoted in *The New York Times,* July 7, 1963, p. 39].

Both professional associations and unions are insisting upon the right of teachers to participate with boards of education in determining the policies of common concern, including salary and other conditions of professional service. According to one source, New York teachers' contracts soon will specify how and when a principal or supervisor may talk with the teacher about classroom activities, and principals will not be permitted to observe or rate tenured teachers (Ball, 1966, p. 10). So, the issue is who should control and at stake is the power structure of American education. But the lay boards of control have shown few signs of concession thus far. A resolution was adopted by the National School Boards Association in Philadelphia in May, 1961, stating:

The National School Boards Association believes that . . . it would be an abdication of their decision-making responsibility for school boards to enter into compromise agreements based on negotiation or collective bargaining, or to resort to mediation or arbitration, or to yield to threats of reprisal; and that concern for the public welfare requires that school boards resist by all lawful means the enactment of laws which would compel them to surrender any part of this responsibility.

American school administrators have not been much more tolerant:

We believe that the right to discuss pros and cons and to participate in developing a program does not imply the right to make decisions. Although consensus should always be patiently sought and will often prevail between staff and school board, the board must retain its responsibility and legal right to make decisions [American Association of School Administrators, 1963, p. 13].

Yet, both the immediate and the long-range prospects are prophesied in this superintendent's assessment:

We must realize conflict is here. Education is vital and anything vital has conflicts. In the future, I think we will have professional negotiators representing the board and professional negotiators representing teachers and a committee which comes behind and makes the decisions [Ball, 1966, p. 10].

Professionalism in Bureaucracies

These undercurrents of unrest spring from a familiar tangle of issues which teaching has only now begun to face up to in new ways. Most of these in one way or another involve conflict between professional and bureaucratic principles of authority. These principles clash on the importance of rules, procedures, impersonality, specialization, and ways of organizing authority. The complexities boil down to a few fateful sets of alternatives for organizing public schools. Specifically, the choices open to teaching are limited by (1) the degree to which work is standardized, (2) the degree of centralized decision making, and (3) the degree of specialization in the work performed. Each of these characteristics may be visualized as a separate continuum ranging from highly bureaucratic at one extreme to highly professional at the other. The bureaucratic-employee status will dominate where there is[2]

1. A high degree of standardization of work
   (a) Stress on the uniformity of clients' problems.
   (b) Personnel are treated interchangeably.
   (c) Highly specific and uniform rules and uniform work procedures.
2. A highly centralized decision-making process, in which employees
   (a) Have little responsibility for decision making.
   (b) Owe primary allegiance to the organization and its administrators.
3. Emphasis on a task-oriented type of specialization where skill primarily
   (a) Is based on practice or experience.
   (b) Involves the accomplishment of a set of tasks.
   (c) Stresses efficiency and technique.

On the other hand, the professional status receives more support in organizations that are less standardized and centralized and in which work is organized on a functional basis.

The scheme just outlined pertains to the characteristics of organizations and does not attempt to classify individuals, who can maintain orientations inconsistent with their existing positions and can use segregating mechanisms that enable them to uphold both orientations simultaneously. This is obviously a caricature, but the point is that the opportunity an organization affords its personnel to act professionally and the amount of pressure it exerts on them to act as employees depend upon the configuration of these characteristics. When both sets of principles are simultaneously present, tension is likely to be present, and compromise will be a force toward change.

PREVIOUS RELATED RESEARCH IN EDUCATION

Unfortunately, most previous studies of professionalization within teaching have focused on the individual characteristics of the teachers involved rather than on the context of organizational processes. However, some of these studies are at least marginally related to the concerns of this study, and a brief review of some of them will illustrate the present state of our knowledge about this matter.

Despite the public's growing awareness of the significance of the professionalization of teaching, very little is known about the dynamics involved. One small study of 100 Chicago teachers indicates that their preference for the professional role is associated with their ethnic background (Kornacher, 1966). Jewish and Irish teachers leaned toward the professional definition—that is, academic, subject orientation, and strong identification with professional principles; Italian and Negro teachers were more child-centered and stressed total individual development. Also, relatively more males than females were classified as professional, especially in the Jewish and Irish groups. Neither the subject taught nor the amount of education distinguished the two groups, but persons educated in parochial secondary schools did have a stronger professional orientation.

In a study by Cole (1969), five demographic background characteristics of teachers were found to influence their predisposition toward a strike. The strike was more favored by males, those under 40 years of age, democrats from the working class, and by Jews than by other groups compared. However, some of the teachers did not act according to their predispositions. It is significant that they were more likely to demonstrate support of the strike in some social contexts than in others, namely when they received support from colleagues and were not under cross-pressure. This indicates that social background factors in themselves do not necessarily explain conflict apart from the social context.

Lowe's (1965) investigation of one school district revealed that men were more inclined to join the AFT local and women were more inclined to join the NEA, but that over-all, male teachers were significantly less likely to be organized. Rosenthal (1966) found, on the other hand, that in Boston and New York City males were more likely to join a teachers' organization than women, but he did support the conclusion that men, more characteristically than women, join unions. On the basis of evidence from both cities, furthermore, teachers, including women, were more likely to join unions in a predominantly male school than in a female climate; the latter findings illustrate the effect of school climate on behavior. Members of the two organizations did not differ in age; AFT teachers apparently are not brash youngsters. Membership in unions was also correlated with size of faculty, teaching load, and proportion of nonwhite pupils—that is, precisely the most bureaucratic settings where teaching is most difficult.

In one of the few studies of its kind, Colombotos examined how the social backgrounds of teachers are associated with their professional orientations (1962). Using an "index of professionalism" based on the teacher's emphasis on technical competence, autonomy, and the service ideal, he found that the more professional teachers come from higher social class backgrounds, that Catholics are the least professional while active Protestants are the most professional, and that academic males are more professional than men teaching in nonacademic areas. Teachers with advanced training were found to be more professional than those less well educated, and liberal arts graduates were more professional than graduates of teachers' colleges. There was a relationship between the professionalism of men and the extent of their participation in the American Federation of Teachers, though not with their participation in the NEA, and there was no difference between the members of the AFT and the NEA.

But the teachers' conduct probably depends as much on the opportunities provided by their present situations as on their own backgrounds. Colombotos found an increase in teachers' professionalism (reported as they looked back on it) correlated with the school's professional "climate" (based on the descriptive component of the professional index items). This finding supports the idea that a faculty's professional orientation, regardless of background, can be influenced by the type of climate in a school. Professional climate, in turn, was found to be directly associated with the socioeconomic status of the student body ($t = .71$).

Colombotos found that professionalism is inversely associated with "proceduralism," a one-item scale concerning whether teachers overlooked the rules. A complementary study of 31 public school systems in Wisconsin by Eye and his colleagues (1966) revealed that the number, quality, and implementation of curriculum plans increased with the extent of teacher participation in the decision-making process. The quality of curriculum plans was found to be negatively related to the amount of control ("initiating structure") exercised by the superintendent, while implementation of plans by teachers was positively related to the consideration shown by the superintendent to his teachers.

The professional role orientation scale developed by the present writer for the study to be reported in this volume was administered by Robinson to teachers and principals in 29 schools randomly selected from all British Columbia schools having ten or more teachers. Faculty professionalism was compared to school bureaucratization, as measured by a school organizational inventory, based on the perceptions of teachers. There was not a significant over-all difference between schools in staff professionalism, but there was an indication that certain schools more frequently attract and retain professionally oriented teachers. Teachers with a university degree collectively exhibited more professionalism than those without degrees. There was a positive and significant relationship between teachers' professional scores and the perceived desirability of certain bureaucratic characteristics—namely, an emphasis on specialization and technical competence and impersonality. However, no significant relationships were discovered between teachers' professional scores and the perceived desirability of hierarchy of authority, rules for teachers, and procedural specification. Female teachers, both married and single, showed more preference than males for rules for teachers, procedural specification, and impersonality. Finally, there were indications that the more professional schools actually did place more emphasis on specialization and deemphasized hierarchical authority, rules for teachers, procedural specification, impersonality, and technical competence; but it is important to note that none of these results was statistically significant.[3]

Role Conceptions of Teachers[4]

Peabody (1964) compared school teachers, police officers, and welfare workers on the stress each group gave to two logically opposed bases of authority—the formal (bureaucratic) authority of position and the professional authority based on technical competence. Elementary school teachers and welfare workers placed more emphasis on responsibility to clients than the police officers. It was concluded that the most striking contrast among these three groups was the relative importance that elementary school teachers attached to authority based on professional competence. Yet, although teachers were more likely than police officers to discuss questionable practices with superiors and seek explanations, it was concluded that their typical reaction to conflict was likely to be acquiescence to authority, particularly among the less experienced teachers in the sample.

Professional role conflict was one of three areas of role conflict in teaching identified by Getzels and Guba (1955) from extended interviews with 41 teachers in four school systems. Major problems involving the "professional" role were related to professional-employee role conflict—that is, the teacher's authority was constantly encroached upon by the administration or the public.[5]

After analyzing the Organizational Climate Description Questionnaire developed by Halpin and Croft in 48 schools, Watkins (1968) concluded that the principal-staff relationships in the public schools probably differ from the hierarchical relationships found in business and industrial bureaucracies. As might be expected, staff size was positively related to "disengagement of the staff" and negatively related to their *esprit* and openness. But the "openness" of the organizational members and their morale declined as "psychological distance" between the principal and his staff increased. The fact that principals generally perceived the school to be more open than it was perceived by their staffs suggests a likely precipitant of conflict.

Such misconceptions about organizational roles tend to be widely shared. Biddle and his associates (1966) discovered that outsiders see teachers as more self-indulgent and as more conservative than they actually are. The hierarchical nature of schools, the history of teacher complacency, and restricted opportunities to observe and communicate with them makes teachers vulnerable to this inaccurate conservative image. The result is that laymen and administrators probably underestimate the degree to which teachers in large-scale organizations are predisposed toward change. When tradition and stability are partially based on shared ignorance, reductions in social distance could invite instability and conflict along with the greater openness.

Role Conflict Among Administrators

Studies of role disagreement among school administrators have shed some additional light on professional-employee conflicts. Gross and his associates (1958), using a sample of 105 superintendents and their school boards in Massachusetts, found that superintendents often disagreed among themselves (interposition dissent), and members of each school board also disagreed among themselves on specific role obligations (intraposition dissent). Role consensus between the two groups was low on 63 percent of the items tested. In general, school board members and superintendents each assigned greater responsibility to their own position than to the other, and each group sensed different obligations to the community.

Gross and Herriott (1965) investigated some organizational and interpersonal variables which influence the professional leadership of principals as evaluated by teachers. They found that the performance of teachers and teacher morale are both associated with the leadership styles of principals.[6] The professionalism of principals, in particular, was, up to a point, related to the morale and performance of teachers and to pupils' rate of learning, but their leadership capacity regressed when the principal stressed either the professional or administrative tasks to the neglect of the other. A principal was judged to be exerting more professional leadership when his immediate superior had high leadership ability, when the principal participated in the selection of teachers, and when teachers were involved in the principal's decisions and had a share of determining, for example, the level of satisfactory student performance, student discipline policies, and supervision practices. Also, the more egalitarian a principal's relationship with his teachers, the greater degree of support he provided his staff, the more he was supported by teachers, and thus the greater his evaluated leadership abilities.

These data begin to expose a few of the many potential problems lying just beneath the surface of most schools. For example, if a principal is not backed by his own supervisor, it will be difficult for him to support his own teachers, and the degree to which he is able to involve teachers in decision making depends upon how much authority he himself has. In short, administrators are subjects of the system and do not always control the situations that are most conducive to even their own professionalism —to say nothing of their teachers' professional authority.

Empirical Approaches to Overt Conflict

By contrast to the vast literature on role disagreement, the study of these overt conflicts has been relatively ignored. However, a few detailed case studies of specific episodes have begun to appear. Descriptions of a few major conflicts have been compiled by several sources (University Council of Educational Administration; The University of Alabama Press; Culbertson, Jacobson and Reller, 1960; Sargeant and Bailse, 1955). A survey of the collective activities of teacher organizations by Perry and Wildman (1966) provides a more systematic step toward analyses of the formal structure of teacher-administrator conflict and negotiations. They found the AFT proportionately stronger in larger districts, especially in the Great Lakes states (the vicinity of the present study). Relationships between the school administration and teacher organizations were also more likely to be formalized in larger districts, where persistent disagreement or impasses also were relatively more frequent. Few collective bargaining documents mention specific issues, but those mentioned (usually in AFT agreements) were most frequently the bread-and-butter issues—salary, grievance procedures, sick leave, sabbatical leave, interschool assignments, insurance, dismissal procedures, and so forth. The authors concluded that the provision of collective bargaining agreements in education has so far emphasized the communication of facts, and seems to assume that the underlying problems are due to a lack of consensus. They imply, instead, that power is the critical problem: "Misunderstanding rather than basic conflict is implied to be the source of disagreement. Power is rejected as a means of settling disputes" (Perry and Wildman, 1966, p. 148). Of course, the reluctance of educators to admit that conflict exists is no proof that it does not exist.

One of the most notable attempts to date to study actual "trouble cases" in educational institutions is reported by Lazarsfeld and Thielens in *The Academic Mind* (1958). In the late 1950s, near the end of the McCarthy era, 2,451 randomly selected social science professors in 165 American colleges and universities were interviewed and asked to describe instances in which their own academic freedom or that of their colleagues had been threatened in any way. They were also asked to relate instances of "civil liberty cases" and "problems" on the campus, and of local events that had stirred up strong feelings.

The term "incident" was used by the authors to describe an episode, long or short, in which an overt verbal attack, direct accusation, or specific criticism was made against a teacher, group of teachers, or the school as a whole, and which could be documented. It was found that the majority of charges involved political issues. The total number of incidents found in any one school varied from zero to 28, with over half of the schools reporting two to ten incidents. About a fifth of these social scientists reported perceived increases in pressure from outside groups, the largest percentage of them located in large, private universities.

IMPLICATIONS

When viewed against this background of change and conflict, much of the recent history of educational administration amounts to vain efforts to preserve an outmoded hierarchical coordination system against growing diversity and to resist the almost certain elevation of experts to new positions of influence. The school system as we know it was bred in small-town America, but it has since matured within a context of urban revolution. Urbanization has left its marks, but it is clear that schools are not yet well adapted to their new environment. Superintendents and school boards unrealistically refuse to face the full implications of the complex systems that have evolved around them. They continue to insist upon reviewing each decision at every point in the system and suspiciously regard the demands of teachers for more authority as insidious plots to usurp their own legal public trusts. Principals continue to pride themselves on being "the instructional leaders," equating leadership itself with official rank. Teachers wonder whether it is "professional" to argue among themselves or to dispute openly with the administration. And everyone futilely strives to achieve a state of efficiency and uniformity in an inconsistent and probabilistic world.

General confusion in education about the meaning of a profession is partly responsible for these vain dogmas. But when it is sorted out, the "teaching profession" turns out to be not one but several groups of people. Principals have their own profession, superintendents theirs, and there are dozens of teaching professions. Teachers cannot identify closely with administrators who control their salaries any more than principals can be "the instructional leaders" of a dozen different curricular areas; nor can any one teacher for that matter. The school board is no more legally obligated to approve all hiring than teachers are obliged to approve administrators, and the superintendent is no more omniscient than the English department.

This picture, of course, is overdrawn. A few adventuresome administrators either defiantly or reluctantly delegate responsibilities, invite teachers to "participate" in making decisions, and push through some pet innovation against the defensive resistance of suspicious faculties. But this does not alter the principal fact that what has emerged are irreconcilable structures: a set of procedures for enforcing compliance awkwardly imposed upon a system that requires autonomy and initiative in order to function. For, in practice, the occupation of teaching is such that administrators cannot possibly exercise close surveillance over teachers, nor realistically assume final responsibility for all decisions; they cannot, in other words, either prevent all mistakes or be responsible for making all improvements. Yet, implicit in the principle of hierarchy is an assumption that teachers are incompetent and will make mistakes if left to their own devices. One writer has facetiously formulated this assumption as an explicit principle of hierarchy: "In a hierarchy, each employee tends to rise to his level of incompetence: every post tends to be occupied by an employee incompetent to execute his duties" (Peter, 1967, p. 340).

In the scheme of things, administrators and teachers serve different structures and different functions. Administrators presumably are responsible for coordinating the system, over-all planning, and representing the school system to the community. It is left to the teachers, on the other hand, to make the day-to-day adjustments to problems and adapt the system to the individual child. Conflict arises when this division of labor is not observed. If the system were completely controlled by administrators, there could be no room for teachers to exercise initiative and to make their own interpretations, and the system would be directly responsive to lay control through the school board's control over the superintendent. But if the system were dominated completely by teachers, it would be subject to internal cleavages and would remain well insulated from lay influence. Either group, if left entirely to its own devices, is as likely to foster its own vested interests and special viewpoint as it is to promote some broader vision of the "social welfare." One can only hope that a new vision will be forged out of the tensions between the two.

NOTES: Chapter 3

¹ The primary enemies of the professions originally were the state and commercialism (Marshall, 1939). Commercialism undermines the service ethic and encourages competition among professionals for clients. The political power of the state represents a major threat to a profession's decision-making autonomy—so much so that it is necessary for a profession to control political machinery, that is, accrediting agencies and licensing boards. Marshall contends that, in comparison to the threat of state control, the status of professionals has not been jeopardized by their employment in bureaucracies. But Marshall is talking about the fact that it is not necessary for a professional to be economically independent in a practice of his own in order to maintain his status, which is very true. Bureaucracies are as menacing to professional decision-making authority as government itself. Both the administrative system and the control exercised by laymen and their legal representatives on regulating boards usurp the authority of modern professions.

² This brief characterization can be elaborated along the following lines.

Standardization. In a bureaucracy, each person is assigned responsibilities according to his position, which must be executed according to designated procedures. Persons with professional status, by contrast, are assigned broad spheres of authority in accordance with their specialized knowledge and given final authority to make decisions. The latter system permits initiative and imagination in solving clients' unique problems. While the assembly-line worker and the surgeon, for example, are both specialists, the degree of initiative expected of each differs markedly.

The professional is also bound by rules, of course. In comparison to the employee's status, rules guiding the professional are perhaps less specific and more abstract and diffuse. But rules can support the professional and provide him with assurances necessary for carrying out his decisions. Moeller (1962) found that teachers in more bureaucratized systems expressed a greater sense of power than those in less bureaucratized systems. In the latter, where particularism and lack of policy are typical, individuals probably have less opportunity to exert influence than when they know the rules and their loopholes and can anticipate what action the administration will take.

New knowledge and innovations are important elements of the professional role. Professions rely upon research as a primary source of change. Therefore, it is significant that educational research has been increasing from both local and federal sources. Over 200 million dollars is available for research and development at the federal level alone. But that figure is not a proportionately large share of the total cost of formal education in this country, which is close to five billion dollars. American industry has found it practical to devote 3 to 10 percent of its expenditure to research and development. If education adopted the minimum formula, it would mean that at least one half billion dollars should be made available for these needs. Most of this will probably have to come from federal funds because local systems are reluctant to support the kind of long-range research that is needed. But if this money is to be used wisely, it also will be necessary to prepare teachers and other social scientists to take educational research roles, and for federal funding agencies to adopt a better balanced and integrated research program than now exists.

Decision-making authority. The rule-bound bureaucratic system limits the professional employee's autonomy over his work, but he has another basis of authority he can appeal to, namely, expertise. (The final authority of professionals, of course, resides in the colleague group rather than in individual preference.) Blau and Scott (1962, p. 35) point out that one of the major dilemmas of modern organizations originates in this dual basis of authority. One of the major characteristics of a good employee is his willingness to suspend his own judgment and to follow the directives of superiors, whose primary claims to authority are the official positions they hold (Gouldner, 1959; Parsons, 1956). By comparison, in the status system of professionals there is more respect for an individual's knowledge and his personal competence independent of his official position. In bureaucracies, Solomon (1957, pp. 253–264) observes, the superior has the right to the last word because he is the superior, while in professional matters, the last word goes to the person with greater knowledge or the more convincing logic.

In bureaucracies, specialists of distinction are evaluated by administrators who may or may not be fully skilled and knowledgeable in new procedures and developments in a particular field (Gouldner, 1959). It should be acknowledged that many people believe that there is a general set of teaching principles which can be applied regardless of field specialization, but others feel that competence to teach depends more upon knowledge and procedures specific to the subject matter being taught; it is this latter situation that produces strain between specialized teachers and the administrators who evaluate them.

While many teachers consider themselves to be professional in one sense or another, the fact is that in the vast majority of schools they are advanced on the basis of their seniority in the system (that is, their loyalty to the system) rather than their demonstrated professional competence. Teachers have notoriously little control over many of the important standards of their work—such as hiring and evaluating colleagues, subjects taught, materials used, criteria for deciding who should be admitted, retained, and graduated in schools, forms of reporting pupil progress, school boundary lines, and qualifications for teacher training. The meager authority of teachers is reflected in the "chain of command" which locates authority in the administrative rather than in the professional sphere. This means not only that critical decisions are made or reviewed at levels of authority above teachers, but that policy is made by the person most removed from the daily problems of teachers, students, and classrooms. The ability of teachers to increase their status probably depends more upon their ability to challenge the present decision-making structure than on any other single factor. But they will not be able to make much headway unless the assumptions behind the present authority system are altered.

Specialization. Employees are evaluated for their efficiency in performing given tasks and have no particular responsibility for the total product; professionals, on the other hand, are evaluated for their service to clients and do have responsibility for the over-all objectives. The surgeon, for example, is rewarded primarily for his part in caring for a patient; the length of time his operation may take is largely irrelevant apart from this primary consideration. Within the limits of his competence, a professional is responsible for any facet of a client's life that has a bearing upon the outcome of his administrations. Yet, as schools have become specialized, fewer teachers know the "whole student." The problem, which is greater for the higher grades, makes it difficult to hold individuals responsible for the total development or failure of students "as persons." It is easier to evaluate a teacher's specific teaching procedure, his or her ability to "cover" material, maintain discipline, and operate a smoothly run and efficient classroom, than to assess his impact on his students' character development.

Professionals also can be distinguished from craftsmen by their emphasis on training in theoretical knowledge, as compared to relying upon practice as a basis of developing skill in specific techniques. The stress that traditionally has been placed on "methods" courses in teachers' training programs perhaps places teaching closer to other crafts. On the other hand, specialized training in the psychology of learning, the history and philosophy of education, or the sociology of education for administrative science is more in accordance with professional education. Only if education finds a body of knowledge (as opposed to a set of techniques) to monopolize, will it gain full professional recognition.

It may be significant that in a study of professionalism in nursing, the writer found that in comparison to hospital-trained nurses, the more professionally oriented collegiate nurses were more critical of the hospitals that employed them (Corwin, 1961b).

The fact that professionals are obliged to serve the best interests of their clients, regardless of other considerations, can come into conflict with the idea that employees should seek to protect the interests and reputation of the organization they work for. Yet, there are cases where teachers have taken a strong professional stand against adverse practices in a system, as when they support a school consolidation which may require the complete destruction of their present organization. Carr-Saunders (1966, pp. 2–9) observed that "The school teacher, for instance, can be devoted to his pupils, but he is limited in what he can do for them, since he must follow his employer's views on these matters or lost his post." The question some teachers are beginning to ask themselves is whether there are other alternatives.

[3] Sorensen (1965) also developed scales modeled after Corwin's to measure the professional and employee role conceptions of accountants employed in 24 branch offices of four national public accounting firms. He found direct increases in bureaucratic orientations and decreases in professional orientations, with rank from junior through partner. Less experienced persons in the lower positions felt that there was too much bureaucracy, while the more experienced people in higher positions felt that there was too little. He also found that job satisfaction was affected more by bureaucratic orientation than by professional orientation; the less bureaucratically oriented CPAs consistently tended to be less satisfied. Migratory and nonmigratory CPAs differed little in professional orientations, but differences in bureaucratic orientations were distinct, with those planning to change jobs having significantly lower bureaucratic orientations than those planning to remain with their current firm.

[4] Professional-employee role conflicts have been identified in a variety of public organizations. Brown (1954), for example, found that professional employees in a government laboratory resisted rules made for them by persons outside the professional group. Even many of the engineers in development and testing work, who recognized the need for rules, circumscribed usual procedure and identified instead with professional colleagues, which apparently served as an incentive to resist the bureaucracy. Wordwell (1955) believes that the principle of delegated authority is especially detrimental to professional authority and that bureaucracy causes professionals to treat their clients too impersonally.

Other writers place less emphasis on the consequences of role conflict for clients, and instead stress the creativity, effectiveness, and long-range modifications of the organizational structure that can result. McEwan (1956) notes that the incongruities between the professional researchers and the bureaucratic roles of military persons stemmed from the fact that the professional research person's self-conception as an individual capable of critical ability and capacity for original thought could only be superficially followed in the structure of a military organization. He believes that the standardization and subordination by rank are, in practice, incongruent with the need for creative thinking and equality relations which prevails among professionals.

Individuals vary in the salience of their professional and employee conceptions. According to one typology, a man who seeks recognition from his professional group rather than from his employers has been termed a "functional bureaucrat" by Reissman (1949). For him, the quality of his work is more important than his ability to use bureaucratic procedures. The "specialist bureaucrat," on the other hand, is procedurally conservative and identifies primarily with the people with whom he works. He is normally unaware of differences between bureaucratic and professional roles. The "service bureaucrat" accepts the bureaucratic means but also seeks recognition from outside professional groups that support his professional objectives. The "job bureaucrat" uses professional skills only as entrance requirements into a bureaucratic job, from which he seeks departmental recognition and material rewards.

Marvick (1954, p. 34) was able to identify three career types in a federal agency carrying on a research-coordinating and research-subsidizing program for national defense: (1) institutionalists—almost all were not professionals in the first place, and their entire orientation was that of the organization; (2) specialists—slightly more than half were professionals to the extent that they had higher degrees, and most tended to maintain their professional orientations; and (3) hybrids—less than half had higher degrees and seemed to have neither a professional nor an organizational orientation, but their behavior was governed mainly by what was most expedient for their own individual careers.

Ben-David's (1958) typology of the medical roles of physicians employed in a bureaucratic setting is more elaborate. Those physicians primarily concerned about therapeutic efficiency he termed "bureaucratic" doctors; "service-oriented" physicians were closely identified with a circle of patients; "science-oriented" doctors sought more external status, had less regard for patient relationships, and tried to dominate the patient more than did the service-oriented physicians. The significance of this particular typology is that it begins to differentiate between professional persons who are oriented to colleagues and those oriented to clients and other specific reference groups.

[5] An analysis of the personal backgrounds of the teachers in the sample shows that role conflict was associated with the teacher's social position outside of the school. Among other findings, there were differences in the patterns of role conflict between male and female teachers, between those with different numbers of dependents, between those who held part-time jobs and those who did not, and between those who perceived that the community in which they taught was different from their original community and those who did not (Getzels and Guba, 1955).

[6] Convergence between teachers' and administrators' definitions of administrative roles was found by Bidwell (1957) to be related to teachers' job satisfaction. Although no relation was found among the high satisfaction schools, teachers' expectations in low satisfaction schools did diverge from perceptions of how administrators behaved, which in turn was associated with dissatisfaction with teaching. Both the deprivation of expectations in practice and the incongruence between role partners' conceptions represent significant types of role conflict.

Corwin (1961a) also found that nurses who simultaneously held both strong professional and employee role conceptions expressed a greater sense of deprivation of their ideal roles in actual practice than those having other styles of role organization. Sorensen (1965) also found that the CPA who simultaneously holds high professional and high bureaucratic status orientations experiences relatively strong status deprivation.

REFERENCES: Chapter 3

American association of school administrators. *Roles, responsibilities, relationships of the school board, superintendent, and staff.* Washington, D.C.: AASA, 1963. P. 13.

Ball, Lester B. Reactionary board pushes teachers to extreme measures. *The Ohio School Board's Journal,* 1966, **10**, 10–11.

Ben-David, Joseph. Professional role of a physician in bureaucratic medicine: A study in role conflicts. *Human Relations,* 1958, **11**, 255–274.

Biddle, Bruce J., et al. Shared Inaccuracies in the Role of the Teacher. In Bruce J. Biddle and Edward J. Thomas (Eds.), *Role theory: Concepts and research.* New York: Wiley, 1966.

Bidwell, Charles E. "Some effects of administrative behavior: A study in role theory." *Administrative Science Quarterly,* 1957, **2**, 163–181.

Blau, Peter, and Scott, W. Richard. *Formal organization.* San Francisco: Chandler, 1962. Pp. 24, 35.

Brown, Paula. Bureaucracy in a government laboratory. *Social Forces,* 1954, **32**, 259–269.

Bucher, Rue, and Strauss, Alselm. Professions in process. *The American Journal of Sociology,* 1961, **66**, 325–334.

Carr-Saunders, A. M. Professionalization in historical perspective. In Howard M. Vollmer and Donald L. Mills (Eds.), *Professionalization.* Englewood Cliffs, N.J.: Prentice-Hall, 1966. Pp. 2–9.

Clark, Burton R. Faculty organization and authority. In Terry F. Lunsford (Ed.), *The Study of Academic Administration.* Western Interstate Commission for Higher Education, 1963. Pp. 37–51. Reprinted in Howard L. Vollmer and Donald L. Mills (Eds.), *Professionalization. Op. cit.* P. 286.

Cole, Stephen. Teachers' strike: A study of the conversion of predisposition into action. *The American Journal of Sociology,* March, 1969, **74**, 506–520.

Colombotos, John L. *Sources of professionalism: A study of high school teachers.* Ann Arbor: Department of Sociology, University of Michigan, 1962.

Conant, James. *Slums and suburbs.* New York: McGraw-Hill, 1961.

Corwin, Ronald G. The professional employee: A study of conflict in nursing roles. *The American Journal of Sociology,* May, 1961a, **66**, 604–615.

Corwin, Ronald G., and Taves, M. J. Professional disillusionment: A study in hospital nursing. *Nursing Research,* Summer, 1961b, **10**, 141–144.

Culbertson, J. A., Jacobson, Paul B., and Reller, Theodore I. *Administrative relationships: A casebook.* Englewood Cliffs, N.J.: Prentice-Hall, 1960.

Dimmock, Marshall E. Expanding jurisdictions: A case study in bureaucratic conflict. In Robert K. Merton, A. P. Gray, B. Hockey, and H. C. Selvin (Eds.), *Reader in Bureaucracy.* New York: Free Press, 1965.

Eye, Glenn, et al. Relationship between instructional change and the extent to which school administrators agree on the location of responsibilities for administrative decision. U.S. Office of Education Cooperative Research Project No. 5-0443, 1967.

Friesdam, H. J. Bureaucrats as heros. *Social Forces,* March, 1954, **32,** 269–274.

Getzels, J. W., and Guba, E. G. Role conflict and effectiveness: An empirical study. *American Sociological Review,* 1954, **19,** 164–175.

Getzels, J. W., and Guba, E. G. The structure of role and role conflict in the teaching situation. *Journal of Educational Sociology,* September, 1955, **29,** 30–40.

Goode, William. The librarian: From occupation to profession? *Library Quarterly,* October, 1961, **31,** 306–320.

Gouldner, Alvin W. Organizational tensions. In Robert Merton (Ed.), *Sociology today.* New York: Basic Books, 1959. Pp. 400–428.

Greenwood, Ernest. Attributes of a profession. *Social Work,* July, 1957, **2,** 44–55.

Gross, Neal, Mason, Ward S., and McEachern, Alexander W. *Exploration in role analysis: Studies of the school superintendency role.* New York: Wiley, 1958.

Gross, Neal, and Herriott, Robert E. *Staff leadership in public schools: A sociological inquiry.* New York: 1965.

Halpin, Andrew, and Croft, Don B. *The organizational climates of schools.* U.S. Office of Education Cooperative Research Program, 1962.

Hughes, Everett Cherrington. *Men and their work.* New York: Free Press, 1958. P. 44.

Jordan, K. Forbis. Who shall be the effective voice for American teachers? *The American School Board Journal,* July, 1963, IV (147), 38.

Kaufman, Bel. *Up the down staircase.* New York: Avon, 1966. Pp. 200–208.

Kornacher, Mildred. *How urban high school teachers view their job.* U.S. Office of Education Cooperative Research Project No. 5-8144, 1966.

Kornhauser, William. *Scientists in industry: Conflict and accommodations.* With the assistance of Warren O. Hagstrom. Berkeley: University of California Press, 1962. P. 8.

Lazarsfeld, Paul, and Thielens, Wagner, Jr. *The academic mind.* New York: Free Press, 1958.

Lowe, William T. Who joins with teachers' group? *Teachers' College Record,* April, 1965, **66,** 614–619.

Marshall, T. H. The recent history of professionalism in relation to social structure and social policy. *Canadian Journal of Economics and Political Science,* August, 1939, **5,** 325–340.

Marvick, D. *Career perspectives in a bureaucratic setting.* Ann Arbor: University of Michigan Press, 1954. P. 34.

McEwan, William J. Position conflict and professional orientation in a research organization. *Administrative Science Quarterly,* 1956, **1,** 208–224.

Moeller, Gerald H. Bureaucracy and teachers' sense of power. *Administrators' Notebook,* November, 1962, **11,** 1–4.

The New York Times, January 16, 1964, 88.

The New York Times, July 7, 1963, 39.

Parsons, Talcott. Suggestions for a sociological approach to the theory of organization. *Administrative Science Quarterly,* 1956, **1,** 54–63.

Peabody, Robert L. *Organizational authority.* New York: Atherton Press–Prentice-Hall, 1964.

Perry, Charles A., and Wildman, Wesley A. A survey of collective activity among public school teachers. *Educational Administration Quarterly,* Spring, 1966, **2,** 131–151.

Peter, Lawrence J. The Peter principle: We're all incompetent. *Phi Delta Kappa,* March, 1967, **48,** 340.

Reissman, Leonard. A study of role conception in a bureaucracy. *Social Forces,* March, 1949, **27,** 305–310.

Rosenthal, Alan. The strength of teacher organizations: Factors influencing membership in two large cities. *Sociology of Education,* Fall, 1966, **39,** 359–380.

Sargeant, Cyril G., and Bailse, Eugene L. *Educational administration: Cases and concepts.* Boston: Houghton Mifflin, 1955.

Solomon, Benjamin. A profession taken for granted. *School Review,* 1961, **69,** 286–299.

Solomon, David N. Professional persons in bureaucratic organizations. In Walter Reed Army Institute of Research *Symposium on Preventive and Social Psychiatry.* Washington, D.C.: U.S. Government Printing Office, 1957. Pp. 253–264.

Sorensen, James Elliot. Professional and bureaucratic organizations in large public accounting firms. Unpublished doctoral dissertation, The Ohio State University, 1965.

Steffensen, James P. *Teachers negotiate with their school boards.* Bulletin No. 40, U.S. Office of Education. Washington, D.C.: U.S. Government Printing Office, 1964.

Superintendent of Schools of New York City. *The New York Times,* July 7, 1963, 1–39.

Watkins, J. Foster. The OCDQ–An application and some implications. *Educational Administration Quarterly,* Spring, 1968, **4,** 46–60.

Wordwell, Walter I. Social integration, bureaucratization and professions. Social Forces, May, 1955, **33,** 356–359.

FROM TALKS WITH TEACHERS *on community relations*

THERE IS *a spirit in some towns and communities that precludes the fact that school teaching is not a very important thing, that anybody can do it, and that we are not specialists. So everybody gets into the act and tells you how to do it. I always say to people: "Well, I didn't spend as much money for my education as a doctor would in order to have someone tell me how to run my business."—a teacher*

THE PRINCIPAL *called me in about some parents calling him about their children and their work. I teach biology. It's a technical subject. Parents can't for the life of them get it through their heads the fact that there has to be something other than just idle talk in a recitation or just writing something when they come to class. What we're trying to do is search for truth; this is what science is all about.—a teacher*

THE ADMINISTRATION *of the school is very sensitive to the feeling of the public. It is much easier for a group of parents outside the school to get something done in the school than it is for the people within the education general picture to get the same thing done.—a teacher*

I CAN *think of an example in a math class which wasn't being taught as a parent thought it should be because the teacher was not fulfilling the prescribed outline of the course and was using a different textbook. The administration got wind of this and asked the teacher to change.—a teacher*

HE HAD *a mother who believed that he [the son] was always right and the school was always wrong, and as a result, any time he would get an unsatisfactory grade on his report card, his mother would come in and blame the school. One day the woman decided to call me up. She said: "What are you running? a kindergarten?" and caught me completely off base. Now, most administrators that I know would sit there and take the abuse. I don't happen to be built that way. So I made up my mind that when I'd see this woman, two days after our phone conversation, that I was not going to start anything with her, but that the minute she opened her mouth and said something that I considered to be out of line, I was going to come down on her like a ton of bricks; and you may rest assured that I did. And her husband was caught completely by surprise. He said to me: "You can't talk to my wife this way." And I said: "Oh, I see, we're operating on a double standard. I can't talk to her this way, but she can abuse me over the phone, is that correct?" I said: "The trouble with you is, you've been used to talking to too many mealy-mouthed people that sit there and take it. Well, you've come up against another this time, and you've got one who isn't going to take it." He said to me: "A man in your position shouldn't talk to me this way." I said: "That's quite right, I shouldn't!" Incidentally, it did help. We never had a bit of trouble from those people again. Never!—an assistant principal*

4. *Procedures*

> *I have had my solutions for a long time, but I do not yet know how I am to arrive at them.—Gauss, 1964, p. 58.*
>
> *Where would anatomy and surgery and dependent specialties be if Mondino, Leonardo, Vesalius, and others had entirely honored the absolutes of their day instead of haunting cemeteries and gibbets in their search for cadavers?—Dalton, 1964, p. 60.*

Problems of research design are not merely technical matters; socio-research is not governed by absolute procedural doctrines; and rigid moral standards are not always useful for resolving the problems that confront a researcher in the field. The reasons are related to the fact that the social scientist and his research design are subject to some of the same social forces that govern the behavior of the subjects he is studying. At certain stages a research project sometimes seems to take on a momentum —a life of its own. The reason is that its personnel are at the mercy of the will and interests of others, who either cannot be controlled or whose control raises serious ethical questions.

Since both procedural and ethical principles in themselves originate in, and are consummated by, a social context, they must be looked upon as part of an incomplete and still-developing system, a system fashioned from compromises for which each research investigator must assume some responsibility based on his day-to-day field experiences and his own values. This sense of indeterminateness and lack of clarity makes research viable. At the same time, it leaves almost any decision open to criticism. Perhaps, then, the least that can be expected is that a researcher fully recognize the unsolved problems his research has raised. Some of these problems will be considered in this chapter.

THE PEOPLE AND THE PLACES

Our conclusions will be based upon information gleaned from over 1,500 lengthy questionnaires and 737 tape-recorded conversations with the teaching staff and administrators of 28 public high schools located in Ohio and adjacent states; information was obtained from more than three fourths of the nearly 2,000 faculty members in these schools.[1]

Our Mr. Sears (referred to in previous chapters) turns out to be a fairly typical Midwestern teacher. He comes from a city of nearly 100,000 persons, is now teaching in a state where he graduated from high school, and he attended college in the same state as well. Half of his colleagues lived in their present community before they took teaching jobs there. He is thirty-seven years old, married, and employed full time. He has taught in two other systems and has been in the present system eight years, but in the present school less than four years. His salary in 1965 was $7,000, but the salaries of his colleagues in different school systems varied from $3,500 to $7,600. At that time, also, he had only one chance in four of earning over $8,000 a year; and in any event he believed then and probably still believes that he should be earning more than his present salary. He has about five years of education beyond high school, and over one third of his colleagues have earned a master's degree. However, about one third of his colleagues report that they frequently or occasionally have taught courses outside of their college majors. Our man belongs to a teachers' organization and subscribes to at least three professional journals and devotes five hours a month to reading them.

Most of the people in our sample are similar to Mr. Sears and reasonably representative of other teachers in age, years of experience and education, marital status, and activity in professional organizations. The proportion of males and their salary level is a little higher than usual, however, and teachers with master's degrees are underrepresented for Ohio, although for the nation as a whole, they are accurately represented.[2] The schools in the study are not typical. They are unusually large. This was deliberate because, for our purposes of relating variation in organizational characteristics to incidents of conflict, heterogeneity was more important than a completely representative sample of the schools of a particular region. But even though the schools in this sample are disproportionately large, it is important to realize that the typical teacher in this country today is employed in a relatively large school.[3]

THE STATE OF THE ART

There are some problems associated with this study which one should keep in mind when interpreting the results.

Sampling the Fieldwork Problems

One set of problems goes back to the sampling and procedures used in the field, namely, the sample's size and representativeness, the lack of control over some elements of fieldwork, and occasional respondent antipathy.

Sample size

Although over 1,500 respondents answered questionnaires, only 28 organizations are involved. This, of course, limits the organizational analyses. But this type of research is costly and time consuming; larger samples would require a sacrifice in the scope and intensiveness of analysis that was permitted in this sample. The sample, in any event, is a great deal larger than the single case studies and comparisons involving two or three organizations that typify organizational research.

Representativeness

There is an element of self-selection on the part of school administrators who chose to participate in the study.[4] This problem, however, is not unique to the topic and sample at hand. Blau (1964, p. 25) has concluded that "Perhaps self-selection makes it inevitable that the organizations we study are those in which bureaucratic rigidities are least pronounced."

The highest proportion of refusals (two thirds of those contacted) is in the "large" (but not the largest) category of schools (87 to 106 teachers). Many of these schools have their own research staffs already imposing on teachers' time; in a few cases, the invitation was forwarded to the director of research for the system, who probably considered this study to be in competition with their staff for the time of teachers.

It is conceivable that a problem like staff conflict would distort the sample's representativeness. However, there is no simple answer. Some administrators, curiously, seemed so confident that no problems existed in their schools that they participated partly in order to demonstrate this fact. On the other hand, three principals who had accepted the invitation reconsidered after they saw the questionnaire. This latter situation, however, does not mean that the most conflict-ridden schools necessarily refused to participate. At least three principals who were involved in serious conflict with their faculties and/or superintendents were apparently coerced into participation, and all three yielded low rates of questionnaire return (as low as 33 percent).[5] In one of these, where the rift between the faculty and principal was particularly acute, teachers either were against the principal and for the study, or for the principal and against the study; needless to say, it was difficult for interviewers to establish rapport in these situations.

Because the study itself sometimes became marginally involved in certain conflicts, the reliability (and perhaps the validity) of the findings probably were jeopardized by the very conflicts being studied; unfortunately, schools with the most intense conflicts, which are the ones of interest to us, yield the least reliable data. The question is whether to omit the biasing organizations, or to include them because they represent certain types of conflict that otherwise would be neglected and hence cause distortion in the sample. In view of the difficulty of gaining access to the most "conflictual" schools, we decided to include them.

Compromise and lack of control

A few administrators stipulated conditions for their participation, some of which would have had the effect of modifying the research design. One principal wanted to circulate the questionnaire and a statement of hypotheses among the faculty before the study. He had good reasons, but because teachers in other schools had been instructed not to discuss the study among themselves, the school in question was excluded in the interest of comparability. But in the schools that were included it was not possible completely to control the amount of information that administrators might have communicated to teachers.

Every participant in the study was explicitly informed that information about particular schools would be guarded in strict confidence. Nevertheless, after the fieldwork had been completed, administrators from two schools requested information pertaining to their schools, and another questioned an interviewer, implying that he would like information about several teachers whose contracts might not be renewed. One principal candidly sought what he believed was only a "fair return on the time his school had invested in the study," pointing out that the information collected about his school would be of immediate practical benefit to both administrators and teachers (for example, to reward teachers judged by colleagues to be "superior" on an evaluation form that was included). However, there was already reason to believe that some teachers in the region suspected the project had been instigated by their school boards for devious reasons.[6] Hence, we feared that *any* information communicated to administrators, however innocent and well intentioned, would serve to confirm such suspicions. At the cost of an opportunity to be of practical service to a cooperative administration, the school was denied the information it sought. This remains one of the delicate dilemmas of doing institutional research.

Respondent antipathy

The wisdom of this decision already had been confirmed during the first year of the study. At that time, some personal "contacts" had been used to secure the participation of a few of their schools. For example, we took advantage of the fact that one of the project members was acquainted with a principal in one of the schools invited to participate. But when a teacher in that school learned of this acquaintanceship, she and two others became suspicious and angrily withdrew from the study. This was notwithstanding the assurances by project personnel of the professional integrity of the parties involved. Hence, a personal contact, which initially had been useful for securing the administration's cooperation, eventually alienated some of the participants and perhaps biased the findings.

Problems in the Field[7]

Most of the people cooperated during the interviews; some, in fact, were apologetic about not having conflicts to report. However, some problems did arise in the field. A few people invited refused to be interviewed (less than 1 per cent), and an additional (negligible) percentage were not wholly cooperative during their interviews. While these problems were not large in number, they are perhaps symptomatic of some underlying issues, the implications of which are worthy of further consideration. At least three types of issues appear to have been in the minds of at least a few teachers: personal distaste for the subject of conflict, fear of reprisal from the administration, and ethical considerations.

Personal distaste for conflict

For some interviewees the subject of conflict was too repugnant to discuss. However, it was repugnant for different reasons. For at least some this aversion must have stemmed from loyalty to their school or other organizational interests; for some it was related to concern about their own image. One respondent complained that the entire study was "too negative," that it seemed designed to make teachers think that small problems were of gigantic proportions, and that it could have a negative reflection on the school. In a few schools, entire departments seemed to have agreed not to cooperate, apparently in order to hide departmental problems (which we usually learned about through other sources).

In at least one school the problem was more immediate: some of the teachers resented the fact that their lounge was being used by the project staff for interviewing. Another source of reluctance could be traced to the fear on the part of a few people that the intent of the study was to evaluate them, and not just to analyze a social organization. These problems are not particular to public schools, of course. One writer observes that

It seems clear that all persons recognized some norm, however amorphous or splintered, for all involved to take pains to conceal what would be denounced. In some cases, part of the official code is a dead letter except as it is used politically to control others. However this may be, the researcher who is obliged to get at all relevant behavior may obviously offend some persons in the organization. . . . The researcher, and not a remote part-time ethicist who cannot say where his personal code comes from, must size up the moral issues peculiar to his problems and bear responsibility for reconciling the diverse moral commitments he assumes in and out of his office. Naturally, he may involve himself and others in trouble . . . [Dalton, 1964, pp. 59–60].

The implications of this issue can have considerable import for the design of research. Laymen tend to base their opinions about the appropriateness of a study on whether they anticipate that the conclusions will be favorable to them. They would believe, for example, that a study of abortion among middle-class families is not permissible unless the study promises to offset negative implications of abortion by stressing the positive features of middle-class people. For the laymen this criterion is realistic, since theoretically a study can be used out of context for propagandistic purposes, contrary to the interests of the people in the study. But it puts the social scientist who is not able honestly to guarantee beforehand what his conclusions will be in an untenable position. Any attempt to neutralize the conclusions can be as biasing and propagandistic as any other kind of manipulation. The dilemma is that laymen live in a propagandistic situation which researchers, as outsiders, can afford to ignore and as social scientists are obliged to ignore.

Fear of reprisal

One of the major reasons that some of the interviewees may not have confided fully was their sense of intimidation and fear of reprisal from the administration.[8] The same pressures of organization responsible for the qualms of some of the respondents about their school's image would also produce feelings of intimidation. Some respondents faced a dilemma. They felt pressured by the administration to participate, and yet they were aware that the very same pressure could be brought to bear if some of their statements became known to the administration. They had to choose between playing the role of interviewee and the role of employee, between candidness and caution. This element of risk is normal, but it was especially acute in one school where participants suspected that the administration was "behind" the study—that is, had secretly commissioned it. An art teacher was extremely blunt in expressing his suspicions. He gave our interviewer a badge labeled "Chief Investigator." At another school a teacher who was suspicious that the study was backed by the administration said that the whole study "smacked of Fascism, where you are asked to inform on your fellow teachers."

These suspicions were responsible for some of the fieldworkers' interpersonal problems. Originally, they had planned to use whatever opportunities were available during the week to observe the school informally

—to eat lunch with the faculty and otherwise to become acquainted and establish rapport. However, it soon became apparent that interviewers were jeopardizing this neutral position by seeming to be "chummy" with certain faculty members or administrators.

Ethical problems

In the majority of schools at least one or two people expressed the belief that it would be unethical for them, even in confidence, to discuss problems involving their colleagues. One of their concerns was that the study could create problems for them and their colleagues. They were correctly aware that when outsiders intrude into an on-going system with the purpose of studying it, their very presence can alter the situation. One respondent, in fact, wanted to know if the objective of the study was to "stir up trouble"; he maintained that many teachers were resurrecting problems that had already died down. And it is true that at times the interviewer did, by the nature of his questions, inadvertently hint of problems. After being interviewed, one teacher decided that she was naive, saying:

I didn't know that all these things were happening, and that all of these disputes were in progress. Evidently they are, or otherwise you wouldn't be asking all these questions. . . . Maybe I will keep my eyes and ears open; maybe there is more going on than I know about.

Another teacher, unaware that several faculty members already knew of her problem with the administration, erroneously accused the interviewer of "spreading the gossip" to them. But if the study did increase the consciousness of some teachers about their schools' problems, it is also possible that, by the same token, it helped them to put their problems in a sociological perspective. For the whole direction of the questions was to locate the "blame" for problems in social situations rather than in the specific persons involved.

Some participants seemed disturbed about the apparent invasion of their own and others' privacy. Invasion of privacy has become a sensitive issue with Congress and government funding agencies. Some critics of the American scene, such as Whyte and Packard, have complained about the growing invasions of privacy implicit in personnel policies and electronic eavesdropping devices. With the recent development of national data banks, personal information is becoming more accessible to government and private agencies. The social sciences appear to play a role in these developments.

The personal privacy of individuals must be balanced against the fact that there are always justifiable reasons for investigating the personal lives of people, namely to protect another individual's rights and to benefit the community as a whole. A lawyer's investigation of a divorce suit, a physician's inquest into a case of venereal disease, or a psychiatrist's efforts to unlock the mystery of alcoholism may all lead the investigators to the secrets of innocent third parties. For similar reasons, social researchers sometimes investigate personal situations if these can assist with solutions to social problems.

There are ways of protecting the rights of individuals, which are presently available to us—for example, securing the consent of the persons being studied and a personal code pledging researchers to treat their information in confidence and to protect their informants. Also, it should be noted that in a diversified society the fact that public opinion itself is not easily crystallized removes some of the stigma which traditionally surrounded many personal problems. The society as a whole is more tolerant and is learning to cope more directly with its problems. Open recognition of problems can be therapeutic for the persons involved and pave the way to better mutual understanding.

The distinction between purely private and public matters has itself come under closer scrutiny in recent years in regard to such questions as discrimination in the sale of real estate and other goods and services. Society is so geared to information gathering and retrieval and is so interdependent, that society finds it difficult any longer to regard certain types of information (such as venereal diseases) as the private concern of individuals. The important question is not whether a third party has the information, but whether he is prepared to use it constructively for socially approved ends and can assure its confientiality.

In any event, in a study of social organization such as this most conflicts are not likely to be purely private matters. The organizational problems of a public organization such as a school involve differences in philosophy of education, questions about the proper status of teachers and the distribution of work loads, and indeed the very future of public education. These are issues of vital concern to every citizen and educator, not just to the individual teachers involved in this sample. In these semipublic organizations it is not surprising that even the most closely guarded secrets were known by several members of the system. "Gossip" in some sense had already made the events partly public, and no doubt the membership had formed opinions long before the study. The study, then, could have served to explicate shared opinion in some cases, but it did not expose purely private matters.

As a study of relationships, not individuals, the primary ethical issue in this study, then, is not the individual's privacy, but his status and the organization's reputation. There was something at stake, but it was the interests of the organization and the status and defenses of the groups within it. An inquiry into the competition between two teachers for a student or the pressures brought to bear by teachers on a principal to lower teaching loads is not comparable to an investigation of a person's history of mental illness or his love for his mother. The respondent's dilemma was whether to reveal to outsiders the knowledge that was generally available to insiders. Not surprisingly, because problems were organizational, solutions, too, often were organizational: groups of teachers sometimes boycotted the study, and in some cases administrators exerted pressures on teachers to participate.

The right-to-privacy issue itself, insofar as it involves implicit mistrust of the social scientists, develops from a larger dilemma which now confronts social science. On the one hand, social science is postulated on the integrity and objectivity of each and every investigator. But on the other hand, under pressure from the public to justify the utility of their research, social scientists frequently identify with influential groups seeking to promote their own viewpoints and interests. They have eagerly hired themselves out to government agencies and school administrators to alter a situation, help some group achieve its objectives, or protect someone's interests. The persons who have employed social scientists in the past have not necessarily had the interests of teachers and other subordinate groups foremost in mind, and because social scientists claim that the information they gather can be useful to someone, teachers understandably will be wary and justifiably will want to know how the information will be used and whose interests the social scientist represents.[9]

Ironically, then, in seeking to be "useful to society," social scientists have become identified as employees of certain vested-interest groups. Laymen do not readily distinguish basic from applied research and so will be suspicious of all social-science projects. Applied, or so-called "social action," research has made social science publicly acceptable to those people who hire them, but it also has made it extremely difficult for basic researchers to establish their credentials as independent, relatively neutral investigators interested in theoretical knowledge with no particular "ax to grind."

MEASUREMENT

Turning from sampling and field procedures to measurement is merely to substitute one set of problems for a different kind of problem. Upon first impression, different school systems cannot be easily distinguished. They all have a hierarchy of teachers, superintendents and principals, similar courses, and standard operating procedures. Yet, teachers and students will testify that schools are very different from one another. The question is, are these differences capable of being identified and measured? In an attempt to do just that, several yardsticks have been fashioned for the purposes of this study.[10]

But the instruments are admittedly crude; indeed, if premature rigor is a scientific sin, this study is guiltless. One of the major problems is that this research, concerning as it does a comprehensive overview of ways in which structural arrangements are related to conflict, opens onto a vista of concern so wide that a thorough examination of each of them would require an unlikely methodology that is thorough, broad in scope, and efficient. Some efficiency was compelled by financial and time limitations, but sometimes it has been necessary to compromise thoroughness in the interest of scope. Confronted with the unfeasibility of having field observers systematically participate in all 28 schools, plus working within the limits of a lengthy self-administered questionnaire and brief interviews, it was necessary to lean heavily on respondents' reports of their own behavior.

However, someone has said that it does not take a razor to cut warm butter. However crude and tentative, the measures developed here have some degree of reliability and at least take into account a wide range of relevant factors. Hopefully, the reader will be satisfied that the measures to be described have been pondered sufficiently to demonstrate their relevance to the notions they are supposed to represent. In most cases they have been subjected to analyses more rigorous than required for the uses that will be made of them; the measures usually will be treated as ordinal estimates to rank-order schools rather than to calibrate the magnitudes of differences among them. All that can be expected is that our measures can support the weight of a short step in the intended direction.[11]

A TYPOLOGY OF MEASUREMENT

Sociological variables can be classified on the basis of their relationship to personality and social structure (Barton, 1961; Lazarsfeld and Menzel, 1961). Beginning with the most personal variables and proceeding to the inherently structural characteristics, six levels of analysis can be identified which are commonly employed in sociological research:

1. Personal orientations of members—for example, the job satisfaction of a teacher
2. Personal behavior of members—for example, the number of professional conferences an individual has attended during the last year
3. Demographic characteristics of members—for example, a person's age and level of education
4. Official and informal relationships between two positions—for ex-

ample, the number of times a principal visits a teacher's classroom
5. Distributions of member characteristics throughout the organization (which can include any of the above characteristics)—for example, the proportion of a teaching faculty with a master's degree
6. Structural properties not derivable from member characteristics—for example, the number of levels of authority

Generally speaking, the first three categories pertain to individual characteristics and the last three apply to organizational ones. But, also note that the first three can be converted into organizational variables by treating them as distributions. For example, by averaging the job satisfaction of all individual employees in an organization, job satisfaction then becomes a property of the organization not possessed by any particular person. The strictly organizational variables deserve more attention than they customarily have received.

With some justification it can be maintaned that a group is no less real than the individuals within it, and that individual personality itself is a hypothetical construct inferred from the consistency of individual responses. Group properties can be inferred from individual reactions to the group, just as temperature of the sun can be inferred from the reaction of other objects and human beings to it. As Scott points out (1965, p. 130): "Just because an individual is used as a source of data is no reason that the data must describe his own characteristics rather than the characteristics of some external system to which he is . . . responding."

The measures and indices developed for this study will be described in terms of each of the above six categories.

Personal Orientations

The term "orientation" refers to a person's understanding of his relationship to a selected part of his total environment—for example, lower-class and middle-class children are known to have typically different orientations toward school. Orientations are part of a value system. As such they are normative, representing a person's beliefs about what ought to occur (although they are less diffused than attitudes, which in addition to beliefs, include feelings and emotions).[12]

A role orientation (or conception) is limited to orientations that pertain specifically to relationships between members of an organization. As mentioned, a role is a shorthand way of talking about the norms that regulate relationships between positions. A position, in turn, is a composite of roles. It is called a "position" in the sense that the pattern of rights and obligations associated with it determines the social placement of teachers, students, parents, and so forth in relation to one another.[13] Each teacher develops conceptions of the roles he is required to perform, and these are to some degree shared with other people.

Professional orientation

A teacher's conception of his professional role was measured by a 16-item "Likert-type" scale consisting of four subscales: orientation to students, orientation to the profession and professional colleagues, a belief that

Table 4-1. Significance of differences between high and low employee and professional validation groups for employee and professional orientation scales

Employee Validation Groups	N	Mean Employee[a] Scale Score	Test of Significance
High criterion group	44	77.3	
Low criterion group	19	88.0	$t_{18} = 2.48$[b] (high vs. low)
"Known" (high) professional group	19	96.2	

Professional Validation Groups	N	Mean Professional[a] Scale Score	Test of Significance
High criterion group	29	53.1	
Low criterion group	30	48.4	$CR = 10.7$[b] (high vs. low)
"Known" (high) professional group	19	60.1	

[a]For the employee scale higher scores indicate lower orientation. For the professional scale higher scores indicate higher orientation.
[b]Significant at $p \leq .01$ (one-tail test).

competence is based on knowledge, and a belief that teachers should have decision-making authority.[14] An example of each type of item appears below in the order mentioned; the complete scales are reproduced in Appendix 1B:

(a) It should be permissible for a teacher to violate a rule if he or she is sure that the best interests of the students will be served in doing so.
(b) Teachers should try to live up to the standards of their profession even if the administration or the community does not seem to respect them.

(c) Teachers should be evaluated primarily on the basis of their knowledge of the subject matter that is taught and their ability to communicate it.

(d) Small matters should not have to be referred to someone "higher up" for a final answer.

For each item, there are five possible alternatives, ranging from "strongly agree" to "strongly disagree," and weighted from five to one. Total scores were computed for each respondent.[15] The corrected split-half reliability of the scale is $r_n = .65$.[16] A school's professional orientation was represented by the average professional scale scores of its faculty. Each scale discriminates at $p \leq .01$ between select groups of respondents representing extremes in professional and employee behavior.[17] Also, both (a) a group of teachers in a university high school with the reputation for professionalism and (b) the least employee-like groups scored near the expected extremes on each scale: they were among the most professional and least bureaucratic groups in the study.[18] (See Table 4–1.)

Employee orientation

A teacher's conception of his obligations as an employee was measured by a 29-item Likert-type scale consisting of six subscales: loyalty to the administration, loyalty to the organization, a belief that teaching competence is based on experience and the endorsement of treating personnel interchangeably, endorsement of standardization, emphasis on rules and procedures, and loyalty to the public.[19] An example of each type of item appears below in the order mentioned. (See Appendix 1A.)

(a) Personnel who openly criticize the administration should be encouraged to go elsewhere.
(b) What is best for the school is best for education.
(c) Pay should be in relation to experience.
(d) The work of a course should be so well-planned that every child taking the same course throughout the state will eventually cover the same material.
(e) Rules stating when teachers should arrive and depart from the building should be strictly enforced.
(f) Teachers should take into account the opinions of their community to guide what they say in class and in their choice of teaching materials.

A school's employee orientation was represented by the average employee scale scores of its faculty.

On the professional scale, the intensity of professional orientation increases with the magnitude of the scores; but the employee scale was scored in the reverse direction. Like the professional scale, this scale discriminates between select groups of respondents representing extremes in professional and employee behavior.[20]

Job satisfaction

The *linear scales* just described presuppose an underlying variable measured in equal units; *ordinal scales* assume a definite hierarchy of qualities (or ranks) without regard to the distance between them. By comparison, an *index* can be formed from the sum of separate indicators of a concept without making assumptions about the form of the underlying relationship among them, except that they are additive (Lazarsfeld and Menzel, 1961). It should be cautioned that an index is not equivalent to an operational definition; an index does not define a concept in the way that years of schooling, for example, can be considered to be a definition of education. Rather, an index is a substitute for something that cannot be measured directly, in the sense that a test score, for example, is an index of education rather than education itself.

A teacher's satisfaction with his present job was estimated from an index of three items having relatively high intercorrelation.[21] The items concerned whether the teacher felt that the school administration accepted him as a professional expert, his present satisfaction compared to his expectations of the job, and his satisfaction compared to other teaching jobs. The alternatives, weighted from four to one, ranged from "very well-satisfied" to "very dissatisfied." A school's level of job satisfaction is reflected in the average job satisfaction scores of its faculty.

Career satisfaction index

This index consists of two items on which teachers were asked to compare teaching with other types of work and to indicate whether they would enter the field of teaching if they had it to do over again. The alternatives to each item were weighted from four to one. A school's level of career satisfaction is reflected in the average career satisfaction scores of its faculty.

Personal Behavior

Under some conditions, perhaps, behavior can be expected to be consistent with personal orientations. However, a variety of circumstances can intervene between belief and action. When external penalties for deviation are high, or when alternatives are otherwise restricted, the association is likely to be less complete and quite complicated. Accordingly, behavioral measures were developed parallel to the orientation measures just described. Two compounds of behavioral indices were devised using specific practices that seemed relevant to the professional and employee roles.

Professional behavior

Nine criteria were used as an index to assess a person's professional behavior, including number of years of college completed, time devoted to professional reading, participation in professional activities, and the like. Schools were ranked on the accumulative proportion of a faculty scoring high on nine such criteria.[22]

The professional conduct of a faculty does not reflect its professional orientation in a completely linear fashion; the tau is low and not statistically significant. However, the lack of correlation is partially due to the inability of the professional behavior index to discriminate in the middle ranges of the scale.[23] For, the schools in the top quartile of professional behavior do have a significantly higher professional orientation than those in the bottom quartile ($t \leq .05$, one-tail test). Also, schools having a predominantly "high professional-low employee" orientation rank significantly higher on professional behavior (with the rank of 16.3) than those classified as "low professional-high employee" (with a rank of 8.3).

Employee behavior

Five criteria were used in the employee behavior index:

(a) Salary required to move a person from his present position (more than $3,000; more than $1,000; more than $500)
(b) Number of days absence from work during the year (0–2; 3–7; 8–9)
(c) Number of agreements with five unfavorable statements made about the principal (none; no more than two; 3–5; and no agreements with favorable statements)
(d) Number of agreements with nine favorable statements about the principal (3–9 and no agreements with negative statements; up to two; none)
(e) Loyalty to the administration, as rated by the principal (excellent; good or average; below average or poor)

Schools were ranked on the accumulative proportion of faculties scoring high on these criteria. There is a significant positive rank order correlation ($t = .42$) between the average employee-orientation of a school and the average number of times its faculty scores high on the employee-behavior index. Hence, by contrast to professionalism, a faculty's orientation seems to be reflected in parallel behavior patterns, even though imperfectly.

Initiative-compliance scale

Another scale was developed to estimate the tendencies of teachers to use "initiative" or to show "compliance" with respect to their administrators. It consists of 11 hypothetical incidents in which a teacher finds himself

Table 4-2. A typology of initiative and compliance of public high school teachers

Type of Behavior Pattern (N = 1,432)		Anticipated Action[a]	Predicted Constraint[b]
I. Rebellious	(17%)[c]	Initiative-taking	Severe
II. Contrary	(17%)	Initiative-taking	None-moderate
III. Defiant	(17%)	Discreet support-seeking	Severe
IV. Cautious	(18%)	Discreet support-seeking	None-moderate
V. Realistic	(16%)	Compliant-compromising	Severe
VI. Submissive	(16%)	Compliant-compromising	None-moderate

[a]The labels for anticipated action are based on responses to the question "What would *you do* in the situation described above?"
"Initiative"—ask for an investigation by a professional organization; or, refuse to comply with request; or, quit the job.
"Discreet support-seeking"—seek support of colleagues.
"Compliant-compromising"—comply with superior's request; or, try to compromise.
[b]The labels for predicted constraint are based on responses to the question "What do you anticipate will happen to you if you do not comply with the above request?"
"Severe constraint"—loss of deserved promotion or salary increase; or transferred to less desirable position; or, dismissed from the school system.
"None-moderate constraint"—no disapproval or mild disapproval from the principal; or, loss of reputation.
[c]Figures in parentheses indicate the proportion of 1,432 public high school teachers, for whom information was available, whose responses placed them in each cell.

opposed to the administration; the incidents are based on actual conflicts reported in public schools. One item reads: "The assistant principal told a teacher that he was too 'outspoken' in criticizing certain policies of the school, and that this was causing unrest among the faculty members."[24] The complete scale is reproduced in Appendix 1G.

Respondents were asked to imagine themselves in each situation and to indicate (1) what they would do, and (2) the sanctions likely to be imposed against them for failure to comply with the administration's wishes. A typology of initiative and compliance was formed by comparing each respondent's total scale scores on the two parts; the split-half reliability of each is above $rn = .85$ when corrected with the Spearman-Brown Prophesy formula. Because respondents were not asked for their beliefs, but to anticipate their behavior in specific situations, the typology pertains to probable behavior under specified situations and is not considered to describe general personality traits or personal orientations. Six types of role behavior were identified. (See Table 4–2.)

Only 17 percent of the sample would take extreme measures under conditions of severe restraint (that is, the "rebellious" reaction), and one in three is either "rebellious" or "contrary." On the other hand, more than one in three teachers would "comply" and almost one in five would comply without the threat of external sanctions (the "submissive" pattern). One third of the teachers would be more "discreet" and oppose the administration by seeking the support of colleagues. The pattern of response provides advance evidence of the militancy of a substantial minority of teachers. Because a small minority typically spearheads militant movements, the fact that nearly one in five teachers is rebellious is significant.

Demographic Characteristics

Each person in the sample was asked to provide information on a large number of questions that would serve to place him demographically in the formal structure. These questions included age, gender, level of education, and so forth.

Relational Measures

In one sense all sociological variables imply relationships. However, in the case of personal orientations, the relationships are viewed from the separate perspectives of each particular group of people involved. At the other extreme, the significance of structural variables depends upon the pattern formed by relationships between pairs of members. Relational properties cannot be completely derived either from the personal characteristics of the parties involved or from the official structure. While individuals enter into the relationships, and their personal predispositions certainly have an influence, the relationships among them are not determined by their personalities. Relationships are a distinct property of organization, although not necessarily an officially sanctioned one. Four types of relational properties have received attention in this study: informal leadership, socioeconomic status, prestige and esteem, and supervisory practices.

Influence

Several questionnaire items were used to identify the "informal leaders" of each school. Each person in the study nominated three teachers in his school whose ideas and opinions seemed to have received the most support from other teachers over the past year. He also named the teachers with whom he had consulted most frequently since the beginning of the school year for advice about a problem in connection with classroom teaching. People who reported having held office in professions, union, or community organizations served as an independent criterion of leadership. In the first-year sample it was found that each index does a reasonably good job of identifying at least the three or four most influential people in each school. The overlap between the first two indices ($r = .40$) and between each of them and the external criterion of holding office (57 percent of 91 officers in teacher and community organizations were mentioned at least once as having been consulted and 53 percent were mentioned as having the most support) suggests that they are each measuring some common basis of informal leadership.

Sociometric structure

Three simple procedures were used to identify the clique structure of schools: (1) teachers were requested to name their three best friends at school, (2) they estimated the frequency with which they saw one another socially outside of work (rated on a five-point scale), and (3) they reported on the frequency they normally lunched with each other member of the school (rated on a five-point scale). School averages were obtained by multiplying each weight by the number of respondents receiving it and dividing it by the number of respondents.[25]

Esteem

A teacher's esteem was tabulated from the number of times he was nominated by other respondents as one of three teachers in the school whose ideas about public education are most respected. In the first-year study this measure was correlated with the number of nominations for the most support from other teachers ($r = .50$).

Supervisory practices

A crude index of supervisory relationships is based on teachers' reactions to a series of five negative and nine positive statements drawn from Halpin's Leadership Behavior Questionnaire which describes the behavior of a principal: "He acts without consulting"; "He is one of the most competent educators in the system"; and the like.[26] Schools were ranked on the average number of positive and negative statements agreed to by their faculties.

Close supervision

The amount of surveillance by principals and central-office administrators was measured with a Guttman quasiscale of close supervision constructed from 14 items answered by principals and teachers.[27] The questions pertained to the number of classroom observations normally made by the administrators, as well as the nature of follow-up and consultation (afterwards); whether permission must be obtained to discuss controversial issues; the amount of supervision by the central office, including the frequency of the superintendent's visits to the school plus the number of reports required by the central office; and the fairness and accuracy reported by teachers of their administrator's evaluations of them. (See appendix 1E.) It is a quasiscale, with a coefficient of reproducibility of .85 (which is below the desired .90); its minimal-marginal reproducibility is .71.

Distributional Measures

All of the personal orientation and behavioral measures so far described can be converted into organizational properties by computing their distributions for each organization; for example, schools can be classified according to the average professional scores of the individual faculty members. In addition, several measures were developed exclusively as distribution properties.

Indices of conflict rates[28]

Several indices of organizational tension and conflict were developed from both questionnaire data and the interviews.

Questionnaire measures: Each respondent indicated on a checklist of the names of faculty members and administrators in his school the colleagues with whom he had "severe" and "moderate" disagreements. He also estimated the "degree of tension" (that is, severe, moderate, slight or none, weighted from 4 to 1) existing in his school among 12 types of roles. Schools were ranked on the average rate of conflict per person and on average tension.

Interview measures: Specific conflict incidents were described in tape-recorded interviews with teachers and administrators. They were asked to describe any "difficulties, problems, friction incidents or disputes" involving themselves or other members of the faculty that had occurred during the academic year or in the recent past. An "incident" is defined as a description of a concrete episode in which a verbal attack or criticism was made against a teacher, group of teachers, or the school as a whole. A single episode was counted as one incident, regardless of the number of teachers involved in it or the number of times the same incident was mentioned by different teachers.[29] Each incident was classified in several ways by three of the graduate students who were the people who did the interviewing.[30] Its form was categorized as one of the following:

1. Complaint
   (a) General complaint (for example, "I don't like the way things are run here.")
   (b) Complaints against a specific group or individual
   (c) Complaints about policy
2. Overt Incident
   (a) Open dispute between two people
   (b) Dispute among three or more people, usually involving an administrator
   (c) Two or more heated discussions
   (d) A major incident—one involving others in addition to the initial parties (usually a substantial segment of the organization and members of the community) in a heated dispute
3. Impersonal Competition—not involving face-to-face confrontation but involving known tension between two or more parties due to their opposing positions or ideas

Also, the general content of each incident was classified into one of seven general categories; these in turn were divided into a total of 26 subcategories.[31]

The indices of organizational conflict are based on the number of each type of incident reported per interview. For convenience, the number of each type of incident reported per interview will be referred to as an incident ratio. For most analyses the following incident ratios were used: the gross incident ratio (that is, the number of incidents reported after complaints were deducted from the total); the dispute ratio; the major incident ratio; the ratio of incidents involving authority issues; and the teacher-administrator incident ratio. Analyses show that the measures derived from questionnaires and interviews tap somewhat different dimensions of conflict. But although the measures cannot be treated interchangeably, there are relatively modest positive correlation coefficients among them, which suggests that the measures are also tapping a common underlying dimension.[32]

Heterogeneity index

A variety of "latent" roles and value systems are introduced to most organizations by the different social backgrounds, experiences, and training of their members. A simple profile of the heterogeneity in these background factors was constructed for each school by dichotomizing 13 characteristics (such as sex, age, educational level, urban residence, and so forth) and computing the ratio of faculty members in each category.[33] A school's total score is the sum of these ratios. Subtotals were computed in the same way for local and cosmopolitan characteristics included in the index.

Properties of the Formal Structure[34]

The outstanding feature of formal structure is that it is relatively uninfluenced by the particular members who implement it. For the same reason, however, it cannot be directly derived from either the personal characteristics of members or combinations of them. Of course, integral properties of organization have a fundamental bearing on all relationships, but these properties are distinguished from the relational aspects by the fact that they are subject to relatively severe official sanctions (including a legal process and dismissal procedures), and are relatively more stable, often capable of enduring complete replacements of personnel. In practice, whether a characteristic such as standardization is a formal system property or whether it is a reflection of a few authoritarian administrators who have been in power for a long time may not be immediately apparent. One test, however, is whether the practices of different organizations, having different members, can be predicted from their structures; another is how much change in relationships occurs with turnover of personnel.

Indices of centralization

Centralization of authority, like several of the other concepts employed in the study, is complex and difficult to assess with the simple indices that could be employed within the scope of this study.[35] But a crude index of the level of authority at which policy decisions are made was constructed by asking teachers to indicate (a) who should have the final authority to approve each of 32 types of decisions, and (b) who actually does approve each type of decision. The possible alternatives were: the individual teachers involved, the teaching faculty, the principal in consultation with teachers or with an appointed committee, the principal, the superintendent, the school board members, or the state department of education. (See Appendix 1C.) Levels of authority were given numerical weights (from 1 for the individual teachers involved to 7 for state departments of education), and the weights were multiplied by the number of respondents specifying each level. The mean position of each school was computed for two parts of the instrument: one set of decisions seemed to be especially desirable to the most professionally oriented group of teachers; they were called the "professional" decision items; the other items were called the "nonprofessional" decisions.[36] The two parts of the scale, professional-type decisions and the nonprofessional ones, are significantly correlated ($t = .45$).

To get at another dimension of decision making, teachers were also asked about their degree of authority to make day-to-day routine decisions which normally arise in the course of their teaching. This measure is based on three global items in the descriptive part of the professional role scale, pertaining to the amount of authority delegated to teachers.[37] Responses were weighted from 5 (strongly agree) to 1 (strongly disagree) and averaged for each school. The correlations of this measure with centralization of nonprofessional and professional policies are inconsequential.

The autonomy of a faculty was calculated by using the average frequency with which its members report consulting with the administration about decisions concerning their classroom work. Faculties were considered to have less autonomy in schools where the rates of consultation (per teacher) were higher. Finally, teachers and principals were asked to estimate the number of levels of authority in their school and in the total system. The average of this estimate was used as an index of the extent of the hierarchy.

Standardization

Standardization is also a complex concept, which is perhaps one reason that there are few reliable measures of this concept available.[38] A

Guttman quasiscale was developed; it consists of 15 questions answered by the principal and teachers of each school, which pertain to the amount of discretion permitted in lesson plans, the role teachers have played in their preparation, teachers' authority to choose textbooks, and their options over the use of textbooks. (See Appendix 1F.) The scale has achieved a coefficient of reproducibility of .84 and a marginal reproducibility of .74.[39]

This measure was supplemented with one of the subscales pertaining to rules taken from the descriptive part of the employee status scale. It consists of five statements about the existence and enforcement of rules and teachers' familiarity with them.[40] This index shows only a slight and statistically nonsignificant correlation with the rules subscale ($t = .14$). These appear to be largely independent dimensions of standardization.

Specialization

The use an organization makes of its more specialized personnel depends upon both the amount of specialized training initially required of them and whether their special training matches the jobs to which they are assigned. The use of teachers as specialists was inferred from the proportion reporting that they are teaching courses in which (a) they have not majored in college and (b) they have neither majored nor minored.[41] These two items will be used as indices of a faculty's level of specialization. The two measures tend to rank schools in a similar, though hardly identical, way ($t = .40$); although they are perhaps measuring related characteristics, the measures cannot substitute for each other.

Complexity

Specialized uses of personnel should not be confused with the "division of labor." The latter term refers to the number of separate work *units* in an organization without regard to their position in the chain of command. It is possible for an organization with an intricate division of work to make little use of any specialized training its personnel may have. In fact, refinements in the division of labor often reduce the level of skill and authority needed by an employee (for example, the assembly line).

Organizational complexity is perhaps the most troublesome concept to assess of any in this study. A Guttman quasiscale was developed that used 17 variables concerning the number of distinct organizational parts in a school system. The scale items (all but one of which were answered by principals) include (a) the estimated number of levels of authority in the school and in the system; (b) the estimated number of weeks it normally would take to effect a curriculum change; (c) the number of staff in the school and in the system; (d) the percentage of part-time teachers, clerical personnel, and administrators in the system; (e) the number of classes in the school with ability grouping; and (f) the number of separate programs and classes in the school. (See Appendix 1D). The coefficient reproducibility is .85 and the minimal marginal reproducibility is .65.

IMPLICATIONS

Laymen are sometimes just as impatient with long-winded discussions of procedures as social scientists are disturbed when their colleagues take shortcuts to describe their work. But it should be clear that practitioners have as much to gain as social scientists in familiarizing themselves with methodological procedures and problems of doing this kind of research and in helping to find better ways of studying organizations. Everyone is becoming more aware that methodologies must be appraised in view of the context of actual situations, that social scientists cannot reasonably be required to conform to unrealistic absolutes, and that knowledge based on any set of standards and procedures must be regarded as conditional.[42] In view of the normal difficulties of sampling complex organizations, together with the sensitive problems being investigated here, the customary sampling procedures and the usual precautions against respondent bias are unrealistic and not of much use as guidelines. The standard procedures available were originally developed for the purpose of sampling populations of individuals rather than of organizations. All three of the issues that arose during the course of this research—reluctance to discuss conflict, fear of reprisal, and ethical considerations—have in common the fact that organizational pressures can distort the responses of individuals. The problem, then, is that most existing methodologies do not help much to resolve the distinctive problems created by sampling organizations and investigating problems within organizational contexts. There are not yet available sufficiently reliable and standardized instruments to measure most organizational variables. Experiences with this project emphasize the need for a set of ethical standards as well as better methodology procedures that are better fitted to populations of organizations. We badly need better techniques to estimate, discount, or overcome the type of bias inherent in fieldwork conducted under these conditions. Practitioners should be alert to the kinds of problems involved in doing this kind of study before they begin to utilize, or to criticize, its findings. Perhaps they, above anyone else, should be aware of the limitations in the data when interpreting the findings.

Despite some of the problems discussed here, in perspective, it should be emphasized that, on the whole, the measurements developed do have some face validity. They have seemed to us to help in understanding organizations—that is, to make some sense.

Some interviewees were cooperative and most appeared to endorse the aims of the study. In fact, the candidness of most teachers who had problems to report is remarkable in view of the issues that troubled a few of them. Some teachers appeared to appreciate the opportunity to discuss their problems with a neutral observer and a sympathetic listener; others, seeming to feel that their problems probably had already been reported by others, appeared to appreciate the opportunity to present "their side" of the story; a few seemed willing to discuss a problem with the hope that our staff would have the power to help them do something about it. But most respondents in the study appeared to cooperate because they sincerely wanted to be of assistance. This fact speaks well for the interest of educational practitioners in improving our long-range understanding about the dynamics of organizational problems.

NOTES: Chapter 4

[1] The number of schools from each state is as follows: Ohio (24), Michigan (2), Indiana (1), and Pennsylvania (1). The data were collected in two phases. Seven schools were included in a one-year feasibility study, conducted during the spring of 1962, which served as the basis for developing most of the instruments and procedures (Corwin, 1963); and an additional 21 schools were visited between November, 1964, and April, 1965. The two samples were treated separately in the preliminary analyses, but because the conclusions reached from both were uniform, they were combined. The breakdown of schools by sizes is as follows:

Number of Teachers	Number of Schools Included
107–168	5
87–106	6
52– 86	6
40– 51	4
14– 39	7

A letter of invitation was sent to school superintendents, who in most cases forwarded it to the school's principal for a final decision. Of 78 schools invited, 31, or 40 percent, agreed to participate (scheduling prevented including all 31). By comparison, Delany (1961) was able to obtain only a 60 percent rate of participation of public agencies after securing prior approval of the questionnaire and deleting controversial material.

Three fourths of the respondents returned their questionnaires, although six schools fell below the average rate for both questionnaires and interviews; in two schools one third or less returned questionnaires. Nearly one half of those who returned questionnaires were interviewed in tape-recorded sessions lasting from 20 minutes to more than an hour. A stratified random sample (of as many as 36 faculty members) was interviewed. Nearly all of the faculty members in smaller schools could be interviewed, but in larger schools interviewees were randomly selected from each academic department as well as from special education, driver education, extracurricular activities, counselors, supervisors, athletic coaches, and drama and music teachers. It occasionally was deemed advisable to include some teachers who, though not randomly selected, were otherwise known to be good informants or involved in major incidents. Interviewees were given a precoded list of all faculty members in the school and instructed to refer to other teachers by the code numbers listed beside each name. The interviews were open-ended and loosely structured. Interviewers were instructed to direct the interview in whatever direction seemed most relevant and productive.

[2] To be more specific, our sample is roughly comparable to national samples of secondary teachers on: age (37 compared to 36 for the nation as a whole); years of experience (12.5 compared to 11.4 for the rest of the nation); marital status (74 percent compared to 70 percent); years of college (5.1 compared to 4.9); proportion of teachers with a master's degree (38 percent compared to 35 percent); proportion of teachers classified as active in professional organizations (59 percent compared to 56 percent); proportion of teachers in the union (8 percent compared to 10 percent nationally). This sample is also close to other teachers in Ohio on the sex ratio (60 percent male), years teaching experience (12.5), and years of college completed (4.9). However, the sample overrepresents the proportion of teachers with a master's degree in Ohio by 10 percent. Also, the proportion of males in the study is about 7 percent over the national average, and the study overrepresents the proportion of

teachers who have attended private institutions of higher education by 14 percent. Also, the median salary for teachers in this sample ($7,000) is $600 above the 1965 figure for Ohio secondary teachers and $500 above the national median (although this discrepancy may be due to lags between collecting and publishing these figures).

[3] Although the size of a teaching faculty is not strongly related to the relevant organizational variables, it is modestly associated with many of them (see Chapter 5), and for that reason school size appeared to be the single most efficient sampling criterion. Because the purpose of the study was to examine varying types of organizations in relation to conflict in the teaching profession and not to assess the prevalence of conflict in the region, the sample does not reflect the actual distribution of high schools within the region. This fact, together with the small sample size, of course, reduces the validity of statistics. Although the sample is not very different from a random sample of high school teachers in many respects, generalizations must be drawn cautiously. The sample could be looked upon as 28 case studies.

[4] The distribution of staff size in Ohio public secondary schools was tabulated from a 30 percent random sample of schools listed in the State of Ohio *Education Directory* (school year 1962–63). For purposes of the study, this distribution was arbitrarily divided into five categories. Three or four schools in each category were selected at random and invited by letter to participate in the study. To reduce community influences, most schools selected were from middle-income neighborhoods. Some variation in economic base was unavoidable because of differences between small towns and large cities; the support for schools in the sample varies from as low as $250 per pupil to $450 per pupil. The schools also vary in the proportion of total receipts derived from state subsidies (from 50 percent to 15 percent) and in the proportion of graduates who go to college (from 90 to 60 percent). There is a somewhat higher participation rate in the "very large" schools, which also have self-contained research units, but greater specialization could help to alleviate time pressures in the schools.

[5] At another school where the principal admitted to some pressure from the superintendent to participate in the study, a committee of teachers hostile to the study was appointed. The principal and the committee were able to devise a polemic against participating that apparently convinced the superintendent.

[6] In one system the board had previously recommended that students evaluate their teachers, using a form similar to the one used in the study. The coincidence aroused the suspicions of a few wary teachers. It was rumored at one point that the local teachers' organization was considering an investigation of the study; however, the president of the teachers' association involved was reportedly in favor of the study, and no official complaint was filed.

[7] A graduate research assistant visited each school for an average of five days (see Acknowledgments). On the first day of his visit questionnaires were distributed and procedures for completing them were explained during a faculty meeting. The six-part questionnaire requires two to three hours to complete. Due to the length of the questionnaire, respondents were permitted to complete them at their convenience during the week; although they were requested not to discuss their answers among themselves, there was no way to control this element. They were assured that their participation was voluntary, that the responses would be completely confidential, and that their questionnaires would not be seen by anyone in their school or that their school would not be identified in any of the published data.

[8] The presence of a tape recorder did not appear to inhibit most interviewees, although some of them may have felt constrained to submit to it because they knew that other teachers were using it. One interviewee refused to discuss a problem freely during the interview, but she did discuss it after the tape recorder had been turned off; that situation involved an illegal report made by the administration to the state department of education falsifying the teacher's qualifications to teach a subject. But, on the whole, the tape recorder did not seem to be an important factor.

[9] Some social scientists do not acknowledge a distinction between pure and applied research. However, such a distinction can be made on the basis of such criteria

as the specificity of objectives of the research, who determines those objectives, the source of the hypotheses, the degree of change intended by the research, the lapse of time expected before the effectiveness of the research can be evaluated, the criteria used to evaluate the research, and the degree of control exercised by the funding agency over research policy and operation.

[10] Most instruments and procedures described here were developed in a feasibility study supported by the U.S. Office of Education, Contract Number 1934, in anticipation of this project (Corwin, 1963).

[11] At least since the American soldier series during World War II, social scientists have been conscious of the seriousness of the problems connected with measuring organizational characteristics. Some indices have been developed which seem to be reliable for specific purposes. Barton's (1961) comprehensive review of empirical measures for studying college characteristics provides one of the most useful current references. In a search of over 100 studies, nearly 150 separate measures of in-put, out-put, environmental characteristics, organizational structures and members' attitudes plus activities were identified. While this heritage is in some respects lean, it can be cultivated. We shall profit from it in considering the more immediate problems of measuring the organizational characteristics of public schools.

[12] There is variability in the way similar roles are conceived and performed in different organizations, and also from situation to situation within an organization, depending upon the values of different members. These differences cause tension which eventually can modify the role system itself. For that reason, despite its many ambiguities, the concept of role orientation can be of substantial utility in studying conflict in complex organizations. For a review of the variety of meanings associated with this concept and some associated problems see the review of literature by Biddle and Thomas (1966).

[13] In addition to their component roles, positions can be divided into "segments." Whereas a role includes all norms relevant to a relationship between two positions, a role segment is a selection of norms shared in common with several roles. The same norms, for example, that define teachers as "disciplinarians" with respect to students make disciplinarians of principals with respect to teachers. Several professional and employee norms, which govern the appropriate amount of initiative and compliance, are commonly incorporated in many different roles. A role segment constitutes a kind of recognizable position, too, albeit an unofficial and latent one in the sense that it is not deliberately created and quite often is not officially recognized. The value of this concept is that it permits comparison between similar norms incorporated in different systems as well as comparison of similarities throughout different parts of the same system. Parallels between the professional segment of the nurse-physician role in hospitals, for example, and the corresponding aspects of the teacher-principal role in a different system can be bridged through this concept.

[14] Interrelations among the subscale scores of individuals range from .50 to .70, and the correlations of the subscales with the total scale score range from .76 to .91. The rankings of a school on orientation to colleagues and decision-making authority also are correlated with its total professional score ($r_s = .68$ and .62, respectively). Because the subscales are designed to measure different dimensions of a complex concept, it is not necessary that they contribute equally to the total scale score as long as they are logically related and there is some degree of empirical relationship to the general concept. Nevertheless, it is notable that a school's client orientation is not significantly correlated with its total professional scale score ($r_s = .16$) despite the fact that this subscale is correlated with the total scale scores of the individual teachers ($r_s = .54$). This fact indicates that, at the level of school-wide climates, schools that are professional in some respects are not necessarily client oriented. Client orientation will be analyzed separately for some purposes.

[15] Selvin and Hagstrom (1963) suggest as an alternative to scaling individual scores that group data should be scaled by averaging the responses to each question separately for each group and then combining questions only after the individual data have been transformed in this way. The procedure is appealing, but its disadvantage is that the scales cannot be used for the dual purpose of simultaneously measuring

individual orientations and organizational climates; nor is there evidence that the conclusions reached using each procedure would differ.

Of course, two respondents could verbally "agree" while using incomparable standards in fact. Rosen and Rosen (1955) have found, however, that Likert-type scale scores can be treated by both parametric and nonparametric techniques with comparable results. For this study the nonparametric technique was used. The final sets of items in each scale were tested for internal consistency, using critical ratio and scale-value-difference techniques. The scale-value-difference ratio is the ratio between the maximum difference theoretically possible (computed between the groups at the extreme quartiles on each item) and the actual difference between these extreme groups on the total set of items; only the items with a scale-value-difference ratio of .32 and above have been retained in either scale; most of them have discriminative power above .50. With the method of internal consistency, an item is acceptable for inclusion in the final scale when it discriminates between respondents whose total scores on the combined set of items place them at each extreme of the distribution. Only items accounting for most of the differences between the two extreme groups have been retained. The critical ratio scale-value-difference method roughly selects the same items as first order intercorrelations among the items (Webb, 1964, p. 65).

[16] Neither the scales developed by Webb to measure the professionalism of elementary teachers nor the professional scale developed by Sorensen (1965) for application to accountants achieved much better reliability than was achieved by the professional scale developed for this much. The lower reliability of the professional scale could be due to factual inconsistencies in the opinions of teachers about professionalism. It should be recalled, however, that the reliability figures report pertains to the measurement of individual subjects, not to large groups of subjects, which would appear to demand less interindividual reliability.

It is also possible that by an outside criterion the schools in the study are clustered within a limited range of the maximum existing range of organizational characteristics. The assumption of equal intervals, which is implicit when the measures are used, makes sense only for comparison among the data at hand. For these reasons, in most cases, ordinal, or rank-order, measures were used instead of cardinal measures having a precise zero point.

[17] The 29 most professional teachers in the sample were selected because they placed high on all criteria: five or more years of education (excluding those trained at normal schools); subscription to two or more professional journals; reading professional journals more than five hours a week; publication of two or more articles in professional journals; officer in a professional organization or active contributor to professional committees or meetings. The 30 least professional teachers in the sample have generally opposite characteristics.

The 44 teachers chosen to represent the most bureaucratic teachers met these criteria: judged by the principal as an excellent employee; one or more standard deviation below the sample mean on a check list of criticisms against the school and its administrators; would not leave the school for an increase up to $3,000 per year; fewer than five days sick leave during the year. The 19 teachers in the least bureaucratic employee group have generally opposite characteristics.

[18] Colombotos (1962) used a four-item index of teacher professionalism; it pertained to technical competence, the autonomy of teachers, and the service ideal. Teachers were asked how important each of these elements were when they began to teach and also about current importance. The seven junior high schools in his sample were ranked according to the average scores of their faculties. The low rank-order correlation ($t = -.05$) between professional climate and past professionalism of teachers, together with a tau of .43 between professional climate and net increase in professionalism, seemed to support the interpretation that the professional working climate of a school has an influence in shaping the orientations of its teachers.

Webb developed more elaborate multiple-item, Likert-type professional and employee scales to measure the orientations of 200 elementary school teachers in Central Ohio. The employee scale is geared to four bureaucratic principles: technical specialization, vertical differentiation, office-based integration, and uniformity due to rules. Four parallel scales were developed to measure allegiance to four professional principles: functional specialization, horizontal differentiation, competence-based integration, and uniformity based on general principles. (The interitem correlations among the eight subscales ranged from $r = .55$ to $.79$, and the interitem reliability of the two total scales was $r = .88$ and $.84$.) A low inverse relationship between the two total scales ($r = -.16$) indicated some conflict between professional and bureaucratic modes of organization. The bureaucratic scale was related positively to a person's loyalty to the local school system and inversely to his belief that standards and requirements for teacher certification should be raised; the professional pattern was related inversely to loyalty to the local school system and positively related to the belief that standards and requirements for teacher certification should be raised.

[19] Linear correlations among the subscale scores of individuals range from $.37$ to $.79$, and correlations between the subscale scores and total scores of the employee scale range from $r = .55$ to $r = .85$. Administrative orientation and rules orientation are most highly correlated with the total employee scale ($r = .85$). Because the subscales are designed to measure different dimensions of a complex concept, it is not necessary that they contribute equally to the total scale score as long as they are related empirically and logically to the general concept.

[20] In an analysis of more than 1,500 respondents, the total scores of the two scales (taking into account the reverse scoring on the employee scale) were found to be inversely correlated ($r = -.57$). In contrast to the correlation of individual scale scores, a Spearman rank-order correlation between the average professional and employee orientations of schools was not significant ($r_s = -.07$). At the level of organizational climates, then, the scales are measuring distinct variables and not opposite ends of the same continuum as they tend to do in the case of individuals.

[21] The two indices of work satisfaction developed are based on five items from a more inclusive scale constructed by Gross and his colleagues (1958):

1. How does teaching compare with other types of work?
2. If you "had it to do over again," would you enter the field of teaching?
3. On the whole, are you satisfied that the school administration accepts you as a professional expert to the degree to which you feel you are entitled by reason of your position, training, and experience?
4. How satisfied are you with your present job when you consider the expectations you had when you took the job?
5. Please check the statement which best expresses your feeling concerning how *satisfied* you are with your job when you compare it to other teaching jobs.

The first two items pertain to satisfaction with a career in the vocation of teaching, while the latter three items pertain to satisfaction with the particular job. Because the two sets of items are not highly intercorrelated, they will be used as two separate measures.

[22] The index of professional behavior is comprised of these criteria:

(a) Number of years of college completed (5–8; 4; 0–3)
(b) Highest college degree (M.A., Ph.D., or Ph.E.; B.A., B.S., or B.Ed.; none)
(c) Type of college (liberal arts; college of education; normal school or teachers college)
(d) Hours per week devoted to professional reading (11 or more; 5–10; less than 5)
(e) Activity in professional organizations (held office, active on committees or contributed to programs; attended conferences regularly; none—membership or dues member only)
(f) Number of workshops or conferences attended during the past two years (4 or more; 2–3; 0–1)
(g) Number of professional journals subscribed to (5 or more; 1–4; none)
(h) Number of articles published (3 or more; 1–2; none)
(i) Employed full time (yes; no)

Respondents were assigned weights from 3 to 1, depending upon their position in the total distribution. Each respondent was scored on each of the nine criteria and rated according to the total number of times he scored in the "high" category. Schools were ranked on the accumulated proportion of faculty scoring high on each of the nine criteria.

[23] The problem of validating orientation measures is at best complex. The appropriateness of a particular outside criterion depends upon the type of relationship that is assumed to exist between personal orientations and specific observable behaviors. Must groups known to behave professionally necessarily express professional orientations, and vice versa? If a discrepancy between behavior and orientation is possible, then what is the basis for validating a normative scale against groups known to behave differently?

[24] Similar items describe an attempt of a principal to determine course content and methods of teaching; the participation of a teacher in local school board elections against school board rules; the efforts of a principal to change a grade given by one of his teachers; the efforts of an administration to prohibit the use of a standard textbook because it is "socialistically" inclined; teachers' disapproval of the administration's proposed change of the course of study; a teacher who takes a public stand on the issue of water fluoridation in a community divided on the issue; a teacher who refuses to move into the school district where he is teaching; and discrimination against women in a school.

[25] Weiss and Jacobson (1955) developed a much more formidable (but difficult to use) matrix analysis for identifying the structure of work groups in a specific organization on the basis of respondents' identifications of their co-workers. It was possible to relate the structural differences in size of work groups and extent and type of contact among workers to different divisions of the organization.

[26] The number of positive statements about the principal is associated with a faculty's employee orientation ($t = .34$), and even more closely associated with its level of employee behavior ($t = .66$), but is not highly associated with their professional orientations ($t = .17$ ns); there is a clearer tendency for faculties which behave professionally to show respect ($t = .25$).

Halpin (1956) developed two scales to assess the supervisory patterns of 50 Ohio school superintendents, one measuring "initiating structure" (for example, clear communication channels), and the other "consideration" (for example, friendship and mutual trust). Only 19 of them were described by their staffs as being high on both measures. In a later study Halpin and Croft (1962) designed a 64-item questionnaire to characterize the "climates" of 71 elementary schools in six regions of the country. Six organizational climates were identified along a continuum defined as open at one end and as closed at the other.

[27] This and other programs used for Guttman scaling were written by the Health Services Computing Facility, UCLA. Twelve variables eventually were dichotomized (scored 1 and 7, respectively) and two were trichotomized. The schools were ranked according to the Cornell technique on the bases of scale patterns. Their scores ranged from 66 to 74.

[28] A variety of methods have been used to study organizational conflict. One study relied on the judgments of an organization's members concerning the over-all "tension" in the organization (Zald, 1962); Lazarsfeld and Thielens (1958) used the number of incidents involving academic freedom reported by professors; Haas (1963) recorded incidents as they arose in hospital work groups. Flanagan (1954) has used the critical incident technique to infer the state of relations in school systems. An attempt at a more complicated measure, "authority conflict," specifically in the public schools was reported by Anderson (1964), who surveyed teachers of English, science, and industrial arts in a stratified sample of ten junior high schools. A 15-item scale with a split-half reliability of $r = .67$ was developed. Average correlations among the items ranged from .01 to .61. The index was based on the degree of teacher satisfaction with such diverse considerations as administrative backing and recognition of teachers, class assignments, transfer requests, faculty room and dining room provi-

sions, and the teachers' attitudes toward collective bargaining and union membership.

[29] Few incidents (10 percent) were corroborated in the sense that two or more respondents described the same particulars; however, in the interest of collecting a large variety of incidents, respondents were not specifically asked to do so. Because there was clear convergence in every school on the frequency with which certain types of incidents were mentioned, it is likely that many noncorroborated incidents could be attributed to small samples and the failure to probe rather than to distorted reports. Moreover, nearly half of the incidents in the first year's study were either corroborated or reported by "reliable" respondents—that is, those mentioning a corroborated incident. The frequency with which validated, reliable, and nonvalidated and nonreliable types of issues were mentioned was not significantly different as tested by chi square. Finally, while some champions of participant observation tend to view reports of behavior which they themselves did not observe with a jaundiced eye, it seems equally plausible that estimates accumulated from respondents' detailed descriptions of specific events are more reliable than reports based on the personal observations of a single investigator.

[30] The coders first worked independently and then rechecked each other's work, discussing their points of disagreement until they reached a joint conclusion. Sometimes only incomplete information was available or statements were so vague that their implications were unknown; it was sometimes more desirable to force an incident into the available categories than continually to expand the taxonomy; and some conflicts had so many ramifications that it was difficult to determine which of their several possible dimensions was primary. Because the coders' ability to agree on the *specific* classifications is the most stringent test of intercoder reliability (the general subcategories are automatically defined once the specific content has been determined), that index was computed. Using a stratified random sample of 172 incidents from 28 schools, the two principal coders, working independently, agreed on the content type of 87 percent of the incidents when they were reexamined; but 10 percent of these agreements, curiously, differed from the original coding, leaving a total consensus of 77 percent between the two coders on the first and second coding of 306 specific categories. The agreement on reclassification of the form of conflict was lower—68 percent. Considering the fact that for most purposes these specific categories were combined and enlarged, and assuming that most of the disagreement occurred within the broad categories rather than between, the coding reliability seems to be reasonably satisfactory.

[31] These are the seven general categories:

1. Authority problems—Control over curriculum and classroom work, control over general school policy, competition for official authority and for social prestige, chain-of-command problems, incongruity among status, overlapping authority problems, insubordination, supervision problems, and misuse of authority.
2. Activity problems—Distribution of teaching assignments and other duties, scheduling of shared facilities and of students, problems involving enforcement of rules, lack of policy, problems involving change, and problems involving the distribution of rewards.
3. Personal interaction and communication problems—Problems involving the official system of communication, social isolation and socializing problems among members of a school, methods of communication, and school-community problems.
4. Valence-sentiment problems—Problems involving alienation, lack of cooperation, and personality clashes.
5. School finances and facilities—Problems involving lack of money, school bond failures, shortages of faculty, and the like.
6. Value conflicts—Problems of moral and religious impropriety, economic and racial bias, appropriateness of disciplinary measures, and the like.
7. School philosophy—Differences of opinion about philosophy of education, general objectives, general merit of different programs, and the like.

Procedures

The categories were refined even further, so that 306 specific conflict-types were identified.

Each incident was also classified according to the parties involved—for example, teachers versus administrators, teacher union versus state professional associations, and the like. And, finally, consideration was given to several other factors, including reactions of the parties, disposition and resolution of the issues, and who won or lost.

[32] The measures were compared with one another for consistency. Generally speaking, each of the questionnaire measures of disagreement and organizational tension is correlated with several of the measures derived from interviews. However, none of the rank-order correlations among the 28 schools is higher than $t = .38$:

1. The correlations between disagreement rates and organizational tension and the number of conflicts, complaints, and competitive relations reported per interview range between $t = .23$ and $t = .31$.
2. The correlations for individuals tend to be higher, ranging from $r = .52$ to $r = .78$.
3. All of the measures of severe, moderate, and total disagreement from the questionnaire correlate with the dispute ratio, calculated from the interview data ($t = .34$ to $.38$). Some of the disagreement indices also correlate with teacher-teacher and teacher-administrator conflict rates.
4. The major incident ratio is not significantly associated with severe disagreement among teachers; in fact, it is negatively associated with their total disagreement rate, although, at the same time, it is positively correlated with tension with the principal ($t = .31$). Major incidents, in other words, are indicative of problems between teachers and administrators rather than of problems among teachers themselves.

Tension between principals and teachers is higher in schools with proportionately more personal complaints and heated discussions ($t = .24$) and with less impersonal competition ($t = -.26$); it is associated with authority problems ($t = .28$) rather than with either scheduling or distribution problems.

Although it would perhaps be desirable if the correlations between the questionnaire and interview measures were higher, in view of the differences in the two procedures it is notable that they are correlated at all. For, they are necessarily tapping different dimensions of the problems. The interviews included only a small proportion of any one faculty and were necessarily selective of only the more salient problems which had come to the attention of others. In the questionnaire, on the other hand, which was answered by the vast majority of teachers, the minor disagreements could be tapped as well.

[33] The total index consists of the sum of the ratios of faculty members on the following characteristics:

(a) Sex ratio—male/female
(b) Age ratio—under 30/over 45
(c) Marital status ratio—single/married
(d) Urban background—graduated in a city of under 10,000/over 10,000
(e) Mobility ratio—number of jobs/years of experience
(f) Staff expansion and turnover ratio—number hired in past two years/faculty size in past two years
(g) Education ratio—M.A. or better/B.A. or less
(h) Ratio of activity in teacher organizations—union/professional associations
(i) Ratio of number of years in the system—over 9 years/under 9 years
(j) Ratio of previous residence in county where now teaching—yes/no
(k) Ratio of office holders in community organizations—yes/no
(l) Ratio of number of systems taught in—one or less/two or more
(m) Ratio of those attending college in the same state where teaching—yes/no

[34] Hemphill's work (1956) is one of the most diligent efforts to measure organizational variables. Although his monograph was published a decade ago, the fact that

it remains one of the most advanced statements to date is a disconcerting indication of the languid pace at which methodology in this field has progressed. A questionnaire consisting of 150 Likert-type statements was used to measure 13 group dimensions, such as autonomy from other groups, control over members, flexibility, and so forth. Intercorrelations among the various dimensions were relatively small, with the exception of a negative correlation between control and autonomy ($r = -.55$). A school in the sample was described by teachers as relatively autonomous, stable, and exercising moderately high control over the conduct of its teachers, but it had little emphasis on stratification, less intimacy than the standard population, a heterogeneous membership that was difficult to join. The school was important to the group and did require considerable participation.

Hall (1963) devised similar measures of several organizational variables. Using 82 global Likert-type statements which were answered by organization members, six scales were then devised, including scales to measure the hierarchy of authority, division of labor, rules, procedural specifications, impersonality, and technical competence. Scale reliabilities in ten organizations ranged from .80 to .90. A few of Hall's items were adapted for use in the professional and employee scales developed for this study.

The difficulty with the global-statement approach used by Hall and used in a few of the principal scales of this study is that respondents estimate only the aggregative characteristics (for example, "how much" authority the faculty has), leaving the investigator with virtually no knowledge of the specific incidents on which respondents have based their conclusions. Nevertheless, MacKay (1964) found that although staff members of schools desired more bureaucratization, their observations of particular schools were not related to either their desire for bureaucratic characteristic of their position in the school. The fact that teachers and administrators agree on what they see suggests that bureaucracy impinges on them in similar ways.

Stern (1963) attempted to measure college characteristics from 300 true-false statements concerning college environments answered by respondents. These statements are somewhat more specific and immediately observable than those used by either Hemphill or Hall—for example, "Faculty members and administration have clearly and definitely posted hours," and "Professors usually take attendance in class." The problem with Stern's index is that because most of the scales were designed on a personality model they are not necessarily directly relevant to a theory of organizational structure. An index modeled upon personality structure will not necessarily tap the significant organizational characteristics.

One of the few comprehensive inventories of the organizational characteristics of schools was developed in 1966 by MacKay and Robinson for their study of Canadian schools. It contains 54 items pertaining to possible overlap of authority, opportunity for teachers to make decisions, competence of the staff, assignment procedures, and rules for teachers.

[35] Tannenbaum (1961) devised a profile based on the descriptions of an organization's members, describing the level at which certain types of decisions normally are made. A "control graph" was constructed that described the pattern of control. The number of levels of authority, the amount of control exercised by each level, and the total amount of control exercised throughout the system portrayed a complex picture of organizations. Of more direct relevance to our measures is a study by Eye and his associates (1966) who developed a decision-making instrument for public school systems similar to the one developed here. It consists of short descriptions of 80 highly specific problem situations, such as who approves the daily teaching schedule, who places students in classes, who determines whether a student needs to repeat a grade, and so forth. Respondents were asked to identify the person who would make these decisions—the principal, the superintendent, the school board, and so forth.

[36] In the pretest, the responses of the most professionally oriented teachers in the sample were compared with the group estimated to be the least professional (that is, the groups used to validate the scales). The decisions on which these two groups differed significantly have been labeled "professional policy decisions"; they are pri-

marily decisions that directly affect classroom work, such as assignment of material, supplementary reading matter, and the like. The remaining decisions are labeled "professionally nonrelevant policy decisions" because they pertain more to broader spheres of the school or the system, such as hiring and promoting teachers and adding or dropping a program of courses.

After the items were classified, the descriptive parts were scrutinized for their power to discriminate among the schools. Statements were omitted if there was little agreement. In the remaining items, it was assumed that the proportion of teachers who indicated that a specific decision was made at a particular level reflected the actual frequency at which they are made.

[37] The three items on the descriptive part of the professional decision-making scale are

(a) At my school, teachers are allowed to make their own decisions about the problems that come up in the classroom.
(b) At my school, small matters need not be referred higher up for final answer.
(c) At my school, the ultimate authority over the major educational decisions is exercised by professional teachers.

[38] Anderson's (1964) "index of impersonality in teacher-student relations" has reference to the standardized treatment of students by teachers. But his "departmental rules scale" is similar to the one developed for this study; it inquires about the authority of teachers to choose lesson plans and curriculum guides, their role in preparing them, the procedures used to select textbooks, and the rules regulating discussion of controversial topics, grading students, and assigning homework. Unfortunately, the reliability of this scale is only .22, with intercorrelation among the items ranging from .10 to .59.

[39] The scale scores of each school (rather than the scale ranks) were used to rank the schools on this measure. The measure will be referred to as an index for that reason. Its utility is also qualified by the fact that it cannot be applied to the seven schools in the first year's study because some of the required information was not available.

[40] The six descriptive items in the rules sub-scale are as follows:

1. Nearly all teachers at my school are completely familiar with the written descriptions of the rules, procedures, manuals and other standard operating procedures necessary for running the classroom.
2. The school has a manual of rules and regulations which are actually followed.
3. Rules stating when the teachers should arrive and depart from the building are strictly enforced.
4. To prevent confusion and friction among the staff, there is a rule covering almost every problem that might come up at school.
5. There are definite rules specifying topics that are not appropriate for discussion in a classroom.
6. When a controversy arises about the interpretation of school rules, teachers at my school typically do not "stick their necks out" by taking a definite position.

[41] Such measures, it should be noted, are based on the questionable assumption that the proportion of members who agree with the statement reflects the existing amount of the variable in question, and that the majority's estimate is the most accurate estimate. The procedure, at times, also makes heavy demands on the respondents when they are asked to estimate aggregative characteristics of the entire faculty —for example, does faculty opinion "usually reflect" that of the administration (Leonard, 1959).

[42] Any methodology has its advantages as well as its price. Rather than engaging in impressive polemics designed to substantiate the validity of one methodology to the exclusion of the rest, social scientists must be ready to assess the state of the art in order to identify the advantages and problems associated with alternative pro-

cedures. Combining interview and questionnaire methods permits a relatively large number of cases concerning sensitive issues to be examined with relatively low expenditures of time and effort in comparison to participant observation methods, but at the risk of oversimplification of complex problems. One dilemma is that a measure or an instrument that can be used across many types of organizations is often not sufficiently refined to analyze variations in a specific type of organization. Also it has proved difficult to measure such dimensions as standardization, centralization, and organizational complexity, particularly because these variables, extremely complex in themselves, were but a few of the many variables being investigated. It has been even more difficult to simultaneously treat the more than two dozen organizations representing different locales with specific histories, and yet to quantify the findings sufficiently to at least tantalize the sociologist's taste for generalization. Further, it has been difficult to maintain a balance between structural variables and counterpart information on individuals. And finally, as usual in such studies, an unbelievably large number of variables that should have been controlled were not.

REFERENCES: Chapter 4

Anderson, James George. An empirical study of bureaucratic rules in the junior high school. Unpublished doctoral dissertation. John Hopkins University, 1964.

Barton, Allen H. *Organizational measurement and its bearing on the study of college environments.* New York: College Entrance Examination Board, Columbia University, 1961.

Biddle, Bruce J., and Thomas, Edwin J. *Role theory: Concepts and research.* New York: Wiley, 1966.

Blau, Peter M. The research process in the study of the dynamics of bureaucracy. In Phillip E. Hammond (Ed.), *Sociologists at Work.* New York: Basic Books, 1964. Pp. 16–49.

Colombotos, John L. *Sources of professionalism: A study of high school teachers.* Cooperative Research Project No. 330, U.S. Office of Education. Ann Arbor: Department of Sociology, University of Michigan, 1962.

Corwin, Ronald G. *Development of an instrument for examining staff conflicts in the public schools.* Cooperative Research Project No. 1934, U.S. Office of Education. Columbus: Department of Sociology and Anthropology, The Ohio State University, 1963.

Dalton, Melville. Men who manage. In Phillip E. Hammond (Ed.), *Sociologists at Work. Op. cit.* Pp. 50–98.

Delany, William. Some field notes on the problem of access in organization research. *American Sociological Quarterly,* 1961, **5**, 448–457.

Eye, Glenn, et al. *Relationship between instructional change and the extent to which school administrators agree on the location of responsibilities for administrative decision.* U.S. Office of Education, Cooperative Research Project No. 5-0443, 1966.

Flanagan, John C. The critical incident technique. *Psychological Bulletin,* July, 1965, **64**, 327–358.

Gauss, K. F. As cited by Melville Dalton. *Op. cit.*

Gross, Neal, Mason, Ward S., and McEachern, Alexander W. *Explorations in role analysis: Studies of the school superintendency role.* New York: Wiley, 1958.

Haas, J. Eugene. *Role conception and group consensus.* Research Monograph No. 117. Columbus: Bureau of Business Research, The Ohio State University, 1963.

Hall, Richard H. The concept of bureaucracy: An empirical assessment. *American Journal of Sociology,* June, 1963, **69**, 32–40.

Halpin, Andrew W. *The leadership behavior of school superintendents.* Columbus: The Ohio State University, 1956.

Halpin, Andrew, and Croft, Don B. *The organizational climates of schools.* U.S. Office of Education Cooperative Research Project, 1962.

Hemphill, John K. *Group dimensions: A manual for their measurement.* Monograph No. 87. Columbus: Bureau of Business Research, The Ohio State University, 1956.

Lazarsfeld, Paul F., and Thielens, Wagner, Jr. *The academic mind.* New York: Free Press, 1958.

Lazarsfeld, Paul, and Menzel, Herbert. On the relation between individual and collective properties. In A. Etzioni (Ed.), *Complex organizations: A sociological reader.* New York: Holt, Rinehart & Winston, 1961. Pp. 423–440.

Leonard, Robert. The incidence-intensity fallacy in sociological research. *Berkeley Journal of Sociology,* 1959, **5**, 111–118.

MacKay, David Allister. An empirical study of bureaucratic dimensions and their relation to other characteristics of school organizations. Unpublished doctoral dissertation. Edmonton: Department of Educational Administration, University of Alberta Printing Department, September, 1964.

Rosen, Hjalmar, and Rosen, R. A. Hudson. A comparison of parametric and nonparametric analysis of opinion data. *The Journal of Applied Psychology,* 1955, **39**, 401–404.

Scott, William, with Scott, Ruth. *Values and organizations.* Chicago: Rand McNally, 1965.

Selvin, Hanan C., and Hagstrom, Warren O. The empirical classification of formal groups. *American Sociological Review,* June, 1963, **28**, 399–411.

Sorensen, James Elliott. Professional and bureaucratic organization in large public accounting firms. Unpublished doctoral dissertation. The Ohio State University, 1965.

Stern, George C. Characteristics of the intellectual climate in college environments. *Harvard Educational Review,* Winter, 1963, **33**, 5–41.

Tannenbaum, Arnold S. Control and effectiveness in a voluntary organization. *The American Journal of Sociology,* July, 1961, **33–34**, 46.

Webb, Thomas William. Classification of teachers by bureaucratic and professional normative orientations to educational issues. Unpublished doctoral dissertation. The Ohio State University, 1964.

Weiss, Robert, and Jacobson, Eugene. A method for the analysis of the structure of complex organizations. *American Sociological Review,* 1955, **20**, 661–668.

Zald, Mayer N. Power and conflict in correctional institutions. *Administrative Science Quarterly,* June, 1962, **7**, 22–49.

part II. The pugilistic pedagogues

FROM TALKS WITH TEACHERS *on status*

I WOULDN'T *say rank has its privileges, but I would imagine that someone that has been here awhile and is reasonably intelligent is contributing more to the school. He should have an opportunity with the better students. It is a matter of practicality and not a principle.—a teacher*

THE SECOND-CLASS *status students are attributed to the business department. You end up with a student that no one else can teach. This means that you yourself are inferior—in this particular philosophy. Nothing that you can put your finger on, or that people come right out and say.— a business teacher*

I KNOW *that sometimes they (counselors) will load a class up just to get a kid credit. They just plump him into an area and say this is the only thing open, take it and sit there until June and then get your one-half credit and you can graduate.—a teacher*

WE'RE CRAFT *teachers and we don't associate with the English teachers and those people. I mean we associate with them, but we're looked down upon. . . . We're not the academic people.—an industrial arts teacher*

IT SEEMED *that the math teacher had a special session after school and said the boy couldn't go to the track meet this time because he had to attend this. . . . The math teacher's reasoning was that the boy was not good in track.—a teacher*

ONCE IN *awhile I get a little disgusted with [a counselor] telling people they are too smart to take my courses. I teach mostly elective courses, but I feel that these courses are important to the development of the student. I know of one counselor here who has told two students not to take Business English. It's too easy for them. I felt, "That's really great. No wonder my classes are so low, if they're all getting this kind of counseling."—a teacher*

SINCE RUSSIA *put Sputnik in the sky, there has been such a tremendous emphasis on science, math and chemistry—everybody's going to be an engineer and everybody's going to college. Well, these kids that don't want to go to college, they're sent to dumping grounds. Look at the National Defense Act of 1958. They supported science, math, physics, and chemistry—what did they do for industrial arts? So, consequently we are a dumping ground, not because of school administration but because of the federal government.—an industrial arts teacher*

5. Confrontations

The great question is not whether teaching can become a profession, but whether teachers can be persuaded to act like professionals.—Stinnett, 1964, p. 20.

OVERVIEW

Though it is, of course, hazardous to generalize from selected, off-hand comments of teachers—they are direct participants in the system—we would be remiss not to indulge in speculation based on our talks with them. Even in advance of more systematic information, it is safe to say that many schools are not peaceful workplaces.

While it is true that Mr. Sears and most of his colleagues seem to be resigned to if not content with their place in the system, a number substantial enough to act as irritants are convinced that they deserve more authority; a handful, in fact, seem determined to increase their power even at the risk of insubordination. In the typical school the average person had been involved in at least two or three overt incidents of one kind or another during the year. Nearly half of all incidents were classified as authority problems; one out of four involved authority problems directly between teachers and administrators, the largest single category of conflict; about 100 of them specifically involved teacher insubordination, and insubordination was implicit in many of the various other authority issues.

Certain individuals and groups of teachers, especially athletic and some types of academic teachers, already have achieved a disproportionate amount of influence in most schools. Of course, many administrators do not subscribe to, nor do some even comprehend, these pretensions; they envision such teachers as nothing but obedient employees. Teachers feel that they are not adequately protected from parents and school boards and, particularly, students. (But as we shall see, the norm advocating that teachers must always be defended regardless of the circumstances would create a real danger if it were observed with any consistency.)

The interviews uncovered a number of tensions between counselors and teachers; not the least important is the tendency of counselors to take the part of students in mediating with teachers. They even exercise surveillance over teachers to protect their students. But one cannot escape the impression that at times the counselors' primary concern seemed to be to get the troublemakers through school and out of everyone's hair. Also, many counselors seem to feel at least as obligated to teachers as to students.

One of the major surprises of the study was the extent of competitiveness among teachers for control over and distribution of students. The most sacrosanct resource that teachers must share is the student. They are, of course, abundant, but from the teachers' viewpoint there is an oversupply of unable delinquent types and a shortage of academically superior types. To old hands at teaching it probably would come as no surprise that despite teachers' talk about salaries and facilities, it is good students that are really in short supply. Teachers, therefore, insist upon authority over students, not only over their academic performance, but over their personal lives as well. They go to some lengths to assure that their colleagues do not violate their territorial claims to certain students.

Obtaining a fair share of able students is only one side of the coin; controlling discipline is the other. Control of discipline means control of the classroom. Teachers grow bitter toward their more mischievous charges who upset their classrooms, make their jobs more difficult, and distract other students. Only some resent the prerogatives of students enough to wonder openly whether students should have any rights at all, but most clearly resent an administration that is lax on discipline. Of course, the act of disciplining students in itself is time consuming, unrewarding, and onerous. It is a responsibility teachers would like to slough onto their wary administrations. But they are not willing to compromise their final authority to determine what the discipline policy is to be, because to many teachers discipline lies at the heart of a successful classroom. Yet, it must be wondered, when teachers act as both prosecution and judge, are students as likely to receive vengeance instead of justice?

The quality of a teacher's students reflects upon his stature. Therefore, at the core of their fight for authority over students is a struggle to gain a fair share of preferred status and at least to avoid consignment to "dumping grounds." Extracurricular activities play a key role in problems involving the distribution of students. The fact that they often are taken from class reflects upon the status of the activities concerned, and activities teachers compete among themselves to have good students join their programs; indeed, the competition for students among extracurricular activities teachers is more severe than among academic teachers, especially in the least bureaucratic schools—music and athletics are the biggest contenders.

Although some academic courses serve as dumping grounds, vocational courses are most frequently used for this function, which is resented by vocational teachers. Counselors, partly from conviction but encouraged by outside pressure, play a decisive role in these allocation problems because they often use their influence to steer good students to academic courses and away from music, art, writing, and vocational courses. The most fortunate teachers see dumping grounds simply as a matter of specialization; however, the problem is that no one wants to specialize with the undesirable students. They also justify dumping grounds in terms of their utility for the student, the difficulty of teaching them, the maintenance of their own status, and empire building. Among the strategies available for competing for students are exerting pressure on the counselors, developing rules of competition and claims to territory (such as equalization policies), setting admission requirements, controlling assignment procedures (including informal recruiting), and attempting to change the scheduling system itself.

Not all of the authority issues and distribution problems concern insubordination of and competition for students, however. Teachers fight among themselves and with their administrators over curriculum content and teaching methods. At stake, in many of these cases, is the convenience of some administrator or the prestige of a department or teacher. The personal sense of obligation of some teachers to guard students from immoral influences, their indifference in many cases, and especially their concerted efforts to forestall possible public displeasure—all play a part in shaping a curriculum. In fact, their sensitivity to outside public opinion was responsible for a substantial share of the conflicts. Teachers and administrators alike are, therefore, sensitive to public relations. Although the study focused on conflicts within schools, 10 percent of them involved school-community relations; this is indicative of the importance of the community context for understanding organizational behavior. Teachers resent parents' efforts to influence grading; some prefer to avoid becoming familiar with parents so that they will not have to take their problems into consideration and can avoid their wrath. School board members were criticized for political interference and for lack of sympathy for teachers, and in many communities political conservatism was a source of irritation.

Grading brings out the worst in school-community relationships and it does not help teacher-administrator relationships either. Administrators are less willing than teachers to grant that some students are not capable of learning. Teachers whose prestige weighs heavily on the performance of their students are more likely to believe that their students are not trying hard enough. But few teachers or administrators seem to blame failures on the quality of teaching, except for the fact that a few teachers are criticized for being too interested in subject matter; even fewer teachers attribute the difficulties involved to the system itself. But it is, nevertheless, clearly understood that part of the problem is that no one wants certain students who have been stereotyped at a particular level of ability.

The authority problems, then, like a large share of the student disciplinary problems, revert to the competition among teachers as they try to monopolize the preferred students and slough off the undesirable ones. The grading problem, however, also reflects much larger difficulties surrounding academic standards. Standards, in turn, are part of a prestige system that determines the criteria for judging teaching competence. Competence is a controversial topic, partly because of disagreements about what it is, and partly because individuals are sometimes less responsible for their own incompetence than are certain features of their jobs—such as promotion and job-assignment policies and an evaluation procedure under which administrators are under no compulsion to observe their teachers in the act of teaching before evaluating them. The irony underlying this system becomes evident when schoolmen attempt to convince parents that all teachers are equally competent, while at the same time they privately complain about one another's teaching incompetence and negligence.

Therefore, in addition to creating "dumptenders," job-assignment procedures raise other problems, such as those connected with assigning teachers to courses for which they are unqualified and with unequal work loads. Incidents involving scheduling of physical facilities also occur in most schools. Extracurricular activities, especially band and football, usually compete for facilities; and in the least bureaucratic schools they seem to find some difficulty in sharing classroom space.

It is problems such as these that make teachers appreciate certain rules. Although they do not like red tape, and they object to some rules —such as those creating what sometimes seem to be unbearable deadlines and regulating their work habits—they know also that they are vulnerable without them and so are willing to put up with anything that helps to clarify their jobs.

Underlying many of these incidents are status problems. Inconsistencies between age, experience, education, sex, and other social positions with official positions often lead to problems. Persons with inconsistent statuses are particularly open to charges of favoritism and to criticisms for obtaining an unfair (by some criteria) share of the rewards.

A number of conflicts, too, involved personal values, philosophies of education, idiosyncracies, and personal irritations and weaknesses. And, finally, it should be pointed out that many teachers had no problems to report. Some did not think that conflict is professional; others simply avoided it or did not socialize with their colleagues; and in some cases the size and ecology of their schools was responsible for minimizing contacts among teachers, and, thus, the opportunities for conflict.

AUTHORITY PROBLEMS

With this as background and before we consider the question of whether, or in what sense, it is professional to become engaged in conflict, we shall in this chapter attempt simply to capture some of the flavor of the rich pot-pourri boiled down from our talks with teachers. We cannot claim that the statements selected are representative of the opinions of teachers, and, in fact, they were sometimes selected because they represent an extreme position. But insofar as conflict is concerned, it is precisely the extremes that should interest us. Taken as a whole, what will be reported provides a fair sample of the range of concerns expressed by teachers.

Five of the ten highest ranking specific types of problems involved authority issues.[1]

Lack of Authority

In general these problems concerned the proper balance of authority between teachers and administrators, with a widespread feeling among teachers that they did not have enough authority. One teacher explained:

I think the teachers feel that they are being treated as underlings, and they are not sufficiently consulted. I know so many times, for instance, that teachers put down a list of things that they considered to be essential in the English department. This list was cut, and they were not consulted. In many instances, teachers have not been consulted in areas of their own speciality.

Another teacher added: "We can express our views, but they will be politely deferred. We don't have a great deal of weight as far as being considered, so people have gotten to the point where they don't speak up for anything."

An incident reported in one of the smaller schools illustrates the situation as described by several teachers:

We used to have an activity council represented by the teachers who would pass on policies and give special permission to go to the Washington Cherry Blossom Festival, and the activity council denied them the privilege because it would involve some school time. The Board of Education overruled them and said they could go. The teachers do a lot of committee work with not too many results.

The teacher added that they have since reduced the committee to an advisory capacity.

Some teachers confined their complaints to specifics, such as the administration not permitting a married couple to teach in the same school, or the case in which teachers complained about the fact that the administration permitted students to smoke outside of the school building and teachers were "told not to observe that type of thing." But other teachers were more willing to generalize. A teacher from one of the largest schools in the sample reported that her school has one of the lowest costs per student in the state, adding: "It was probably true, but we also had some of the poorest education."

A number of reasons were given or implied in the interviews to explain why teachers have no more authority than they do. One reason, implicit in the remarks of several teachers, such as the one cited above, is that they regarded their administrators as dogmatic and dictatorial in their use of authority. There are also indications that other teachers feel the same way. One reported this incident:

I was carrying Cokes down the hall from the teachers' lounge to the faculty office, which we've done all year. She [an assistant principal] told me in front of the students that I was not to carry Cokes in the hall. I said: "all right." I'm on the faculty committee between the faculty and the principal, and others said she told them how to dress, interrupted their classes, etcetera. So, we talked to the principal about her and he said that we could carry Cokes in the hall. She didn't have the authority over it.

However, other reasons were cited too. Sometimes it was simply not feasible to delegate authority because of time pressures, a reason given by this administrator:

Many times when things are done there is not a detailed explanation of why it has to be done. But, really, in an operation of this size, sometimes you just have to go ahead for what's good. You just can't put it off for a faculty meeting in every case. I find that since I am working in administration a lot of things I, as a teacher, used to think, "Why do I have to do this or that?" are things where they have no choice.

A related reason is that administrators have a communication advantage that gives them access to information that many teachers do not have. But, possibly even more important, the major decisions were often simply defined as the prerogative of administrators. One teacher resigned himself with the fact that "Of course, these are administrative matters, and the teachers have nothing to say as far as administrative matters are concerned. You're a teacher, and that's it. The school policy is determined by someone else." But, a possible result of this policy is noted by the person who said, of counselors specifically: "Sometimes a teacher can help a child, but if we are never told about it [his problem], we never know a thing. We are never told about anything. It seems to be a policy. It has always been that way."

Administrators seem to believe in their decision-making prerogatives, too, and zealously guard them. An assistant principal inadvertently made a comment to a teacher that might reflect a sentiment that many administrators feel, even if not so vehemently:

I said: "If you think that the time is going to come when the assistant principal is going to hold his hat in his hand to one of his faculty members to talk things over, then you're going to have to think again, because I'll suffer the consequences that come from it."

Such administrators employ standard tactics to discourage teachers from taking a more active part in policy decisions. A few of these tactics are revealed in this teacher's description of an incident in which his colleague disagreed with the assistant principal over a matter of policy:

He [a colleague] wouldn't raise his hand because, as I told the assistant principal, anybody who raises his hand and says something at a faculty meeting, one of two things will happen to him—he is either made fun of or he is scolded, as I was. That is my general impression of the faculty meetings.

But if teachers feel they lack authority, it is not entirely the fault of administrators, for administrators themselves are squelched by strong school boards. Those administrators not in a strong position to defend their own authority can hardly be expected effectively to defend their teachers from board control. Speaking of his administrator, this teacher in a large school said: "They're scared to death of school board members and they're scared to death of citizen's groups. They shake in their boots when they see them. . . . They don't seem to get too shook over the faculty." An assistant principal expressed his resignation this way: "Sometimes I feel like General MacArthur—you know, he disagreed with Truman—and I always used to side with Truman because I say: 'Anyone that's in the army has to take orders from the Commander-in-Chief and keep his mouth shut.'"

While some teachers want more authority over certain matters, the resignation of many, even most of them, to their fate is a major reason why they have not achieved more authority. One teacher observed:

It's really the teachers who have to bear the blame because of their fear, cowardice, and their stupidity, and their not seeing that they certainly have a claim to dignity which has been denied them—not only in this system, but in the other two systems in which I have worked. I think it is basically fear, fear of losing a job. . . . but all of the people who can best lead us are the older people, and they don't assume this leadership.

Another teacher concurred: "Teachers as a group are lethargic and insecure. They feel vulnerable to a very high degree, and as a result, teachers don't respond. They don't take an active part in things. They are too scared to do it."

The acquiescence of many teachers is reflected in this teacher's praise of his school administrators: "I think these people are highly qualified, and if they suggest an improvement, a teacher should follow without any doubt." Their faith in their administrators, however, is no greater than their faith in the system by which they have been recruited. Said one: "Our administrators have been appointed by their superintendent, and they have proven themselves to be educated and efficient in their jobs or they wouldn't have been appointed." Another teacher's personal philosophy reinforced a complaint attitude: "I think that any employee, if he is going to work at a place, should make an effort to get along in that situation; and if the situation becomes unbearable, instead of griping about it, you better get out and find a situation that suits you better." This one spoke for many teachers when he said: "I go along with the one in higher authority." And another adds simply: "I respect the chain of command."

Some teachers, in fact, tend to equate compliance with professionalism. For example:

It is my belief that we have a pretty good crew of teachers here, and I think anyone that is professionally trained and mature enough to be a school teacher should have the ability to get along, as we do here. I think differences of opinion never get that far. They are talked out. I think most people feel they can ask the principal anything and respect his judgment.

But one teacher sensed more of the dilemma involved: " I have been very active on the national level of the National Association of Biology Teachers, so . . . I know what the country-wide demands are, what we should be doing, and what we should not be doing." Teachers with these sentiments find this situation a puzzle: "Teachers are more of an authority, and yet it seems that the school is trying to please the community rather than the faculty." The paradox is summed up by one teacher:

The point is, you are talking about educational problems and it would seem to me that the people closest to the situation are the classroom teachers. It seems to me that they are the people who have the least to say about school policy. In my way of thinking, this is not the best way to operate.

Insubordination

The very fact that some teachers do sense a lack of authority provokes a few of them to challenge the existing authority system. Insubordination problems involving a challenge to authority account for nearly 4 percent of all the incidents and are typical of the most bureaucratic schools. Counselors often find themselves compelled to defy the authorities when they are asked by the administration for certain confidential information regarding pregnancies, and the like. In some cases teachers worked together and forced the administrator to rescind an unpopular decision. For example, in one large suburban school an incident arose because the administration made a record of the fact that certain teachers had refused to pass out public relations literature supporting a school bond levy. Speaking for the irate teachers involved, this teacher reported:

We petitioned the teachers who didn't go, and found that they didn't think it was fair, either, that we should be knocked down because we didn't go along with this. As a result of the petition, the administration later removed the record from the personnel folders of the teachers involved because of opposition from the local teachers' association.

In another school several informants told of a "pretty serious-minded group that met periodically over a period of two or three years, which has expressed concern over the leadership, in particular, of the high school principal."

In some instances, teachers exercised their power more subtly. Their passive resistance was effective in this case:

One principal was brought here to straighten the school out. He was a tough one. One day he told the teachers that when the class bells rang he wanted them out in the hall observing what was going on. Nothing happened. So, he told them again. No one was in the hall. He told them to get out in the hall, that he was coming through. But, there are some things where teachers will not cooperate.

Probably most cases of insubordination did not involve organized groups but instead involved particular teachers in opposition to an administrator on a certain matter. In describing the case of a band teacher who refused to give a piece of sheet music to a student who had been sent to borrow it by an assistant principal, the administrator involved said:

The point was that in front of the student messenger, he threw quite a king-sized tantrum for a grown man. In so many words he told the student, who was a little eighth grade girl, to tell me to go jump in the lake or, perhaps, to a place that's a little hotter. This was the part that wrangled me—the student saw all of this. So, I decided that I would go directly to the superintendent. When he was informed of what had happened, he agreed with me that he should not have done it but, beyond that, there wasn't going to be anything done about it. I, therefore, decided that I was going to take the matter into my own hands, and I did. I went to the president of the school board.

An assistant principal of another school reported this case of insubordination:

We had to ask this teacher, as we did other people, to cover a class during her planning period, which she felt she should not have to do since that was her planning period. The planning period is not part of the contract, although it is in the school policy. With this, I gave her an alternative to teach or I would consider this insubordination and treat it accordingly. After this pressure she agreed to do it, but I am sure she did it unwillingly.

Although most cases of insubordination occurred between teachers and the administration, in a few instances, nonprofessional staff members would challenge teachers. For example, a teacher reported that "We had open house last fall. I asked the janitor to mop the floor in my room and he said: 'Well you can do a much better job than I can; I'll get you the mop.'"

Probably far more cases of attempted defiance of authority were aborted than succeeded. A failure occurred in one of the largest schools when the faculty members met to discuss ways to defy certain members of a school board whom they thought were unethical. One of the teachers involved reported:

That meeting was invaded by representatives of the local teachers' association who had not been invited. Although they were vociferous in their displeasure, they did nothing. They didn't sign a petition and they didn't vote for censure. They were afraid, understandably, I suppose. They were all quite afraid to assert what were supposed to be their rights. Some vague kind of compromise arose. It was finally drafted by the teachers' association in the Code of Ethics for Board Members. But that is a kind of wishy-washy solution. It meant, in effect, that she [a board member] had gotten away with it. Most of the community, most of the faculty, and most of the administration had condemned her actions and called them unethical. But, there was no reprisal by anyone.

A few clues were obtained in the interviews as to the identity of the leaders of these challenges. One teacher identified them as males. Another informant identified the militants as the more competent teachers: "These people who I think are the most dynamic teachers, the best teachers, are the ones who most frequently get involved in these conflicts. They are so keyed up all the time." But some teachers, such as this one, have misgivings about the trouble that these teachers cause, competent or not: "I have often questioned whether it is worth it to have an excellent teacher when she [or he] causes such friction."

Dominance of particular groups

Even in those schools where teachers complained the most about the lack of decision-making authority, some of them were said to have a disproportionate amount of authority and were able to dominate certain matters. One teacher said simply: "At this school, sports are what makes the system go." Athletics, in fact, tend to dominate the extracurricular activities programs of most schools in comparison to the relative emphasis on activities such as drama or music (76 percent of the extracurricular incidents involved athletics; 24 percent, other areas). An English teacher in one of the bureaucratic schools estimated the situation like this:

The athletic director's wishes, wants, and desires are considered first and everything else is secondary. . . . No one is even considering the dramatic society on the same par with the athletic group or even with the coeducational athletic group such as the marching girls.

This emphasis on athletics is resented by many teachers who feel that it impinges on the quality of the academic program. In one school the athletic program was maintained after an important school levy was defeated. The coach was aware of the sentiment of many teachers:

Well, many of the teachers resented this [the fact that the athletic program was maintained] because even though there was no money for textbooks and materials, we still had money for our athletic program.

But, he explained his justifications: "Of course, they didn't stop to realize that we were paying our own way, we were paying the mileage on the buses, paying the bus drivers, and paying for everything." He obviously does not feel that his money should be used for the academic program. The domination of particular groups or individuals in school affairs was more prominent in the least, rather than the most, bureaucratic schools. In one of these, a math teacher reported: "One teacher [a coach], whose father-in-law is the big wheel in the Republican party, manages to get pretty much what he wants. We rather envy him, and he is probably the most influential man in the school." Reputedly, the "old timers" of one school were in a position of dominance, even to the extent of violating the wishes of the administration on the grounds that they "wouldn't find out what was going on anyway." Teachers are not the only ones who gain an upper hand. One teacher complained that "The secretaries have been here longer than I have, so I am reluctant to do anything to them. They are very bossy, but the principal isn't aware of my feelings about the secretaries."

An underlying source of tension and competition arises in most schools from the attempts of entire departments to dominate a school. This teacher gave her opinions about the academic teachers who dominated her school:

We have considered ourselves a college-oriented high school, and even though a great number of kids *do* go on to college, there is a large proportion who are in need of vocational guidance or courses that will help them as average citizens, because this is what they will be. I think that we do an adequate job of preparing the students for college, but it is the other students who are not being adequately prepared.

The power of academic teachers seems to be derived in part from community backing; for, she added: "Parents are forcing their children to take courses which would prepare them for college without considering their ability or desire. We need community learning."

For all of the influence a few teachers may have, some feel they are hardly even on a par with secretaries—let alone students, whose power some teachers view as a real threat. One went so far as to say:

I feel that this is like any other community—the student can hire or fire. I feel that they have a great deal of influence. They carry home stories to the parents who carry these stories to the Board of Education—the Board of Education in many instances takes stock in these statements and the result is that they do have the power of consent.

Indeed, in one school it was reported:

The student council put out a little leaflet yesterday in which they wanted the students to bring any grievances that they had with the teachers before the student council, and they would present it to the administration, and then the teacher would be brought in for a discussion. I don't know whether this is a good thing or not.

Lack of Administrative Backing

The teachers' lack of authority is further aggravated by the failure of administrators to protect them from parents and students. Two dozen incidents (over 1 percent of the sample) directly involved the failure of administrators to support or back teachers, and the same element was present in many others. Regarding the lack of backing by the administration, one teacher said:

That's an over-all picture of the whole system. The teachers do not have the backing they should have in relationship to parents. When I first came here the superintendent would always stand right between the parent and the teacher, do or die. Now, the teacher contacts the parent directly.

Many teachers want more defense because they feel helpless against public pressures, but several of them agreed with a teacher at one school who accused his principal of being more concerned with the reactions of the general public than with those of the teachers. This teacher's comments are typical of the feelings of teachers in several schools:

Well, the opinion I get is that this community is, you know, very wealthy and they don't seem to want a very strong administration. They want to run this thing directly and that's about what they do. A parent calls up and this thing is done. I've even had the superintendent come to me asking about grades of some political big-wig's son.

Their comments also revealed fears that students have too much influence with the administration: "He [the principal] goes to the students first for their feeling and for [suggested] changes before he will go to his own faculty." Another teacher complained: "They [the administration] buy wholesale, in many cases, what the kids say over what the faculty would say or what the faculty does." One teacher commented that "You really feel, of course, they [the administration] are on the student's side."

The president of a student council at one school complained to the principal about a long assignment he had received from an English teacher; the teacher felt that the principal had not listened to her side of the story. A teacher told of an incident involving a girl who "had taken her term report and copied it directly from someone else." He continued:

But they took the girl's word for it, dropped her out of his [the teacher's] class and gave her an A. This is the reason for some of the disturbance in that department. They upheld the girl because the principal knew her family very well in church, knew the girl's older brothers and sisters. She was supposed to be an outstanding student. However, in this case, she was wrong.

Some of these problems will be illustrated in greater detail in connection with the discussion on disciplinary problems and school-community relations.

It is understandable that teachers are delighted when they feel they have administrative backing against such pressures. Their pleasure at being spared the intrusion of outsiders is revealed in statements made by teachers whom administrators had backed:

Administration has always put the teacher first. In other words, if a student problem arises, the teacher is considered and if the teacher says that something is true, then the administration backs it.

This school board member thought the people in the English department were not requiring enough written work. One of our English teachers said he [the board member] didn't know what he was talking about. The principal in this case backed the teachers. He is one of the few men in the whole system who will stand up to the board member and set him straight. The superintendent won't.

The teacher is automatically taken to be right, and the student as wrong. Therefore, this is good.

Finally, this administrator said: "I always stick up for the teacher because I think this is best for the child and the school."

But, is it best for the child? When teachers are backed by the administration on blind faith, students may be left without a defense regardless of their guilt or innocence. That faith is often blind is implicit in this description:

There was an instance where the teacher gave a student a poor grade. During the summer the parents came in and wanted to know what the story was. The teacher wasn't here at the time. The administration tried to stick with the teacher as best as it could, saying maybe there was a discipline problem or something else. In other words, they will back the teacher all the time.

But not all administrators are so willing to condemn the children without a hearing. Sensing that students may be victims of a power coalition, at least some administrators consider it their duty to protect students from teachers. Such a stand was taken by one principal who said:

The only person that I feel that I have really an obligation to—and I'll do everything in my power to do a good job for—is the student. This is why we are here. Now, I'm not going to change just to satisfy a teacher because it is easier for him, nor will I change my course of study so I can supervise more easily; this is not my function. The function is to give the student the best you can and the best that is available in our system.

If anyone in the school had assumed the role of defending students from teachers, it was likely to be a counselor, a fact that is a point of contention between teachers and counselors in many schools. This teacher's complaints about students are really pointed at the counselors supporting them:

The student is always right, you know. They [counselors] will let them drop courses. They will let them audit courses in typing just so that they won't get a bad grade. My department is very much against this. It makes the working relationship [between teachers and counselors] somewhat strained.

And this teacher felt equally intimidated by counselors: "I think students use them as a crutch whenever they get into trouble. If I reprimand a student in study hall and tell him to sit down and be quiet, he immediately wants to see the counselor." Some counselors do go out of their way to monitor teachers in interests of the students, such as this one who said:

On Fridays, they have current events. Last Thursday, she [a student] didn't take her book home from school because we were having current events on Friday. In the meantime, we had a snowstorm and she didn't have her book at home. Therefore, she didn't have some written work done today. The teacher refused to accept it after today, and the student felt it was not quite fair. So, I told her that I would speak with this particular teacher.

But counselors, it should be recognized, are under equally powerful pressures from teachers to protect the teachers vis-à-vis the students, and in some cases apparently do so, as evident in this teacher's admiring comment: "I think the counselors try to explain the point of view of the teacher and help the child to understand that the teachers have certain responsibilities and that the child must comply."

Conflict over Students

Implicit in some of the preceding comments is the fact that a substantial number of problems entail overlapping authority over the students plus disciplinary problems that involve students. Six and one-half percent of all incidents in the sample, in fact, concerned, in one way or another, competition among teachers and administrators and parents for control over student behavior; and there was an additional 2.10 percent involved in problems regarding student discipline. The first type of problem was twice as frequent in the least bureaucratic schools (12.58 percent compared to 6.9 percent in the high bureaucratic schools). Discipline problems also seemed to be lower in high bureaucratic schools.

Control over unofficial student behavior

In one fifth of the conflicts involving competition for control over students, there were attempts to influence their behavior outside of the official classroom performance. In one school teachers complained about high-heeled, pointed shoes and tight pants and long haircuts for boys. One teacher commented: "Yes, sir, I had to kick a boy out of study hall the other day for doing this (wearing a Beatle haircut)." One incident involving a girl who was sent home because her dress was too short reached the mass media. The tendency of teachers to interfere in students' personal lives is illustrated by this teacher's report: "The daughter of one of my friends was called in by one of the counselors and told that she should allow her daughter to have more outside activities—dates, in other words. This friend of mine told her that she would take care of personal problems."

Sometimes, the school can exercise sanctions of considerable weight against disapproved personal behavior. This teacher laid down the law:

This student sort of assumed the attitude that work is far more important than school. He's a senior and had gotten to the point where he would just go out and work and not show up at school on the days when he was supposed to be part time in one place and part time in another. The things on which he spends his money have taken precedence over either school or work. Now, between his employers and ourselves, we are cutting off the job completely. If he can make it between now and the end of the year, he'll probably graduate. If he can't, if he decides to get another job somewhere and ignore the whole situation, he'll probably be dropping out of school. It's one of these situations. You get full cooperation from the counselors on this.

Control over classroom performance

More of the incidents involved control over the official classroom performance of students. The amount of homework assigned was a particularly sore point of contention in three schools when a teacher assigned heavy homework loads and caused students to neglect other teachers' courses. This coach observed:

I have some of the same athletes in both football and track that she has in her seminars. I don't know how many hours she expects them to work on that, but . . . as far as I'm concerned, it's very unreasonable. The kids feel that this course is supposedly preparing them for college and they rate it very high. But, yet, I have some real good athletes this spring, one in particular, a two-year letterman, who did not come out for track because he couldn't keep up with track and her course too. . . . Kids will actually skip school to go down to the library and study all day to work on that stuff.

An English teacher in the same school also complained: "In one of my particular classes, there were six people absent. I discovered they had spent the whole day in the library. I think research is great, but it should be kept in the bounds of the high school."

At one school a librarian and an English teacher were at odds due to their overlapping control of students' academic programs. The librarian insisted that students should have a library card and be allowed to come to the library two times a week for a full period; at other times they were to be allowed, on a pass from the teacher, to come to the library for only ten minutes at a time. The English teacher felt that students should be permitted to come to the library at any time that they wished. The rivalry became even more bitter when the head of the English department rejected a student's design for a yearbook because it was too "modernistic"; it turned out that an art teacher in the same school had assisted and encouraged him.

A related source of rivalry developed over efforts to control the policy for admitting students to class and for determining their eligibility to participate in after-school activities. This teacher complained:

I didn't feel the student should have been allowed to take the advanced class, as she had done so poorly in the beginning class. She [the counselor] was writing a report to the parents and she called me down one time and wanted to know if I could change the report because she couldn't send that to the parents. I said, "No, I couldn't," because I said I didn't think the girl should be in the advanced class. I think she was a little disturbed with me.

A related incident in the area of extracurricular activities developed over eligibility rules—a disagreement as to how stringently they should be enforced. A teacher said: "There were a couple of times that I felt that he [the athletic coach] was lax in pushing eligibility rules, and I would get on his back about this. He felt I was too strict. He said that other schools don't enforce these rules." The last statement demonstrates that coaches and classroom teachers have different standards of reference—that is, the conference teams' norms versus the rulebook.

Faculty members, too, are very sensitive about each other's attempts to control students out of their "jurisdictions," as illustrated in this indignant report involving two study hall supervisors:

He prides himself on perfect discipline. He has the section [a study hall] two doors down from us. He observed someone in my section and without saying anything to me, he came up and took that person and moved him to his study hall. He did that not only with me but with the teacher on the other side, too.

A similar incident, involving an industrial arts teacher, was reported by a counselor who found it necessary to speak to several of his students about minor disciplinary disturbances: "He [the industrial arts teacher] is in charge of the work-study program. These are, in effect, 'his boys.' He is overly sensitive about any criticism of these fellows, which I think is due to the fact that he is very dedicated to this program."

Not all of the conflicts over the control of students are confined to teachers. This band teacher's comment illustrates the well-known tug-of-war between parents and teachers: "A parent wanted me to release a band member after halftime, and I wouldn't do it. I don't break my rules for anyone. Because if I break them once, then I will have to break them again."

The consequences for students pushed and pulled by overlapping authority figures are implicit in this account:

The assistant principal wouldn't accept a pass administered in the office because it had my name on it. And, even if I'm in guidance, it didn't seem legal enough. There was some doubt in his mind that I was eligible or qualified or was in the correct capacity to do this. He sent the student back three times until someone else signed it.

Student discipline problems

Student discipline problems are exceptionally high in the four least bureaucratic schools compared to the most bureaucratic schools (.73 percent compared to 2.19 percent). Maintaining discipline is important. One teacher said: "I think a good teacher knows how to take care of his discipline problems." But, they still have some trouble. A teacher in one of the least bureaucratic schools complained that "Students constantly question authority. I feel this is a reflection of the underlying conflict—the questioning of authority. The students constantly ask: 'Why do we have to do this, or why can't we have this?' " The gravity of the underlying tension is reflected in comments such as this:

They're just a bunch of nomads. The average caliber of the individual that comes from Kentucky and Virginia, we get them in class, and they come to school drunk and they smoke in school; they quit about the sophomore year. They probably do more destruction before they quit than ten custodians can fix up, and that's my only complaint.

And, this even more innocent description: "And you've got kids that really belong in prison." And, of course, it was always better in the old days:

It's not just the school system, it's all over and, of course, I went to school some years ago, which makes a difference too. You know, we have a totally different relationship now, the student and the teacher. Back there we were in awe of the teacher, and would never attempt to get away with anything 'cause we knew that you couldn't. I guess we recognized authority. Whereas, here, and it's not just this school, you get away with what you can.

As already pointed out (although briefly), these discipline problems, like other authority problems, often revolved about the reluctance of administrators to back their teachers because, at times, administrators have sided with the recalcitrant student. In fact, several teachers in one school reported that when a student called one of the teachers an obscene name in the classroom, the vice principal in charge of discipline not only did nothing about the problem but later implied in public that he tended to agree with the student.

What can be done about the situation? In one school, because of the reluctance of the administration to back their teachers on matters of discipline, the faculty formed a committee to "talk to the principal." A member of the committee said:

There was some kind of pressure being put on from the top to ease up on the disciplining. Just recently we heard that the person in charge of assigning people to detention halls had been called on the carpet for being too harsh on the students. So, we went down with the idea of backing up the principal. His reaction was that he was in charge and that we had nothing to do with it and had overstepped our bounds.

Other teachers react toward the students. One teacher said: "I maintain that students don't have rights. I have never been much for student government." And his colleague concurred:

I don't want to be undemocratic, but I have a feeling that the less you get the kids involved, the better off you are. I am all for student council, these type of things. But, if you ever get to the point where the kids have too much to say, I don't think it is good. They are still fifteen and sixteen years old.

But, the teacher who said, "Sometimes you just don't 'see' quite as well as you do other times," is probably typical.

The issues regarding student discipline, like other conflicts among teachers, involved competition among teachers for the control of policies regarding disciplinary matters. Describing one case that arose, a teacher said:

I kicked the boy out of class and he was sent back with an admittance pass for being tardy. And I thought they were being a little bit funny, so I sent him back. Then he was sent back up, and I sent him back down. I wouldn't honor the pass because it didn't explain why they kept sending him back to me. Finally, the counselor brought him up. We had a few words. The boy was not admitted that week.

A counselor said: "This teacher would not let him be removed from his control," and explained that when students are either admitted or removed from a teacher's classes without his permission, he takes it as a personal affront.

The above counselor put his finger on what was possibly the underlying problem in these cases. In the first place, administrators and counselors quite often do not want the responsibility of disciplining students, a fact that was indirectly apparent in this teacher's comment: "It spoils a teacher's reputation to keep sending kids to the office"; and in this administrator's philosophy:

I've never bothered them [the teachers]. I've let them teach the way they want to teach as long as I know they're doing a good job. The only thing I ask in return is that they not bother me unless it's something that is absolutely necessary. But, to handle every person who sneezes out of tune or looks cross-eyed, to assume that this is a job for a disciplinarian, is the most ridiculous thing I've ever heard of, because the minute a teacher sends kids to the office for sneezing, that teacher has lost a lot of respect.

Teachers, on the other hand, do want administrators to assume the responsibility, but at the same time they are unwilling to grant them final authority for disposing of these problems. This counselor reported that teachers often complained that he was too easy with students, and added:

If a child is referred to a counselor by a teacher, I feel strongly the counselor should be given the ultimate authority to handle that problem. If the teacher could have coped with the problem in the first place, he wouldn't have sent it to the counselor.

Administering discipline, it seems, is part of a teacher's "dirty work," which no one wants to perform, but which everyone wants to control because it is as crucial as it is unpleasant. Teachers are not really willing to relinquish to an outside party something so vital to their classroom as discipline. However, in the long run there may be a certain advantage in giving administrators final authority over discipline problems, as this teacher was willing to admit:

The punishment of students is being handed out by the principal, which to me is a good thing, because I think it keeps personal prejudices of the teachers out of the picture. Some student that isn't doing too well or some student that rubs the teacher the wrong way is then protected. The teacher doesn't enter into it as much.

The teacher, it might be added, has an additional advantage—students turn their resentment toward remote administrators.

Participation in Formulating School Policy and Control over the Classroom

The underlying crux of all these problems involving authority is the fact that many teachers feel excluded from the policy and decision-making process. In the least bureaucratic schools, problems involving control over school policy (not directly involving the classroom) occurred at a rate nearly twice that of the most bureaucratic schools, whereas problems involving control over curriculum and classroom work occurred with about equal frequency in both types of schools. Together, both problems involving control over the classroom and over schoolwide policy account for 10.4 percent of all incidents in the sample.

General school policy

Unlike the issues involving control over the classroom (reported in the next paragraph), issues involving school-wide policies not directly affecting the classroom were twice as prevalent in the least bureaucratic schools. A teacher's observations, speaking from the perspective of one of the smaller schools, gave a general picture: "I think this is universal in our country, don't you? I don't know of any school system where teachers make policies." More specifically, they complained because they are not consulted on such key promotion policies as whether outsiders should be considered, and they disputed over whether students must have participated in outside activities in order to be eligible for the Honor Society; countless other issues were mentioned.

Control over the classroom

These issues were generally as prevalent as those involving school-wide policies. Issues involving control of classroom procedures and methods of teaching were more typical of the least bureaucratic schools, while incidents involving control over teaching materials were more typical of the most bureaucratic schools; problems involving control of the subject matter to be taught were not typical of either extreme type of school. All three types of issues, however, accounted for less than 2 percent of all the incidents. The issues did include a large range of problems—from discussions about whether recipes for the home economics class should be copied by students or mimeographed, to a major incident between a science teacher who wanted to introduce engines into a course for slow, lower class seniors and a principal who insisted on traditional physics. Many teachers were criticized by colleagues teaching advanced courses because they were not "covering the material they should be."

There were several disagreements over the way to approach lower class children, such as this one:

I made the statement that you had to use a different approach for the lower class than you would teaching students with middle class values, that you couldn't superimpose your values on them because they would rebel. They [other teachers] said it was our job to introduce them to our culture and we should follow the traditional curriculum.

Two industrial arts teachers in one school were involved in a conflict because one of them, who reputedly had been "brought up under the old schooling of industrial arts where you had nail driving contests and the like," wanted the other one to go back to the old manual training theories, and so he rebelled.

An incident developed between two teachers over the items that should be included in a departmental examination for geometry; apparently, one wanted to include items the other had not covered in his section. In another case a teacher met resistance because he introduced a laboratory course in biology which the head of the science department and the vice-principal thought was far beyond the students' capabilities.

A notable clash occurred between a principal and a social studies teacher who was also a city commissioner. The teacher refused to pass out the required textbooks for his course because he did not like the book. As a respondent reported: "So, here we are going into the ninth week of school and he has not yet passed out the textbooks." The principal in this situation, reportedly reluctant to stand up to the social studies teacher, directed the teacher's department head to enforce compliance; the department head felt he was being made the "heavy" in the situation.

One of the most violent disputes in the entire study occurred because the administration refused to accept a new math program that several younger teachers wanted to introduce. One of the teachers reported:

We had three younger teachers in the math department who were very enthusiastic about the newer approach in mathematics, and the administration and the Board of Education no doubt went along with the superintendent who did not want the new approach brought in suddenly. They preferred to stick with the old established program, and this brought on the conflict. . . . Our best math teachers left as a consequence. . . . They were all three very brilliant people.

While this study was in progress, a petition was being circulated behind the scenes to oust the principal.

Occasionally, a dispute over the control of an activity would get out of hand, such as one that arose between two teachers involved with the direction of a play:

There was something about the last curtain that she didn't like. It was a difference of esthetic opinion—was the final curtain too fast? Well, we no sooner had gotten the curtain closed when she started screaming, "You pulled that curtain too fast," and that touched off the dispute in back of the light board. She wound up swinging her purse full from the hip, with me ducking and saying, "No more swinging or I will have to put you out." She didn't swing the bag in playfulness, and I didn't threaten to pick her up and dump her out of the stage door in playfulness. We were serious. She stomped off in her direction, and I went off in mine. . . . The cast came and dragged her back and told her, "You can't walk out two separate doors." The stage crew shoved me into her and the cast shoved her into me and we met somewhere in the middle. She ceremoniously handed her purse to some students to indicate that she had no more weapons in her hand. We have since been in each other's homes for dinner.

Many of these disputes over curriculum and related activities apparently arise because of administrative convenience, outside pressures, prestige, and other logically incidental concerns. An administrator, for example, praised the change in an annual promotion policy because it cut down clerical work and made his life easier. An English teacher, complaining about team teaching, reported:

I heard that our school received funds for the school building, but only if they would incorporate team teaching into the plan, and that was one of the deciding factors as to why we have it; I also heard that it was a feather in the ex-superintendent's bonnet.

One teacher complained that not only were many curriculum decisions being made by the administration, but the administration had failed to prepare teachers for the change. Instead, this teacher said: "The administrators were the ones who went to the conferences for team teaching; but *no teachers* were ever sent."

Then, too, some requirements for courses apparently are established with an eye on maintaining a department's relative status. A business education teacher complained that students in his department were allowed to transfer out of a course if they had failed the first semester rather than continuing for the full year, and concluded: "It's too easy for them to fail. Their counselor will give them a course that they can get through in the second semester if they fail in the first." Some of the repercussions of liberal transfer policies on a department's image are clear in this science teacher's comments:

I've had some question raised by some students who would have liked to drop certain courses and weren't permitted to. For instance, a student trying to get out of chemistry to get into my physical science class; this is usually not advisable when they are on an academic program. They are advised to take chemistry instead of physical science. If they were allowed to transfer, then it would seem that everyone could get out of a difficult course too easily.

One teacher, complaining that the administration would buy only one brand of typewriter, commented: "But what can you do when the typewriter salesman is taking the administration and the school borad to his estate during the summer? They go fishing and hunting together."

Academic freedom

Because only five incidents centrally concerned freedom of speech, and with only eight others involving censorship of books and teaching materials, the problems of academic freedom do not appear to be prevalent. But, they are so vital to the authority of public school teachers that the ones that do arise deserve special attention. One teacher was charged with "putting too much emphasis on sex"; a social studies teacher in another school was accused of "getting a little too far to the left"; another teacher was censured by the administration because he was active in politics and was elected to the city commission.

A number of books were removed from the library shelves as well. This English teacher reported:

I had a few books that he requested me to take off the shelves. *1984* was one of them, and I was surprised because he had been a history teacher. But, he said that parents had called and complained. Some of the other books were *Exodus* and *A Bell for Adano*. The board member [the one who had complained] left the board. This was finally resolved by leaving the hardback copy in the library, but taking the paperback copy out of the paperback book store. The students can't buy it, but they can read it.

Librarians play an important part in censoring books. This enviable librarian had an ideology to justify her role:

There have been a few times when I didn't get a book for the English teachers because I didn't feel that the language was suitable for high school students. It was a controversial book. It is possibly good for college but not for high school. The book was *Catcher in the Rye*. I don't believe in censorship of any kind; I do believe in *selection* of books.

This teacher expressed a sentiment typical of many in the study:

I have as much freedom as anyone could have. There has never been anyone to say that you must teach this or teach this way. Now, if I were selecting a play to present I would keep in mind the limitations of the community—such as, I wouldn't pick *Tom Jones*, which was one of the suggestions in a book I have.

Another librarian simply relied on other members of the faculty to select innocuous books. She said: "It is supposed to be the kind that everybody can read [the book on the list], and there won't be anything on there that will cause the parents to call in, supposedly." This teacher's cautiousness speaks for a large number of his colleagues:

When you figure that we are working with high school students, you must be very, very cautious. I think they [the administrators] are very subtle in choosing what they think is the right thing.

Grading and academic standards

A number of conflicts over control of classroom procedure specifically involved grading. Inherent conflict between teachers' academic standards and community expectations is reflected in a teacher's comment: "The standards of the school, I think, should always be higher than the standards of the community, and, therefore, what is requested of the student in school should be, in many cases, higher than what is expected at home."

Perhaps that is one reason why, in several schools, teachers were reprimanded by their public opinion-conscious principals for failing too many students. Reported this principal:

I think most of my problems result from the fact that I try to talk to teachers about their grades. I know that the teacher gives the grade, and I am also aware of the fact that the administration has to deal with the community, and I try to do some of these things for the protection of the students. IBM provides us with a record [each marking period] of the percentages of each grade that is given. And when it seems abnormally high at the lower end of the scale, why I feel it necessary to call in the teachers.

In another school an English teacher was upset because the administration made all of the teachers keep very specific accounts in their gradebook in order to "prove the grade they give in case the parent should question it." This teacher felt that the administration should trust the teacher's judgments.

Teachers and administrators tend to disagree about how much can be reasonably expected from a student who is doing poorly. Reflected in the following reports is the fact the administrators often feel that the student can't do any better and so should be passed, while teachers feel that the students are not trying:

The opinion of the counselor was that this boy could take the course 50 times and would never pass it so I should go ahead and pass him anyway. Well, I disagreed with this. My feeling was that maybe this boy would never obtain a high grade, but if he would put forth the effort, he could obtain a *minimum* grade. The boy felt that he had been pushed through other courses, and that he could get through this one in the same way. This is probably one of the reasons why the boy went to the counselor originally; he felt that this would be a fellow who would act as a go-between, and he could sit there and do nothing.

Another teacher reported that "The assistant superintendent said that the student must be exposed to the subject [second-year algebra] and that if he is cooperating in the least, he should be passed. Then, he has a chance to take trigonometry."

Teachers are often accused by administrators of being too subject-matter oriented. Teachers quite often do frankly admit that they prefer to teach only the bright students. An English teacher reported this of her colleague:

> She made the statement that she had no time to spend with the student who is not bright, and I said that this was not fair. She is unwilling to give any extra time to the student who had come into the composition class because, she said, she would be wasting her time with him because he wasn't going to get it anyway. He was an average student. I said that I disagree with this, and I believe the general student has as much right to see us as the superior student.

The above comments reflect the tendency of some teachers to stereotype students. For example, this teacher said of her colleague: "She feels that only those who are doing academic or that type of work should be given A's." That teacher went on to say that her colleague did not feel that most students in remedial classes should be given A's for their effort.

One of the reasons that some teachers stress high academic standards and stiff grading policies must be attributed to the fact that they are evaluated by their colleagues and compete for prestige on this basis. The importance of academic standards in the teacher's self-image is reflected in these statements: "My feeling about education is that it is not what anyone thinks about me personally and how he evaluates me right at the moment, but what they eventually are going to say about me when they get into college." An assistant principal lamented:

> I do see a conflict occasionally when a nonacademic department is trying to maintain academic standards, and they do this because they want to be sure everyone understands that what they have to contribute is just as important—that is, that woodworking is as important as physics. Then, the teacher's standards become unrealistic.

Competence

The issue of academic standards raises other questions about the professional competence of teachers, which is a basic issue because competence is presumably the primary source of professional authority. Issues involving personal competence occur with relatively high frequency (twice as frequently in the least bureaucratic as in the most bureaucratic organizations—2.73 percent compared with 1.09 percent of respective totals). Teachers criticize one another's competence quite openly. Teachers were more than willing to admit the inferiority of their colleagues. "Well, she feels inferior to me and it is a feeling that I can't do anything about. You see, I have more experience in education than she has. I feel her training was not as good as mine and she admitted this."

An English teacher reported an incident in which he was accused of incompetence by a history teacher:

This student had been working on a term paper for a history teacher, and he had come to me for some help within the term paper area. I had given him an alternative suggestion about bibliography. The boy came back a day later and said that I was absolutely wrong about this particular area, that the history teacher had mentioned the fact that he would not do it this way. So, I talked with the man a little bit later, and I said that I didn't think there should be this kind of conflict. . . .

An industrial arts teacher told a social studies teacher, who was complaining that her students did not live up to her standards, that she was not teaching the course well enough and not disciplining the students sufficiently. He told the teacher that the course was not being made interesting enough for the students, and that actually she shouldn't be teaching this type of course in the first place. In another case a counselor criticized a science teacher for giving a boy an "E" on the final examination; the teacher apparently had not noticed that the boy had withdrawn the second week of the semester.

Many of these problems, while perhaps reflecting personal disagreement, can be traced to flaws in the system of promoting and allocating teachers. For example, the nature of promotion is such that a person is often promoted out of an area in which he has demonstrated competence. The assignment of teachers to courses for which they are not prepared often contributes to the fact that teachers are sometimes less effective than they otherwise could be. This English teacher reported that "It came to my attention that the girl did not have much background in drama, and she had been assigned to this task last year prior to my coming to the school. I think the girl was put in a poor situation." In another incident, to be reported subsequently, a principal was accused of falsifying a report to the state department of education in regard to his use of an unqualified teacher to teach a language course.

Part of the problem, however, is that teachers are not sure what competence means. Some of them charge that college training does not necessarily assure competence either. In fact, some believe that too much reliance on academic background, in comparison to sympathy for the students, produces incompetence. This teacher said:

There is one thing that seems to bother me. It is the hiring of teachers that have done excellent work in colleges gradewise, and maybe feel the youngsters aren't as important. In other words, I think there are a number of teachers who go into teaching because they like to go to school. . . . There are some courses that just come naturally to teachers, and I think that they think youngsters should get it that easily or maybe they should be so enthused in taking the course—that they should *be as enthused as the teacher*. They just don't realize that pupils don't have things come too easy for them.

Occasionally, entire categories of personnel will be singled out for criticism; in this case it was the counselors:

I personally think that it is the biggest farce that has ever been placed upon the public educational system—or any other place. I think that if they put those people [counselors] back to work in the classroom, it certainly would solve a lot of the shortage of the teacher problem.

Some of these problems are aggravated by the fact that principals are aware that the competence of teachers varies to some extent but, unable to cope with it, are reluctant to admit it publicly. The public, for its part, is unwilling to accept the school's public statements to the effect that teachers are equally qualified and, therefore, pressure the school to assign their children to "good teachers," in violation of school policy. The school, of course, prefers to let the parents take their chances in order to maintain complete control over these assignments. This principal said:

About 95 percent of the students are scheduled without regard [for teacher competence] because we feel all our teachers are qualified. So that's all we can do about it. We say to the parents: "We are sorry." We have a lot of pressure to change, but we don't change. Once the youngster is handed his schedule, that's it. There are dozens of pressures. The main pressure we sense is that of the parent on the child to get good grades, and this is an insidious thing that we can't control. This causes a lot of unhappy kids, and parents too.

Ironically, it should be noted, the same principal complained earlier in the interview that one of his biggest headaches was: "Some teachers don't do the kind of job they should be doing with the kids."

Neglect of responsibility

Neglect of responsibility is a special kind of "incompetence," which reflects less on the person and more on certain situations and is especially native to bureaucratic situations. An example is a type of "buckpassing" involved in 1.86 percent of the incidents; it occurred with nearly equal frequency in both the most and least bureaucratic schools:

About five years ago we were supposed to set up a curriculum guide for all of the different areas. I worked on one for physical education, and our's was accepted. Then one day the head of the science curriculum for the system said that I was in charge of getting the science curriculum guide done. It was supposed to have been turned in two years ago. Someone else had been appointed for the job and apparently didn't do it. It looked to me like they were "kind of passing the buck."

This desire of teachers to avoid responsibilities they do not consider rightfully theirs was also reported in a case where the teachers in an English department refused to learn to run movie projectors because they would be responsible for maintaining the equipment. The head of the English department explained:

To be specific, I have women in the department who have absolutely refused to learn how to operate the motion picture projectors, and this is very simple. Their argument is that it is the audiovisual director's responsibility to get somebody to operate them. We used to have students volunteer to do this sort of work, but there haven't been enough students recently. Consequently, my answer is that if they refuse, no films.

Supervision Problems

Over 80 incidents, including overlapping authority, dogmatic administration and close supervision, lack of supervision (4 percent), and others involved what some teachers regarded as improper methods of supervision and measures of authority.

Close supervision

Only three incidents in the study were specifically about close supervision. However, the incidents that did occur revealed some of the difficulties involved in attempting to coordinate a large staff of professionally oriented people. A teacher in one of the less bureaucratic schools reported this situation:

There have been times when the principal has gone to a position in the window so that he could watch the parking lot as some of us were arriving, and I suppose I do arrive late. But I have a senior class and things are always under control. So I had been talked to about that, but it is in the manual, so I accepted.

Lack of supervision

There were actually more incidents (eight) involving lack of supervision than close supervision. Probably this teacher reflected the attitudes of a number of his colleagues when he said: "My personal feeling is that we have *too much* academic freedom. I think there is a lack of supervision." Another teacher complained: "No one ever came in the classroom. Nobody's been in my classroom for years. The superintendent has never come in all the years he has been here."

Evaluation problems

One reason why teachers complain about lack of supervision is connected with the way they are evaluated. They object to being evaluated without being observed because they consider irrelevant any evaluation criteria not based on their performance in the classroom. A teacher complained: "I was rated and never given an observation. I objected to it twice. When I was called in for the evaluation, I asked how I could be evaluated without an observation." The following teacher's story suggests a common difference of opinion between teachers and administrators as to the legitimacy of an evaluation criteria not based on classroom performance:

I didn't turn in certain forms. I told him why they weren't turned in. He said that he was rating me as a teacher; I thought the way he was doing it was most unjustifiable. I presented the question: "How can you rate me on teaching? You or your predecessor have never observed me. I haven't seen you up on the third floor."

Overlapping authority

Many of these supervision problems stemmed from, or were aggravated by, a structural situation—that is, where two or more persons were in a position to supervise the same subordinate. In describing the unenviable position of teachers in a conflict with the principal of one school, this teacher commented:

The thing is, the superintendent did not hire this principal. The superintendent and principal both came here to the system the same year. There was a power play, as I understand it, to get rid of the superintendent that was here. The old superintendent hired the principal and the board hired the superintendent.

Teachers sometimes become hopelessly entangled in these overlays of inconsistent authority figures. For example, an instrumental music teacher complained:

The band was supposed to play and the football team was supposed to play in the beginning of the season for a preview; and it had rained a little on the night before. Someone thought we shouldn't be on the field and someone else thought we should. So then we got the superintendent, the assistant superintendent, the music supervisor, and the athletic director, and they all had to decide as to whether we should go on the field or not.

In some cases an administrator would undermine a teacher's authority by going directly to his students, as in a case described by an extracurricular activity teacher:

I have a group that I have worked with from each home room. It is really hard sometimes to put your finger on what these girls accomplish. . . . He [the principal] didn't know whether we should go on and schedule this for another year or not, and so he called all the girls together. This was without my knowledge. He put this up to a vote and didn't consult me on it.

Red Tape and Rules

In some of the incidents the underlying authority system itself was less critical than the specific elements of the routine bureaucratic machinery undergirding the whole system.

Red tape

If they could not think of anything else, teachers would then complain about the clerical work and paperwork loads. This distaste for red tape is reflected in the comments of an industrial arts teacher who tried taking his class into the hall to do some sketching: "I ended up by writing 30 individual hall passes. He was within his rights, but I thought this was a lot of nonsense, taking up my time doing this when I could have been teaching."

Larger schools are especially subject to complaints about impersonality and red tape. For example, one English teacher was criticized over the loudspeaker by an assistant principal because he sent his students to the health center without a pass. The teacher involved reportedly said: "If a student is really sick, I am not going to take the time to write out a pass. The administration's attitude is 'Go ahead and faint, while I make out a pass for you.'"

Time pressures

Meeting deadlines is another headache. In one case an industrial arts teacher and his administrator had a dispute. Said the administrator:

The drawing people are anxious to have a new book. They came here and said they neeeded 36 copies of this textbook. Now this is kind of ridiculous because they could have known this back in September. Our texts have to be approved by the board of education, and this is usually done in the summer and purchased in the fall. We can't rush a board adoption now.

"Getting grades in" on time, in particular, assumes the proportions of Golden Rule in many schools, as illustrated in this report of a heated discussion:

It was over getting grades done on time. We had until Monday to get them out for the semester. But the assistant principal contended that he [an American government] teacher gave out so much work that it was impossible to get them done on time. He gave book reports. I guess they had about 128 to grade at the last minute. To be more explicit, he blew his stack.

Rules

These incidents usually concern the interpretation of rules. Quite often in these incidents the teachers involved will add that although they understand the reasons for a rule, it is being enforced too strictly in their particular instance. However, at least one reason for the strict enforcement was revealed in an interview in which it became clear that the administration had used strict interpretations of rules as a defense against pressures from teachers—for example, pressure to get rid of unwanted students. There are similar indications in this case reported by a science teacher:

I thought that they should be permitted to drop. By this time, the assistant principal had developed a hard and fast rule: "We don't drop anyone after the first six weeks." So this was a real conflict. To him, you do something because you are following the rules in this school and nothing can be done that goes against the rules. Now to me, it is more important to have a kid educationally where he belongs rather than to follow the rules. It was really heated. I still have the kids.

Rules are also used by the administration to maintain close control over the work habits of teachers. A principal complained:

Getting here on time seems to be a problem with adults. For instance, this morning we had small assignments for teachers trying to keep kids from loitering in the halls. One teacher wasn't here on time and I reminded him that the whole system would run smoother if assignments were carried out, and he agreed.

However, teachers can be even more vulnerable where there is a complete absence of rules, as this teacher's comments suggest: "The rules around here have been very vague, and I don't know what I can or can't do. I mean that I don't like to be scolded or bawled out for something that I didn't know was wrong because there is no rule." The lack of rules is a source of irritation not only between teachers and administrators but among teachers as well. This teacher complained that "Much of the time extracurricular activity is left up to the person who is engaged in directing the activity. But should you do something which is considered improper, you are generally notified only after it happens." Therefore, teachers tend to demand certain rules as a means of protecting themselves from administrative caprice and from the ambitions of their own peers. One teacher went so far as to demand a rule prohibiting a specific way of playing a game: "I have always thought we should have a rule in our regulations that seventh graders cannot use zone defense." He added, proudly: "We added the rule."

Ambiguous definitions of the job

When the ambiguity from lack of rules becomes widespread, the job itself becomes ambiguous. Job ambiguity accounts for some of the incidents. As an example, a counselor reported that

I am in charge of eligibilities. I take care of the week-by-week reports. But there are big reports that go to the state, and I try to keep out of that particular clerical work. Because I wouldn't assume the whole job and do it as he [the head basketball coach] wanted me to, he got mad and in the restroom in front of the other teachers he cussed me out and kicked a wastepaper basket across the room.

Attempts to institute new procedures are especially conducive to ambiguity. Leaders of newly instituted teaching teams complained about the ambiguities of their roles. Said one:

I was asked to be leader and to organize the team. This I did. But after the organization, where are you? You still are the team leader, but then there is a disagreement as to what should be taught and how it should be taught. I asked for help from my supervisor and the curriculum coordinator at that time. It never occurred to me that the limits of his authority were not fixed either. But I found out at a later date that he was in the same position as I was.

In order to alleviate some of these ambiguities, teachers are sometimes willing to accept more administration, especially if it is closer to their control and will provide them with structure. This teacher suggested that: "Here's the problem—there is no chairman in our department. Four people in our department with no leader, so to speak; no one to make the final decision; no one to take the final blame or punishment if that's what is 'needed.' "

SCHEDULING AND DISTRIBUTION PROBLEMS

Problems involving the distribution of functions and scheduling of facilities and students jointly constitute about one fifth of all of the problems in the sample, and the distribution of rewards and salary problems constitute an additional 8 percent. Taken together, the "activity" problems, which also include a group labeled "structural maintenance and change" problems, constitute nearly 31 percent of the sample. These types of problems are almost equally typical of the most bureaucratic and the least bureaucratic schools, although there are some minor and subtle differences worth noting.

Allocation of Students

The largest single type of scheduling problem involved the scheduling of students (10 percent). There were 210 of these incidents, which occurred with almost equal prevalence in both the most bureaucratic and the least bureaucratic schools (9.5 compared with 7.8 percent).

As might have been anticipated from the types of authority problems that arose among teachers, the bulk of problems involving the scheduling of students (6.1 percent of the total) was concerned in one way or another with the allocation of and competition for students. For example, some of the incidents essentially involved competition for students' time by using homework assignments. Several incidents involved pressures from colleagues against certain teachers who were assigning "too much" homework and forcing students to spend more time on their courses than on their colleagues' courses. Other incidents involved students transferring between teachers, or dropping unpopular courses; these accounted for about 1 percent of the total and were equally prevalent in the most and least bureaucratic schools. As an example of the disruption created when students transfer from one class to another, a business education teacher complained that students are often admitted a week or two after classes begin, which creates added work for him. He then added:

They are generally the type of persons that are going to have enough trouble just passing the course if they are there every minute of the day, and they need all of the advantages they can get. Now, certainly, it is not their fault in many cases, because there is no place else to put these people, and because they come in late or are high school dropouts who come back.

A teacher generalized: "I think the main difficulty that I have seen is, for instance, one group wants something that interrupts the schedule. When something special arises, it seems to throw both the adults and the students off schedule." Most of these disruptions involved taking students out of class. The degree to which this practice upsets teachers is evident in these comments:

Mrs. A. [a counselor] unilaterally excused a number of students from my class without permission. Then she brought them back in the middle of a rather dramatic point in my presentation, disrupting my class. I became furious, went to the person and told her to stay out of my life for good. . . . It certainly doesn't behoove this person to excuse students from my class. And to make bad matters worse, I was told by the office that whenever this person wants students excused, I was to excuse them.

But it is not merely that the classes are disrupted when students are taken out that bothers teachers. For when students are taken from one class to work with another teacher, it reflects on the relative status of the two teachers' activities, as this comment suggests:

That teacher just detained her [a student] to clean up the room. It was in home arts. It seemed to me that it was a rather unjust detention. She was assuming that her work was more important than my class. So I did speak to the lady about it afterwards.

The underlying status problem is revealed even more clearly in another comment:

He [a student] didn't show up in class, so the next day I asked the student where he was, and he said that the other teacher wanted him to make up a test. That teacher didn't really feel that my class was that important. He had *commented* that it wasn't important if they attended my class.

Curricular versus extracurricular activities

The vast majority of these disruptions are created by extracurricular activities programs. Six and one-half percent of the incidents in the sample involved either distribution or authority problems concerning extracurricular activities, one half of which specifically involved competition for students. One-sixth of the extracurricular problems specifically involved taking students out of class for practice or participation in an activity. Of the total number of incidents in which extracurricular activities were involved in one way or another, about one half specifically involved conflict with academic teachers, while slightly over one half involved extracurricular activities teachers in conflicts among themselves.

An example of a conflict between extracurricular and academic teachers involved an attendance officer in a less bureaucratic school who was accused by an academic-type teacher of not doing anything in regard to a student who was flunking a math course, and according to the math teacher, other courses as well. The student wanted to take time off to go to Iowa for a swimming meet during school time. The administration agreed with his parents, who felt that it would be "good experience." Spring musical productions also are sources of tension, as in one school where

Mrs. C. has an operetta in the spring, and she takes children from our classrooms. I may have a class of 25, and she'll take 15. That leaves me with 10. I'm a business teacher, and I'm sure if I wanted 15 children, the office wouldn't stand still for it at all. We all appreciate the fact that she's doing a great thing, but we often feel she takes advantage of it.

These problems seem to be associated with all extracurricular activities. For example, the Junior-Senior Prom in one school was the subject of widespread complaint.

The position of extracurricular activities is often one of privilege, which does not necessarily require reciprocity when academic teachers want to take students from extracurricular activities. A math teacher threatened:

One day I had wanted some people from his class during the last 10 minutes of the period. At the last minute he didn't let them go, and then I said: "Well, you're an athletic coach and someday you'll want somebody to help." This was an emergency, or else I wouldn't have asked for it.

One teacher, pondering the general problem, concluded: "There are so 'doggone' many events in all areas that they can't possibly do this without a conflict. You know, we always have conflicts with test dates and our music competitions, etcetera. Something like that just can't be avoided." But some teachers, at least, feel that as a consequence the academic program suffers. This teacher reflects a general sentiment when she said:

I am a great enthusiast for learning English, and I feel that it is the most important course taught in this school. I sometimes have a feeling—and to be completely realistic, we do have sharp band shows, a beautiful choir, and a winning football team—that the fact is that a student *can't* put a sentence together. This doesn't show, and I sometimes have the feeling that English is somewhat slighted. There seems to be money for everything but that.

Of the incidents that arose among extracurricular activities teachers themselves, over one third specifically involved persons in the music department and the athletic department. An informant reported: "The music people might say, 'We want so-and-so for music practice after school,' and the athletic team says, 'Well, we want him too; he's got to practice with us after school.'" An incident involving a music teacher and an athletic coach was summarized by a teacher like this: "There's a kind of bad feeling between the music department and the physical education department. Mr. L. kept a boy from going to a track meet, and now there is friction between the two because Mr. M. lost the track meet."

When these conflicts come to the attention of the administration, policies are sometimes developed for regulating the student's decision. Such a policy was described by this coach:

The board actually had a policy that if a boy had a conflict with a [basketball] tournament and any other activity, the boy should go to the tournament. I could have taken a definite stand and told the boy that he couldn't go to choir practice, but I didn't because the boy is such a wonderful boy. He told the supervisor of music last year that everything was going to basketball; he wasn't going to take part in the operetta this year. And then, when school started, he [the music supervisor] talked him into it, taking a part against his wishes [Corwin, 1965, pp. 89–90].

Sometimes there is a tinge of commercial interest underlying these conflicts between music and athletics, as indicated in this statement:

On the night the band puts on a show for one of the basketball games, the administration will allot 20 percent of the net gate receipts to the band. There's been some remonstrance on the part of the coaches. Some of them have even gone so far as to get a tab on the crowds and try to show the administration that the band wasn't responsible for that proportion of the gate.

However, not all of the incidents arising between extracurricular activities teachers involved music and athletics. Debate, speech, and drama also played their part in these situations. This particular debate and speech teacher, in describing a conflict between himself and an instrumental music teacher, reported a grim situation: "If I don't get a particular student that I want, it is fine with me. It does upset the instrumental teacher a great deal, however, and he used to call me at least once a week to impugn my ethics." He found the solution, however: "I put a stop to this by telling him that as far as I was concerned, my philosophy was that a marching band was a complete insult to the intelligence of a child."

These problems surrounding the extracurricular activities program are more typical of the least bureaucratic schools than of the most bureaucratic ones. In the most bureaucratic schools such problems occurred at only half the rate at which they occurred in the least bureaucratic schools. (This type of incident represented 3.3 percent of the incidents in the least bureaucratic schools compared to approximately 6.0 percent of the incidents in the most bureaucratic schools.) The proportion of incidents involving competition for students, either generally or specifically in extracurricular activities, was similarly low as compared to the least bureaucratic organizations (1.45 vs. 2.19 percent). The most bureaucratic ones, in comparison with the least bureaucratic, are equally underrepresented in incidents involving conflicts among extracurricular activities teachers (.72 vs. 2.04 percent; and .73 vs. 2.34 percent, respectively). It would appear, then, that bureaucratization, perhaps together with a larger supply of desirable participants in such schools, reduces competition and clarifies the relationship of extracurricular activities to the total program, and perhaps provides mechanisms for routinizing disruptions that do occur.

Academic versus vocational education teachers

The source of real contention between academic and vocational teachers is the competition between them for the most desirable students. Vocational courses and some less-academic electives such as art often are used as dumping grounds for unwanted students. Therefore, although there was competition among academic teachers for desirable students, competition of this kind was ten times as frequent between academic and vocational teachers (4.8 percent compared to .33 percent of all incidents, respectively). (Competition for the most able students and rejection of the least able and the disciplinary cases constituted 2.1 percent of all incidents.) As mentioned, they were more typical of the least bureaucratic schools (1.92 vs. 2.73 percent of the respective totals), because there are likely to be proportionately more good students in the bureaucratic schools—in part because the policies governing students are more clearly defined, and in part because the supply of good students may be more favorable in relation to the number of activities involved in the more bureaucratic ones.

Industrial arts has the reputation of a dumping ground in many schools. Students often are scheduled into vocational courses to enable them to graduate, or at least vocational teachers think so. Said an industrial arts teacher in a less bureaucratic school: "Well, this is the attitude. If a kid fails history or geography, 'We'll send him out to industrial arts.'" This teacher summed up the problem:

I don't care what department it is, they all want the good students. And we have students that have to be taken care of that aren't as good. Industrial arts feels that they have always been the dumping ground, and this is one of the departments, by the way, that has needed assistance, and the equipment has been lacking. Now that they are getting it, we have a pretty good shop, but even the shop department wants the "A" students.

The role of counselors

Guidance counselors, who are often officially responsible for scheduling and, in any event, are in a position to influence the decisions of students, play a vital role in the competition among teachers for desirable students. The comment of one counselor, while it is not necessarily typical of their philosophy, revealed the potential significance that these conflicts may have for the careers of students. He proclaimed ominously:

The academic courses are required of the more able student. He has a certain responsibility because he has been fortunate enough to have this greater ability, and therefore, the responsibility to society and to himself to achieve this. While I don't demand that a good student move into the academic area, I will make my strongest pitch for this. I have been refused, but I will make this pitch for the academic areas by the more able student.

Another counselor gave emphatic support to this philosophy:

I think it's certainly incumbent on the counselor to encourage the student to live up to his greatest potential, and if someone plans to be a secretary when they have the potential to be a nuclear physicist, I think we're really missing the boat if we say: "You be a secretary, and this is fine." There isn't any use beating around the bush. I think we do have some responsibilities here. We've probably kept some nuclear physicist out of the commercial department. This isn't the complaint, really. They're [the commercial teachers] talking about the student with a 110 IQ who is wavering between a terminal education in high school and a college education.

In view of these remarks it is understandable when a music director complains: "We have had occasions where it came to us that they [the students] were discouraged from participating in chorus or orchestra or band. They were encouraged to carry heavier academic loads." This teacher was more vociferous:

These kids are stereotypes and shoved into an area by the counselor. I'm not for the method they use. All the kids take these tests and are evaluated, and then she asks them to pick a course that they would like to take. But, by that time, they have had the idea so pounded into them that they will take the same course that the counselors want them to take. Eighth grade kids with low IQs will end up in industrial arts, home economics, etcetera. It is pretty well cut and dried for them.

In nearly every school studied, at least a few teachers, and in some schools many teachers, complained about the role of counselors in steering the better students out of their courses and the poorer ones into them. The following remarks illustrate the general tenor:

I had one specific case of that last year, where the youngster did want to enroll in bookkeeping for this year. He was definitely steered out of this course and into one he would need to get into college.

I happen to ride to school with a teacher in the business department. He gets quite irked sometimes because a lot of students are pushed into academic programs when instead they would make good stenographers, even though they have the intelligence. But because of parental pressure, or because of a counselor's advice, they are put into academic programs where they can succeed. But maybe they don't have the opportunity to go to college because they don't have the money. They end up going into stenography anyway after they are out of school. It seems rather useless, but how are you going to decide ahead of time?

I had the experience, several years ago, of a boy who wanted to take the commercial course, and his counselors refused to put him into the commercial course because they said he was too bright. And as a result, the boy was leaving here and going into college in a commercial course for which he had no background. And this was a counselor I know. I feel this is going past the authority of a counselor—then you are a dictator and not a counselor.

With views such as these well represented among teachers, it is understandable that many of them hold counselors largely responsible for the fact that their courses are treated as dumping grounds. This art teacher accused with this statement:

They want to put him in here to get this credit. Well, this is one way to help him graduate. . . . It's a matter of getting these counselors to realize that we need students in here who do have the ability. I just don't think they fully realize what kind of student should go into it.

Sometimes students and teachers have to go to great lengths in order to circumvent the "advice" of counselors, as this account demonstrates:

There is a tendency for the guidance people to direct anyone who seems to have good ability into the academic courses. And, to some extent, it may be justifiable. But I have even heard of one young lady who wanted to take the commercial course, and she had not intended to go to college, and she insisted on taking this. They wouldn't give her the permission. At least, they effectively deterred her from taking it. She finally had to bring a note from home that her parents wished to have her take the commercial course. She was a very good student. Maybe the guidance people had her best interests in mind, but I felt this was perhaps too much pressure.

While most of the dumping grounds are in the vocational areas and art, they also develop within certain academic areas, such as biology or journalism. When a particular teacher's course becomes defined by his colleagues as the one into which to steer the least desirable students, that course will be emphasized. This journalism teacher said:

There are some of my colleagues who encourage the C and D students to take my course, not realizing that if they can't write, I can't teach them to write journalistically. We have a grouping, where the better students are in the other classes, and so it's almost as if the "A" students were plucked out of the class.

Sometimes the pressures that steer students from the more demanding teachers into the care of the "dump tenders" are quite subtle. In one school, for example, a biology teacher complained that because another biology teacher was assigning abnormally large amounts of homework, the counselors were transferring the complaining students from that section into her own biology class. The teacher said: "The guidance department becomes a real problem. They take those students out of his classroom and I get them. I've gotten about nine this year."

Many teachers become resigned to their fate, such as this one:

Oh, once in a while we [he and the counselor] discuss a student. I may not be happy with the progress a student is making in class. There's not much you can do sometimes. He may not be prepared for the subject I teach, but there's no place to put him, so I keep him.

And this teacher resigned himself with this statement:

You can't win when they come in and say: "Mr. A., I am going to have to drop band because I have this advanced biology course, or I am going to be a doctor." What are you going to do? Of course, the main thing that you are here for *is* the academic, and we try to go along. It is awfully hard to compromise there.

One industrial arts teacher, however, had a more positive definition of his function:

Many times they will do the same test and show poorer results on the fifth try than they did the first time. And that same kid may go out of here and start running his own service station, get married, raise a family, be a voting citizen; the first thing you know he is an elder at his church. Now should I, as a shop teacher, complain because that kid has been shoved on me in shop? No. . . . Now there is said against the opinion that maybe we should have some brains in here so that you can teach more than you can teach these kids.

But while some teachers have resigned themselves, the system itself remains, and the consequences of "dumping grounds" make it difficult for some teachers to reconcile with their professional mission. This teacher comments, with sarcasm, on the philosophy that "If the student hasn't the reasoning ability for academic achievement, surely he can work with his hands." But he added:

Some students who have a reading comprehension of the fiftieth percentile, the counselors place them in the vocational classes. What I would like to know is, what happens to the average student that doesn't intend to go to college? Industry doesn't want a lot of this type of student as an employee either.

Ideologies behind "dumping grounds"

What reasons do teachers give for wishing to possess only the ablest students and for sloughing off the rest to defenseless colleagues? Several overlapping ideologies could be detected from the interviews: the utility of certain courses for the student, the difficulty of teaching less desirable students, reflections upon the teacher's status, empire building and maintenance, and the need for specialization.

1. *Utility for the student.* Several teachers in dumping grounds of snap courses rested their case for better students on the conviction that their courses could be as beneficial to able college-bound students as to potential dropouts. For example, a home economics teacher said:

We feel that many college students need more [of home economics]. If they marry in college, which happens frequently, they need to know how to make that dollar stretch as far as it will stretch, and they have no background unless they have some home economics, or business education, which will help in this.

An art teacher repeated a similar theme:

I would like to see an opportunity for a student to have an acquaintance with more subject areas. In other words, of the students who graduated from high school, a majority had no acquaintance with art although they have gone through 12 years. I would like to see them have more cultural opportunities.

And, of course, industrial arts teachers expressed the same sentiments about their program:

I feel that all individuals could take an industrial arts course because they are going to, at one time or another, have to use it. They should take it either as an elective or for half a semester so they could get familiar with paints and varnishes and develop a hobby.

But, interestingly, other teachers also use almost the same reasons to justify keeping the least desirable students in their courses. For, as this music teacher pointed out: "This teacher thought the boy shouldn't be in orchestra because he didn't deserve to be there due to his actions in other areas. It was my contention that this is the only thing that the boy could do well."

2. *Difficulty of teaching.* Whereas the preceding comments are predicated on the welfare of the students, other teachers are more frank in admitting that they don't want the lower ability groups because it makes it difficult for them. A teacher explained: "It is horrible to try to teach *Julius Caesar* and *Silas Marner* to slow students."

3. *Status maintenance.* Besides the sheer difficulty of teaching a standard curriculum to a unique group, tenders of dumping grounds also suffer statuswise, as this comment revealed:

There is some slight friction between the teachers of the general subjects and those of the honors. They sometimes tend to put themselves on a pedestal, and if they are asked to teach a basic class, they don't like it. They are too smart for those "dumb-heads" down there. There is some feeling—I suppose it is natural—that "People who teach the lower levels are tending to lower themselves. The ones who teach the honors [therefore] must be the real brains of the faculty."

The comments of this teacher about rewards suggests that the lower esteem for such teachers is built into the system itself:

Everyone likes to work with the outstanding student. You receive more rewards for your efforts. If you teach the noncollege students and they don't perform well, you get discouraged to some extent. . . . Some would argue that we have too much tracking and grouping.

4. *Empire building.* Teachers also are concerned about getting the proper number and type of students in order to maintain an established program or to expand one. This instrumental music teacher threatened with this:

One thing that would drive me away from here [is that] I can't see where there will be any band in five years with noncredits [that is, the fact that students do not receive any credit for band]. It used to be that we had all of the better grades in the bands, and now we have leveled off quite a bit. In fact, we have some of the lower ones because the better ones are on a more or less accelerated program.

An industrial arts teacher lamented:

I am leaving this school because for the past 13 years I have been able to get a fair amount of kids that have average ability; but now, in order for me to form a nucleus for students in my trade program, I must leave [so that I can place kids in industry every year as I have done for 12 years]. I have been placing from 33 to 50 percent of those kids in jobs. I am leaving the profession for many things. One of the major reasons is that I do not get the type of kids with which I can form a nucleus to produce fairly good craftsmen. . . . They are encouraged by the counselor, who may have been in turn encouraged by the administration, to egg those boys into college prep, and that is making the good craftsmen suffer.

Some courses are on very shaky grounds and need students simply to continue, which is the case of a foreign language course described by an assistant principal:

Very briefly, there were three students that she wanted to take out of German II and move into German III at this time of year. As I analyzed it, they were bright students. However, there was only one reason she wanted to do it; she had one student in German III and she wanted to make sure she had at least four to create a fourth-year following, so we won't say she doesn't have enough students to carry a class. I don't think they're as bright as she analyzed. We had a disagreement. She claims I'm being unfair—I'm being against students.

5. *Specialization.* Underlying the entire issue is the question of the feasibility and desirability of specialization in the public schools. This teacher pointed to the problem of attempting to apply a standard curriculum to all students:

They are divided more or less now, but because of scheduling, they sometimes get mixed up and we have a few slow ones in with the good ones and the other way around. It is just that we are trying to teach them all the same material from the same textbook.

But also involved is the question of the proper criteria for allocating students into the specialized programs once they are established. Many teachers, like the following, seem to be fatalistically resigned to the incompetence of large segments of people, stereotyped for assignments on a logical basis:

Our principal's philosophy is that we're training them to gain employment. We do get a lot of them good employment, and they stay. But about one half of the class, I'd say, is not teachable to the point where they're going to work in a trade.

This teacher, too, was bewildered by the logic of it all:

There are some boys that we aren't getting at all. Some that they are putting into biology and science have no business in there, and they do have good manual dexterity. Then there are some boys that they should put into a special class, and also there are some that just can't read.

But despite the problems associated with dumping grounds per se, this teacher put his finger on one of the major advantages of a specialized institution for nonacademic students:

I think there should be training schools for certain fields, something like industrial arts. I feel that the students in the business and industrial arts areas are being neglected. The *whole school* has to be an atmosphere of learning and not just one section of it.

So perhaps the real problem is not the existence of specialized programs, but the inflexible ways in which people are allocated to them, the lack of support for them once they are established, and the often-times sterile and unimaginative programs designed only to tend those who do not fit into the major programs (until they go on to their predestined fate).

Strategies for competing for students

However, if the system itself can be criticized for a lack of imagination, the teachers competing for students within it certainly cannot. Although they are not always successful, they have evolved a number of strategies, some of them quite imaginative, for grabbing the students they want. The strategies range from subtle pressures on counselors and institutionalized rules for competition to gaining more control over admission policies.

1. *Pressure on counselors.* The remedy for the shortage of able students mentioned most frequently in the interviews was to exert more pressures on counselors. This teacher placed her hope in "better counseling":

We have a couple of courses—note-hand and personal typing—and we have more or less the run-of-the-mill type of student. I think that now, through the guidance and counseling program, we can eliminate stick wood. We want the type of student in there that is going to college, the type of student that will be typing compositions. . . . We are trying to eliminate this type of problem with cooperation with our guidance program. We do get students who possibly aren't of the higher intellectual group, but at the same time, we do get a lot who are good students.

This teacher saw the problem as one of "educating" counselors who are unaware of what they are doing:

I think it is just a matter of getting the advisors and anyone else in the position to place these students . . . to realize that we need students in there that have the ability. I just don't think that they fully realize what kind of students we need.

One industrial arts teacher even wanted to formalize the educational program for counselors, suggesting that they "should have a sort of seminar with us—all of your tradespeople and teachers—on what these students go through, what they have to learn, and where they're going to be placed on a job."

    2. Institutionalized competition. But some teachers are not content to leave matters in the hands of counselors, and call for rules that would regulate the competitive situation and equalize their advantage. There is a suggestion in certain comments that some teachers have staked off boundary lines, or territories of possession, which they consider to be "off limits" to their peers. For example:

This person had charge of a certain activity where they had groups of boys organized with the basketball team, and he was a basketball coach at the school. I would go to the playground during the summertime and play with them. We would go into the gym and then he got the principal after me. They had made up some rule which they never had before, and said it wasn't right for me to be with these boys, since he was the basketball coach and I wasn't. . . . It seemed to me that he didn't want them to be friendly toward me since he was their coach and he wanted to teach them everything, and I was teaching them something. I didn't know what it was, but I didn't like it at all, and I told him about it. We haven't been very friendly since then.

    A counselor reported on a similar conflict that arose between him and another counselor who had complained about the fact that the students weren't coming to him:

I said: "I have never complained about when my boys like to come in and talk to you. If I feel you are helping them in any way, fine." I said: "I can't understand why you feel the way you do, jealous because they talk to me instead of you."

    In one school a rule (described in the following account) was established which had the effect of curbing competition after the beginning of the school year:

We have a policy that a boy must stick to what he started with at the beginning of the year. If he starts in athletics, he can't change over to music. I would pick this policy as being good. Several years ago when the football team wasn't doing too well under another coach, the music department was accused of having all of the big boys.

A number of teachers also expressed preference for a policy under which the less desirable students would be distributed equally among all teachers instead of dumping them on particular persons. Such preferences are revealed in this industrial arts teacher's comment:

Against my advice, they put all the T and I boys in one class, even in history. Of course, they didn't consult me about that until it was done. Always before, they spread them around to various classes so nobody had all of them. That worked out pretty well. Now we got them all in one class. They're a bunch of energetic boys who don't want to do anything, and it makes it kind of a problem.

But, apparently, some progress is being made toward equalization; at least this home economics teacher thought so:

Sometimes college-bound students do not take home economics and as a result they get the slower, stupid students in home economics which she [another home economics teacher] feels is being overcome, because many of the college-bound students are now being worked into the home economics program.

A special plan for equalizing the work loads without doing away with dumping grounds themselves was volunteered by one teacher: "I made a recommendation several years ago that we should have one basic class as a maximum load for any teacher." But, of course, those teachers not responsible for tending dumping grounds prefer to leave the chore to "specialists."

3. *Admission requirements.* The idea of rules limiting the ratio of undesirable to desirable students is so appealing to teachers that some of them advocate establishing admission standards for their courses which would, in effect, routinely exclude the unwanted students and select the ablest ones. For example, a principal pondering the fact that an art teacher was getting pupils who were taking art for an easy credit, uncovered the solution: "The principal felt that perhaps we should resort to giving written examinations in art, just for the sake of keeping out some of the people who should not be taking art." This art teacher, though in another school, gave his wholehearted support:

I do get a lot of people in there who shouldn't be in there. . . . They just don't have the aptitude or the ability for it, and they are there, and it is always stated by the principal that she thinks that it should be like this—an elective. But I feel that I should be able to sort through these people and take out the ones who are better. Twelfth graders, it seems, just want to pick up the credit, which I don't mind, but they think that it is an easy credit.

Teachers of industrial arts, too, have ambitions to raise their sights beyond the common students. Said this drafting teacher:

As a matter of fact, I think the industrial arts is sort of a "dumping ground" for students who have done poorly in the academic curriculum. And I am opposed to that. I teach drafting. And the kids who don't have very good grades in other areas don't get good grades in my area either. If he [sic] does get good grades in other courses, he will do a good job in mine. . . . I don't think that counselors are well enough informed about industrial arts subjects. They don't know the caliber of pupils that we should be taking. I don't think they understand fully what is needed to make progress in industrial arts. This is as important as any other area.

Then he proposed a remedy: "I think that we should have a counselor who is an industrial arts teacher also. We are not represented there at all." If the industrial arts teachers feel this way, it is not surprising that social studies teachers have the same idea: "I think we should get together with the counselors, tell them what we want and what we can take—exact requirements, instead of just the boy who is causing trouble or is lazy."

One teacher had an elaborate justification for establishing academic standards for her language course:

We finally got together a couple of years ago and decided that since all our professional organizations said that there was a definite correlation between ability in foreign language and ability in English, that we would like to require that no student would be allowed to take foreign language who has ever had, at any time, less than a C grade in English. When we did that, the guidance people accepted it, the administration accepted it, and all thought that it was a fine idea. Since that time it has been better. We still miss, and I still have people in class who shouldn't be there—who are not capable, but with those people, I try to work on the basis that if they try honestly, they can get through it.

There is some indication in the above comments, however, that teachers are not entirely agreed on the criteria for selecting and excluding students. Some of them mentioned written examinations, others referred to progress made in other courses, and this teacher would use IQ scores as a basis. "I looked up their IQs. I found that there were several students who should not be in geometry. Their aptitude tests showed that they shouldn't be in there. Now these other counselors will take them out." Still other teachers, such as this one, looked to outside opinion to clarify their claims:

We wrote [to the state department of education] for an interpretation of a "service occupation," and they said if the student was hired primarily to do mechanical work, then he should come under DCT, but if he was hired mainly to sell merchandise then he would come under DE.

4. *Control of assignment procedures.* Some ambitious teachers envision going beyond simple rules and gaining more of the actual control of the machinery by which students are assigned to courses. A band teacher, for example, seemed to wish for more opportunity to consult directly with students in the process of choosing their courses:

Once in awhile, because a student wasn't doing too well in band, the student would think: "Well, next year I won't make the good band, so I may as well quit." He would be on the point of discouragement. But many times after they had withdrawn, I would talk to them and they would want to continue and go on anyway. I think if they had me talk to them in the first place [instead of the counselors] maybe I could have allayed their fears.

And the fact is that teachers are in a position to exercise a certain amount of control over students' choices, and a few are very direct in their use of this power. For example, a band teacher admitted this:

Some of the students that wish to drop, I try to save and keep them in the program, and so I refuse to sign their change. They could carry it to the counselor. I don't know whether they do or not. I can't think of a time when a counselor has come back to me and said I would have to sign this or anything like it.

Some teachers use their ingenuity by recruiting the most desirable students early in the season before they reach the counselors. This incident, reported by a basketball coach, involved athletics:

The baseball coach, who is new this year, had been stepping on my toes as far as athletes are concerned. During the basketball season he would go out and talk baseball and take youngsters to various baseball activities during basketball season. In other words, he was talking baseball to the guys who were practicing in basketball, which I don't do during football season; so I expect the same respect. The boys weren't actually leaving the team, but he was diverting their attention. I talked to him a couple of times, not heatedly, and it slowed down.

And informal recruiting occurs in fields other than athletics, too, as this vocal music teacher's description of a debate teacher testifies:

He gets the better students because he goes out into the junior high school, and when he finds a student who is an all "A" student, then he tries to encourage them [sic] to take his class, which is a very funny technique for recruiting debaters. There is fault to be found with it in my estimation. Some of the teachers may feel that they don't get the cream of the crop.

5. *Changing the course scheduling system.* Finally, some of the remarks indicated an awareness on the part of teachers that certain courses were at a disadvantage because of the scheduling system. At least one teacher took matters into his own hands for a time and found a way around the fact that students often lack time for electives, but his idea was usurped by another activity:

I have always had a boys' choir before school began in the morning. So this year they instigated an early class to start at 7:30, which meant that many of the boys who want to be in choir couldn't be. And it was for the benefit of the athletic program; so that they could go to early class and get out early in the afternoon and practice. Now I can't have them before school or after school.

Even in cases where teachers were not in a position to change the system, their remarks shed some insight on certain structural factors which encourage at least some dumping grounds. For example, a music teacher attributed his disadvantage in the competition for students to the fact that too many subjects are required in the sophomore year, leaving them little time for electives. Another structural factor, one that is perhaps even more important than a course's elective status, was alluded to by this teacher:

This hits me right now because we've just had a change of schedule due to the large numbers of students enrolled in half-credit business education subjects, so that a student who has failed math the first semester could go on and pick it up. [As a result] the discards from the other departments find their way especially into this. But, the only solution I could see would be a change in curriculum. If there would be a [second semester] math class of some kind, or an English class of some kind so that these students could step into something that would be within their range.

Sensing that it was unlikely that the course structure itself could be changed, one teacher advised:

Students should not have the opportunity to fail a course and then take another one. They should have to stay with the course the entire year. The way it is now, if you fail the course at semester time, you do not go on and take it the next half, but pick up another course. It's a half-semester course, and this is where it hit our business subjects.

Assignment of Teacher's Work

Not surprisingly, the status problems implicit in allocating students are paralleled in the assignment of teachers' work loads. One teacher said simply: "The most desirable courses are the highest level courses." Another, an English teacher, was more specific: "Now the big question is this 'prize plum' called Senior English. This is a conflict that is looming in the background." One teacher believed that promotion policies should officially recognize the desirability of working with the better students by giving the more experienced teachers the better students. But other teachers, such as the one just cited, object to having to start at the bottom of the ladder at all. Hoping to specialize with the better students, she advocated:

I feel that I could teach other tracks and be effective and do a good job, but I don't feel there is any particular reason for a policy that a teacher should be in a general class or a low class for two years, or something like that. No more than a doctor shouldn't be able to specialize and work with just a particular area of his practice. I, as a teacher, like and enjoy and find a challenge in teaching the honor students. I don't really see any justification for a policy of teaching general classes for a few years.

The problem is, of course, that most of her colleagues feel the same way.

How, then, do principals induce teachers to take the unwanted students? One uses a volunteer method, but he has learned not to be too optimistic. He said:

We attempt working very closely in order to schedule these classes so that the teachers are not put in a position [to teach them] unless they volunteer to end up with all one group. For example, we have a man teaching low ability tenth grade, but he wanted it. He asked for it. But along late in the spring, he said: "Can you bail me out?" We have a man in the eleventh grade who insisted that he wanted to do it this year. We had him talk to this other gentleman, and I told him: "I think you had better consider this very carefully." He was still convinced that he could do a good job. So I said: "If it is agreeable with the principal and the assistant, we will give it to you with the stipulation that if you change your mind before the year is out, you can get out of it before the end of the year." And interestingly enough, he has come to me.

In another school, however, the principal is more arbitrary. One of his teachers decried: "I know the first-year teachers get the worse courses. I think this is the worst thing they can do. Because I think it is very discouraging to first-year teachers to have the terrible classes. They are not qualified to handle them." *Neither is anyone else.*

Not all of the incidents that arose over job assignments, however, were concerned with obtaining the prized courses as such. Some of them originated because teachers were assigned to courses outside their specialties. Take, for example, this report:

It [an incident] happened when coaches who were assigned to teaching jobs and were given the courses they wanted even though there was another teacher involved who wanted it. For example, some years ago, I was to teach some bookkeeping, for which I had preparation. This particular coach, who had been hired, would not teach American history. He might possibly have felt that he wasn't qualified. The result was that he wanted to teach commercial, particularly bookkeeping. So I taught American history that year, which gives you an idea of some of the things that happened. I wasn't particularly qualified.

Another teacher reported a similar incident:

I'd like to drop Latin and have a straight German schedule, which is right up my alley, my main field really. He mentioned, at the time, that this probably wouldn't be possible, because Latin teachers are hard to find. So if they get anyone to lighten my load, it will probably be in German. We had a disagreement here, because I feel German is my forté. I did all my graduate work in it.

The sentiments of many teachers might be expressed by the teacher who said: "If I have a job, I want a chance to do it right."

The practice of assigning teachers to courses for which they are unprepared leads, in one school, to a breach of law. A Spanish teacher in a small school reported this conflict involving herself, the principal, and the superintendent of schools:

So I came in [to the superintendent's office] and he asked if I were interested in Spanish. I said: "No, thank you." This went on all summer long. Then I said: "Well, if I ever want to teach social studies at M. [this is my husband's home town], I'd better go in and say I would teach Spanish for a year. To make a long story short, I did. I worked my old head off that year. I stayed one page, not a chapter, ahead. And I know I didn't do a good job in the second-year classes. I couldn't. The first year I had three Spanish classes and one English class. The next year I had four Spanish classes and one English class. The next year I had no English classes. I taught all Spanish. I know for a fact that the information that went on the North Central report said that I was teaching four classes of English and only one of Spanish. I was not.

A few assignment problems involved unequal or too heavy work loads. An English teacher said:

The major problems are with teachers' loads and curriculum, and things of this type. My major problem is that I have been sick this year with a very, very bad case of nerves. I had this problem with my stomach, which my doctor said was nerves, because I teach five different classes. I had play, I had the newspaper. It was just a headache. If I were in a larger school, to which I was accustomed, I don't think I would be involved in all these things, because the newspaper would be handled by the journalism department, the drama department would take care of the plays, and you would be a teacher within your field. I don't feel I have time to devote to my classes.

From this principal's point of view:

There's always the tendency for a teacher to compare her load with another teacher. And "load" is rather hard to define. Educational experts have tried to develop a formula. The only problem you run into is that many of these things look good on paper. Some people work at it, others don't. So on paper, it may look equal, but in actual results, there is quite a difference. This is where the formula doesn't measure human reaction. Some teachers go into their classrooms and really knock themselves out working at their jobs. Others go in with just the notion that "I'm here for 55 minutes and I have a job to do." It's a pretty cold-blooded thing. They sometimes take exception on the grounds that they are doing more, when in reality the other person may be doing much more because of the nature of the two people. The bigger the school, the bigger the problem gets.

The resentment that develops when some of them show too little commitment to their jobs was described by a teacher who said:

Conflict between coaches who teach social studies and the person who teaches a full load of social studies is common here. The conflict comes because you have in-service meetings and they [coaches] are tied up with practice. We have had this series of in-service meetings for the whole city. This is just the second year we have had it, and with the result that many of the coaches cannot go to these in-service meetings because of practice.

Scheduling of Facilities

In addition to competing for students and favorable job assignments, teachers compete among themselves for other scarce resources, especially physical facilities.

Scheduling space

The most frequently specified type of scheduling incident concerned scheduling two or more classes or groups using the facilities of the same room or area. There were 49 of these incidents in the sample, accounting for 2.33 percent of the total.

The proportions of such incidents in both the most and the least bureaucratic schools were similar. In the most bureaucratic schools, however, this type of problem was confined largely to extracurricular activities, and especially to athletics, music, and drama, all of which use the same auditorium, gym, or practice field. At one school, for example, the basketball coach became aggravated because the track coach began his indoor practice too early in the season, placing the programs in competition for the use of the indoor gym facilities at choice times. The track coach accused the basketball coach of using his position as athletic director to emphasize basketball. Teachers are very adamant about their claims to scarce facilities. A drama teacher reported:

My people had been here for rehearsing music many nights after school, and I think I met them at night once. The day of the final rehearsal, he said to me: "Will you please give me an hour for rehearsal time for my orchestra, because some of my people have never played the music before." I didn't answer him, because I had said: "I will try to do everything I can for you." So I deliberately thought this thing out, and made up my mind that I was *not* going to give him an hour at the expense of my students. If it were my personal expense, I would do this. But I had a responsibility to my youngsters. They come in after school and they deserved to have a smooth program.

Such incidents, at almost every school, became very incendiary when they were between the band and football teachers. At one school a band director was unable to gain access to the football field in order to rehearse formations for the halftime show. The reason given by the athletic director was that marching band practice ruins the grass. Such disputes center around titles to territory and jurisdictional rights, underlying which is the implicit claim to the importance and priority of the activities involved. An analysis by a football coach is particularly enlightening:

There is usually a conflict between band directors and coaches. Each feels that *his* program is the most important. But when you come right down to it, there would not be any of these things without football. They would not have any place to perform or any other reason to perform.

Besides the fact that this coach did not feel compelled to explain his program in terms of the over-all school philosophy or student welfare, for him the band had obviously become a subsidiary of the football program without independent justification. His whole case for monopolizing the practice field was based on the influence of the athletic program.

Similar incidents arose between athletics and intramural programs. Said one intramural coach:

It's a question of who limits the facilities and who can use the facilities. And in this case it's athletics and intramurals. The question is, "Which is more important, athletics or intramurals?" I think that the gym should be available down there every afternoon after school for *all* the boys and girls, for at least an hour.

The fact that these conflicts entailed more than a simple shortage of facilities became most apparent when it was realized that the band in the case cited above refused to use another "dusty" practice field that was available, because of its inconvenience and lack of maintenance. Similarly, at another school, where the gym was shared jointly by the basketball coach, wrestling coach, physical fitness teacher, and intramural director, the latter refused to use a less desirable gym in an old high school building because he felt he would have trouble recruiting the bigger boys who preferred not to practice there.

In the least bureaucratic schools the scheduling of shared facilities appears to be an equally prevalent problem, involving mainly the same issues, but with one added dimension. Scheduling problems in these schools spilled over even more into the academic program. This teacher reported the kind of scheduling problem that arises in nonbureaucratic schools:

I was originally scheduled by the administration to have biology in the art room. It is bad enough to teach biology in a room that is not equipped for biology itself, but this is the second best thing because we are short here. The art teacher, however, was very perturbed that I was there. I was in that room, and nobody said anything to me. Then the department head spoke to me and said that the art teacher wanted his room back. The next day I heard in the announcements that my biology class had been switched to a study hall, which is where my class is now.

Similar incidents occurred in other schools. For example:

The person with whom I share one of my rooms is very individualistic. He is that type of person. There are two bulletin boards in our room, and I sometimes get disturbed about them. I thought that since there were two, I could have one and he would have the other one. He didn't agree.

Some of the disputes over facilities also involved the lack of adequate office space or parking facilities. For example, this exasperated teacher moaned:

The people who park there first are janitors and others who come early. I never have trouble getting a place to park because I am here early. But some of the folks who don't get here early have to park out in the student lot. They don't have a special place to park. We often wonder why we're not permitted to park out here in front.

Lack of money

Many teachers attributed the problems associated with the scheduling of facilities to the lack of money and unwillingness of the communities to support their schools. At times the money pinch becomes very tight, as this report demonstrates:

My conflict comes with the top administration of this school. We had some awful arguments last year over the budget. They told us they were going to cancel our contracts [because the community did not support the bond issue]. We called in Mr. ——— from the OEA and he told them they couldn't cancel our contract, it's against the law. I think sometimes that there's too much money spent in the administration and not as much on teaching aides and equipment and facilities.

Some teachers, however, maintain that raising money is no longer entirely the responsibility of communities, that administrators and teachers should be doing more to build their own programs. One teacher advocated:

If the science people want to push the science program, why don't they go out and develop a program and get a grant, if this is what they want. There is a lot of government money floating around, waiting for people to get it. . . . You can't sit back and wait for the superintendent of the school or the principal to do it. They have too much to worry about. You know the "squeaky wheel gets the oil." This year we had a problem. We felt something had to be done, so we went together and got a workshop to share. . . . I don't think it's fair to say the science department is suffering because of the industrial department, because they aren't. That's not the same money.

And, to the dismay of the less fortunate departments, some programs are in a position to obtain outside support for their programs. Those who service outside groups are in a particularly favorable position. For example, although industrial arts is sometimes the neglected stepchild, in one particular school it was in a favorable position due to its support from influential industrial leaders, as indicated in this principal's account:

Industry has gotten together and they have given us, I suppose, over a million dollars worth of equipment, and we in turn do turn out pretty much of a finished product so that industry *can* come in and hire these people. You know we have had 100 percent success in this program. In fact, our whole department was recognized just last week in New York at the National Convention of the National Association of Manufacturers. This has gotten a lot of publicity. It has been written up in professional magazines; we have had radio television publicity on this program.

Although lack of facilities and equipment was frequently a greater source of trouble in the least bureaucratic rather than in the most bureaucratic schools, (2.73 vs. .73 percent of the respective totals), the way in which available funds or property are used was disproportionately a problem in the most bureaucratic schools (2.55 vs. .55 percent). An American history teacher reported:

A few years ago we had arranged for maps, and then we were told that there wasn't enough money available for them. We had to have trees and shrubs, and a gardner had to be hired for the campus. That is what I mean by the money being spent on nonessentials instead of essentials. We have American history being taught in rooms where there isn't a map of the United States, but we can't do without trees and shrubs.

Another teacher in the same school related a similar dispute about the way money was used:

They [industrial arts teachers] thought it was a shame that we got a music building, and not an industrial arts building when the campus was built. I can justify that, because there was enough money to erect a building to house the music department, but the type of building that it would take for industrial arts, including the drawing rooms, would need more money.

Coordination problems

Underlying some of the problems stated above is a general lack of coordination between departments. Some coordination problems are illustrated in this remark:

When the students come to me from the lower grades, I feel that they have not been properly prepared. But perhaps the person who has had them before me feels that he had done his job. When the students get to high school my requirements are one thing, and the school and the community requirements may be something different. As a result, my program isn't growing. It lacks coordination.

This lack stems from the absence of a general policy, and in turn creates further policy problems. One of the general complaints arising from the lack of coordination was that teachers are inconsistent in their use of discipline. An assistant superintendent in charge of discipline in one of the smaller schools in the study said: "My biggest problem is that the discipline in each class is different. Then when they get caught, what am I to say—if they can chew gum in one class and get kicked out of another because they do?"

Competition for Status

In many, perhaps most, of the preceding incidents, there were indications of struggles for status among various individuals and groups of teachers, struggles which at times lay buried beneath the surface of seemingly trivial problems, but which at other times became more manifest. It is, therefore, somewhat arbitrary to select certain incidents as involving competition for status among teachers, except that it serves the purpose of focusing attention on the problem.

Occupation-based status competition

Some of the incidents involved competition for status between persons on the basis of their positions in the occupation of teaching or of a particular job. One type of officially based status competition integrally involved the evaluation system. Some teachers expressed concern over the fact that their merit could not be evaluated fairly and accurately by the administration; they preferred instead a system of seniority. But teachers do insist on evaluating one another informally. This situation creates ambiguities about the importance of merit at promotion time, which opens the field to a broad range of people contending for any vacancy, some of whom consider themselves more qualified than their experienced colleagues. In fact, teachers espousing the merit criterion will openly challenge the right of persons to continue to hold positions gained through seniority. In one school it was reported that a teacher "indicated that he would like to take someone else's job who had no intentions of leaving the system" because he felt the person in the position was incompetent.

One unspoken basis of esteem is the way a teacher's students perform on standardized tests. As this teacher explained:

> There is sometimes, I think, competition among teachers in the same area, let's say for social status. Perhaps I have a class in American history and Mr. M—— has a course in American history, and we're taking these state tests [which I won't mention]. They are given to almost every pupil in the district. And whether we realize it or not, we are in competition with each other as to how well students do, and I can see where the administration can see that Mr. M—— is doing better than I am in teaching American history.

But perhaps the most critical evaluation a teacher can receive does not concern his teaching competence at all, but the prestige of the function he performs. Two teachers, for example, one in English and the other in shop, at a noon hour became involved in a fist fight over who was teaching the most important subject. Within the field of English, grammarians compete for prestige with literature and humanities teachers. And one cooperative education teacher maintained that a distributive education teacher was placing his students in office jobs for which her girls were better trained.

A number of teachers complained about the fact that certain departments or groups dominated the school. Athletics tend to dominate the extracurricular activities programs of most schools. Complaints and incidents involving an overemphasis on either drama or music encompassed, respectively, .76 and .24 percent of all incidents. An English teacher in a bureaucratic school assessed the situation at his school like this:

The athletic director's wishes, wants, and desires are considered primary and everything else is secondary. . . . No one has even considered the dramatic society on the same par with the athletic group or even with the coeducational athletic group such as the marching girls.

However, the dominance of athletic activities is not universal. In two or three schools the music department seemed to be at least as important as athletics. This science teacher described the situation at his school as follows:

You know, we have so much emphasis on music. They have a big program and a lot of power and they don't try to hide the fact; they use it whenever they can. This is the general feeling, that the department is too powerful. This is sometimes called the B——— Conservatory of Music.

As illustrated previously, many teachers of vocational subjects feel that too much emphasis is placed on academic subjects, with one arts-and-crafts teacher offering this opinion:

I think that some teachers who are teaching vocational subjects feel that too much emphasis is placed on academic courses and subjects, whereas a considerable proportion of the high school doesn't go on to college. We are not permitted to have anyone "above average."

And from another school comes this observation from someone at the low end of the "totem pole": "Art is still on the bottom of the ladder of the curriculum. Because of circumstances due to college pressure and college requirements, it doesn't seem to fit in, plus other local factors—the community supports the college courses."

Socially based prestige

Teachers also compete for prestige on the basis of their social backgrounds and personal connections, as this counselor's comments reveal:

The amount and type of education are important determinants of a teacher's prestige. I am also a guidance counselor. My master's degree is in guidance. So I feel that I am also a threat to [another counselor], plus the position I am in, and also the informal atmosphere that I have with the girls.

From another school comes the report that the head of the home economics department, who does not have her master's degree, is afraid that a colleague with this particular degree will try to take over her department.

The *alma mater* seems to be as important as the amount of education in some cases. For example, one teacher noted: "It is rather amusing to me that there are a few people who are working toward a master's degree at ——— University and they are looking down their noses at people who have degrees from ———."

One or two teachers complained that the federal fellowship program, under which teachers are paid to return to school, is upsetting the status system, particularly because popularity with students is being outweighed by academic criteria in grant awards. This teacher complained:

I do not feel that a teacher should be given such a great reward. Granted, he has gone to school all of this time and has devoted himself to the teaching profession. This would assume that he is a good teacher. Yet, the way I've heard students talk [because of the informal nature of my classes and my close connection with the students], I have a pretty good idea of who is a good teacher in the students' opinions. And a number of these teachers who are not good teachers in the students' opinions are the people who would fall into the fellowship deal. I think you can have all the degrees in the world and still not know anything.

Status inconsistency

In many of the instances the underlying problems are status inversions and conflicts of interest with the organization—that is, inconsistencies between a person's social and official positions. For example:

She shouldn't be teaching because she is a board member's wife. I don't care if she wants to go and spoil someone else's system. She should be able to be a teacher here plus a board member's wife, but she is unable to separate herself. She is first a board member's wife and, secondly, she is "possibly" a member of this faculty.

One teacher, "whose father-in-law is a big wheel in one of the political parties," reputedly "manages to get pretty much what he wants." One teacher said of him: "We rather envy him, and he is probably the most influential individual in the school."

Often a group with a disproportionate amount of authority has a more persistent type of status incongruity as well, or inconsistencies of status. For example, in the less bureaucratic schools, board members often have lower levels of education and more authority than the teachers. In a similar vein a teacher reported:

The secretarial staff in the office seem to be the main target of the teachers; they seem to feel that they are not treated properly by the secretaries. I feel that I am usually quite tolerant. The two major secretaries have been here longer than I.

Incongruity between a person's age and experience and his position created other problems. An anguished teacher admitted:

It was mentioned to me that they [other faculty members] wondered how I was put in this position since I was a new teacher. They could see no justification in it. I was only here a little more than a year and was placed in this position, which upset some of the teachers who had a longer tenure. There have been times when I made a purchase for something that would suit our purpose, and [one of her subordinates] has made complaints to my superiors.

This teacher said prophetically: "You always have the age-old problem in schools, where the younger man is promoted over somebody who had been around for a long time, and you will always get a conflict."

Promotion to administration without teaching experience is a related problem that arose in a couple of instances, as for example, when an assistant superintendent was criticized for having only one year of classroom teaching experience.

Occasionally, a dispute would occur which seemed to be provoked by the fact that men were subordinated to women supervisors as in this case:

I had a woman for a principal in my first year as a teacher. I felt that she didn't do the job, not because she was a woman, but the boys didn't respect her because she was a woman. She would say something and then she would change her mind. She would sort of "give in" to the students.

Finally, there seemed to be tension whenever a person or group in an officially subordinate position obtained more privileges and rewards than their official superiors. The following remarks illustrate the problem:

She said that there was one parking lot near the administration office, which was reserved exclusively for the administration, the cooks, the counselors, and the custodial staff so that the regular faculty were not permitted to park there. They had to park much farther away from the school proper. She feels this was not right.

Favoritism

In view of the several forms of status competition among teachers, it is not surprising that dominant groups attempt to claim disproportionately more privileges and resources for themselves; at least they are accused of doing so. A girls' physical education teacher complained that all of the attention was being given to the boys' football team, and the girls' sports program was neglected, adding: "The football field is always supposed to be maintained; but not the playing field for the physical education classes. They have men out there working on the field for a game Friday night, but we can't even get the grass cut." An English teacher complained: "Everything is given to the advanced placement and honors program, even the new textbooks." Another teacher, noting a lack of parking space for teachers, complained: "The teachers actually get a place to park after everyone else is assigned a spot—custodians, staff, clerks, everyone involved. They get the places they want. What's left is for the teachers who drive."

There also were rumors of favoritism in the hiring of administrators. In one school it was maintained that "no new administrators or coaches would be considered if they are not from a particular state." In one of the largest schools in the sample several teachers complained that girls were deliberately being counseled out of physics. Racial discrimination was rumored in another school where a counselor reported:

I have heard several comments to the effect that the DCT program coordinator will not accept colored students. But he did accept one this year, so that kind of "shoots" that idea down. However, this boy that he accepted is a fine athlete and a very good boy.

Finally, a case was reported involving the waiver of a prerequisite to a course for a superintendent's son against the objections of his teacher, who said:

The superintendent's son was taking a course, and they were supposed to require students to take a certain course as a prerequisite. The superintendent's son had just about enough time to call his father, and his father to call the principal, and he had time to call me. This was within a half hour, and this whole policy was reversed full circle.

PERSONALITY CLASHES

Some incidents that seemed to involve no more than human foibles, personal irritations, or pet peeves were labeled as personality clashes. For example, two teachers at one school became involved in a fist fight on the school grounds after one of them insulted the other, implying that his outside job at a service station required little intelligence; two women physical education teachers became involved in a heated quarrel when one of them could not find her gym shoes; and one principal reprimanded a teacher because he wore sports shorts to school and another reprimanded a teacher because he failed to remove his hat in the building; one teacher became involved in an incident because he was allegedly an alcoholic; a teacher reported an incident between herself and a male colleague who made improper sexual advances in public; two English teachers had feuded for years over whether a window should be open; two teachers argued over the repossession of some office furniture; and a teacher argued with her colleague because she parked her car too close to hers.

One teacher was chided because he

. . . takes the *Time* magazine covers that we use for bulletin boards and draws faces on them, cuts them out, and puts them up all over the room. He distracts my kids while I am trying to teach them about the joy and beauty of art. He puts glasses on people without glasses, and so on.

Another teacher was censured for being

. . . very lax in the care of equipment, typewriters, adding machines, in the whole classroom. . . . For example, we have had banana peels and apple cores in the typewriters. Then I have had to get on him three or four times about leaving the room quite torn up, papers on the floor, desk completely disorganized, all kinds of problems on the board that he never takes off, and that type of thing.

LACK OF CONFLICT

Some teachers accepted conflict with philosophical reserve. But the reader should not get the impression that teachers do nothing but fight. Many of them had no problems at all to report. Some schools, and probably most teachers, are relatively peaceful in comparison to the most militant among them. One teacher, for example, when asked if she had any disputes, pondered the question for a while before finally replying: "Only with my husband—he's on the staff also." Indeed, perhaps one of the most important theoretical questions is why conflict is not more prevalent than it already is. As one teacher wondered: "I am amazed that there haven't been more disputes than there have been, because I am not easy to get along with." Many teachers, too, insisted that things at their school are very harmonious, and that if there are any complaints, they either are unaware of them or make it a point not to get involved. One teacher said: "We make a special effort not to have disputes . . . it just doesn't seem professional to get into these disputes." Another elaborated: "If teachers can't set an example of cooperating and working together without these radical disputes, then there is something wrong with this as a profession."

Those teachers who avoided conflict were among the most task oriented and less sociable ones. Said one English teacher:

You would think with a staff as large as we have, I could rattle them [conflicts] off by the dozens, but it isn't like that. It is like a job where you come and go, and you do your job and go home. Perhaps if I spent more time in the faculty room I would be able to relate more. Really, I sort of avoid the faculty room in the respect that if there are any disputes, if they come up anyplace, it will be in there.

This teacher also found teaching a very peaceful business:

All I know is that I don't like to mix socially with the people I work with. I find that my life is better when I work eight hours here and then have eight hours away from school. Therefore, I see no one socially. I don't go out after work with any of the teachers. I know many of these teachers meet socially; I think it is because they like them. I think it is very difficult for single girls to have companionship with any of the married faculty.

Avoidance with outside activities is a related factor:

I don't care to become involved in any activities. I think most frequently the problems arise with teachers in activities after school. If I work with a person in the same building five days a week, from eight to three-thirty every day, I don't care to fraternize with them at night.

Size of the school and ecology were mentioned by some teachers as important reasons for lack of conflict. For example: "Size is a factor, and layout of the building, because certain teachers here may go a month without seeing each other." Finally, this teacher, a male naturally, attributed his peace and quiet to the fact that he doesn't associate with the women:

If everyone does his job and has a free period, about the only time that you get to see them is during the lunch period. And they rotate that, so you are only there about 20 minutes. You don't get to socialize with these teachers too much. Men teachers are probably a little more reluctant to spread rumors or gossip or this sort of thing. As a result, things happen that we are never aware of. I don't feel that it is any great loss.

IMPLICATIONS

The most fundamental characteristic of the status system connected with public high school teaching is that those teachers who most closely emulate the higher levels of academic teaching are the most highly regarded and rewarded. Their status is directly related to the difficulty of the subject matter they teach, which in turn depends upon the ability of their students. The best students, and the positions that put teachers in touch with them, are the most coveted because the performance of students reflects upon the teacher's own status. Consequently, teachers will go to some lengths to protect their territorial claims over the desirable students and to increase their share of such students. The competition extends into the extra-curricular and vocational areas of the curriculum as well. Certain courses and activities serve as "dumping grounds" for the less desirable. Many of the disputes over curriculum content and methods have similar status implications; some of these cases reflect the desire of teachers for more decision-making authority, while in other cases it is the convenience of some administrator or the prestige of a department or teacher which is at stake.

From the standpoint of the teachers involved, there is an oversupply of inept and delinquent students and a shortage of the academically superior, highly motivated ones; since their prestige weighs so heavily on the performance of their students, teachers tend to regard such students as being incapable of learning, and they are inclined to blame them for not trying hard enough. But from another standpoint, the fundamental problem is that no one wants to specialize with the "undesirable" students because there is no provision for recognizing teachers who do this type of work.

Under the present system, the status competition among teachers functions to undermine their professional obligations to protect and serve all students. But teachers cannot be blamed for wanting to work with the type of student that brings them the most recognition with fewest difficulties. Competition for the most prized and recognized positions is inherent to social life. The question is, what is rewarded? As long as the academic model prevails as the over-riding basis for receiving recognition in teaching, working with the less able students will not be highly regarded.

But, by using the same principle, an alternative reward system could be established which could serve to channel this competition for status among teachers into more constructive forms of concern for the less academically able students. To identify and institute this alternative status system is one of the formidable challenges to the teaching profession today.

NOTES: Chapter 5

[1] Half of the first ten of the major conflicts involved authority problems, and three of the first ten involved scheduling and distribution problems. However, one of the top ranking problems involved a value conflict—that is, ethical impropriety; and personality clashes also ranked in the top ten types of incidents.

To provide further insight into how conflict fluctuates with bureaucratization, a comparative analysis was made of the incidents typical of the four *least* and the four *most* bureaucratic schools in the sample, as reflected in their total bureaucratization scores. (Two of the schools in each group also had highly crystallized structures—that is, consistent levels of bureaucratization.) Brief accounts of a group of specific incidents that characterize schools at each extreme will perhaps provide deeper insight into some of the implications of bureaucratic conflict. The four most bureaucratic schools yielded 474 separate incidents compared with 183 incidents in the four least bureaucratic schools.

REFERENCES: Chapter 5

Corwin, Ronald G. *A sociology of education: Emerging patterns of class, status, and power in the public schools.* New York: Appleton-Century-Crofts, 1965. Pp. 89–90.

Stinnett, T. M. *The profession of teaching.* Washington, D.C.: The Center for Applied Research in Education, 1962.

FROM TALKS WITH TEACHERS on administrative irritations

HE FINALLY *did give me an office. But I didn't use it, because there are three desks and there is a teacher at each desk, and I have no place to call my own. I have decided this year that security or happiness—what is the word with which Peanuts is associated?—to a teacher is a place that she can lock a drawer. I haven't got that this year, and it's been disturbing to me.—a teacher*

THEY [THE *teachers*] *know the rules and the laws as well as I do. They shouldn't come here and presume that I or Mr. A can shove a thing like this through. Maybe 20 years ago, when we had 1,000 kids in the top four grades and we had 40 or 50 people on the faculty and everybody lived in everybody's backyard, we could have. But [the school] is big business now.—an administrator*

HER TRAINING *is in primary education, and she is a supervisor over* all *areas —primary, secondary, and junior high. Consequently, the majority of the material she hands to us and the majority of her suggestions pertain to primary children. And they don't readily apply to the secondary. The students recognize this to the extent that they are insulted at times. . . . Let's say that she wants the children to become aware of the newspapers. Some of them are already aware of them. She'll bring in a book in which you will cut out an article from the newspaper and paste it in; this sort of thing. They will be insulted, and rightly so.—a teacher*

I MYSELF *am in, oh, I don't know what you call it, a touchy situation. You see, I'm teaching Russian as my major, and also French. The Russian course is one of the new languages and definitely not getting enough students to enroll in it. I don't want to hide the fact that this makes me uneasy . . . I was hired as a Russian teacher. In four or five years Russian has had the same number of students; it doesn't seem to grow. . . . Probably there is something [that is called student-teacher ratio] which has a certain magic number that probably shows the efficiency of the school. If you have a high student-teacher ratio, that shows that those teachers are keeping busy 25 or 30 students all of the time. Now, in my case, the student-teacher ratio would be pretty low, because I have very small classes.— a language teacher*

6. Who are the belligerent professionals?

> The people whom I think are the most dynamic teachers, the best teachers, are the ones who most frequently get involved in these conflicts. They are so keyed up all the time.—a high school teacher
> I have often questioned whether it is worth it to have an excellent teacher when she causes such friction.—a high school teacher

During their discussions teachers would occasionally speculate about the nature of the people who became ensnarled in these disputes. Some of them were quite charitable toward their militant fellows; others were not. We followed some of their leads as we sought to identify the belligerent teachers, their militant leadership, and their adversaries. We shall first briefly survey the general conclusions before presenting the data on which they are based.

OVERVIEW OF THE FINDINGS

We were able to distinguish the more conflict-prone people from their colleagues on the basis of several indices of professionalism and several background characteristics. We developed a typology of professional militancy which helps to explain the results. The following types of teachers were identified:

1. Ultraprofessionals—The most professionally oriented people in the sample (that is, in the upper 15 percent of the professional orientation distribution)
    (a) Moderate militant ultraprofessionals—Ultraprofessionals who have been involved in at least one dispute
    (b) Belligerent militant ultraprofessionals—Ultraprofessionals who have been involved in at least one heated discussion or major incident
    (c) Nonmilitant ultraprofessionals—Ultraprofessionals who have not been involved in disputes, heated discussions, or major incidents.
2. Rank-and-file—Teachers not classified as ultraprofessional (that is, in the lower 85th percentile of the distribution)

(a) Rank-and-file militants—Rank-and-file teachers who had been involved in at least one dispute, heated discussion, or major incident.

Rank-and-File Militants

Professional orientation and behavior

In a previous chapter we conjectured that professionalization is a prime incentive behind personal militancy and the militancy of an occupation. But what does this mean empirically? It could mean simply that professional people are more likely than less professional ones to become involved in conflict without implying anything about the frequency. Or it could be more precise than that—that is, that the more professional a person is, the more frequently he will become involved in disputes. To answer these questions, we examined both whether a person had ever become involved in conflict and his rate of involvement.

Only slight correlations were found between professionalism—measured both by a person's orientation and his self-reported behavior—and most of the measures of conflict; except for major incidents and severe disagreements the correlations for the sample as a whole were negligible. But the extremes provided clearer evidence. The 200 ultraprofessional teachers (that is, those with the highest professional orientations in the sample) tended to have slightly higher conflict rates than the typical person. When teachers were classified into high, middle, and low groups on the basis of their professional orientations, on seven of the eight conflict measures there was a crude statistical tendency for persons with weaker orientations to become involved in fewer incidents than teachers with average or stronger orientations. The teacher with the strongest professional orientation was likely to become involved in twice as many authority issues as his counterpart with a weak orientation. However, the groups were reversed on the average frequency involvement in major incidents—that is, the teachers with weaker orientations became involved in more major incidents than their colleagues with weaker orientations. As we shall see later, this pattern anticipates a parallel finding about organizational climates.

The percentage of teachers who become involved in certain types of incidents also tended to be a little higher for the 30 percent with relatively strong professional orientations, but the differences were not as clear-cut as their average (mean) rates of involvement. It should be noted, too, that for the total sample, correlations of the conflicts measures with the professional behavior index were generally higher than the total sample correlations with professional orientation.

In short, there is a slight degree of linear correlation and the proportion of teachers who become involved in certain types of incidents tends to be a little higher for those with strong professional orientations, but the major difference is that less professional people engage in conflicts less frequently on the average. What separates the least professional teachers from the others is not that they become involved in conflict, but that on the average they become involved in conflict less frequently. Persons with weak professional orientations appear to be less "recidivistic."

Employee orientation and behavior

Although not striking for the sample as a whole, there was a partial tendency for the most employee-oriented teachers, and especially those who were more compliant in their conduct, to be less militant. Persons who were highly professional and at the same time not committed to their employee role had disproportionately high rates of involvement in conflict, while those with the reverse loyalties were less likely to be involved. However, the percentage differences were not large.

Sex and age differences

Professional *orientations* did not differ between the sexes or between the younger (that is, those under thirty-five) and the older age groups; the slightly higher professional-orientation scores of the younger males were not statistically different from the other groups. However, males did show signs of more professional *behavior* than women, with older males excelling in this respect. Younger men also expressed exceptionally low employee orientations. Older women, on the other hand, were extremely loyal. In general, men characteristically were less employee oriented than women and leaned more toward certain types of professional behavior. Curiously, the 'Organization Man' turns out to be an older woman.

These characteristics probably help to explain the finding that men had significantly higher rates of conflict than women on all eight of the conflict indices tested. The average male has been involved in over eight disagreements and between one and two incidents, most of which have been with the administration over issues of authority. By comparison, the average woman has been involved in less than seven disagreements and less than one incident. Nevertheless, the *correlations* with total disagreement rate, severe disagreement rate, and major incidents were all substantially higher for women than for men; slight increases in their professionalism have more visible effect on their militancy than on that of men. (Because males are concentrated in high schools, elementary teachers are not as likely to be militant.)

The younger men had lower employee orientations, but the older ones (who have shown more signs of professional behavior) became involved in statistically more conflicts (on six of eight measures). Perhaps younger men do have less compliant attitudes by virtue of their youth and gender. But it seems to be the older ones who have developed a sense of accomplishment and prestige sufficient to put them in a position actually to challenge authority and openly dispute with colleagues.

The fact that older males are militant seems to indicate that militants do not necessarily leave the field of teaching or mellow with age. Moreover, the militant attitudes of the younger men may forecast a new generation of even greater militant tendencies to replace the present one.

The Leadership

Sex and age differences

The "moderate" militant professional leaders were disproportionately middle-aged (thirty-one to forty-five years of age)—44 percent compared to 36 percent of the total sample. This relationship is probably a product of at least two tendencies. On the one hand, the youngest teachers seem more in touch with new developments than older ones due to the recency of their education; they have less stake in the status quo and generally favor change; on the other hand, until a certain level of maturity has been reached, they are unlikely to have gained the experience expected of leaders, or to be well enough integrated into their informal group structures to have influence.

Other background differences

The militant ultraprofessionals had more support from their colleagues, were more respected, and had more education than either the typical teacher in the sample or the nonmilitants of their high professional conviction. They were more likely to be men than women; conversely, the ultraprofessionals who did not become militant were more likely to be women. (These findings about women fit the more passive stereotype about their gender, but it is also true that some women did contribute to the leadership of a milder form of ["moderate"] militancy.)

Types of conflict

In comparison to the "moderate" militant professionals (that is, those who participated in the less severe disputes), the "belligerent" ultraprofessionals (that is, those involved in major incidents) were more likely to be concerned with scheduling and distribution problems. They also seemed to be as anxious to tangle with their peers (particularly those in vocational education) as with members of the administration. They were more likely to become involved in conflicts with the public as well; this is partly a function of the way major incidents were defined. By comparison, the moderate militants expended most of their energies on authority issues, most of which involved the administration.

The fact that belligerent professionals very frequently became involved in major incidents with their own colleagues might tell us something about the general character of professional movements: teachers willing to take extreme positions and become involved in major incidents do so at the risk of alienating at least some colleagues who are not willing to go that far, or who otherwise are neutral. This tendency of professional movements to become segmented and fraught with conflict among peers seems to be typical of professionalization (Bucher and Strauss, 1961). The fact that belligerent militants were comparatively less concerned with authority problems than with scheduling and distribution problems suggests that in comparison to their counterparts, they were perhaps more involved in a struggle for personal resources than for decision-making authority.

These findings raise a perplexing question which we cannot answer with the data at hand. Do these two types of leaders simply represent alternatives for achieving more professional status, or do they represent two horns of that universal dilemma faced by all professions—the selfish struggle for individual rewards versus the search for group autonomy?

Militants compared to teacher organization officials

How do the informal leaders compare with the officers of teachers' organizations—that is, the acknowledged leaders of the teaching profession? Compared to officers of professional associations, the AFT officers seemed to be more professionally oriented and less committed (both by word and action) to the administrators, and they expressed more defiance on the Initiative-Compliance Scale. However, in practice they were more militant in only two respects—in rates of involvement in authority issues and in disputes. In several other respects professional officers were more militant than AFT officers.

More important, in every respect but one, the informal leaders were more militant than the officers of either organization. Perhaps that one exception is critical, since AFT officers exceed all groups on the rate of involvement in conflicts over authority for teachers. Nevertheless, one cannot escape the impression that much of the leadership for militant professionalism in education has come from behind-the-scenes informal leaders as well as from officers of established teachers' organizations.

The Adversaries

Various types of adversaries of the militant professionals could be distinguished on the basis of their professional and client orientations. There was little evidence of "in-fighting" among militant professionals of equally high professional orientation. But the people most chronically (that is, frequently) opposed to the belligerent ultraprofessional had exceptionally low professional and client orientations—with a major exception: people who were opposed to the belligerent militants in solitary incidents (that is, only once each) whose professional and client orientations were even higher than those of the belligerents; this suggests that the most professionally oriented of the peer-group members, though militant themselves in lesser degrees, do act to hold in check the wrath of their most zealous colleagues.

Also, it is important to note that at least these informal leaders of the professional movement were able to combine militancy with a strong client orientation and were more client oriented than their adversaries. In this sense the militant professional leader counteracted the exceptionally low client orientations of those colleagues who were opposed to him. The fact that the militant professional leaders had high client orientations, and that they were more oriented toward protecting client welfare than their adversaries provides some evidence that professionalization may be to the benefit of clients.

There seems to be in teaching, then, a hard core of resistance to professionalization. For this reason, conflict between militant professional leaders and their reluctant colleagues may be as essential for improving professional status as conflict directly with the administration; for the militancy of professional leaders seemed to be turned against precisely those rank-and-file members who were less committed to professionalism. In the absence of militant professionals their less professional opponents probably would dominate school teaching to an even greater extent than at present.

Work Satisfaction

Finally, it is significant that an individual's satisfaction with his work increases significantly with his conflict rates. The correlations with career satisfaction are in most cases higher than with their job satisfaction. Perhaps only those persons who were already committed to teaching and satisfied with their careers become concerned enough to participate in conflict. But one cannot ignore the possibility that the very act of conflict may give one the sense that he has had part in the long-range development of education, especially if he meets with any success. Whether conflict is unsatisfying probably depends on the significance of the issue and the outcome.

CHARACTERISTICS OF THE RANK-AND-FILE BELLIGERENTS

With this general overview in mind, we can now turn to more detailed considerations. Perhaps it will help first to identify the kind of rank-and-file person who becomes involved in conflict before turning to the more complex problem of describing the militant leaders. Linear correlations, comparisons of means, and frequency distributions were all examined in connection with the hypothesis that a person's professional orientation is associated with his involvement in conflict.

Professional Orientation and Behavior[1]

Correlations*

The correlations of both professional orientation and professional behavior with eight measures of conflict rates are all in a positive direction, but when the sample is taken as a whole they are very low (Table 6–1, "Professional, Total r"). The correlations with professional orientation in particular are exceptionally low (ranging from .00 to .07), with the exception of the total disagreement rate ($r = .23$).[2] But the correlations are substantially higher for particular groups within the total sample. When men and women are separated, the correlations were raised for all types of conflict, now ranging from .14 to .76 (Table 6–1, "Males," "Females"). The correlations between professional orientation and total disagreement rate, severe disagreement rate, and major incidents are all substantially higher for women than for men (respectively, $r = .76$ compared to .55; $r = .37$ compared to .17; $r = .51$ compared to .17). When a person's age is taken into account, there are similar increases in the basic correlations parallel to the pattern represented for each sex.

For the total sample, correlations between the conflict measures and

---

* The correlations reported in this chapter were computed with the Pearsonion r formula. This is a measure of association between two variables which takes into account only the linear aspect of the relationship—that is, the proportionate amount of change in the values of one variable in relation to a similar proportionate change in a second variable. It does not account for disproportionate, or nonlinear, types of association. For a sample of this size most of the relationships are statistically significant at $p \leq .05$, meaning that the likelihood that they have occurred due to chance is less than 5 in every 100 such samples.

Table 6-1. Linear correlations between the professional and employee orientations and behavior of individual teachers and their rates of conflict ($N = 1,511$)

Type of Conflict	Professional						Employee					
	Orientation			Behavior			Orientation			Behavior		
	Total r	Males	Females	Total r	Males	Females	Total r	Males	Females	Total r	Males	Females
Total number of incidents (less complaints)	.04	.20	.14	.21	.50	.59	−.04	−.18	−.23	−.24	−.74	−.23
Number of open disputes	.04	.20	.14	.17	.49	.56	−.04	−.20	−.36	−.19	−.56	−.29
Number of authority incidents	.05	.18	.19	.17	.41	.37	−.05	−.21	−.28	−.25	−.85	−.27
Number of incidents with other teachers	.07	.20	.22	.17	.48	.34	−.05	−.20	−.28	−.08	−.49	−.31
Number of incidents with the administration	.05	.23	.15	.16	.44	.42	−.06	−.26	−.20	−.26	−.68	−.26
Number of major incidents	.00	.17	.51	.09	.29	.25	−.04	−.32	−.54	−.13	−.38	−.37
Total number of disagreements	.23	.55	.76	.06	.31	.21	−.23	−.59	−.68	−.04	−.28	−.27
Number of severe disagreements	.05	.17	.37	.08	.30	.14	−.06	−.39	−.39	−.06	−.37	−.28

professional behavior are generally higher than the equivalent correlations with professional orientations (ranging from $r = .06$ to $r = .21$). These correlations also increase when sex is taken into account. For females, as an example, the correlation of the professional behavior index with the total conflict measure is $r = .59$; for males it is $r = .50$ (Table 6–1).

Analysis of means

While the above correlations are not notably high for the total sample, it would seem possible that professional orientation is associated with conflict rates in a nonlinear fashion not revealed in correlation analysis. To explore this possibility, the 200 teachers in the sample who had the highest professional orientations were examined separately. On the average, they do have statistically higher rates of involvement in (a) the total number of incidents, (b) teacher-administrator incidents, and (c) authority incidents than the typical member of the sample (Table 6–2).* In particular,

Table 6-2. Conflict rates of the individuals with extremely high professional orientations compared to the total sample

Type of Conflict	Mean of the Ultra-Professionals[a] ($N = 200$)	Mean of Total Sample ($N = 1,513$)	Critical Ratio
Total number of incidents (less complaints)	1.40	1.15	1.65[b]
Number of open disputes	.44	.38	.80
Number of incidents among teachers	.81	.72	.85
Number of incidents between teacher(s) vs. administrator(s)	1.11	.82	2.00[c]
Number of authority incidents	.98	.79	1.66[b]
Number of major incidents	.15	.11	1.30

[a] Individuals in the upper extreme 15 percent of the professional orientation distribution.
[b] Critical ratio significant at $p \leq .05$, one-tail test.
[c] Critical ratio significant at $p \leq .05$, two-tail test.

* The critical ratio is a statistic that tests the likelihood that an observed difference between the means of two groups within the sample has occurred by chance. In most cases a probability of $p \leq .05$ is acceptable, meaning that the observed difference could occur by chance in less than five times out of 100 such samples. $\bar{X}$ is the symbol for mean (average).

Table 6-3. Comparisons of the conflict rates of individuals with strong, moderate, and weak professional orientations ($N = 1{,}513$)

	Mean Level of Professional Orientation				
	1 Strong	2 Moderate	3 Weak		Critical
Type of Conflict	($N = 510$)	($N = 535$)	($N = 468$)	F Ratio	Ratio
Total number of incidents (less complaints)	1.53	1.47	1.00	5.82^a	(1, 2) 0.34 (1, 3) 3.17^b (2, 3) 2.98^b
Number of open disputes	0.57	0.49	0.30	8.31^b	(1, 2) -1.09 (1, 3) 3.36^b (2, 3) 3.98^b
Number of incidents among teachers	0.80	0.78	0.56	4.93^b	(1, 2) 0.26 (1, 3) 2.88^b (2, 3) 2.79^b
Number of incidents between teachers and administrators	1.17	1.07	0.75	4.91^b	(1, 2) 0.68 (1, 3) 3.05^b (2, 3) 2.42^b
Number of authority incidents	1.11	1.02	0.63	10.20^b	(1, 2) 0.73 (1, 3) 4.05^b (2, 3) 4.90^b
Number of major incidents	0.10	0.12	0.17	4.12^b	(1, 2) 0.82 (1, 3) 2.58^b (2, 3) 1.93
Number of severe disagreements	0.15	0.11	0.06	2.73	(1, 2) 0.96 (1, 3) 2.16^a (2, 3) 1.85
Total number of disagreements	8.10	8.04	6.56	13.64^b	(1, 2) 0.16 (1, 3) 4.89^b (2, 3) 4.51^b

[a] Significant at $p \leq .05$.
[b] Significant at $p \leq .01$.

the teacher with a strong professional orientation, on the average, becomes involved in twice as many authority issues ($\bar{X} = 1.11$) as his counterpart with a weak orientation ($\bar{X} = .63$) (not shown in Table 6–2). The ratios are similar for rates of involvement in incidents with administrators and for open disputes.

Moreover, when the teachers are classified into high, middle, and low groups on the basis of their professional orientations, there is a crude, statistically significant tendency on seven of the eight conflict measures tested for persons with weaker orientations to become involved in fewer incidents than the teachers with either average or stronger orientations; the low category is more likely than the high category to be statistically different from the average group. (See Table 6–3.) However, the trend is reversed on their frequency of involvement in major incidents; teachers with weaker professional orientation become involved in more major incidents than their colleagues with stronger orientations.

Rates of involvement

As another approach to this question, we examined only whether a person became involved in conflict (regardless of frequency of the involvement). The proportion of people with strong, moderate, and weak professional orientations who have been involved in at least one conflict were each computed and the differences tested by chi square. The direction of the differences was as expected for five of the eight measures tested, but the percentage differences were significant on only two of the chi squares (not reported in tables).[3]

Employee Orientation and Behavior

Except for a correlation with total disagreement ($r = -.23$), the negative relationships between an individual's conflict rates and his employee orientation are negligible for the sample as a whole. But with sex controlled, they increase substantially, up to $r = -.68$ in the case of females involved in disagreements. (See Table 6–1.) Correlations of the total group with the employee-behavior index are somewhat higher than correlations with other totals, ranging up to $r = -.26$ for teacher-administrator conflicts.[5]

Role Organization

There are some indications, then, that a person's professionalism is associated with his involvement in conflict, and that loyal employees are less likely to become involved in conflicts than those who are less loyal. Therefore, it seems reasonable to expect that conflict will be exceptionally in evidence when these two role conceptions are combined in particular ways.

Compared with people having the opposite pattern of loyalty, persons dedicated to the professional orientation and simultaneously undedicated to their employee roles more frequently become involved in major incidents at a rate of two to one (12 vs. 6 percent).[4] Comparable figures for involvement in authority issues are 43 and 32 percent.

A select few persons who simultaneously expressed the most extreme acceptance and rejection of these two roles were examined. The pattern becomes even more prominent. The 42 persons with the simultaneously highest and lowest employee orientations were involved in heated discussions at a rate double that of persons having the reverse extreme conceptions (21 vs. 10 percent). They also differed greatly on the total number of incidents, number of general complaints, number of heated discussions, number of incidents involving impersonal competition, and number of disputes involving more parties.

Identities of the Professional Militants

Professional orientations do not differ between the sexes or different age groups; the slightly higher professional orientation of males is not statistically significant. (See Table 6–4, Total.) However, males show signs of behaving more professionally, with older men excelling the younger ones in this respect. Moreover, men (of all age brackets) and younger people (of both sexes) have statistically lower employee orientations than their opposites. The young men have exceptionally low employee orientations, while older women are extremely loyal employees. (See Table 6–4.) (The employee orientations of both older males and younger females are intermediate.) Men, who are less committed to the employee role and who act more professionally than women, also have significantly higher rates of conflict on all eight of the conflict indices tested. The average male has been involved in eight disagreements and between one and two overt incidents, most of which have been with the administration and over authority issues. By comparison, the average woman has been involved in fewer than seven disagreements and less than one incident.[6] (See Table 6–4.)

The older teachers, who, it will be remembered, show more signs of professional behavior, also become involved in statistically more conflicts than the younger ones on six of the eight measures of conflict. This is especially true of the men. It is possible that young men have more militant attitudes by virtue of their youth and gender, but the older ones apparently are in a better position to actually challenge authority.[7] (See Table 6–4.)

Table 6-4. Comparisons of the mean professional and employee scores of men and women and their conflict rates, by age group

	Men			Women			Total		
	Young[a] ($N=446$) $\bar{X}$	Old ($N=475$) $\bar{X}$	Critical Ratio	Young[a] ($N=241$) $\bar{X}$	Old ($N=349$) $\bar{X}$	Critical Ratio	Men ($N=921$) $\bar{X}$	Women ($N=590$) $\bar{X}$	Critical Ratio
Professional & employee orientation & behavior									
Mean professional orientation scale	55.92	55.82	0.11	54.94	55.22	−0.21	55.87	55.10	0.95
Mean professional behavior index	3.00	3.95	−9.88[d]	2.23	3.58	−12.25[d]	3.49	3.03	5.69[d]
Mean employee orientation scale[b]	78.49	74.46	3.05	75.67	69.88	3.02	76.41	72.24	3.64
Mean employee behavior index	8.65	8.43	0.84[c]	9.03	8.70	1.11	8.53	8.84	−1.51
Number of conflicts per person									
Total no. (less complaints)	1.19	2.07	−4.44[d]	0.72	1.02	−2.32[c]	1.64	0.90	6.15[d]
No. open discussions	0.43	0.64	−2.76[d]	0.31	0.37	−0.92	0.54	0.34	3.70[d]
No. authority issues	0.81	1.43	−4.27[d]	0.55	0.68	−1.21	1.13	0.62	5.49[d]
No. teacher-teacher incidents	0.69	1.00	−3.12[d]	0.46	0.56	−1.26	0.85	0.52	4.96[d]
No. severe disagreements	0.15	0.11	0.80	0.08	0.07	0.47	0.13	0.07	2.36[c]
Total no. disagreements	8.03	8.25	0.67	7.47	6.31	2.38[c]	8.14	6.79	4.82[d]
No. major incidents	0.12	0.19	−2.61[d]	0.05	0.08	0.18	0.16	0.07	4.85[d]
No. teacher administrator incidents	0.89	1.50	−3.77[d]	0.65	0.74	−0.69	1.20	0.70	4.75[d]

[a]Young: 35 or younger.
[b]High scores indicate lower orientations.
[c]Critical ratio significant at $p < .05$.
[d]Critical ratio significant at $p < .01$.

WORK SATISFACTION

Cole reportedly found a positive association between job dissatisfaction and teacher militancy (as reported by Rosenthal, 1966). However, in the present sample, an individual's satisfaction with his work increases with his conflict rates. Without doubt, this fact is one of the most pregnant findings of the study, and, at first glance, perhaps the most puzzling. But a person's satisfaction with his career increases markedly with the total number of conflicts in which he has become involved ($r = .52$), number of authority conflicts ($r = .49$), number of conflicts with the administration ($r = .52$), and open disputes ($r = .40$); career satisfaction is also somewhat related to the number of major incidents in which a person has participated ($r = .28$). (These figures are not reported in a table.) The comparable correlations with satisfaction with the present job are lower (hovering around $r = .15$ to $r = .18$), but they are also in the positive direction.

It is possible that only people who are already committed to teaching and satisfied with their careers and jobs become concerned enough to participate in conflict. It is also plausible that the very act of conflict itself contributes a sense of having played a part in the long-range development of education. This fact also could make conflict satisfying from the standpoint of one's career goals even though from the standpoint of one's present job conflict can be threatening and disruptive.

IDENTITY OF THE MILITANT PROFESSIONAL LEADERS

Professional movements advance in a spearhead-like fashion, with a few leaders paving the way for a lagging, often reluctant, rank and file. The presence of a handful of professional leaders in teaching may have significance for the future status of their profession far out of proportion to their numbers. The most professional of these militant leaders are of particular interest because they are the key that can unlock behind-the-scenes tensions and control the subsequent direction of teacher militancy. We contrasted a profile of militant professional leaders with the rank and file of teachers, expecting to find that the "militant ultraprofessionals" have the distinguishing characteristics of leaders.

To refresh the reader, we shall remind him of the typology described at the beginning of this chapter. For the purposes of this analysis, 200 teachers having professional orientations in the upper 15 percent of the distributions of their respective schools were selected to represent the most professional teachers; they are referred to as the "ultraprofessionals." They, in turn, include the (a) "moderate" militants (that is, those who have been involved in at least one dispute) and the (b) "belligerent" militants (those who have been involved in at least one heated discussion or major incident). We shall refer to the ultraprofessionals who have not been involved in disputes, heated discussions, or major incidents as the "nonmilitant ultraprofessionals." Finally, the term "rank and file" refers simply to teachers in the lower 85th percentile of the distribution of professional orientations.

Social Relations

Compared with the nonmilitant professionals and the rank and file we expected that the most professional people would have the most group support and respect from their colleagues and be better educated and would have higher levels of education. The evidence supports these expectations.

Group support[8]

Militant ultraprofessionals have more support from their colleagues than either the typical teacher in the sample or the nonmilitant ultraprofessionals.* (Table 6–5.) Fifty-six percent of the moderate militant ultraprofessionals and 59 percent of the belligerent militants are identified by their colleagues as having the most support of their respective faculties, whereas only 38 percent of the nonmilitant professionals and the same proportion of the total sample are so identified (chi square $p \leq .01$).

Group respect

Peers also show more respect for the militants than for the nonmilitants. Fifty-two percent of the moderate militants and 68 percent of the belligerents are highly respected by their colleagues. (See Table 6–5.) This compares with only 30 percent of the nonmilitant professionals and 34 percent of the total sample (chi square significant at $p \leq .001$).

Client orientation

A disproportionate number of militant professionals (both types combined) have a high client orientation (74 percent vs. 31 percent in the rest

* Chi square (X^2) is a statistic that computes the likelihood that a difference in frequency among various categories has occurred by chance. Normally, a probability of .05 or less is acceptable, meaning that the observed frequency distribution would have occurred by chance less than five times in 100 such samples.

Table 6-5. Proportions of ultraprofessionals and rank-and-file teachers identified as having the specified social relations

		Ultraprofessionals			Rank and File ($N = 1{,}266$)	Total ($N = 1{,}46$)
		Moderate Militants[a] ($N = 53$)	Belligerent Militants[b] ($N = 34$)	Non-militants[c] ($N = 114$)		
A. Support of Colleagues[d]	Yes	.56	.59	.38	.37	.38
	No	.44	.41	.62	.63	.62
	$X^2 = 13.87$; 3 df significant at $p \leq .01$.					
B. Respect of Colleagues[e]	High	.52	.68	.30	.33	.34
	Low	.48	.32	.70	.67	.66
	$X^2 = 23.87$; 3 df significant at $p \leq .001$.					
C. Types of Initiative & Compliance	Rebellious or contrary	.62	.92	.59	.50	.52
	Realistic or submissive	.38	.08	.41	.50	.48
	$X^2 = 9.64$; 3 df significant at $p \leq .05$.					
		Moderate and Belligerent Combined				
D. Client Orientation	High	.74		.69	.35	.31
	Moderate	.20		.25	.41	.39
	Low	.06		.06	.23	.30
	$X^2 = 196.53$; 4 df significant at $p \leq .001$.					

[a] Ultramilitants (in the upper 15 percent of the professional orientation distribution) involved in putes.
[b] Ultramilitants involved in heated discussions or major incidents.
[c] Ultramilitants not involved in disputes, heated discussions, or major incidents.
[d] Identified by at least one colleague as persons whose ideas and opinions have gotten the most supp from other teachers within the last year or two.
[e] Mentioned by at least two colleagues as a person whose ideas about public education they respect most.

of the sample); more of them have high commitments to students than even the nonmilitant professionals (69 percent; chi square significant at $p \leq .001$). (See Table 6–5.) This pattern could be partly a product of the way the ultraprofessionals were selected, but it also is consistent with the common assumption that "true" professionals are service oriented. The fact that at least the leaders of the professional movement seem to be motivated in part directly out of personal concern for their students, together with the even greater commitment on the part of the militant leaders, is the first indication in the study that this factor is a primary incentive behind professional militancy.[9]

Initiative and compliance[10]

Finally, the most belligerent militants (92 percent) express rebelliousness on the Initiative-Compliance Scale more frequently than either their nonmilitant colleagues or the rank and file. (See Table 6-5.) Because the scale asks respondents to anticipate what they would do under certain conditions, belligerents apparently fully intend to be militant. But it should be noted that, compared with the other groups, the "moderate" militants generally are not any more rebellious or contrary than anyone else. This corresponds with their actual behavior; apparently, they only become involved when provoked by a unique set of circumstances.

Social Backgrounds

Level of education

As leaders of their groups the militant professionals lead their peers in educational achievement as well. Over half of the militant professionals (both types) have a master's degree or better, compared with 40 percent of the total sample. (See Table 6-6; chi square significant at $p \leq .05$.) But the difference between the militant and nonmilitant professionals, while in favor of the former, is relatively small (51 vs. 46 percent).

Gender

Leadership in our society is characteristically exercised by males. Especially in view of the finding that men generally are more belligerent than women, it was expected that the militant ultraprofessional category would be disproportionately comprised of males. This is generally true. (See Table 6-6; chi square significant at $p \leq .001$.) Sixty-five percent of the moderate militants and 79 percent of the belligerents are males, compared with only 45 percent of the nonmilitant ultraprofessionals. However, considering the fact that the total sample is 39 percent female, the fact that there are only a slightly smaller proportion of women (35 percent) among the moderate militants suggests that women take part in milder forms of professional militancy. But women are unlikely to be among the most belligerent professional militants—79 percent of whom are men—whereas the nonmilitant ultraprofessionals are likely to be women (55 percent).

Table 6-6. Proportions of ultraprofessionals and rank-and-file teachers with and without master's degrees

		Ultraprofessionals		Rank and File ($N = 1,266$)	Total ($N = 1,466$)
		Moderate[a] and Belligerent Militants[b] ($N = 86$)	Non-militants[c] ($N = 114$)		
Educational Achievement	Master's degree or better	.51	.46	.38	.40
	Less than a master's degree	.49	.54	.62	.60
	$X^2 = 7.51$; 3 df significant at $p \leqslant .05$.				
		Moderate	Belligerent		
Gender	Men	.65	.79	.45	.62	.61
	Women	.35	.21	.55	.38	.39
	$X^2 = 18.11$; 3 df significant at $p \leqslant .001$.				
Age	21-30	.23	.38	.27	.36	.33
	31-45	.44	.25	.35	.36	.36
	46-75	.33	.38	.38	.27	.31
	$X^2 = 27.53$; 6 df significant at $p \leqslant .001$.				

[a]Ultramilitants (in the upper 15 percent of the professional orientation distribution) involved in disputes.
[b]Ultramilitants involved in heated discussions or major incidents.
[c]Ultramilitants not involved in disputes, heated discussions, or major incidents.

Age

The association between age and the capacity and opportunity for leadership is complex, and for good reasons. The most recently educated teachers are more likely than the older ones to be in touch with new developments, and because they are likely to be the youngest, they probably will have less stake in the existing order. But it takes time and maturity to gain sufficient experience and garner the necessary group suport. These leveling effects would help to explain the finding that militant professionals (both types combined) are disproportionately middle-aged—44 percent vs. 36 percent of the total sample; and that the nonmilitant professionals are underrepresented in the middle-aged (25 percent). (See Table 6–6; chi square significant at $p \leq .001$.) In another analysis, however, no difference was found with respect to the number of years that different types of professionals had been employed in their particular schools.

Selected Types of Conflict

It is instructive to compare the types of conflict in which the two types of ultraprofessional militant leaders have been involved. (See Table 6–7.) (Only comparisons that are statistically significant on chi square at $p \leq .01$ level of significance are reported in the table.) For both types, the teacher-administrator incidents constitute the largest proportion (83 and 88 percent), which is more than double the rate of the rest of the sample.

Table 6-7. Proportions of ultraprofessionals and rank-and-file teachers involved in selected types of conflict

	Ultraprofessionals					
	Militant					
Selected Types of Conflict	Moderate Militant[a] (%; N=52)	Belligerent Militant[b] (%; N=34)	Non-militant[c] (%; N=114)	Rank-and-File Teachers (%; N=1,269)	Total (N=1,469)	Chi-Square Level of Significance
Authority issues	.73	.62	.17	.37	.38	.001
Scheduling and distribution problems	.56	.82	.16	.36	.36	.001
Teacher-administrator incidents	.83	.88	.13	.38	.39	.001
Teacher-teacher total	.50	.83	.16	.36	.36	.001
Teacher-guidance personnel	.27	.21	.06	.13	.13	.01
Academic-vocational teachers	.46	.76	.13	.30	.30	.001
Teacher-Public	.10	.35	.00	.10	.09	.001

[a]Ultramilitants (in the upper 15 percent of professional orientation distribution) involved in disputes.
[b]Ultramilitants involved in heated discussions or major incidents.
[c]Ultramilitants not involved in conflicts, except impersonal competition.

However, moderate militants are less prone than the belligerents to become involved in disputes with other teachers (50 vs. 83 percent).

The two types differ in other respects as well. Compared with the moderate militants, a much higher proportion of the belligerents have been involved in problems involving scheduling and distribution of personnel and resources (82 vs. 56 percent). Conversely, a slightly higher proportion of moderate militant professionals has become involved in authority problems (73 vs. 62 percent). Also, conflicts involving the public and conflicts between the academic teachers and vocational teachers are both far more typical of the belligerents.

On the other hand, there appears to be no differences either between these two types or between them and the rank-and-file teachers in frequency of conflict with students, with extracurricular activities teachers, and with their rate of involvements in value conflicts (not reported in tables).

Comparison with Officers of Teacher Organizations

How do these informal professional leaders compare with the more widely acknowledged leaders of the teaching profession—that is, the officers of professional associations and unions?[11]

First, it should be noted that AFT officers are more professionally oriented and have higher professional behavior scores than officers of professional organizations. While their total employee orientations are not statistically different from other officers, the difference is in the expected direction; AFT officers also have lower employee behavior scores.[12] (See Table 6–8.) The AFT officers express less commitment to their obligations toward students, however.

A statistically larger proportion of AFT officers than union officers are either rebellious or contrary on the Initiative-Compliance Scale (65 vs. 49 percent; not shown in tables), and more important, union officers (one in four) become involved in more authority issues and disputes (about 50 percent more). (See Table 6–8.) These are indeed important types of conflict; however, one cannot say that union officers are generally more conflict-prone, taking all types of conflict into consideration. On the contrary, rates of conflict with the administration and with other teachers, major incidents rates, impersonal competition rates, and total incidents rates were all substantially lower for the union officers than for officers of professional associations.[13]

There are a number of possible reasons for this pattern. For one, the geographical area from where the sample was drawn is dominated by a conservative segment of the AFT (the National Caucus).[14] Also, administrators in medium-sized cities at this particular period of time may be

Table 6-8. Comparisons of the mean professional and employee orientations and behavior of the officers of teachers' professional organizations and unions

Mean Orientation and Behavior Scores and Indices of Conflict	Officers of		Critical Ratio
	Teachers' Professions ($N = 348$)	Union ($N = 307$)	
	$\bar{X}$	$\bar{X}$	
Orientation and behavior			
Employee orientation	77.54	83.60	−0.31
Loyalty to administration	17.96	20.13	−2.36[b]
Employee behavior	18.56	12.86	5.92[c]
Professional orientation	58.26	61.00	−2.70[c]
Student orientation	16.46	11.30	5.68[c]
Professional behavior	19.23	19.91	1.73[a]
Indices of conflict			
Total incidents	8.66	6.87	1.96[b]
Major incident	0.47	0.20	1.96[b]
Disputes	1.50	2.20	−1.86[a]
Impersonal competition	0.49	0.13	2.89[c]
Teacher(s) vs. administrator(s)	3.04	1.57	2.49[b]
Teacher(s) vs. teacher(s)	1.09	0.50	3.72[c]
Authority	3.30	4.73	−1.84[a]

[a] Critical ratio significant at $p \leq .05$, one-tail test.
[b] Critical ratio significant at $p \leq .05$, two-tail test.
[c] Critical ratio significant at $p \leq .01$, one-tail test.

seeking to avert more trouble with the unions in an effort to avoid the difficulties that have developed in the nation's big cities. In addition, the fact that most of the union officers are not in schools with strong unions, or even with official union recognition, is probably critical; grievance structures that could otherwise facilitate conflict relations with the administration are not present. At the same time the professional officers in this sample may be unusually militant; they are predominantly male high school teachers, which is not typical of NEA membership in general (70 percent of the professional officers in this sample are male vs. 80 percent of AFT officers).

Table 6–9 presents a picture of the comparative militancy of the officers under consideration in relation to the informal (ultraprofessional) leaders. Professional officers have become involved in incidents with the

Table 6-9. Comparisons of the percentage of leaders and officers of teachers' organizations involved in conflict

Types of Conflict	Type of Leader or Officer				Chi Square	DF
	Informal Leaders			Officers of		
	Moderate Militant (%; $N = 52$)	Belligerent Militant (%; $N = 34$)	AFT (%; $N = 30$)	Professional Associations (%; $N=348$)		
Incidents involving scheduling people and distribution of resources	55.77	82.35	13.33	41.38	35.60[a]	3
Teachers vs. administration	82.69	88.23	23.33	45.11	53.78[a]	3
Teacher-administration vs. public	9.62	35.29	0.00	12.93	19.44[a]	3
Teacher-teacher total	50.00	82.35	36.67	49.71	16.08[a]	3
Authority	73.08	61.76	90.00	86.78	19.51[a]	3

[a] Chi square significant at $p \leq .01$.

administration nearly twice as frequently as their counterparts in the union (45 vs. 23 percent); but the involvement of belligerent militant leaders in comparable conflicts is nearly twice as high again (82 and 88 percent; chi square significant at $p \leq .01$). Similarly, although professional officers dispute more with other teachers than AFT officers (50 vs. 37 percent), they have still lower rates than belligerent professionals (82 percent); they are identical to moderates in this respect.

However, there is one respect in which the AFT officers are the most militant of the leader groups. American Federation of Teachers officers have the highest rates of involvement of all the groups in authority issues (90 percent). (Oddly enough, the informal leaders are also reversed on this index.)

In short, despite the fact that AFT officers express more professionalism and more defiance on the Initiative-Compliance Scale than the professional officers, they are more militant in only two respects—their rates of involvement in authority issues and in disputes. In most other respects professional officers are more militant. Most important, in every respect but one the informal leaders are more militant than the officers of either organization. Much of the actual leadership for the broad-gauge problems of professionalism in education seems to be coming from the behind-the-scenes informal leaders.

THE ADVERSARIES

Professionalization tends to divide occupations into opposing camps, each with different commitments to professional status and to employers, and each upholding different attitudes toward changing the occupation, the desired rate of progress, and the appropriateness of divergent strategies. Professional leaders, then, can expect to encounter resistance from adversaries in competing groups. Who are the adversaries of the militant professionals? Who resists them? Colleagues? The least professional persons? The typical member? Or do the militant professionals dispute primarily among themselves?

To gain some insight into these questions, the militant professionals'

Table 6-10. Professional and client orientations of the adversaries of moderate and belligerent militant ultraprofessionals

	Adversaries of Leaders	Type of Orientation[c]	
		Professional	Client
$\bar{X}$	Moderate militant leaders[a] ($N = 52$)	70.5	11.3
	Adversaries of moderate leaders ($N = 76$)		
	$\bar{X}$ Solitary incident ($N = 65$)	58.0	9.1
	$\bar{X}$ Chronic involvement ($N = 11$)	57.6	9.2
$\bar{X}$	Belligerent militant leaders[b] ($N = 34$)	68.9	11.5
	Adversaries of belligerent leaders ($N = 133$)		
	$\bar{X}$ Solitary incident ($N = 85$)	58.6	9.2
	$\bar{X}$ Chronic involvement ($N = 48$)	54.3	8.1
$\bar{X}$	Rank-and-file members ($N = 1,438$)	57.9	9.3

[a]Persons in the upper 15 percent of the professional orientation distribution who have been involved in disputes.
[b]Persons in the upper 15 percent of the professional orientation distribution who have been involved in major incidents or heated discussions.
[c]Statistical tests of significance are reported in the narrative.

professional-orientation and client-orientation were compared with their opponents' orientations in various types of conflicts. Adversaries who were involved in a solitary conflict with militant professionals were further distinguished from adversaries who were more "chronically" opposed to them —that is, involved in more than one conflict with militant professional leaders.

Professional Orientation

Both solitary and chronic adversaries of the moderate militant leaders have much lower professional orientations than these leaders ($\bar{X} = 70.5$ vs. $\bar{X} = 58.0$; CR $= 7.5$; and CR $= 6.2$, $p \leq .01$). (See Table 6–10.) Both types of adversaries, in fact, differ very little from the rank-and-file members of the sample ($\bar{X} = 57.9$).

The opponents of belligerent leaders involved in solitary major incidents also have lower professional orientation than the leaders ($p \leq .05$); however, in this case the adversaries have higher orientations than the rank and file ($\bar{X} = 57.9$, $p \leq .01$). The chronic enemies of the belligerents have still lower orientations ($\bar{X} = 54.3$).[15]

Client Orientation

The solitary adversaries of moderates and belligerents also have lower client orientations ($\bar{X} = 11.3$ vs. 9.1 and $\bar{X} = 11.5$ vs. 9.2, $p \leq .01$). Moreover, the client orientations of the chronic opponents of the belligerent leaders are still lower, even below the rank and file ($\bar{X} = 8.1$; $p \leq .01$). This means the solitary adversaries of belligerent leaders, whose client orientations are below the leaders' ($p \leq .01$), are significantly higher than the chronic adversaries' ($p \leq .01$).

IMPLICATIONS

Although the overall correlation between an individual's professionalism and his involvement in conflict is not very prominent, it is in the expected direction, and it becomes more prominent when age and gender are taken into account. While men are more militant, the correlation is higher for women. Therefore, professionalism seems to have a more significant influence on their militancy than on that of men. Probably, too, the low overall correlation can be explained by the fact that the relationship is not completely linear. It is more accurate to say that on the average teachers with low professional orientations become involved in conflicts less frequently than other teachers; the one exception is major incidents, where the pattern is completely reversed. This suggests that improving the professionalism of the least professional people probably has more impact on militancy than increasing the commitment of people already convinced of the value of professional norms.

Because teachers with stronger orientations toward their colleagues are more militant and less client oriented, it seems possible that the quest of teachers for decision-making authority and for more favorable reputations are stronger impulses behind professional militancy than strong commitment to students' welfare. However, it is significant that informal leaders of the professional movement are more concerned than their adversaries about the welfare of their students, especially in view of the fact that they are resisted by a hard core of their own less professional colleagues. Much of the leadership behind professionalization of teaching seems to come from these informal leaders who normally are less visible than the more widely acknowledged officers of professional associations and unions.

Of course, none of these findings demonstrate whether there is a connection between professional militancy and a teacher's effectiveness in his classroom. In fact, for the time being we are willing to accept the possibility that professional militancy may not be closely related to teaching effectiveness. For in the long run the important question is not whether professionals are "good" teachers within the present context but whether they apply their energies to long-range improvement of student welfare. The improvement of teaching as a whole is a much more fundamental process than the ability of any individual to cope with the existing system.

The fact that conflict is associated both with faculty and individual job satisfaction suggests that most forms of conflict (except major incidents) contribute to the morale of teachers; or, at the least, conflict does not reduce existing high morale. One reason for this may be precisely that, within the narrow constraints of many public high schools, conflict provides one means by which individual teachers can become meaningfully engaged in efforts to improve public education. Therefore, it is important to examine the kinds of organizational constraints under which teachers must work. We turn to that problem in the next chapter.

NOTES: Chapter 6

¹ Because it is well known that the same individuals will be encouraged to behave differently under varying circumstances we shall be cautious about imputing a one-to-one correspondence between personal orientation and behavior. It is possible, for example, that a usually militant person would feel restrained in a peaceful organization; while a person not normally inclined to be belligerent could become so among militant associates. Or, to look at it in a slightly different way, one cannot merely assume that what holds true for organizational climates as a whole will apply to individuals. Therefore, organizational climates will be examined separately in the following chapters. But with these caveats as a point of departure, we shall allow the hypotheses developed in Chapter 8 with respect to organizational climates to guide the analysis of individual behavior. The reasoning is that an organization's professional climate is dependent upon the role conceptions of its members, and the members' conceptions are, in turn, modified by the general climate of opinion. In general, then, it seems more likely than not that individual orientations and organizational climates would reinforce one another.

² One reason that the correlations with professional orientation are not higher is the small variance in the conflict measures (which in most cases ranged from one to three conflicts per person) compared with a much larger variation in the orientation measure. Because the measures were developed to assess organizational rates of conflict, they do not necessarily generate distributions applicable to individuals. For one thing only a sample of persons was included in each school, which makes the measures less reliable for individuals than for the school as a whole. Because a large proportion of the respondents were not involved in conflict, and only small proportions were involved in more than one, the distribution, in effect, consists largely of zeros and ones. But for the same reason, the somewhat higher correlation with the total-disagreement rate probably is in part due to the fact that there is more variance in this measure; in addition, because it is based on self-reports, the measure is likely to be more inclusive of all the respondents and of the total population of conflicts.

³ For example, whereas 95 percent of the most professional group report at least one disagreement, 89 percent of the lowest group do (chi square significant at $p \leq .05$); the comparable figures for the rate of involvement in authority issues are 41 and 35 percent (chi square significant at $p \leq .05$). On the other hand, total rate of involvement in incidents of all types for these two groups is identical (46 percent).

⁴ That is, people who are simultaneously in the upper and lower fifteenth percentiles of the respective distributions of professional and employee role-conception scores.

⁵ Some of the correlations of employee behavior with conflict rates are exceptionally high for men compared with women. For example, the correlation between the men's total incident rate and their employee orientation is $r = -.74$ (vs. $r = -.23$ for women); the correlation for the men's employee orientation is $r = -.85$ and teacher-administrator conflicts is $r = -.68$ (vs. $r = -.27$ and $r = -.26$ for women).

⁶ In view of these findings, rank-order correlations were computed between the proportion of males in a school and its conflict rates. The correlations are in the positive direction but are very low; they range from .04 for teacher-administrator conflicts to .17 for disputes. More of the variance is explained by the structural variables and the mean professional orientation than by the proportion of males in the school.

⁷ There is a similar tendency for older women to become involved in more conflicts than younger ones, but only three of eight of these tests are statistically significant.

⁸ Support from colleagues was assessed by asking teachers to mention the col-

leagues whose ideas and opinions had received the most support from other teachers within the past year or two. The criterion used here is that they had been nominated at least once.

Respect was assessed by asking teachers to mention at least two or more colleagues as persons whose ideas about education they respected the most. These people were nominated at least once.

[9] In another analysis it was found that the militant professionals are overrepresented among persons with low employee orientations, but they do not vary greatly from nonmilitant professionals in this respect (chi square significant at $p \leq .001$).

[10] The *initiative-compliance* typology described in Chapter 4 was, of course, originally assessed for its power to discriminate the highly professional and highly militant teachers. Because of the way it was designed, and given the premise of the study, it was to be expected that compared with the other types in the typology, rebellious and contrary teachers would be more professionally oriented and become involved in more conflicts. In general, the rebellious and contrary teachers are both more professional and more militant. Their professional orientations are statistically higher than both the defiant-cautious and realistic-submissive types. They also have the highest client orientations. Rebellious and contrary teachers have higher total rates of conflict and higher rates of teacher-administrator conflicts than the other two groups; they also become involved in more conflicts with other teachers than the defiant-cautious group.

[11] Respondents were asked whether they had ever held any office in a teacher's professional association or union. Thirty people identified themselves as union officers and over 300 identified themselves as having been an officer in a professional association. There is no way to know what positions and organizations were included in the self-designations. Most of the officers were probably in local and state organizations, so undoubtedly many officers in both organizations were not in the mainstream of militant activity, much of which is still focused at the state and national levels.

[12] On a chi-square test comparing officers with high, average, and low employee orientations, union officers have significantly lower employee orientations than officers of professional associations ($p \leq .05$); only 13 percent of the union officers have high employee orientations vs. 32 percent of the other officers.

Accordingly, proportionately more union officers have simultaneously high professional-low employee role organization than the professional officers (chi square significant at $p \leq .05$). Fifty percent of the union officers have simultaneously high professional-low employee role organization, and only 3 percent have the reverse pattern—that is, a low professional-high employee style of organization. The comparable figures for professional officers are 27 and 20 percent. Also, proportionately more AFT officers were mentioned as having respect from other teachers (68 compared to 55 percent), but the two groups did not differ on support from colleagues (55 percent of both groups were mentioned two or more times).

[13] The AFT officers have exceptionally low rates of involvement in scheduling and distribution problems (13 percent); officers of professional associations, who are likely to become involved in these incidents (41 percent), are again similar to moderate militants (56 percent), and once more belligerent militants have exceptionally high rates of involvement in scheduling and distribution problems (82 percent).

[14] I am indebted to Mr. Pete Schnaufner, former director of Research for the American Federation of Teachers, for an informative conversation on this topic.

[15] However, the adversaries of the moderate leaders do not differ in professional orientation from the belligerents' enemies; nor do the chronic adversaries differ from those involved in solitary incidents.

REFERENCES: Chapter 6

Bucher, Rue, and Strauss, Alselm. Professions in process. *The American Journal of Sociology,* 1961, **66**, 325–334.

Rosenthal, Alan. The strength of teacher organizations: Factors influencing membership in two large cities. *Sociology of Education, Fall,* 1966, **39**, 366–370.

part III. *Schools and
their discontents*

FROM TALKS WITH TEACHERS *on politics*

THE SUPERINTENDENT, *I am sure, would . . . not approve of the political alliances of one of our teachers who ran for a city office. I am sure his own service club members make snide remarks like "What are you trying to do, control the city now that you have the superintendency?" So, naturally, these people are putting the damper on his ambitions. He has been disciplined in a number of ways. You can get the rooms with the southern exposure, and maybe you are asked to move from class to class. Many techniques have been used at different times—but very rarely. He is in a precarious situation because he teaches social studies. The whole thing is touchy. I can see the position of the administration. If he were a chemistry teacher, it wouldn't be so bad.*
—*a teacher*

I THINK, *too, that in this particular community, which as I say is very conservative, you would naturally have a conflict with this community and anyone that had any left-wing notions at all. In fact, I might elaborate. I teach speech and debate. And in debate, when we have changes, like Medicare or national health insurance, or something of this nature, we have a difficult time trying to find an affirmative team. That is, if you say the United States should evolve a program of national health insurance, the nasty word [accusation] would be "socialized medicine," I guess. It's difficult to find someone to take the affirmative side. It's even difficult to find somebody to take the affirmative side on adopting the British Parliamentary system of government, or any change in the status quo.*—*a teacher*

I THINK *that probably one of the biggest disagreements here was that the teachers were involved too much in passing the levy. I think the teachers were expected to go out and work for it. We even had a parade trying to get the levy passed. Some of the teachers had a sign on their windshield about giving an "apple to the teacher." I think teachers were probably involved too much in trying to go out and campaign for the levy when it was for an increase in teachers' salaries*—*a teacher*

7. The organization of work

But the larger the group and the more complex the task it seeks to accomplish, the greater are the pressures to become explicitly organized.— Blau and Scott, 1962, p. 7.

System: an aggregate of related interests or activities. . . . Whatever the system, its related character is identified by harmony in operation and the integration of its structure.—Fairchild, 1944, p. 315.

Mr. Sears is vaguely aware of some differences between his present school system and his former one in Excelsior City. It seems to him that there was far more emphasis there on following the rules; they were better enforced and the rules themselves were more explicit, specifying the starting and departure time and other expectations. There were rules governing topics for discussion in the classroom, and in fact there generally seemed to be rules to cover most of his problems. Though the present system is larger and more complex, rules are not as elaborate and specific, but there seems to be more reliance on other impersonal forms of supervision such as lesson plans, the elaborate curriculum guides, emphasis on covering the textbook and using standard tests. Both systems also seem to be alike in several ways: they are highly specialized and have several layers of authority, close supervision is common, and there are few opportunities for teachers to make routine decisions on their own.

Mr. Sears had just become adjusted to his previous school and is now somewhat confused about what is expected of him in this new situation. Nor does he understand why rules are not just as important or necessary in one school as in another. He wonders what kinds of supervision are necessary if a school is to function properly. Trying to get his bearings, he has discussed similarities and differences with some of his colleagues. But they only describe still other differences between this system and others they have known. It is all very perplexing. For his own protection he wishes there were some way to more systematically understand how school systems work.

MODELS OF BUREAUCRACY

Mr. Sears needs a framework for putting different patterns of organization into perspective. Probably, like most other people, he thinks of the "school system" as a system in the technical sense of the word. Unfortunately, the term "system" may be somewhat misleading in this case, for it already implies a selective perception which may not be entirely accurate; a way of looking at something is also a way of not looking at it. Dahrendorf laments (1958, p. 121):

> One of the more unfortunate connotations of the word "system" is its closure. . . . There is no getting away from the fact that a system is essentially something self-sufficient, internally consistent and closed to the outside. . . . it is only a step from thinking about societies in terms of equilibrated systems to asserting that every disturber of the equilibrium, every deviant, is a "spy." . . . The system theory of society becomes dangerously close to the conspiracy theory of history.

It is more accurate to think of a school system, or any bureaucratized organization, as a composite of several models, rather than only one internally consistent set of characteristics. There are several ways of visualizing bureaucracy. In its simplest form bureaucracy can be portrayed as a dichotomous attribute—that is, an organization is considered to be either bureaucratic or it is not; the fact that different concepts are used to describe organization and disorganization, such as anomie in the latter case, seems to reinforce the notion that organization and disorganization are distinctly separate processes. In a more refined version bureaucracy appears as a complex set of distinct characteristics. In the most advanced interpretation permitted within this general framework, each characteristic of the model forms separate dimensions which are considered to be variables. At this point the implications of this general system can veer in one of three different directions. The three models to be discussed represent alternatives within this advanced interpretation.

The Reinforcement Model

In one version of the advanced interpretation, bureaucratic procedures are presumed to be consistent and mutually reinforcing. The implicit assumption is that there is a drive for maximum control in organizations, in which case to the extent that any one characteristic is emphasized, all the mechanisms of bureaucracy will be brought into play in support of one another. Presumably, the variables function in coordination and mutual support of one another—that is, decisions made at high levels will be interpreted uniformly, to interchangeable personnel, through rules and other standard procedures and perhaps enforced by close supervision.[1]

The Independence Model

However, there is some question about whether the various dimensions of bureaucracy are actually consistent with one another. Hall (1963), and earlier Hemphill (1956), reported only low intercorrelations among the characteristics of several organizations, indicating that they were quite independent of one another. (In fact, they were so decidedly independent that Hall questioned whether one variable, which correlated negatively with the others, was for that reason appropriate to the model.) Particular configurations of variables appear to be associated with different types of organizations and their activities, the implication being that some patterns are more rational or effective than others for the performance of particular activities.

The Compensatory Model

This latter suggestion becomes more meaningful when considered in light of a third framework, namely, that certain dimensions of bureaucracy exist in states of tension with one another. Udy (1959), for example, reported that in preindustrial societies, although there were high intercorrelations among some organizational variables, two major dimensions could be identified and these were negatively associated—one identified as "bureaucracy" and the other as "rationality." Some functionalists have become intrigued by the idea that patterned tension and strain are inherent in the relationships among organizational variables. Hage points out (1965, p. 296):

The major theme running through [a particular] axiomatic theory is the idea of functional strains, as discussed in the writings of Parsons, Bales, and their associates, or the concept of organizational dilemma, as it is called by Blau and Scott. This means that an increase in one variable results in a decrease in another variable, or that the maximization of one social means results in the minimization of another. Although this dependence of one variable on another is an old idea, the problem is to specify which variables are in opposition, and perhaps more important, why they are.

In this, the compensatory model, bureaucratic characteristics not only are interchangeable but also can compensate for one another. This means that the variables are inversely correlated; when one is present the others are absent. Each practice presumably functions as a means of resolving particular problems which arise because of inadequate control and lack of coordination which often are consequences of size, complexity, heterogeneity of membership, turnover, and similar disruptive elements. Moreover, it is not always necessary to use more than one form of control to maintain order, either because the situation itself can be easily controlled or because a particularly powerful form of control is used. A particular problem might be resolved in a variety of ways; or a single practice may be relevant for resolving several types of problems. The degree of flexibility in choosing alternative forms of control is probably dependent upon the total pattern of characteristics and the nature of the problem. In short, organizations use bureaucratic controls interchangeably, compensating for the relative neglect of some by emphasizing others and compensating an emphasis on some by relaxing others.[2]

Therefore, it should not be assumed that in organizations there is a compelling drive to maximize all forms of rational control or that the controls will be consistent and in harmony with one another. Rather, organizations appear to mobilize only as much control as necessary to combat the most disturbing elements, and more conflict is permitted with some forms of control than with others. From this particular vantage point the reinforcement model can be viewed as a limited case of the compensatory model and independence model. That is, bureaucratic controls apparently will be emphasized simultaneously only when any one means of control is weak or when unusually disruptive elements are confronted. Otherwise, the different forms of control will be used somewhat interchangeably but largely independently from one another, though in opposition to the disruptive characteristics.

OVERVIEW OF FINDINGS

Our findings indicate that no one model provides a complete picture of the systems in this study.[3] Certain variables seem to reinforce one another, and there is a certain amount of overlap among different sets of variables, but the key variables of one set are not necessarily related to those of another. Before proceeding, a quick review of some of the findings about to be reported in detail may be useful.

Several hypotheses have been advanced in the literature pertaining to the probable relationships among standardization, close supervision, and organizational size and complexity. Triandis (1966) has argued that it is more difficult to maintain close supervision in larger organizations. A reasonable corollary is implicit in Rushing's (1966) suggestion that more use will be made of rules where it is difficult to exercise close supervision—for example, that large organizations will place more emphasis on standardization.

If size is inversely associated with close supervision and directly correlated with standardization, then it logically might be expected that close supervision will vary with emphasis on rules, which is what Anderson (1966) and Rushing (1966) propose. This derivation is based, implicitly at least, on the compensatory model of organization. That is, it is assumed that one form of control acts as a substitute for the other; the presence of one implies the absence of the other.

An alternative is that different forms of control reinforce one another. If so, then close supervision and standardization might be positively correlated with one another (even though they may be independently related to isolated third variables).

Rushing suggests that what is involved is the difficulty of supervising employees. This statement suggests a liberal criterion that might be used to categorize the variables. Organizational complexity and hierarchy, for example, can be included along with organizational size as variables which represent such difficulty.

With this general statement as background, we can return to the findings:

Contrary to the hypothesis, close supervision is not significantly correlated (either negatively or positively) with school size, complexity, or number of levels of authority (although it is inversely associated with size of school system).

However, organizational size, complexity, and number of levels of authority are positively associated with standardization, as the last statement would have indicated.

Also in conformity with the hypothesis, organizational complexity and number of levels of authority are positively associated with emphasis on rules.

In other words, the expectation that standardization and rules would be more emphasized as organizations become larger and more complex is borne out. But the proposition that efforts to supervise employees closely are relaxed as schools increase in size and complexity is not; there appears to be little relationship. This latter finding, of course, affects the derivative hypotheses.

In view of the propositions advanced in the literature, what is most significant is that close supervision is positively related to standardization and rules, and not negatively as hypothesized. This relationship points to the importance of the reinforcement model and cautions against assuming that the presence of one form of control necessarily implies the absence of another. In many cases it appears that instead of retiring weak forms of control under difficult conditions, organizations may actually attempt to maintain what controls they have at their disposal and to reinforce them with still other control procedures.

For the rest of the discussion, the variables used here will be considered under two separate groupings: control mechanisms and disruptive elements.

Control Mechanisms

Using evidence from rank-order correlations, one can say that as schools become more standardized, they become bureaucratized in other ways also: they become larger, more specialized, and more complex; they make more use of close supervision; and they become more centralized in terms of the number of levels of authority and the centralization of routine decisions. This pattern conforms to the reinforcement model. This is not as true of rules. While schools which stress rules make greater use of close supervision and have more layers of authority, otherwise the use of rules is not significantly correlated with other forms of bureaucratization. Whereas rules appear to be emphasized more typically in smaller, less specialized schools, other forms of standardization are used in larger and more specialized ones. Rules and other forms of standardization appear to represent independent strategies of control.

Another form of control, close supervision, is correlated with emphasis on rules and standardization, as well as with the interchangeable use of personnel. Close supervision, in other words, reinforces the other two forms of control. But whereas standardization increases with school size, close supervision is more likely to be used in smaller schools where it is probably easier to utilize. It is more likely to be found in schools where routine decisions are centralized, though it is largely independent of other forms of centralization.

Turning to more centralized forms of control, it was found that centralization, whether measured in terms of professional or nonprofessional policy decisions or more routine decisions, does not seem to be clearly correlated with most of the other bureaucratic characteristics. There are exceptions with respect to specialization, and in the case of routine decisions being correlated with close supervision. Forms of centralization, in other words, seem to play only a minor role in the overall reinforcement pattern.

Disruptive Elements of Organization

Most of the variables just discussed represent forms of control. These can be contrasted with the more disruptive characteristics typically found in bureaucratic organizations—namely, organizational complexity, large size, specialization, hierarchical authority system, heterogeneity, and staff turnover. Many of these disruptive features seem to be closely interrelated, although not entirely. For example:

Large schools are also more specialized and complex, with higher rates of personnel turnover and more levels of authority.

Similarly, more specialized schools are larger and more complex and have more levels of authority.

As the number of levels of authority increase, so do the school's size, complexity, specialization, and turnover rates.

Likewise, more complex schools are larger and more standardized and have more levels of authority.

Schools with the highest rates of turnover are larger, more complex, and more hierarchical.

Controls Compared to Disruptive Characteristics

Some clues about the compensatory and reinforcement features of schools are provided in the pattern of relationships between the two types of variables just considered. In general, it appears that the amount of control is associated with the extent of disruptiveness within the organization. It seems plausible that whether different forms of control are used to reinforce one another or whether they act as substitutes to compensate for one another depends upon the amount of disruption. For example, more complex schools, which also tend to be large and hierarchical, are more standardized and characterized by a greater emphasis on rules, but they are neither any more closely supervised nor centralized than less complex organizations; perhaps in this case rules and standardization help to compensate for the fact that close supervision and centralization do not increase with complexity.

Likewise, as the levels of authority increase, so does standardization. And although control of decision making, emphasis on rules, and measures of close supervision do not increase with hierarchy, there is an increase in the number of supervisors per teacher and the proportion of teachers supervised by control from the central office. Similarly, while schools with higher rates of turnover are not more closely supervised, they are more standardized and more rules oriented, and routine decisions are made at higher levels.

The more heterogeneous a faculty's background, the more closely supervised it is likely to be, though such schools are not any more standardized or rule-ridden.

In all of these cases some forms of control are brought to bear to counteract potential disruption, but in no case are all forms of control used simultaneously. In several cases controls reinforce one another, but on the whole only a few are used at any one time. Typically, one form of control increases in a degree that compensates for the failure of other controls.

It is not easy to anticipate when one form of control will or will not be used, but undoubtedly logistics and feasibility are important factors. For example, close supervision is both more feasible and more likely to be used in smaller schools, which characteristically are more heterogeneous. On the other hand, standardization is probably more appropriate than close supervision in larger schools, which have high rates of turnover.

In general, then, although standardization is associated with almost all of the other bureaucratic characteristics in support of the reinforcement model, most of the other components of bureaucracy are not consistently associated with one another. The compensatory model, which assumes that bureaucratic practices are interchangeable and partially inconsistent, seems more generally applicable. In many cases, of course, the independence model, which assumes that bureaucratic processes are simply independent of one another, must be used to account for relatively low relationships that occurred. In general, organizational controls are used sparingly. A high degree of organization seems to evolve only under serious provocations.

These conclusions will be elaborated in the tables and the discussion that follow. The discussion will be organized around six principal dimensions of organization: (1) standardized procedures, (2) the authority system, (3) supervision, (4) the horizontal and vertical divisions of labor, (5) specialization, and (6) recruitment practices. The first three dimensions represent alternative means of coordinating the system; the others are potentially disruptive in that they refer to divisions within an organization and to outside influences.

STANDARDIZATION

In all schools, rules restrict teachers' discretion over their classrooms, and in some their classroom conduct is virtually determined by them. In over half of the 21 schools for which this information was available, the typical faculty member agrees that there is a "high degree of control."[4] But the sample does not necessarily object to these efforts to standardize. Nearly all agree that a school should have a manual of rules and regulations that is followed closely and with which everyone is familiar. What they do seem to object to is highly specific rules, especially those that curtail their authority over the classroom.[5] Such attitudes are not necessarily inconsistent. Though rules can restrict a teacher, if they are not too strict, they provide guidelines for cooperation and protect teachers from instability, erratic fluctuations in procedure, and injustices in the system of distributing rewards and punishment; lax enforcement can undermine the system and leave teachers vulnerable to the caprices of administrators and colleagues. But it is when rules become excessively specific and threaten to undermine a teacher's authority without necessarily conferring real advantages for him that he is likely to object.

Emphasis on Rules

Presumably, the social and physical distances created by organizational size and centralization increase the difficulty of surveillance. Perhaps rules are sufficient to provide the guidelines necessary for remote administrators to maintain control. Rushing proposes that "the greater the cost of surveillance, the greater the use of formal rules" (1966, p. 431). The fact that rules tend to be emphasized more in complex ($t = .26$) and more hierarchical systems ($t = .21$ ns) adds support to his proposition, although they are not significantly related to size as might have been expected. (See Table 7–1.) MacKay's findings (1964) regarding schools also support these findings.[6] The investigators of another study of 75 diverse types of organizations also found no relationship between size and emphasis on rules (Haas, Hall, and Johnson, 1965). Even the relationship between rules and hierarchy turns out to be largely illusory, for the correlation disappears when organizational complexity has been partialed out. This latter fact, together with the fact that the correlation between rules and complexity ($t = .26$) persists after relevant variables have been controlled, suggests that rules are not responses to hierarchy per se so much as they are ways of coping with many forms of organizational complexity.

Emphasis on rules is also associated with the number of staff additions ($t = .21$) and with the propensity of administrators to treat personnel interchangeably ($t = .31$); rules may even facilitate this practice.

Rules seem to be reinforced by two other forms of control—close supervision ($t = .26$) and centralization of professional decisions ($t_p = .21$; controlling for the centralization of nonprofessional decisions). Rules may help to clarify situations sufficiently to reduce the need for consultations between teachers and administrators ($t = -.19$ ns), or perhaps close supervision provides a way of interpreting decisions made at higher levels and of supplementing and enforcing rules; in any event, rules probably help to accommodate the tensions of close supervision, as Gouldner suggests (1954).

In summing up, rules are emphasized in complex, hierarchical systems where there are frequent staff additions. Such systems are also more centralized and more closely supervised. Though these findings are

Table 7-1. Intercorrelations among bureaucratic controls and other dimensions of organization (Tau)

Organizational Structure	Bureaucratic Controls					
	Standardization	Rules	Close Supervision	Professional Decisions	Nonprofessional Decisions	Routine Decisions
Size: No. of faculty in						
School	.42†	.11	−.07	.12	−.08	−.02
School system	.33†	.12	−.22*	−.01	−.12	−.12
Centralization						
Number of levels of authority (21 schools)	.42† .25a,*	.21 .02a	.01	.05	−.12	−.03
Policy decision-making index						
Professional policies	.21	.14 .21c,*	.01			
Nonprofessional policies	−.11	−.10	−.16 −.23d,*			
Routine decision-making authority	−.21	.14	.34† .17e			
Rate of consultation with administration (autonomy)	.18	−.19	−.13			
Standardization						
Total index (21 schools)		.14 .05a	.26*	.21*	−.11	.21
Rules	.14		.26*	.14 .21c	.25*	.14
Specialization: Proportion of teachers with courses in which they have not						
Majored	−.22	.01	.15	−.02	.08	.27*
Majored or minored	−.31* −.24b,*	.05 .14a	−.02	.08	.29*	.04
Close supervision	.26	.26*		.01	−.16 −.22a,*	.34*
Complexity	.36*	.26*	.03	.10	−.18	−.03
Heterogeneity	−.21	−.02	.22*	.00	.12	.40†
Staff additions	.39*	.21*	.15	.13	.04	.27*

*Rank-order correlation significant at $p \leq .05$.
†Rank-order correlation significant at $p \leq .01$.
Key for control variables:
[a]Complexity scale.
[b]Percent of courses not majored in.
[c]Centralization of nonprofessional decisions.
[d]Rules.
[e]Routine decision making.

consistent with the reinforcement model, that model is incomplete by virtue of the fact that such systems are not necessarily more standardized. Again, not all of the available controls are used to reinforce one another, though perhaps because of the enormously disruptive tendencies within such organizations, more than a minimum of reinforcement is used.

Standardization

Rushing proposes (1966, p. 441) that "As an organization grows, rules and regulations will increasingly replace direct surveillance of organizational control." It already has been shown that rules are not significantly associated with size of school, but for the 21 schools for which this information is available, other forms of standardization increase with school size ($t = .42$) and size of system as Rushing's proposition would imply ($t = .33$). (See Table 7–1.) These findings again correspond to those of Haas, Hall, and Johnson (1965). Standardization also increases with several other disruptive characteristics. Standardized schools tend to be more specialized (that is, fewer promiscuous assignments; $t = -.22$ and $t = -.31$); they have more staff additions ($t = .39$); there is less agreement in supervisors' instructions to teachers ($t = -.32$); and they are more complex ($t = .36$). The fact that the correlation between standardization and number of levels of authority remains significant after organizational complexity has been partialed out ($t = .25$) indicates that standardization is a function of increases in the hierarchy—more so than of organizational size and complexity per se. In this respect standardization functions in a manner exactly opposite to rules, which are more closely associated with organizational complexity than with hierarchy. Rules appear to be used to compensate for complexity, while standardization is more likely to help offset increases in the hierarchy.

Consistent with the reinforcement model, standardization also is associated with several other forms of control. It tends to increase with centralization in both professional policy decisions and routine decision making ($t = .21$ ns and $t = -.21$ ns, respectively) and with more close supervision ($t = .26$ ns), though these latter correlations do not quite reach statistical significance for a sample size of 21. They are also reinforced by more remote supervision from central office administrators ($t = .26$), and perhaps as a result fewer teachers report that their committee recommendations are followed by the administration ($t = -.30$).

Standardization, then, appears to be a pivotal variable associated with most other bureaucratic controls. The reinforcement model seems particularly applicable to standardization. Perhaps this indicates that standardization is, by itself, a relatively ineffective form of control which requires reinforcement. However, it is equally plausible that reinforcement develops because standardization is involved in precisely those highly disruptive large, hierarchical, centralized, specialized, and complex systems with high rates of turnover where it is most difficult to maintain control.

THE OFFICIAL AND INFORMAL STATUS SYSTEMS

Responsibilities in complex systems are divided vertically into administrative echelons, each with responsibilities for coordinating the work of subordinate levels. The official hierarchy is the backbone of the system, but overlaying it is an informal system of influence among subordinates, a many-faceted decision-making structure, plus networks of administrative-subordinate relations, central to which are patterns of supervision and evaluation. The resulting status system can be as complex as the lateral division of labor.

The hierarchy presents a special anomaly. For, although it is designed as a mechanism for coordinating activities, the separate layers of authority create further divisiveness which only contributes to the problem the hierarchy was designed to remedy. We shall emphasize the divisiveness of separate levels of authority. But first we shall consider the less formal dimensions of schools' status systems.

Informal Status

Teachers—college educated, hired and assigned to a complex system of courses and extra duties only in part on the basis of their special training—share a somewhat uniform position in an official hierarchy which offers them little opportunity for promotion.[7] But underneath this façade of uniformity in official status, teachers are highly differentiated from one another in informal ways. Some of the frustrations created by the official status system are probably compensated to a certain extent, but aggravated in other ways, by these auxiliary informal status systems.

Teacher organizations

For one thing, membership in competing teacher organizations separates teachers. This study suggests that there is a grain of truth in the idea that professional teacher associations are dominated by employee-oriented "company men" (Lieberman, 1956). The larger the proportion of faculty having simultaneously low professional and high employee orientations, the more of them who are "active" in their professional association ($t = .21$). However, faculties with more union members are no more professionally oriented, though on the average they behave more professionally.[8]

Prestige

Invidious distinctions also develop between teachers on the basis of the prestige and importance attached to their jobs. In all of the schools English is considered to be the most important course area (on the basis of the proportion of teachers nominating it as the last course that should be eliminated from the curriculum). The autonomy of teachers (that is, the frequency with which they contact the principal) does not always coincide with their prestige, however.

Informal leadership

Schools also differ considerably in their patterns of leadership, particularly in the proportion of faculty who are acknowledged as leaders by their peers. As the size of a school increases, the proportion of teachers receiving five or more nominations from their colleagues for being respected and for having the support of peers declines ($t = -.27$ and $t = -.44$, respectively).[9] In other words, smaller systems have consolidated leadership structures, while larger systems have relatively nucleated power structures, probably because differences of interest tend to develop in more complex systems. It is also significant that the frequency with which teachers talk to the principal declines sharply with school size ($t = -.66$). Consequently, even though more leadership positions are available to the rank-and-file teacher in larger schools, his influence with the administration is weakened by a diffuse system of informal leadership, and he is less likely to have opportunity to talk with, and thus directly influence, the principal.

Interpersonal relations

Interpersonal relations among faculties and their sociability also vary from school to school. The proportion of faculty lunching together shows only a slight (and not statistically significant) tendency to decline with system size ($t = -.17$ ns), but whatever loss there may be, on-the-job sociability is more than compensated for by the increases in the off-the-job social occasions in larger schools ($t = .37$).[10] Lunching cliques probably remain constant in size regardless of an organization's size, if only because people in larger schools have more specialized interests and school size presents more formidable scheduling and ecological problems in getting together during school hours; but perhaps larger faculties can sustain a larger number of off-the-job cliques and parties.[11] These findings illustrate the way in which the formal structure can influence the informal setting.

Centralization of Power and Authority

No matter how important they are, however, these informal status systems cannot fully substitute for the official authority of teachers, which is a function of the level at which decisions are made.

Number of levels of authority

The number of levels of authority between the faculty and the administrator who can give a final answer to a teacher's request, for a curriculum change, for example, is inversely related to the system's size.[12] Seven of the eight schools where it is necessary to go through as many as four or five levels are small; while seven of the nine where only one level is interposed are large (chi square significant at $p \leq .05$); the same pattern occurs where system size is concerned. Ironically, then, it is the small organizations that appear to be capable of making decisions at the top; teacher influence may actually increase as the organization becomes too large to control from a central office.

A slightly different way of looking at the authority system is simply in terms of the total number of levels of authority in the official hierarchy. According to the estimates of teachers, the schools in the sample range between one and three levels of authority; the number of levels in the total system ranges from three to seven. The mean number of authority levels estimated by teachers (in 21 of the schools for which the information is available) increases with school size ($t = .71$) and size of system ($t = .69$). (See Table 7–2.) Other investigators found a similar relationship between organizational size and the length of hierarchy of 75 organizations (Haas, Hall, and Johnson, 1965).

The number of levels of authority also is positively associated with specialization (that is, negatively associated with the proportion of teachers teaching outside of their majors or minors) ($t = -.40$ and $t = -.38$); and with organizational complexity ($t = .76$ or $t_p = .54$ when school size is controlled). (See Table 7–2.) McKay (1964) found a similar relationship in the schools he studied.

Perhaps new echelons evolve as a system increases in size, specialization, and complexity because administrative work is progressively delegated as a way of maintaining a manageable span of control at each level; this would require more echelons at the intermediate levels. Assuming that the number of subordinates supervised by a single supervisor

Table 7-2. Intercorrelations among divisive characteristics and other dimensions of organizational structure (Tau)

	Divisive Characteristics					
		No. Levels of	Specialization		No. Faculty	Hetero-
Organizational Structure	Complexity	Authority	Majored	Minored	Hired	geneity
Size: No. of faculty in						
School	.68†	.71†	−.29*	−.24*	.61†	−.12
School System	.54†	.69†	−.39†	−.27*	.36†	−.32†
Centralization						
No. of levels of authority (21 schools)	.76† .54a,*		−.40† −.07b	−.38† −.21b,*	.67† .18a	−.19
Policy decision-making index						
Professional policies	.10	.05	−.02	.08	.13	.00
Nonprofessional policies	−.18	−.12	.08	.29*	.04	.12
Routine decision-making authority	−.03	−.03	.27*	.04	.27*	.40†
Rate of consultation with administration (autonomy)	.05	.24	−.13	−.28*	.15	−.22*
Standardization						
Total index (21 schools)	.36†	.42† .23b,*	−.22 −.05c	−.31* −.24d	.36*	−.21
Rules	.26*	.21*	.01	.05	.21*	.02
Specialization: Proportion of teachers with courses in which they have not						
Majored	−.38†	−.40†			.15	.17
Majored or minored	−.31*	−.38†			−.02	.17
Close supervision	.03	−.01	.15	−.02	.15	.22*
Complexity		.76† .54a,†	−.38†	−.31* −.19d	.46†	.15
Heterogeneity		−.15 −.19	.17	.17		
Staff additions		.67†	.15	−.02		

*Rank-order correlation significant at $p \leq .05$.
†Rank-order correlation significant at $p \leq .01$.
Key for Control Variables:
aSchool size.
bComplexity.
cLevels of authority.
dPercent teaching courses not majored in.

remains somewhat constant, larger organizations require longer chains of command, and the intermediate line-and-staff administrators are coordinated at progressively higher levels. It should be noted, however, that these particular developments are partly based on the ideology that subordinates must be controlled.

With the increasing distance between administration and teaching faculty, with more levels of authority, a larger proportion of the faculty belives that the superintendent is too removed from daily events to be familiar with their programs ($t = .42$). One out of three teachers in the median school expresses this belief, and in one school over half the faculty indicates agreement.

Perhaps largely because of the higher administration's remoteness, there seems to be a very slight (not statistically significant) tendency for nonprofessional policy decisions to be delegated downward ($t = -.12$ ns); such decisions are made at lower levels in nine of the 13 systems which have six or more levels of authority, whereas they are made at higher levels in six of the seven systems that have three or fewer levels of authority (chi square significant at $p \leq .06$). Teachers in systems with longer chains of command do not lose decision-making authority; indeed, they may actually gain.

But the administrators of hierarchical systems seem to retain other forms of control. Standardization ($t = .42$, $t_p = .23$ with complexity controlled), emphasis on rules ($t = .21$), and rate of consultation between teachers and administrators ($t = .24$) all increase with the number of levels of authority; MacKay (1964) found an even higher relationship between hierarchy and the use of rules in Canadian junior high and elementary schools. Hierarchical systems, however, are not likely to be any more closely supervised ($t = -.01$), perhaps because the social distance makes personal surveillance less feasible. But there are indications of increase in the amount of supervision by remote superiors in hierarchical systems; as the number of levels of authority increases, the proportion of teachers who report being supervised by a central office administrator increases ($t = .62$).

Related to the above, there is a similar rank-order correlation between proportion of faculty supervised by an administrator from the central office and size of school and system ($t = .42$ and $t = .37$, respectively). It is noteworthy that disagreement between supervisors' instructions also appears to increase with both measures of organizational size ($t = .60$ and $t = .50$, respectively).

To summarize, organizations seem to evolve progressively more levels of authority in response to the problems of size, complexity, and specialization in order to control their increasing scope of activity. But because at least some key decisions cannot very well be elevated to correspondingly higher levels of authority and because the hierarchy produces social distance, administrative control is jeopardized and supplementary controls are utilized. The slight tendency for nonprofessional decisions to be decentralized in such systems is more than offset by increased consultation, remote supervision, and standardization.

Centralization of policy decisions

The number of levels of authority and similar structural characteristics establish only the gross distribution of power. The real spine of an organization lies along the point where key decisions actually are made. Therefore, it will be useful to form an impression about the role teachers play in the decision-making process itself.

Policy decisions of the schools in our sample are made at administrative levels, and although teachers frequently are consulted, there is little evidence that they are influential. They report that, on the average, the professional policy decisions are made by the principal. Although these decisions are usually made in consultation with teachers or a committee of teachers, and although teachers have more authority in some schools than in others, they seldom have final authority. Nonprofessional decisions are made even further up in the hierarchy. On the average, the sample locates the source of these decisions somewhere between the principal and the superintendent, but in many schools the superintendent's office is ultimately responsible for making this type of decision.

Though centralization of professional decisions is not highly correlated with increasing organization size and complexity, there is support for the idea that centralization is accompanied by more formalized attempts to control employees; standardization increases ($t = .21$) and rules are enforced more strictly ($t_p = .21$, controlling for centralization of nonprofessional decisions). (See Table 7–1.) Centralization of nonprofessional decisions is also accompanied by increased emphasis on rules ($t = .25$); though in this case employees are less closely supervised ($t_p = -.22$, controlling for complexity).

In other words, the centralization of policy decisions tends to be reinforced by some form of standardization, except that close supervision is either not emphasized, or, in the case of nonprofessional policy decisions, it actually becomes relaxed. Such organizations are necessarily more bureaucratized in other ways—such as size, number of levels of authority, and specialization (which declines). To the extent that supervision is relaxed in centralized systems as emphasis on rules increases, the compensatory model seems to be appropriate.

Routine decision making

Of course, even within the limits set by basic policy decisions, there is still room for teachers to make routine day-to-day decisions about matters that arise in their classrooms. The fact that teachers work alone in classrooms within relatively autonomous school units should guarantee them some authority. Yet, the descriptive decision-making subscale provides an indication of the amount of authority teachers have over their day-to-day work and it reveals some alienation. (See Appendix 1B.) Whereas 70 percent of the sample believes that the ultimate authority over the major educational decisions should be exercised by professional teachers, only 43 percent see themselves now in such positions. Even more teachers (90 percent) believe that they should have the authority to make decisions about problems that arise in the classroom and that small matters should not have to be referred to someone higher up for a final answer; again, substantially fewer of them (only two thirds) report actually being permitted to make routine decisions.[13]

There is more opportunity for teachers to make routine decisions in the more heterogeneous organizations ($t = .40$), those with higher rates of staff turnover and additions ($t = .27$), those that are less standardized ($t = .21$ ns), and those that have less specialized staffs ($t = .27$, with the proportion assigned to courses outside their major). This latter finding does not correspond with prevalent assumption in the literature that specialists have more decision-making authority. (See Table 7–1.) This would be a portrait of potentially unruly organizations, except for the fact that they are more closely supervised ($t = .34$).

It already has been noted that standardization and emphasis on rules may help to compensate for decentralization of policy decisions. Similarly, close supervision seems to compensate for the disproportionate amounts of routine decision-making authority of teachers.

Autonomy

The autonomy of teachers, or the lack of it, also reflects upon their decision-making power. As the term "teacher autonomy" is used here, it means infrequent consultation between subordinates and the administration. The index used is the rate which teachers consult the administration about their decisions and their problems.[14]

During a year's time the average teacher in the typical school consults with his principal about a decision or problem approximately only eight times. Autonomy does not appear to be related to organizational size (not reported in tables). However, the frequency with which the faculty "talks" with the principal (as opposed to consulting) was found to decline with school size ($t = -.66$) and system size ($t = -.62$). The rate of consultation does tend to increase with the number of levels of authority in the system ($t = .24$ ns), and it declines with a faculty's heterogeneity ($t = -.22$).[15]

An image begins to form of the position of teachers in the decision-making structure. They seldom make major nonprofessional policy decisions, and they participate only in a tangential way in the professional ones, although the majority have enough discretion to make routine classroom decisions. Many would like to have authority in this respect. Also, the freedom they otherwise seem to gain in larger systems is limited by the constraints of standardization, rules, and close supervision and by increased rates of consultation with the administration.

SUPERVISION

Teacher-Administrator Relations

Despite the problems that could be read into the authority system as it has been described thus far, relations between teachers and their administrators are, on the whole, not bad. In general, teachers respect their administrators and appear to "get along" with them relatively well; in 11 of the 28 schools, the average teacher reported no conflicts with his principal during the previous six months. A faculty's willingness to rate its principal as one of the best educators in the system and as an excellent leader increases sharply with the proportion exhibiting employee behavior ($t = .47$ and $t = .53$, respectively). Yet there is tension in such relationships, which becomes especially explicit when administrators attempt to maintain close supervision. As the amount of close supervision increases, the proportion of faculty who are negative on five statements about the principal's style of supervision also increases ($t = .21$); as a parallel, the proportion who are favorable increases as standardization declines ($t = -.26$).[16] There may be a reinforcement pattern at work—that is, bureaucratic procedures are used by administrators to control employees who are critical of them, which causes employees to resent them even more.

Teacher-Administrator Ratio

The ratio of school administrators to subordinates provides another indication of a system's capacity to supervise its employees.[17] Larger systems in the present sample have proportionately fewer administrators than smaller ones (chi square significant at $p \leq .05$). Six systems in which administrators comprise between 11 and 26 percent of the personnel are all small (that is, below 240 teachers), while 14 of 20 systems having an administrator-teacher ratio of 10 percent or less are large. However, the reverse relationship begins to emerge with respect to size of school, although the chi square is not statistically significant. Six of eight schools with between 10 to 20 percent administrators are large; while seven of ten schools with an administrator-teacher ratio of 7 percent or below are small.[18]

This apparent reversal of pattern between schools and school systems may occur because the minimum number of central office administrators necessary to run a system remains somewhat constant regardless of the number of schools being administered, whereas a school's administrative and staff functions probably increase disproportionately to number of students (which in turn is reflected in number of teachers).

Remote Supervision

Most teachers work under relatively complex supervisory patterns. The average teacher receives instructions from two or three people; in some schools each person must satisfy three or more supervisors. However, most respondents report that their instructions seldom, or only occasionally, disagreed.

Teachers are supervised by administrators in their own schools and by remote central-office supervisors. The number of the latter increases with number of levels of authority ($t = .64$) and with school size ($t = .41$). Most teachers (58 percent of the faculty in the median school) are subject to a central-office administrator who is authorized to supervise their course areas, and the number of teachers involved increases with the number of levels of authority in the system ($t = .47$). The vast majority of teachers had been contacted at least once during the preceding six months by a central-office administrator giving them advice or requesting something of them; in all but one of the 21 schools for which information is available, the majority have been visited at least once by such an administrator during their tenure, and in five schools, one third of the faculty received two or more visits.

Close Supervision

Teacher status is probably affected more immediately by the amount of direct surveillance over them than by the number of central-office supervisors. It is probably easier to check up on subordinates in smaller, less centralized schools than in larger, complex ones. Hence, Triandis (1966) hypothesizes that the larger the size of the group, the lower the frequency of the leader's monitoring of the behavior of individual group members. As he predicts, close supervision declines with system size ($t = -.22$), though the correlation with school size is not statistically significant. (See Table 7-1.) It also diminishes with the proportion of faculty who believe that the superintendent is too removed ($t = -.37$, not reported) and with the centralization of routine decisions ($t = .34$) and professional decisions ($t_p = -.23$, controlling for emphasis on rules); these findings are contrary to Triandis' prediction that it would decline with decentralization.

Anderson (1966), like Rushing (cited earlier), implicitly uses the compensatory model when he hypothesizes that bureaucratic rules and similar controls vary inversely with the amount of supervision given to subordinates. However, using the measures developed for our study, the reverse seems to be true. Close supervision apparently is not a substitute for rules, but tends to be reinforced by rules ($t = .26$) and other forms of standardization ($t = .22$). In other words, supervision, like several other forms of control, appears to need reinforcement.

The fact that there is more supervision in more heterogeneous schools ($t = .22$) and where routine decision-making authority is more decentralized ($t = .34$) suggests that close supervision may be adopted as a way to control potentially unruly situations. However, it is noteworthy that close supervision does not appear to be associated with organizational complexity, especially in view of Rushing's (1966) prediction that direct surveillance will be supplanted by rules and regulations as an organization undergoes increasing structural differentiation.

Evaluation

Frequent evaluation represents still another means of maintaining close checks on subordinates. In four schools a near majority are evaluated three or more times a year, but in most schools they are evaluated by their principals no more than once. Only 8 percent of the sample believe that their administrator's evaluations of them are unfair and inaccurate, and perhaps the reason is that the average rating given by most principals ranges between "good" and "excellent" ($\bar{X} = 4.2$, on a five-point scale). One third of the faculties fall below the "good" rating, but none of the principals rates his faculty over-all as "average." Principals also believe that most teachers are loyal to the administration ($\bar{X} = 4.2$, on a five-point scale).

Professional and Employee Norms

From the self-descriptions of actual on-the-job behavior, one gets the impression that teachers are as compliant and loyal, and lacking in discretionary authority, as some writers have portrayed them (Lieberman,

1956; Friedenberg, 1962). For example, teachers express strong loyalty to their administrators and their communities. Approximately two thirds or more agree that teachers in their schools adjust their teaching to the administration's vews of good educational practice; are obedient, respectful, and loyal to the principal; look primarily to administrator's judgment for guidance in case of community disputes (controversies over a textbook or a speaker); are completely familiar with written descriptions of the rules, procedures, manuals, and other standard operating procedures connected with running a classroom; and would not publicly advocate a position on the place of religion in the school if it differed greatly from the community's majority opinion. Even higher proportions of teachers believe that they should conform to these practices.

More than one half of the teachers also agree that their school administration is better qualified than they to judge what is best for education; that rules stating when teachers should arrive and depart from the building are strictly enforced; that teachers in their school are usually guided by community opinions in deciding what to say in class and in choosing teaching materials; and, in general, that teachers conform to the accepted community standards. Even higher proportions of the sample believe that most of these practices are desirable.[19] One half of the sample also agrees that teachers who openly criticize the administration should be encouraged to go elsewhere, that local control over schools by school boards represents the most fundamental form of democracy in public education, and that the criterion of a good school should be how well it serves the needs of the local community.

On the other side of the coin, less than one half believe that the ultimate authority over the major educational decisions should be exercised by professional teachers or that they should try to put their standards and ideas of good teaching into practice even if the rules or procedures of the school prohibit it. Only one third or less agree that a teacher should consistently practice his ideas of the best educational practices even though the administration preferred another view, that it is permissible for a teacher to violate a rule if he is sure that the students' best interests will be served by doing so, or that a teacher should refuse to do anything that may jeopardize the interests of his students ragardless of his instructions or what the rules state; only one out of five teachers reports that colleagues actually refuse to do what they are told unless they are satisfied that it is best for the student.

Positions taken by teachers toward these issues, then, indicate a telling degree of compliance and lack of initiative on their part. However, there is another side to the story. In some respects teachers have a certain amount of freedom. They seem to have a great deal of regard for this discretion and express tendencies toward self-initiative. For example, less than one quarter of the teachers in the sample report that teachers of the same subject in their systems must follow the same lesson plans; that course work is so planned that every child taking the same kind of course throughout the state would eventually cover the same material; that there are rules covering almost every problem that might arise in the school; that definite rules exist specifying topics inappropriate for classroom discussion, or that their colleagues avoid controversial issues (such as abolishing the House Un-American Activities Committee) which could jeopardize the school's public relations. Only slightly more (one third) report that teachers try to keep out of "hot water" by following the wishes of the top administration, teach their course in such a way that a substitute can take over at a moment's notice without serious interruption, or avoid "sticking their necks out" when a controversy arises about the interpretation of school rules.

Moreover, over two thirds of the sample agree that teachers in their school are able to make their own decisions about classroom problems, that small matters in their school do not have to be referred to someone higher up for the final answer, and that the ultimate authority over the major educational decisions is exercised by professional teachers. Approximately one of every two teachers reports that in his school, teachers try to live up to what they think are the standards of their profession, even if the administration or the community does not seem to respect them. In all of these cases even higher proportions of teachers believe that teachers should live up to these practices.

In summing up, then, there is a distinct eagerness on the part of teachers to comply with their superiors, yet they are not completely dominated by their organizations either; indeed, there are issues on which the majority would take a firm stand in opposition to the administration.

Professionalism and Bureaucratization

Several writers have alluded to the probability that modern bureaucracies are adapting in various ways to the demands of professional authority structures (MacKay, 1964; Scott, 1966; Clark, 1966). In this sample the more professionally oriented schools seem to have accommodated to professionalism in at least one important respect: the more professionally oriented faculty members are, the more authority they assume for routine decisions ($t = .34$). (See Table 7–3.) Yet, there is little evidence that any of the other bureaucratic characteristics are associated to any significant degree with professionalism.[20] Neither is there a clearly discernible attempt to regulate the more professionally oriented faculties any more closely; there is a low positive correlation with close supervision, but it is not statistically significant ($t = .14$ ns), and there is no correlation at all with emphasis on rules or standardization.

Table 7-3. Professionalism and employee characteristics and organizational structure (Tau)

Organizational Structure	Professionalism and Employeeism			
	Professional Orientation (N = 28)	Professional Behavior (N = 28)	Employee Orientation (N = 28)	Employee Behavior (N = 28)
Size: No. faculty in				
School	.04	.14	−.19	−.29[a]
School system	.02	.01	−.21[a]	−.27[a]
Centralization				
No. levels of authority (21 Schools)	.17	.12	−.38[b]	−.28[a]
Policy decision-making index				
Professional policies	−.12	−.04	.19	−.02
Nonprofessional policies	−.14	−.10	.16	−.02
Routine decision-making authority	.34[b]	.16	.36[b]	.24[a]
Rate of consultation with administration (autonomy)	.06	−.24[a]	−.25[a]	−.18
Standardization				
Total index (21 schools)	.04	−.01	−.29[a]	−.35[a]
Rules	.03	.12	.26[a]	.29[a]
Interchangeability	−.02	−.06	.27[a]	.08
Specialization: Proportion of teachers with courses in which they have not				
Majored	.09	.16	.24[a]	.33[b]
Majored or minored	−.16	.00	.14	.17
Close supervision	.14	.10	.29[a]	.23[a]
Complexity	−.01	.15	−.23[a]	−.18
Heterogeneity	.17	.07	.14	.12
Staff additions	.17	.26[a]	.07	−.04

[a] Rank-order correlation significant at $p \leq .05$.
[b] Rank-order correlation significant at $p \leq .01$.

A faculty's employee orientation, by comparison, is more closely associated with organizational variables. It increases with close supervision ($t = .29$), with emphasis on rules ($t = .26$), with decentralization of routine decisions ($t = .36$), and with the centralization of policy decisions ($t = .19$ ns), and it declines with consultation with the administration.[21] Though employee and professional orientation are associated with more routine decision-making authority, there are probably different reasons.

In more professional faculties decentralization could be simply in recognition of their technical competence, whereas in employee faculties it may be in recognition of their loyalty to the administration, especially because close supervision and emphasis on rules in these organizations provide the administration with other safeguards. (There are similar patterns for employee behavior.)

In sum, compared with its professional orientation, the average faculty's employee orientation is more systematically associated with bureaucratic characteristics, with the important exception that the more professional faculties have proportionately more authority to make routine decisions. In general the professional orientation seems to be less bound to specific organizational characteristics. The most loyal faculties are found in the more bureaucratic schools despite the fact that they logically would seem to require less control. It is not clear to what extent more bureaucratic organizations simply attract reticent people who will submit to control and to what extent bureaucratization represents an accommodation to employee expectations.

SPECIALIZATION

The term "specialization" refers to the use an organization makes of the special training acquired by its employees.[22] In addition to taking specialized education courses, most high school teachers have concentrated on a major area of academic work. In this sense, large organizations are more specialized.[23] That is, the practice of assigning teachers to their majors becomes less frequent as size of school and size of system increase ($t = -.29$ and $t = -.39$, respectively); the corresponding correlations for those who have neither majored nor minored in courses are also statistically significant ($t = -.24$ and $t = -.27$, respectively).[24] (See Table 7-2.)

Specialization also increases with organizational complexity ($t = -.38$ and $t = -.31$, respectively). (See Table 7-2.) More elaborately organized systems probably require greater technical competence, but, in addition, complexity permits tasks to be duplicated so that a specialist can concentrate on a specific activity in a way that he cannot in smaller schools where a rudimentary division of labor must be maintained regardless of the number of people on the staff; the fact that small schools are required by law to "cover" a minimum number of functions regardless of the people available means that each person may have to handle several duties.

More specialized schools are more standardized. The rank-order correlation of standardization with the proportion of teachers assigned to courses in which they have not majored is $t = -.22$ ns; and with the proportion of those who have neither majored nor minored it is $t = -.31$. (See Table 7-1.) But because standardization seems to be more consistently associated with degree of hierarchy than with specialization per se (because it partials out), it is more reasonable to assume that standardization is a way of coping with the problems that arise due to the increasing social distance between subordinates and higher administrators rather than as a curb on specialized employees.

Although less specialized schools are less hierarchical ($t_p = -.21$, controlling for complexity), in that context the level at which nonprofessional policy decisions are made tends to be higher in schools that more frequently assign teachers to courses in which they have neither majored nor minored ($t = .29$). Also, the more teachers are assigned to courses outside of their majors, the less routine decision-making authority they have over their classrooms ($t = .27$). [Although those assigned outside both their major and minor do not consult with the administration as frequently ($t = -.28$).] The fact that authority over certain types of decisions is retained at higher levels in less specialized schools may be one way of compensating for the lower competence that threatens to develop when specialists are not fully utilized.[25] This pattern is consistent with several studies which have found the parallel fact that specialized organizations tend to be decentralized.

Division of Labor

Specialization refers to the personal training of employees. Division of labor refers to the way the work itself is divided; it is part of the role system and a property of the organization.[26] The complexity of schools is reflected in the variety of nonteaching and teaching duties of teachers and committees and the proliferation of separate courses, departments, and special programs found in most of them.

Nonteaching duties

Overlaying the structure of courses and departments is the system of standing committees, the number of which exceeds 10 in six of the 28 schools. Most teachers in the sample are active on at least one or two committees, and on even more in two schools.[27] In addition, they spend an average of 10 hours a week supervising extracurricular activities, the average ranging from as much as 24 hours a week to only four hours a week in different schools. The proportion of faculty responsible for extracurricular activities varies, but in the median school about 40 percent claim such duties. Higher proportions tend to be responsible for extracurricular activities in smaller compared to larger schools (over 60 teachers).[28] Though Barker and his associates (1962) maintain that small schools permit more student participation than larger ones, they fail to consider the other side of the coin: the added burden that extracurricular activities imposes on teachers in small schools and the possible distractions from their academic duties.

Course structure

In the academic realm, too, schools are segmented along several lines. The complexity of the course structures varies considerably. One school in the sample offers only 28 different courses, while several offer 100 or more. Some of these also have adult-education programs, and in still others there are ability groupings within courses and content areas, or double sessions for all or a portion of the courses (in nearly half the schools); though there is a slightly disproportionate occurrence of double sessions in the larger schools, the relationship is not statistically significant. In all but six of the 28 schools the curriculum is also divided into separate curriculum tracks; 10 of the 28 have more than three tracks, and three of those have at least five programs.

Departmentalization

In about half the schools separate subject-matter fields are organized into departments in the charge of official "heads"; two schools have as many as 10 separate official department heads.[29] One study found that the number of subdivisions within organizations is related to size (Haas, Hall and Johnson, 1965), and in this study, too, larger schools have significantly more officially recognized departments, although the relationship is not entirely uniform.

Special programs

Nine of the 28 schools are using experimental programs and testing newer developments not yet fully incorporated into the traditional system.

All nine are using team teaching in at least one classroom (but only four of them use it in five or more classes), and six also are participating in advanced programs. There seems to be a slight tendency for professionally oriented schools to have more experimental programs; in six of the nine schools with such programs the faculties have above average professional orientations, but the chi-square value is not statistically significant.

Total complexity

Considered together, the variety of nonteaching duties, the complex course structure, tracking systems, departmentalization, and specialized programs provide an estimate of an organization's over-all complexity. Organizational complexity increases with the number of teachers in a school ($t = .68$) and in a system ($t = .54$). (See Table 7–2.) This supports the findings of another study (Haas, Hall and Johnson, 1965). As already noted, complexity is positively associated with specialization, which conflicts with a negative relationship found by MacKay (1964) between schools' division of labor and technical competence. The number of levels of authority, of course, increases with complexity ($t_p = .54$, controlling for school size), because the number of levels of authority is part of the complexity measure.

To the extent that separate groups of specialists are likely to develop distinct goals, special interests, and resources, organizations that are large, hierarchical, complex, and specialized will be difficult to control. If bureaucratic controls ever need mutual reinforcement, it should be in complex organizations. And this is the case. As schools become more complex, more emphasis is placed on rules (t = .26). This finding supports MacKay's findings in Canadian schools. Also, proportionately more faculty members are supervised by a central-office administrator (t = .49); and there is more standardization ($t = .36$). (See Table 7–2.) But perhaps partly because complex organizations are difficult to control from the top, the level at which nonprofessional decisions are made tends to decline with organizational complexity (although the measure is not quite statistically significant: $t = -.18$ ns).

In other words, whatever loss of control may occur because complex organizations are large, hierarchical, and decentralized tends to be compensated for by a disproportionate emphasis on rules and standardized procedures and by more remote control from the central office. The divisive characteristics of complex organizations are at least partially compensated for by the emphasis on controls. Indeed, in view of the potential lack of control that could otherwise arise in such schools, it is perhaps remarkable that their members are not controlled even more closely.

RECRUITMENT

Heterogeneity

When an organization's members are recruited from heterogeneous backgrounds and have different values, perspectives, and commitments, one might expect that control problems would be aggravated. One might also expect the larger schools to recruit more widely from diverse backgrounds. But, in fact, heterogeneity seems more typical of smaller school systems than of larger ones ($t = -.32$). (See Table 7–2.) Perhaps it is partly because heterogeneous schools do not have the problems of size and complexity to contend with that they actually place less emphasis on certain kinds of controls. More heterogeneous schools tend to be less standardized ($t = -.21$ ns) and more decentralized (as reflected in teachers' routine decision-making authority) ($t = .40$), and their faculties consult less with the administration ($t = -.22$ and $t_p = -.18$ ns, controlling for specialization). They also appear to be more closely supervised ($t = .22$). The closer supervision and the centralization of some types of decisions could help compensate for losses of control from heterogeneity and the greater routine decision-making authority of teachers in such schools.

Staff Additions

Faculty turnover and expansion represent still other potentially disruptive factors which are likely to require compensating controls. Some schools hire faculty members at the rate of 30 or 40 per year, while one school in the sample had hired only eight new people during a five-year period. The schools that have the most problems—that is, the larger, hierarchical, complex schools—are the ones most likely to be disrupted further by staff turnover and expansion. The number of faculty members hired during a five-year period increases sharply with organizational complexity ($t = .46$), number of levels of authority ($t = .67$), school size ($t = .61$) and (to a lesser extent) system size ($t = .36$). (See Table 7–2.) Also, as faculty additions increase, so does their authority over routine decisions ($t = .27$). Given the potential disruption that turnover and expansion can create in a school system already large and complex, it is understandable that increases in staff additions are compensated for by tighter controls—in this case, emphasis on rules ($t = .21$), and standardization ($t = .36$).

IMPLICATIONS

Although schools can be loosely characterized as bureaucratic in both method and intent, the bureaucratization of education has not been an entirely coherent or uniform development. It consists of more or less discrete practices which have become related in a variety of ways. These patterns are complicated further by the inherent tensions between pressures for group autonomy and for integration. A delicate tension exists between the latitude necessary for employees to take initiative and solve some of their own problems and the compelling pressures on them to comply for the sake of coordination and control. These internal processes are further influenced by constraints imposed by the external environment, especially through recruiting practices.

Different dimensions of bureaucracy appear to operate on somewhat different principles, but each of the three models considered in the first part of this chapter is of some use in interpreting organizational patterns involving different variables. The reinforcement model seems to be most applicable to the control types of variables; the compensatory model, on the other hand, fits the divisive variables better, or, more accurately, it applies to the relationship between the divisive and the control variables. Divisiveness in an organization calls for controls to offset it; and, accordingly, the greater the divisiveness, the more likely that more than one control measure will be used in order to provide reinforcement.

A significant minority of teachers seem to be dissatisfied and, in some sense, alienated. Teachers have little prospect of being promoted and not much greater hope of a substantial salary increase; they are being rewarded for experience when they believe that they should be more directly rewarded for their teaching competence. Teachers make few nonprofessional policy decisions, and though they participate in the professional decisions, they seldom have final authority. Even though they have discretion to make routine classroom decisions, they desire more authority than they have at present. Perhaps under these conditions it is understandable that one in five teachers regrets his choice of career or job.

Given what is from the viewpoint of teachers the inadequacies of the official system, teachers' informal associations could play an important part in improving their own lives. However, in the larger schools the potential influence of informal groups is largely dissipated by the nucleated and diffuse clique structure, and by the fact that there are few opportunities to work directly with the principal. Moreover, the company man seems to predominate in teacher organizations. Therefore, it would appear that in the long run teachers will not be able appreciably to increase their authority without basic modifications in the schools' informal and official structures.

But it is our contention that bureaucracy is neither an insidious plot to stifle employee initiative nor an insatiable natural growth of organization. It is probably difficult for the typical individual to grasp just how complex and potentially disruptive the large school is and the magnitude of its problems until he has had occasion to reflect upon the organization as a whole—its division of labor, specialization, degree of hierarchy, and turnover. Viewed in that context, bureaucracy will be seen as an often nominal and purely defensive response to these disruptive factors rather than an excess.

It is true that the opportunity for individual initiative and professionalization can be easily compromised in the process of controlling other forms of divisiveness; the opportunity for employees to act professionally depends largely upon the outcome of the tug-of-war between control and divisiveness. Yet it is precisely the most divisive, complex organizations —in which attempts to maintain control are also the most concerted— that are otherwise most favorable for the growth of initiative and professionalization. In these organizations there may be more control mechanisms, but the controls are not likely to be oppressive precisely because such organizations initially permit so much freedom. It is significant that the most centralized schools are not the largest, but rather the smallest ones, and that the authority of teachers to make routine decisions increases with a school's rate of faculty expansion and turnover. That teachers have the most opportunity to participate in decision making in the most bureaucratic and unstable organizations indicates that at least a limited amount of authority accrues to professionally oriented teachers as an organization develops. The irony is that it is in the situations where the threat of being controlled is the greatest that professionally oriented teachers have the most opportunity to exercise authority, at least over the routine decisions.

Because the more bureaucratic schools tend to employ more employee-oriented teachers, the potential conflict between professionalism and bureaucracy is not as great as it could be—if it were the professionals who gravitated to bureaucratic situations. Nevertheless the fact that there is not more accommodation of bureaucracy to professionalism, even where the faculty is strongly oriented in this direction, is a forewarning of the severe tensions that may develop in the future if professionally oriented faculties do begin to gravitate to the most bureaucratic schools.

More information is needed about how present school systems can be made more appropriate for professionally oriented faculties. Certainly, several of the forms of control traditionally used in bureaucracy have become relatively ineffective. Many of the present anomalies are created by the persistence of administrators in attempting to impose these outmoded forms of control. For example, neither close supervision nor the personal evaluation of teachers by remote administrators seems practical in most large school systems, though there are efforts to continue both practices. The idea that personnel must be "supervised" is probably responsible for the growth of hierarchy, with resulting remoteness of the officials and even more internal divisiveness created by the hierarchy itself. Our data suggest that if administrators are to develop good relationships with their teachers, it may be necessary for them to exercise less direct control and surveillance over their teachers.

There are several alternatives to present forms of bureaucratic control. (1) Some of the divisiveness responsible for bureaucracy can be reduced—for example, by minimizing the number of layers of authority or reducing turnover. (2) New forms of control might be developed through a more equitable distribution of authority—for example, by relying more on peers to evaluate one another and to make other internal decisions. (3) Schools can learn to live with divisiveness by calculating the costs of inefficiency and disruption in comparison to the costs in the form of risk taking, change, and diversity implicit in many forms of control.

NOTES: Chapter 7

¹ Triandis (1966) exemplifies this point of view when he proposes that "the taller the organizational structure, the closer the supervision." The sheer esthetic appeal of symmetry provided by an internally consistent system is not the only reason for believing that bureaucratic dimensions might be mutually reinforcing. Bureaucratic elements sometimes actually seem to propagate one another. This is suggested in Gouldner's (1954) observation that impersonal rules are used to disguise the element of personal power relations between superiors and subordinates —and hence partially to accommodate the tensions that arise from the close supervision of specialists. On the other hand, it seems as plausible that the over-all tensions would be reduced as effectively if some bureaucratic characteristics were relaxed to the same degree that others are stressed.

² There are at least three reasons why organizations might use substitute measures. The first is simply to conserve scarce resources. Each time a bureaucratic practice is used it requires at a minimum an expenditure of time and energy, which restricts its ability to make maximum use of the potentially available control procedures. Scarcity of resources limits an organization's power to cope simultaneously with equal effectiveness with all of its problems and forces it to emphasize a few practices applicable to selected problems while neglecting others. Once resources have been allocated in a particular way (for example, emphasizing close supervision), resources available for other alternatives will be thereby limited. Second, some situations will require only a minimum effort to maintain control; hence it may not be necessary to use more than one form of control. Third, in some cases subordinates are already sufficiently loyal and homogeneous or otherwise compliant, making it unnecessary to impose official control.

³ Models themselves are not appropriate subjects for research. A model's validity depends upon whether it helps to interpret the way organizations function. It can be regarded as a convenient construct likely to be supplanted eventually by still more advanced concepts. It should be remembered, too, that these data were drawn from only a handful of organizations which represent only one type of social organization, and that broader social trends, supply and demand ratios, and interorganizational relationships were not taken into account.

⁴ The faculty of one school "agrees" that the six items on the decriptive rules subscales accurately portray their school, while at the other extreme one faculty is "undecided." Only 15 percent of the teachers in the sample work in situations where persons in the system teaching the same subject must follow the same lesson plans, but three fourths work in schools having manuals of rules and regulations to follow; one half report strict enforcement of rules specifying the times for teachers' arrival and departure from school. And although two out of three teachers are not required to file lesson plans or curriculum guides with the administration, half of those who follow them frequently or very frequently have not had any part in preparing the plans. It also should be noted that one out of every two teachers works in a situation where tests are required, but most schools do not observe the practice on the whole.

⁵ Two thirds of the teachers in the sample even recommend strict enforcement of the rules specifying when teachers should arrive and depart from the building. But as evidence that they object to rules that curtail their authority over the classroom, it was found that only one fifth agree that there should be definite rules specifying topics inappropriate for discussion in the classroom; only one third want rules so specific that they would cover almost any problem that would arise; and only one fourth believe that teachers of the same subject throughout the system should follow

the same lesson plans. Yet, it should be recognized that even in these latter cases substantial minorities do not object to being closely regulated.

[6] Throughout this chapter the symbol t refers to the Kendall tau rank-order coefficient between two ordinal variables. The corresponding values computed with the Spearman formula are usually higher—for example, tau of .30 equals .43 when computed with the Spearman formula for a sample of 28. For an N of 28 the tau must reach .21 to be statistically significant at the .05 level of probability. The corresponding tau for 21 cases must reach $t = .25$. Where correlations that are not statistically significant are reported in the discussion, they will be identified with an "ns." Each of the rank-order correlations reported in this chapter was computed several times, each time controlling for other relevant organizational variables related either to the dependent or independent variable. These partial correlations are reported as t_p. The partial correlation will be referred to in discussions only where it makes a substantial change in the interpretation.

[7] Most teachers have little opportunity to ascend far on the truncated official status ladder. Despite a wide spread in their years of experience, teachers in this sample range within a narrow salary scale varying in different schools from an average of $4,000 to $8,000 per year. Combined with the emphasis on experience, this limited salary range creates an inflexibly narrow channel of mobility which seems likely to make some of the more competent younger teachers especially impatient.

The fact that there are few intermediate positions between classroom teachers and higher officials creates a hiatus between them so wide that few teachers plan to go into administration. With little variability from school to school, only 5 percent of the sample anticipate becoming administrators wthin the next two years. Only slightly more (13 percent) even hope for a better job in the same school; although over half of the faculty of one school anticipate improved opportunities, and it is not uncommon to find that one fifth of the faculty anticipate improved positions. A few teachers (only 6 percent in the median school) expect to improve their situations by transferring to another school, but the fact that if the opportunity arose more (14 percent) would leave their present jobs for the same or lower salary elsewhere indicates dissatisfaction with the present position. The position of department head, which represents one of the few opportunities for promotion short of full-time administration, is illuminating. Over one half of the schools in this sample do not have department heads, and anyway, there are likely to be no more than 6 to 11 of these positions available in a school. Part-time counselor is another administrative staff position which permits one to teach, but there are only 17 part-time counselors in the entire sample. The power of administrators is emasculated by the lack of these middle-level executive positions and by the single salary schedule.

[8] Colombotos (1962) found that members of the NEA were no more professional than AFT members, although the professionalism of male AFT members tended to increase with their level of participation in the organization. In the present sample, unfortunately, only four of the 28 schools have officially recognized teachers' unions. However, on the average, the schools with the highest proportion of union members (when trichotomized) rank slightly lower on professional orientation than schools with average or fewer numbers of union members (tested by the Kruskal-Wallis one-way analysis of variance of ranks); but at the same time the most unionized faculties report higher levels of professional behavior (as well as employee behavior).

[9] Teachers were asked to identify the colleague whom they most respect. In the median school about 15 percent of the faculty received five or more votes. In one of the largest, however, only 3 percent of the faculty could command as many as five nominations from their colleagues; at the other extreme, in the smallest, one fourth of the faculty was nominated at least five times. Schools vary similarly in regard to teachers nominated as having the most "support" from their colleagues. In one school no one received as many as five votes, while in another over one fourth of the faculty received this tribute.

[10] A more stringent index of sociability would be the proportion of teachers with at least one of their best friends on the faculty. A typical teacher counts at least

one of his colleagues as a best friend, but only a negligible 11 percent have as many as three of their best friends on the faculty. Even in the most gregarious school one out of three does not consider another member of the faculty to be among his best friends. Again, this pattern varies considerably among schools. In one, fully three fourths of the faculty do not have a best friend among their colleagues, while in another, nearly one half have most of their best friends on the faculty.

It is interesting that the proportion of faculty without friends at school is not associated with the organizational size. Perhaps the greater opportunity to develop close relationships in small schools and communities is offset by the larger number of potentially compatible friends available in large systems.

[11] In most of the 28 schools the majority of teachers report having lunch very frequently with at least one other faculty member, but in one not particularly large school only one fifth report this pattern, and in several the proportion varies between 30 to 40 percent. No school reflects a high degree of sociability after school hours, and most teachers do not see even one other colleague "socially"; a majority do see one another at least "frequently" on social occasions, however.

[12] In 21 schools the principals were asked to indicate the number of different levels of authority through which a teacher's request for curriculum change might have to travel. In most cases two levels were considered to be sufficient, but in seven schools it was estimated that three or four levels would be involved. Also, in half of the schools, principals estimated that it would take almost a month to get a decision on such a request, and up to a year in three of them; but in seven schools the "red tape" would take more than ten weeks. Teachers' estimates are a little more optimistic on this point, but unless their estimates are more accurate than the administrators', they may be disillusioned on this point.

[13] Gross and his associates (1958) reported that the majority of school superintendents and boards wanted teachers to participate in major policy decisions. Forty percent of the teachers in that study also felt that their part in policy formation should be increased. But in practice, only 10 percent of their sample said that staff members actually are given the opportunity to consult with the superintendent about filling a vacant teaching position or other matters likely to be of importance to teachers.

The precariousness of teachers' situations is reflected in the present study. Although nearly every teacher serves on at least one committee, between one fourth and one half say that the majority of their recommendations are never followed, although typically substantial proportions believe that they are followed at least some of the time. In all schools only insignificant proportions of teachers perceive themselves as having any authority over faculty meetings, and the vast majority report that the principal or his assistant usually arranges the agenda for such meetings; in two schools the superintendent or school board takes this responsibility.

[14] Over half the sample report consulting with their principals at least once a week, but one in five see him no more than once a month; in some schools this is true of over one third of the faculty. In one school one fifth of the faculty report that they do not see the principal about a problem during a normal six-month period. No attempt has been made to ascertain whether autonomy reduces the opportunity of subordinates to influence administrative decisions through consultation.

[15] Perhaps teachers in hierarchical systems make more attempts to influence decisions made by remote officers; or perhaps they seek more direction from the administration; or, finally, it could mean that the administration requires consultation as a way of maintaining touch with disloyal employees in such systems. This last interpretation, however, is not supported by the fact that faculties with autonomy are more loyal to the administration—that is, as the proportion of the faculty with employee orientations in the upper fifteenth percentile increases, the faculty consults less with the administration ($t = -.24$).

[16] In 17 of 28 schools the average faculty member does not agree with any of the five negative statements on the checklist of 14 statements evaluating the principal. The sample tends to be correspondingly positive toward their principals. In all of the schools the vast majority agree with at least one of the positive statements. Yet not more than one half agree with as many as four of them. These over-all trends are

qualified by variation from school to school. In four schools one fifth of the faculty report conflicts with the principal; and in another one fifth agree with four of the five negative statements and nearly one half agree with two of the five statements.

[17] Terrien and Mills (1955) found a tendency for administrators of public school systems to increase at a faster rate than the student body grows. Also, between 1929 and 1952, the proportion of total expenditures used for administering public schools remained relatively constant (fluctuating between 3.5 and 4.5 percent of total expenditures), while auxiliary staff increased from 4.4 to 7.8 percent. Anderson and Warkow (1961) suggest that the physical dispersion of administrative units, which is typical of the separate schools in a school district, requires more unit administrators to coordinate the work than do organizations located in the same building.

[18] The ratio of administrators to teachers in the sample of schools ranges from 0 to 20 percent. In eight schools more than 10 percent of the personnel are administrators. The ratios for school systems are similar.

[19] Also, when they were asked to whom they looked for advice regarding a proposed school for bright children, one in five teachers referred to their own administrators—the single most frequent response. The sample, as a whole, fluctuate between "undecided" and "agreement," with seven statements maintaining that they owe loyalty to the administration, although they are definitely "undecided" about the loyalty owed to their organization. Very few (4 percent) have been employed by any other school system.

[20] There are, however, slight (not statistically significant) tendencies for a faculty's professional orientation to diminish as professional and nonprofessional decisions become more centralized ($t = -.12$ ns, and $t = -.14$ ns, respectively), while it tends to increase in systems that are more hierarchical ($t = .17$ ns), more closely supervised ($t = .12$ ns), and more specialized ($t = .16$ ns) and that are adding faculty ($t = .17$ ns).

Colombotos (1962) found a weak relationship between professionalism and proceduralism for men; the professionals who scored at the median were slightly less procedural than those who scored neither high nor low on the professional scale. Among women a stronger, more monotonic relationship appeared, but it was not quite statistically significant. A higher proportion of men than women reported that they break rules frequently or occasionally.

[21] The employee orientation of a faculty appears to diminish in more hierarchical, complex, standardized, larger, and less centralized systems ($t = -.38$, $t = .23$, $t = -.29$, $t = -.21$, and $t = -.24$., respectively). But because number of levels of authority, standardization, and proportion specialized are correlated with organizational size, they are reduced below statistical significance when size is partial. When complexity is controlled, the correlation with the system size is reduced also ($t = -.12$), while the correlation with rules is increased ($t = .35$). The correlation with supervision is not appreciably altered by partialing out controls.

[22] The relatively high level of formal education achieved by the typical teacher is one of the unique features of schools. With the possible exception of law and accounting firms, even technical, industrial, or commercial organizations that employ large proportions of technically trained or college-educated personnel cannot claim the average of five years of education per employee which the members of this sample have achieved; the least educated faculty averages 4½ years of education, whereas the one school averages 5½ years. Over one third of the sample have the master's degree. Not even hospitals surpass these figures (especially if diploma nurses without college degrees, aides, and students are taken into consideration). The fact that each teacher attends an average of two professional conferences or workshops a year is further indication that they continue their formal education while in service. However, about half of their training (90 hours in the median school) is confined to colleges of education; and in one school a typical teacher has taken only 45 hours of course work outside of an education college. While it may be debatable that specialized training in education increases teaching competence, the claims made by educators that teachers require a special type of training for their work have some merit. College degrees and specialized training might encourage

teachers to expect a great deal of decision-making authority and responsibility. But some teacher-training institutions may counteract this tendency by emphasizing their obligations as employees and their corresponding dependence for direction upon administrators and laymen. In any event, there is no discernible relationship from the data between a faculty's level of professionalization as measured by the professional-orientation scale described in the preceding chapter and its average level or type of education.

[23] About one third of the teachers in the median school report teaching courses, at least frequently to occasionally, in areas in which they have not majored. This practice suggests a lack of specialization and thus a low degree of bureaucratization in this respect. Over one half of the faculty in one school report this to be a frequent practice. About 12 percent of these people have at least occasionally taught courses in which they neither majored nor minored in college, and in one school this practice involves over one fourth of the faculty. This complete disregard for specialized training of any kind is more characteristic of schools with lower salary schedules ($t = -.23$) and with fewer master's degrees on the faculty ($t = -.21$). Both characteristics might be regarded as negative reflections on academic quality.

[24] But although specialists are utilized more effectively in larger schools, the fact that the correlations are far from perfect indicates that some complex schools also have difficulty in retaining or holding specialists. Some small schools, on the other hand, appear to have found ways to overcome handicaps.

[25] In a study of correctional institutions Zald (1962) found that where specialists were used more, decision making was less centralized. Hage (1965) observed that hospitals with more specialized staffs of physicians tended to be decentralized. Anderson (1966) expected that the standardization of a school would increase as the level of competence increased, but MacKay (1964) found a negative correlation between competency and the hierarchy of Canadian elementary and junior high schools. Also, Rushing (1966, p. 439) proposed that "an increase in the organization skill structure will be accompanied by a decrease in the use of formal rules and surveillance to control conduct." Technical competence, it would appear, gives specialists a disproportionate amount of influence. By comparison, the present data seem to indicate the counterpart of this proposition: less specialized subordinates are in a less favorable position to gain control of their work.

[26] The way work is divided in an organization probably depends to a certain extent on its objectives. Eisenstadt (1958, p. 118) maintains that the extent of specialization required of employees in a culturally oriented organization is far greater than in economic organizations, but that relatively little complementary division of labor is required between their members; members of such organizations perform parallel rather than complementary tasks. The following data are probably limited, then, by the fact that they were gathered from an organization having only one type of goal.

[27] According to one national study at least one fourth of the teacher's time each day is spent in activities unrelated to classroom work, with administrative chores alone consuming 15 percent of a normal day (NEA, 1963).

[28] Of the eight schools in which over 60 percent of the faculty are involved in extracurricular activities, six are small; on the other hand, six of the eight in which less than 30 percent of the faculty have such duties are large.

[29] Of the eight schools with six or more department heads, only one is small (below 60 teachers), whereas 10 of the 15 schools without department heads are small. However, at least one third (five) of the large schools function without official heads.

REFERENCES: Chapter 7

Anderson, James G. Bureaucratic rules: Bearers of organizational authority. *Educational Administration Quarterly*, Winter, 1966, **2**, 7–34.

Anderson, Theodore R., and Warkow, Seymour. Organizational size and functional comlexity. *American Sociological Review*, 1961, **26**, 23–27.

Barker, Rober G., et al. The principals look at the schools. In *Big school—small school: Studies of the effects of high school size upon the behavior and experience of students.* Lawrence, Kan.: Midwest Psychological Field Station, University of Kansas, 1962.

Blau, Peter, and Scott, W. Richard. *Formal organization.* San Francisco: Chandler, 1962.

Clark, Burton R. Organizational adaptation to professionals. In Howard L. Vollmer and Donald L. Mills (Eds.). *Professionalization.* Englewood Cliffs, N.J.: Prentice-Hall, 1966. Pp. 282–291.

Colombotos, John L. *Sources of professionalism: A study of high school teachers.* U.S. Office of Education, Cooperative Research Project No. 330. Ann Arbor: Department of Sociology, University of Michigan, 1962.

Dahrendorf, Ralf. Out of Utopia: Toward a reorientation of sociological analysis. *American Journal of Sociology*, September, 1958, **LXIV**, 115–127.

Eisenstadt, E. N. Bureaucracy and bureaucratization: A trend report and bibliography." *Current Sociology*, 1958, **7**, 99–163.

Fairchild, Henry Pratt. *Dictionary of sociology.* New York: Philosophical Library, 1944.

Friendenberg, Edgar Z. *The vanishing adolescent.* New York: Dell, 1962.

Gouldner, Alvin. *Patterns of industrial bureaucracy.* Glencoe, Ill.: Free Press, 1954.

Gross, Neal, Mason, Ward S., and McEachern, Alexander W. *Explorations in role analysis: Studies of the school superintendency role.* New York: Wiley, 1958.

Haas, J. Eugene, Hall, Richard H., and Johnson, Norman J. Toward an empirically derived taxonomy of organizations. In *Proceedings, research conference on behavior in organizations.* Athens, Ga.: University of Georgia Press, 1965.

Hage, Jerald. An axiomatic theory of organizations. *Administrative Science Quarterly*, December, 1965, **10**, 289–320.

Hall, Richard H. The concept of bureaucracy: An empirical assessment. *The American Journal of Sociology*, July, 1963, **69**, 32–40.

Hemphill, John K. *Group dimensions: A manual for their measurement.* Monograph No. 87 Columbus, Ohio: Bureau of Business Research, The Ohio State University.

Lieberman, Myron. *Teaching as a profession.* Englewood Cliffs, N.J.: Prentice-Hall, 1956.

MacKay, David Allister. An Empirical study of bureaucratic dimensions and their relation to other characteristics of school organizations. Unpublished doctoral dissertation. Edmonton: Department of Educational Administration, University of Alberta Printing Department, September, 1964.

National Education Association. Time devoted to school duties. *Research Bulletin,* 1963, **40,** 83.

Rushing William A. Organizational rules and surveillance: Propositions in comparative organizational analysis." *Administrative Science Quarterly,* March, 1966, **10,** 423–443.

Scott, Richard W. Professionals in bureaucracies—Areas of conflict. In Howard L. Vollmer and Donald L. Mills (Eds.). *Professionalization. Op. cit.* Pp. 265–275.

Terrien, F. C., and Mills, D. C. The effect of changing size upon the internal structure of an organization. *American Sociological Review,* 1955, **20,** 11.

Triandis, Harry C. Notes on the design of organizations. *In Approaches to Organizational Design* James D. Thompson (Ed.). Pittsburgh: University of Pittsburgh Press, 1966. Pp. 72–73.

Udy, Stanley W., Jr. Bureaucracy and rationality in Weber's theory. *American Sociological Review,* 1959, **24,** 791–795.

Zald, Mayer N. Power and conflict in correctional institutions. *Administrative Science Quarterly,* June, 1962, **7,** 22–49.

FROM TALKS WITH TEACHERS *on students*

I WAS *raked over the coals for three hours one night. It was quite a harrowing experience. The superintendent as much as told me that I would have to pass my student. I have just been going along since then, and if they make any effort at all, I pass them. I have lost a great deal of my enthusiasm.—a teacher*

I HAVEN'T *agreed with many of his [the principal's] decisions on discipline problems. I guess it is to his advantage as an administrator to discharge these things as effortlessly as possible. It's kind of hopeless. I am responsible for the kids and have been employed as a teacher, and he should have enough confidence in my judgment to go ahead and do as I request. Instead, he puts the kid on one side and then says: "Now, let's hear your side of it," and I'm not on trial. He puts me on the defensive, which I feel is unjustified in front of the kids.—an industrial arts teacher*

WHEN THERE *is such a small number of students, I find myself getting too personally involved with the student's problems, their personal problems, their home life. You begin to know that this student's parents are separated or they are constantly fighting, and you give a little leeway if they are late with an assignment. You think: "Well, they had to rescue an argument. . . ." I have even had students come to me and tell me these things. I don't feel it is any of my business. I am the teacher, but I don't feel I should be involved in their family relationships.—a teacher*

8. The organizational roots of discord

Too many sociological studies of schools are, in fact, studies of the social life of adolescence, and little count is taken of the more or less tacit demands and pressures of the formal organization or school life and work. Floud and Halsey, 1958, p. 186.

The Mr. Sears' of the teaching world are caught up in the web of organizational relations described in the preceding chapter. Whether they can look forward to a tranquil career or are doomed to a discordant one is as much a product of the way their schools are patterned as their personal predispositions. Each teacher is an individual, of course, which we acknowledge as having some bearing on their choice of a particular school and the pattern of conflict unique to it. But sociology is well beyond that debate and the psychological reductionism that it implies. There is ample evidence of "structural effects" on people; in other words, we already know that there are uniformities of conduct that cut across the board and are associated with social positions regardless of who fills them. At least some of these uniformities produced by the structure are conducive to or produce conflict. Our assignment now is to identify in more specific terms the components of school systems responsible for the strains (and the cohesiveness) in them. That is what this chapter is about.

As a point of departure, we shall identify from the literature three dimensions of organizations that promise to provide some clues to the specific sources of conflict and harmony:

1. *Specialization of personnel and functional divisions of labor and resources are sources of conflict* (Thompson, 1961). Undoubtedly, some conflict occurs because certain parts of an organization develop a degree of autonomy from the others; having distinct functions, they develop their own objectives and norms and compete with one another (Katz, 1964). The simultaneous pressures toward departmental autonomy, on the one hand, and official interdependence of departments, on the other, are persistent sources of strain (Gouldner, 1959). The amount of strain, however, varies with the proximity of departments and the relationships between certain key members of each department (Kahn, 1964), and with the consequent need for joint decision making (March and Simon, 1958). White (1961), for example, found that the drive for departmental autonomy was greatest in those areas where the interrelation of tasks was highest; hostility was also highest at these points. One crucial problem stems from the fact that while departments and organizations have little control over outsiders, they are subject to their criticisms (Kahn, 1964).

2. *Hierarchical conflicts result from interest-group struggles over the allocation of rewards—status, prestige, and monetary returns* (Katz, 1964; Thompson, 1960). Subordinates and supervisors are likely to have different problems and hence different self-interests and values. The people in supervisory positions are further subject to tensions due to anomalies inherent in their positions (Kahn, 1964): the "dual" basis of authority—that is, technical competence as opposed to sheer incumbency of office; pressures from superiors for efficiency in contrast to the professional's veneration of technical procedure; and the fact that executives in complex organizations typically are less qualified than their own subordinates to judge the specialists below them (Gouldner, 1959).

3. *Latent roles of the labor force based on differences in the social backgrounds of an organization's members contribute to conflict* (Thompson, 1960; Becker and Geer, 1960). Because people bring their perspectives, values, and problems to the job, conflicts between the generations, between new and old organizational elites, between males and females, and between "locals" and "cosmopolitans" all converge within organizations (Gouldner, 1959). These background influences also create differences in the loyalty of employees to the organization, to lay audiences, and to their professions.

These three major dimensions can be further broken down into several elementary properties:

1. A set of official positions and their relationships
2. Structural subdivisions and linkages between them
3. Participation of subordinates in the authority system
4. Standards of work and work procedures
5. Professional-employee and bureaucratic-employee principles or organizations
6. Interpersonal structures—especially informal patterns of interaction and collective activities of employees
7. Latent roles of the membership
8. Environmental support

The first four characteristics are part of the official division of labor and internal operating procedures, the second is divisive, and the fourth is integrative. The fifth characteristic refers to competing principles of organization, insofar as they are reflected in the role conceptions of the membership; and the sixth refers to the informal interpersonal system which mediates potential conflict. The last two determine the organization's relationship to the outside society.

Any or all of these eight properties could be associated with conflict. The relationship with conflict takes any one of three major forms (cf. Gamson, 1966):

1. Conduciveness, which refers to variables which permit or encourage conflict (such as the opportunity of a group to participate in the political structure and group solidarity)
2. Strain, which refers to the extent of discontent generated by structural characteristics, and is often created by shifts in the control structure
3. Integration, which refers to structural characteristics that prevent or inhibit conflict, such as overlapping organizational membership, interpersonal relations, and social backgrounds

In particular, it can be expected that strain and conduciveness increase with

(a) Status striving and maintenance of status
(b) The complexity of a structure
(c) Heterogeneity and instability of the membership
(d) Scarcity of resources
(e) Participation of the membership in the official and informal systems of interaction
(f) Inconsistencies between regulating standards and procedures
(g) The number of decisions to be made

The hypotheses we shall advance are necessarily just contrived scaffolding, but, hopefully, they will provide the basis for a more secure foundation as they are successively refined or discarded. Also, the tests are necessarily warped because it has not been possible to take fully into account systemic, regional, or national tensions known to be independently responsible for much internal tension. Finally, the ability to generalize from the data is further restricted by the small sample size, crude measures, and the limits on the number of controls that could be taken into account; unfortunately, these deficiencies characterize the social sciences. However, within these constraints and using several controls, the hypotheses were tested with as much detail as the data would tolerate.

OVERVIEW OF THE FINDINGS

There is ample evidence that conflict is associated with organizational characteristics and with a person's position with respect to those characteristics; in fact, while it is conjecture beyond the evidence, it seems that some forms of organization evolve in response to conflict and that conflict is in turn produced by certain patterns of organization.

Given the apparently growing desire among teachers for more authority, in conjunction with their persistent pattern of subordination to administrators, it is not surprising that authority problems are the most frequent sources of tension and that authority incidents between teachers and administrators constitute the single most frequent type of problem reported by teachers (over one in every four incidents). On the other hand, there is also competition among teachers for a favorable share of resources and rewards; incidents within the peer group more characteristically concern schedule and distribution problems. With the exception of the fact that impersonal competition is more characteristic of peer-group problems than of problems between echelons, the forms of conflict show no other systematic differences.

When the subject matter areas were analyzed separately, it was found that as the prestige of an area increases, its professional orientation increases while its employee orientation declines; reverse patterns tend to exist in the more autonomous areas. There is some tendency for tension within a departmental area to increase with its prestige level, but tension among teachers is more directly related to inconsistencies between their department's prestige and its autonomy. Conflict rates do not appear to be systematically related to the orientation of a department, though they increase directly with its professional behavior index.

The contention that structural arrangements can be sources of tension is supported (though not demonstrated) in a connection found between organizational complexity and conflict. The frequency of several types of conflict increases with a school's size, number of authority levels, number of departments, experimental programs, extracurricular programs, overlapping authority, and total organizational complexity. Also, certain types of disagreements and disputes are associated with specialization. Authority structures, in particular, appear to be less stable in larger, more hierarchical schools. But many of these findings are complicated by relationships with other structural variables, including the level of bureaucratization and professionalization of particular schools.

The way a structure is organized also can either restrict or open the necessary opportunities for those disposed to engage in conflict. For example, the more authority a faculty exercises over routine decisions, the more occasions it has for becoming involved in disputes and so the higher its conflict rates. But probably precisely because they have some authority, there is less need for these faculty members to use the more severe forms of conflict; hence the number of major incidents in the school diminishes with faculty authority even as the rate of other forms of dispute increases. The correlation with centralization over policy questions is lower, although in the more bureaucratic schools there is a more pronounced negative relationship with certain measures of conflict.

The apparent role of various control mechanisms in conflict situations is somewhat puzzling. Controls are designed to minimize conflict, but for that very reason they are likely to be instituted in the most tension-ridden situations and probably provoke resistance; therefore control measures are associated with conflict. Far from suppressing conflict, standardization and rules (though not necessarily close supervision) are positively associated with several indices of conflict. The relationship between increases of standardization and tension is especially high in the more professionally oriented schools and in schools having initially low levels of standardization. Probably, standardization is both partially responsible for conflict and a response to existing conflict. No matter how standardized an organization becomes, when its tasks are not equally routinized, when some of its members are specialists, and when subordinates are self-consciously professionalizing, it is unlikely that all activity can be closely controlled.

We expected, too, that conflict would be associated with the general social climate, and we found that informal interaction, in particular, seems to provide the occasions for conflict. This is especially true of social relations outside of school hours, but to a limited extent it is true of lunching together during school hours as well. In the latter case the relationship holds among the less professionally oriented and older faculties (while interaction over lunch hour actually seems to restrain conflict among the younger and more professional faculties). However, formal employee associations do not seem to aggravate conflict in the way that informal relationships often do. On the contrary, militancy increases with the proportion of faculty members who fail to join the professional associations.

We also expected, and found, that conflict increases with the instability of an organization, as reflected in the heterogeneity of its membership and rates of turnover. Certain types of conflict increase with heterogeneity in the backgrounds of a faculty and the number of staff members added in a given period, and decline with the average tenure of faculty members. In addition, it is also evident that the principal's background plays a vital part in setting the pattern of conflict. But while we expected that schools in which principals were appointed from the outside would have more problems and dissatisfaction than where insiders were appointed, the latter appear to have the higher rates of conflict. The appointment of outsiders is undoubtedly associated with some unidentified factors, possibly consensus with teachers on their respective roles.

It is significant that conflict does not have perceptible detrimental effects on either a faculty's job satisfaction or learning outcomes. On the contrary, the morale of a faculty, as reflected in its job satisfaction, improves as conflicts of most types increase; and there is no evidence that conflict is detrimental to either the student dropout rate or to the proportion of graduates going on to college.

Finally, an inspection of the three most discordant and the three most tranquil schools in the sample showed that the more discordant ones have fewer members active in a professional organization, higher average professional orientations, higher levels of professionalism, and lower employee orientations; also, the members of such organizations are more sociable and express more job satisfaction, though they are more negative toward their principals. The discordant schools, furthermore, are larger and more bureaucratic, more decentralized in routine decision making, and more heterogeneous, with higher rates of staff turnover and expansion. The discordant organizations also place more emphasis on character training and critical thinking, and more of their graduates have gone on to college.

Tranquil schools have older faculties who have been in the system longer and who are more client oriented; they exhibit more employee-type behavior and more of their members have, simultaneously, low-professional and high-employee orientations. The members of such organizations are more satisfied with their teaching careers (as opposed to their specific jobs); they also are more positive toward their principal and speak with him more frequently. These organizations are more complex but more closely supervised and place greater emphasis on rules; and they have higher total incomes. They also place more emphasis on subject matter and vocational training.

Now let us examine the data on which these conclusions are based.

OFFICIAL POSITION AND CONFLICT

Conflict in schools in some measure is likely to be a product of normal status striving and status maintenance. Members holding different positions are likely to have divergent perspectives and interests; and, therefore, the pattern and intensity of conflict will be influenced by the relationship of the positions to one another, the specificity and clarity of roles, the interdependence of functions, the salience and inconsistency of role conceptions.

The concept "status," as used here, includes two elements: the notion of self-direction, and a favorable share of resources and rewards. Incidents involving each of these elements can, in turn, take the form of either overt dispute or impersonal competition. The parties involved may be either of the same official rank or of a different rank. These six categories were used to structure a set of hypotheses.

In general, it was expected that issues between people of different

The organizational roots of discord

ranks would take the overt form of group resistance against administrators because it is their authority that most directly infringes on the teacher's self-direction. The issues are likely to involve teachers' control over the classroom and their authority within the school. This thesis is spelled out more specifically in hypothesis form below.

Table 8–1 summarizes the rates of various types of conflicts reported for the sample as a whole. In 638 interviews 2,099 incidents were reported, a ratio of 3.3 incidents per interview.[1] Thirty-seven percent of those, however, involve impersonal complaints or complaints against specific persons, neither of which entails further overt action on the part of the participants. (See Table 8–1c.) Half of the remaining 1,322 incidents (or one third of total) involve open discussions, one third of which include three or more parties; of the incidents that do not involve complaints, 19 percent (or 12 percent of the original total) include one or more heated discussions and 10 percent constitute major incidents. Can any trends be detected in these incidents?

We do not have comparative information for other occupations, but in view of the apparently growing desire among teachers for more self-direction, it was expected that

Hypothesis 1: Authority issues will be the single most frequent type of problem.

The largest single category of conflict (44 percent) involves authority problems (as described in Chapter 4). (See Table 8–1b.) About one third involve complaints, two such conflicts being reported by each three persons interviewed. By comparison, schedule and distribution problems are less prevalent, but they still account for one fifth of the total. Conflicts involving values, structural enforcement and change, and the distribution of other rewards, by comparison, each accounts for 5 to 7 percent of the total.

Also because teachers are subordinate to administrative officials, especially in view of apparently growing solidarity among teachers, it was expected that

Hypothesis 2: Incidents between teachers and administrators will occur more frequently than incidents among teachers themselves.

It is significant that nearly half of all the conflicts are between teachers and members of the administration (20 percent of these are confined to complaints). (See Table 8–1a.) Eighteen percent of the teacher-administrator conflicts (9 percent of the total) specifically include persons in areas of guidance.

Conflict among teachers is by comparison less frequent.[2] One third of

Table 8-1. Percentage of conflicts as classified by parties involved, intensity of incident, and nature of problem

A. Role-Partners Involved in Incidents[a]

Miscellaneous conflicts	1.2
Teacher and administrator vs. public	7.5
Teacher-Student	2.6
Administrator-Administrator	3.5
Teacher vs. extracurricular teacher	9.6
Academic teacher vs. vocational teacher	24.2
Teacher-Teacher total	33.0
Teacher-Guidance	8.97
Teacher-Staff	.91
Teacher-Line administrator	37.49
Teacher-Administration total	47.1
No data	4.3
Total	100.0

B. Nature of Incidents

Philosophy	.9
Values	6.7
Resources	4.1
School-Community	3.5
Valence-Sentiment	3.6
Communication and socialization	4.6
Structural enforcement and change	6.7
Scheduling and distribution	17.6
Authority	44.3
Distribution of other rewards	6.7
No data	2.9
Total	100.0

C. Intensity of Incidents

Impersonal complaints	11.59
Personal complaints	24.75
Disputes	20.59
Disputes involving 3 or more parties	10.11
One or more heated discussions	10.66
Major incidents	7.03
Impersonal competition	12.31
No data	2.96

[a] All percentages refer to the total number of conflicts.

The organizational roots of discord

all the incidents reported involve teachers in conflict among themselves; one fourth of these are complaints. Over one fourth of the incidents among teachers involve those teachers of extracurricular activities.

Implied in the first two hypotheses is a third:

Hypothesis 3: Authority incidents between teachers and administrators will constitute the single most frequent type of problem.

Half of the teacher-administrator conflicts, or over one out of four of all incidents reported (29 percent), involve authority problems—the largest single category of conflict in the sample (not reported in the tables); 16 percent of these conflicts involve heated discussions or major incidents. By comparison, only 15 percent of all incidents concern authority issues limited to the teachers themselves, a substantial number of which involve academic teachers against those in vocational-education programs, while conflict between teachers and guidance counselors is almost equally divided between authority and distribution problems; among teachers of extracurricular activities, distribution problems occur at twice the rate of authority problems.

If authority issues are vital to the interests of teaching as a profession, it could be expected that conflicts involving authority will provoke more resolute involvement on the part of participants. And so:

Hypothesis 4: A disproportionately larger number of authority incidents, in comparison to other types of conflict, will take the form of major incidents and heated discussions.

There is little support for this hypothesis. The proportion of authority incidents of the intensity of heated discussion and major incidents (21 percent) is only slightly higher than the total sample proportion (19 percent); instead, disproportionately more value conflicts take the more intense forms (26 percent). Similarly, even though nearly half of the major incidents and heated discussions involve authority issues, nearly half of all conflicts in the sample involve authority issues.

Scheduling and the distribution of scarce resources generally involve competition between two parties for the favor of a third who controls the resources. Therefore, direct confrontations between the parties themselves do not seem either necessary or very likely when those types of problems arise. It was expected that

Hypothesis 5: A disproportionately larger number of schedule and distribution problems (than other types of problems) will (a) take the form of impersonal competition; and (b) involve peers among themselves rather than with administrators.

The first part of this hypothesis is unsubstantiated. In fact, compared to distribution problems, a slightly larger share of authority problems take the form of impersonal competition (27 vs. 22 percent). However, impersonal competition occurs more frequently among teachers than between teachers and administrators; 24 percent of all incidents among teachers take this form compared with only 7 percent of the incidents between teachers and administrators.

The second part of the hypothesis is supported. Scheduling and distribution problems are more characteristic of peers than of conflict between teachers and administrators. (The difference is 21 vs. 12 percent when problems involving distribution of rewards are omitted; it is 25 vs. 16 percent when distribution of rewards is included.)

Finally, it was reasoned that open conflict between ranks challenges the entire authority structure and for this reason will be suppressed; consequently, this type of conflict is less likely to be vehement than incidents among the peer group.

Hypothesis 6: Disproportionately fewer incidents between teachers and administrators will involve heated discussions or major incidents than those incidents which occur among teachers themselves.

This hypothesis does not have much support, however. The proportion of teachers who become involved in heated discussions (14 percent) is only 4 percent higher than for teacher-administrator incidents, and it is 4 percent below the sample average; nearly identical proportions of teacher-teacher and teacher-administrator conflicts involve major incidents. The fact that over 10 percent of the latter type of conflicts involve major incidents seems to indicate a certain degree of instability in the authority structure of public schools, but this may not be abnormally high for complex organizations.

Departmental Position

Teachers identified with different disciplines and programs develop special interests, compete for limited resources, and cope with unique problems. As Clark points out in another context (1966, p. 285): "The value systems of the faculty particularly cluster around the individual disciplines and hence at one level of analysis there are as many value systems as there are departments."

Therefore, we hypothesized that

Hypothesis 7: The departments will have systematically different orientations and conflict rates.

The organizational roots of discord 253

We have divided teachers in the sample on the basis of the course area in which they normally teach. For convenience, these groupings will be referred to as departments, although they are not necessarily officially such in all schools. Included are nine types of academic departments, vocational education, counselors and administrators, and a miscellaneous category comprised of driver education, study-hall and corridor monitors, and other less-academic teaching functions.

Status orientations

Our findings correspond to those of Colombotos (1962), who found that academic teachers are more professional than nonacademic ones; because there was apparently little or no difference in the level of professionalism of academic and nonacademic female and male teachers in his sample at the time that they entered teaching, he concluded that their orientations must have been shaped by the academic positions rather than by their prior background experiences.

Generally speaking, we too have found that persons in the more academic departments are more professionally oriented and less employee oriented than those who perform less academic functions. Although the individual comparisons are not necessarily statistically different, it is instructive to look at the ranks of departments on the status orientation. (See Table 8–2.)

Teachers of social science have the highest professional orientation in the sample ($\bar{X} = 59.1$) and the lowest employee orientations ($\bar{X} = 82.9$). Nearly one third of the social-science teachers are simultaneously more professionally and less employee oriented. The English, science, mathematics, and art-music-drama departments exhibit a similar pattern; while teachers of home economics, vocations, and the miscellaneous category rank low on this particular style of role organization. Staff members classified as having miscellaneous duties, or as being in vocational education, administration, or athletics, have the reverse pattern—that is, simultaneously low professional and high employee conceptions. One third or more of the persons in administration, vocational education (who are more employee oriented than even the administrators), and athletics simultaneously hold low professional and high employee orientations. Because professionals seem to be distributed unequally among different departments, the support given a department indirectly determines the amount of support that will be given to the professional role. This means that in order to achieve excellence in some departments it may be necessary to pay the price of higher professionalism.

With few exceptions, client orientation tends to be uniformly high in all departments; though teachers in the area of humanities and English

Table 8-2. Ranks of (mean) status orientations of 13 types of departments

Department	Ranks			
	Professional Orientation	Client Orientation	Employee Orientation	High-Professional Low-Employee Orientation
Social science	1	5	13	1
English	2	1	10	4
Science	3	6	9	2
Math	4	8	11	5
Art, music, drama	5	4	8	6
Home economics	6	3	4	12
Administration	7	13	3	9
Language and humanities	8	2	7	7
Counselors	9	9	12	3
Business	10	7	5	8
Athletics	11	10	6	10
Vocational	12	11	2	11
Miscellaneous	13	12	1	13

outrank social-science teachers. It is perhaps ironic that the administration, many of whom still think of themselves as "instructional leaders," and to whom teachers often look for guidance in educational leadership, rank the lowest of the 13 groups on client orientation. Because they are the furthest removed from students, their reluctance to define problems from the students' point of view is understandable; but the implications are provocative in view of their power over the organization.

In general, it appears that disciplines that have a more practical bent or are more strongly oriented toward the general public, such as athletics and home economics and school administration, are less professionally oriented, while the more academic departments, such as English and social science, are more professionally oriented.

Prestige[3]

In every school it is agreed that English is, by far, the "most important" course in the curriculum, which we shall take as an indication of its prestige. The lowest ranking courses are art-music-drama and some in the miscellaneous category. Courses in both the language-humanities and home economics areas rank lower than athletics. A department's prestige shows signs of declining with its employee orientation ($t = -.31$), although the correlation is not statistically significant. It does increase significantly with the level of professional orientation in the department ($t = .41$), but not with its client orientation.[4] This suggests that the more prestigious departments are more oriented to knowledge, authority, and/or colleagues.

Autonomy

Using the average number of times that teachers in each department have consulted the administration about a problem as an index of their autonomy, teachers in the miscellaneous and vocational categories and those in language and humanities appear to be the most autonomous (that is, they consult least). Consultation increases significantly with professional orientation ($t = .44$) and decreases with its employee orientation ($t = -.49$ for rate of consultation). Perhaps professionally oriented faculties need more control; perhaps they initiate more consultation with the administration; or perhaps the nature of their work (which as just indicated, is functionally very important) requires more consultation.

Conflict rates

Administrators and counselors have the highest rates of conflict of the 13 categories, no matter which measure of conflict is considered. Teachers of social science also rank relatively high on total tension, tension between teachers and the principal, heated discussions, and incidents over authority. Athletics and art-music-drama teachers also have relatively high rates of disputes, of incidents involving scheduling, and of conflict involving authority issues; the scheduling problems of these two departments probably reflect the anomalies of coordinating extracurricular activities with the academic program. Teachers in the vocational and miscellaneous areas have low rates of conflict. Also, home-economics teachers have low total tension and fewer authority conflicts, while members of the language-humanities departments have low dispute ratios and fewer conflicts over authority.

On several of the measures of conflict, a department's conflict rate declines with its client orientation, but neither the professional nor employee orientation of a department appears to have the same degree of connection with departmental conflict that the total faculty orientation of a school has with school-wide conflict.[5] Indeed, there are more definite positive correlations between autonomy (rates of consultation) and conflict rates. In general, the more a department consults with the administration, the higher its rate of conflict. The correlations are particularly high with the dispute ratio ($t = .62$) and conflicts involving authority ($t = .56$). Perhaps conflict is a function of the opportunity created by the sheer rate of contact between teachers and administrators; but perhaps too teachers consult more frequently when there is more disagreement.

Most of the conflict rates for departments are positively correlated with the differences between their rankings on prestige and autonomy. This measure correlates especially well with the dispute ratio and major incident ratio ($t = .55$ and $t = .53$).[6] Inconsistencies among status dimensions, signifying discrepant amounts of deference, privilege, and differences in expectations, seem to be especially important sources of tension and dissatisfaction.

STRUCTURAL SUBDIVISIONS AND LINKAGES

The character of an organization is strongly affected by the complexity of its operation. Complexity, in turn, refers to the delicate combinations of separate but interdependent subunits that make up an organization's fabric. This interdependence forms a "linkage system," which is simply a graphic way of speaking about the points of connection between units. Insofar as cooperation and autonomy among the subunits must be reconciled at these points, it can be expected that the problems of defining boundaries and responsibilities typically arise at the points of linkage. An organization's stability is likely to be adversely affected by the number of linkages because the more interrelations that must be maintained, the greater is the likelihood that it will break down at some point (Argyris, 1954).

For our purposes, we shall assume that complexity reflects the number of linkages and is a source of strain because of the linkage problems. Taking into consideration the implications of these general propositions, we propose

Hypothesis 8: Separate objectives, misunderstandings, and, hence, conflict will increase with the number of separate units in an organization.

Four crude indicators of complexity were used: organizational size, number of authority levels, number of subparts, and degree of specialization. Though they do not directly appraise the linkage system, they provide an estimate which is useful for the reasons indicated above.[7]

Size

In the previous chapter it was shown that school size is empirically associated with the amount of subdivision (that is, both organizational complexity and the number of levels of authority), and related characteristics like specialization, which in themselves are likely sources of tension.[8] Therefore, we expected, and found, that the number of teachers in a school is significantly associated with measures of organizational tension and conflict derived from interviews and questionnaires; seven of ten measures are statistically significant.[9] (See Table 8-3.)

It is noteworthy that authority structures appear to grow less stable in the larger schools; both the number of conflicts reported per interview involving authority ($t = .26$) and the number of conflicts between teachers and administrators increase with the size of school ($t = .41$), while conflicts among teachers do not ($t = .07$).

Controlling for the emphasis that schools place on rules does not appreciably alter these relationships. However, the relationship between organizational size and conflict is conditioned by the level of bureaucratization. Also, the correlations with the measures of both total tension and severe disagreement are reduced when controlling for the number of staff additions made during the past five years. This latter fact is enough to caution us that conflict is not necessarily produced by size, but rather is very much influenced by factors which are in themselves associated with size.

Number of Levels of Authority

The number of administrative echelons is a critical ingredient of organizational complexity. Not only is adequate communication between echelons normally difficult to achieve in hierarchical organizations, but also the fact that each echelon presses on its incumbents distinct role conceptions, problems, objectives, and vested interests further aggravates linkage problems; persons in different echelons are not likely to identify closely with one another's problems (Smith and Ari, 1964; Thompson, 1961). There is a possibility, too, that more echelons get added in the process of mediating conflicts that arise at lower levels of the organization. As Homans explains: (1961, p. 295):

When a dispute arises between equals, which they cannot negotiate, they will refer it to someone higher in status than they. To submit it to someone of equal status is to admit that he in fact is not of equal status. Moreover, it is necessary for the arbitrator to actually be of higher status in order to exert sufficient influence to resolve the conflict.

Table 8-3. Rank-order correlations between organizational size, complexity, number of levels of authority, and specialization and indices of organizational tension and conflict (Taus)

Indices of Organizational Tension and Conflict	No. of Teachers in School ($N = 28$)	No. of Levels of Authority ($N = 21$)	Organizational Complexity ($N = 28$)	Lack of Specialization: Proportion of Faculty Who Have Taught Courses in Which They Did Not	
				Major ($N = 28$)	Major/Minor ($N = 28$)
Avg. total tension bet. all roles (reported by faculty members)	.22[a]	.30[a]	.19	.08	−.07
Rates of disagreement					
Total no. of disagreements per faculty member	.16	.18	.16	.02	−.23[a]
No. of severe disagreements per faculty member	.35[b]	.37[b]	.32[b]	−.18	−.12
No. of incidents reported per interview					
Total no. of all types of incidents (gross incident ratio)[c]	.38[b]	.48[b]	.33[b]	−.03	−.04
Disputes	.27[b]	.32[b]	.27[a]	.01	−.24[a]
Heated discussions	.37[b]	.39[a]	.33[a]	−.06	−.12
Major incidents	.04	.18	.10	−.22[a]	.05
No. of incidents per interview involving the following role partners					
Teacher(s) vs. Administrator(s)	.41[b]	.40[b]	.23[a]	−.05	−.08
Teacher(s) vs. Teacher(s)	.07	.08	.02	−.04	−.10
No. of incidents involving authority problems (reported per interview)	.26[a]	.26[a]	.13	.07	−.03

[a] Rank-order correlation significant at $p \leq .05$.
[b] Rank-order correlation significant at $p \leq .01$.
[c] Complaints are not included in "Total no. of incidents reported."

The data show that the number of the levels of authority is positively correlated with seven of the ten measures of organizational tension and conflict.[10] (See Table 8–3.) For example, ten of the twelve systems having six to seven levels of authority report high rates of severe disagreement, in comparison to only one of seven with three or fewer levels of authority (X^2, $p = .05$). As in the larger schools, the authority structure is less stable in these more hierarchical organizations; that is, the number of authority problems (per interview) and conflicts between teachers and administrators increase with the number of authority levels ($t = .26$ and $t = .40$). Again, the solidarity among teachers is not affected.

These relationships, however, are inflated because hierarchy and conflict measures are associated with still other variables. Hence (except for correlations with the total incident ratio and heated discussions between teachers and administrators), the correlations drop below statistical significance when either school size or complexity is controlled (not shown in tables). This means that centralization, as size, represents a convergence of other factors. More important (with the exception of the severe disagreement rate), it is only in the less bureaucratized schools where the hierarchy is associated with conflict.[11] In other words, it appears that starting an organization on the path toward bureaucratization is associated with more tension than further increments of bureaucratization in an organization already bureaucratized.

Organizational Complexity

The over-all complexity of an organization is a product of its "horizontal" division of labor as well as the hierarchical structure. In fact, one writer maintains that the need to cooperate among parallel subgroups having different functions is largely responsible for organizational conflict (Landsberger, 1961). People working in interdependent but separate units develop distinctive role conceptions and objectives and compete for resources and rewards (Wilson, 1966). We shall examine some of these components before considering one over-all index of complexity.

Departmentalization

Using as an index of departmentalization the number of officially recognized department heads in a school, this variable appears to be associated with the number of moderate and severe disagreements among the faculty (X^2, $p \leq .01$). Seven of the eight schools with more than six departments report more than four moderate disagreements per person in comparison to only three of 15 schools without department heads; a similar pattern exists for severe disagreements.

Experimental programs

It is, perhaps, to be expected that attempts to experiment with new programs will create linkage problems and be sources of disruption and tension, and such appears to be the case. Whereas only two of nine experimenting schools report low rates of severe disagreement (that is, less than .11 per individual), 12 of 19 schools not experimenting have low rates (X^2 significant at $p \leq .05$). There is also a slight tendency for schools using team teaching to report higher average rates of disagreement than schools not using this practice (70 percent compared to 40 percent), but the chi square is not statistically significant for a sample of this size.

Number of curricular programs

When there is a variety of separate academic and vocational programs, distinct goals and other linkage problems are likely to develop. Five of the six schools without separate programs report low rates of total disagreement, whereas 13 of the 22 schools with one or more programs have above average rates of disagreement—that is, two to seven disagreements per teacher ($X^2, p \leq .05$).

Functional overlap

Complex and overlapping supervisory practices also can be sources of conflict. Henry (1954) proposes that the amount of tension between departments will be directly proportional to their power and to the degree of functional overlap between them. Our data indicate that number and consistency of commands received from supervisors are associated with the incident rate between teachers and administrators ($t = .32$) and the rate of incidents involving authority issues ($t = .27$).[12] No relationship, however, was found between organizational complexity and inconsistency of instructions.

Total organizational complexity

The evidence concerning each of these components considered separately suggests that on the over-all index of complexity it will show a definitive relationship. Several of the indices of organizational conflict increase significantly with scores on the organizational-complexity scale. (See Table 8–3.) Four measures of conflict (rates of severe disagreement, total incident ratio, ratio of disputes, heated discussion ratio, and ratio of conflicts between teachers and administrators) are positively associated with organizational complexity.

When the professional climate is controlled, the relation of complexity to teacher-administrator conflict, in particular, increases substantially. Also, because organizational complexity is associated with the size of schools, controlling for size lowers the correlations. Complexity per se is probably only one of several factors accounting for the prevalence of conflict in complex situations.

It is plausible that problems associated with a complex situation could be offset by experience (March and Simon, 1958). For this reason, the mean ages of the faculties were controlled, on the assumption that older faculties have had a longer period in which to work out their problems. However, the relationships just discussed hold up for all age levels, suggesting that experience in itself does not compensate for the problems associated with complexity.

Specialization

Specialization has the effect of aggravating linkage problems by delineating group boundaries and accentuating the barriers between colleagues. The distinctive competence of specialists makes them particularly visible as targets for hostility (Gamson, 1966), and they are more likely than nonspecialists to develop vested interests and monopolistic claims over certain spheres of work, which they stand ready to defend from encroachment. However, when people are assigned to the various tasks indiscriminately and without regard for their special training, these invidious distinctions become blurred and the identifications weakened. Therefore, it was expected that specialization would be positively associated with the incidence of conflict.

Although most of the correlations between conflict and specialization are in the expected direction, only a few are statistically significant. (See Table 8–3.) The proportion of a faculty assigned to courses in which they have neither majored nor minored is inversely associated with both the total rate of disagreement ($t = -.23$) and with the ratio of disputes ($t = -.24$).[13] Also, the number of major incidents reported per interview declines with the proportion of teachers assigned to courses outside of their majors ($t = -.22$). Stated the other way, certain types of conflicts seem to be less characteristic of less specialized faculties.

These conclusions are sustained after school size has been controlled. But the relationship of specialization to certain types of conflict becomes more accentuated in the more bureaucratic and in the more professional schools, whereas the relationship between specialization and major incidents holds only in less professional and in less bureaucratic schools

($t = -.38$ and $t = -.30$, respectively), but not in their counterparts. In other words, specialization seems to be especially disruptive in bureaucratized, professional schools, but it is in settings where neither type of control dominates that conflict moves out of bounds as specialization increases.

But specialization appears to be unrelated to the volume of conflict either specifically involving teachers or between teachers and administrators, and it does not appear to be associated with authority problems. Specialization, in short, shows some relationships with the volume of conflict per se, but if it has a bearing on the type of issues of parties involved, it is not readily discernible.

PARTICIPATION IN THE AUTHORITY SYSTEM

Coleman (1957) has argued that closing the channels of legitimate political expression encourages conflict because people cannot exercise influence by peaceful means. However, Gamson (1966) challenges the assumption that discontent "accumulates in reservoirs," maintaining that open channels increase the likelihood that existing tension will be expressed, and if strain does exist, it will not be eradicated simply by giving employees more opportunity to participate. According to this latter version, the decision-making apparatus provides a channel to communicate existing grievances, and to the extent that employees participate in decision making, they have the opportunity to express irritations that otherwise might have remained latent. Regardless of where the responsibility for decisions resides, using this interpretation it would seem likely that that responsibility will be accompanied by conflict. Following this line of reasoning, insofar as day-to-day decisions are decentralized, the faculty will have both more reason and more opportunity to disagree among themselves. Hence, the more frequently subordinates participate in decision making, the greater the number of occasions that arise for disagreement. Conversely, when employees cannot influence decisions, they will have less to fight about among themselves, but will more easily develop group solidarity and antagonism against the administration.

Hypothesis 9: Organizational tension and conflict are positively associated with the extent to which subordinates participate in the authority system.

In examining this proposition, however, we need to take into account the differences between routine and professional and nonprofessional policy decisions.

Table 8-4. Rank-order correlations between participation in the authority system and indices of organizational tension and conflict

Indices of Organizational Tension and Conflict	Routine Decision-Making Authority ($N = 28$)		Professional Decision-Making Policy Index ($N = 28$)		Nonprofessional Decision-Making Policy Index ($N = 28$)	
	Taus	Partials	Taus	Partials	Taus	Partials
Avg. total tension bet. all roles (reported by faculty members)	.14	.01	.11		.01	
Rates of disagreement						
Total no. of disagreements per faculty member	.17	.09	.13		−.18	−.19[a]
No. of severe disagreements per faculty member	.17	.08	.00		−.25*	−.27[a],*
No. of incidents reported per interview						
Total no. of all types of incidents (gross incident ratio)‡	.17	.19[b]	−.06	−.11[b]	−.04	−.02[b]
Disputes	.39†	.41[b]	.08	.05[b]	−.13	−.11[b]
Heated discussion	.03	.04[b]	−.05	.00[b]	.08	.12[b]
Major incidents	−.38†	−.38[b]	−.03	−.03[b]	.13	.13[b]
No. of incidents per interview involving the following role patterns						
Teacher(s) vs. administrator(s)	.07	.08[b]	.14	.10[b]	.04	.08[b]
Teacher(s) vs. teacher(s)	.12	.12[b]	−.11	−.11[b]	−.04	.05[b]
No. of incidents involving authority problems (reported per interview)	.05	.05[b]	.04	.01[b]	.04	.06[b]

*Rank-order correlation significant at $p \leqslant .05$.
†Rank-order correlation significant at $p \leqslant .01$.
‡Complaints are not included in the "Total no. of incidents reported."
Key:
[a]Socialize very frequently with others on faculty.
[b]School size.
[c]Professional orientation.

Routine Decision Making

The authority of subordinates to make routine decisions gives them some occasion to dispute with administrators, and larger spheres of discretion leave more room for disagreement among themselves. Routine decision-making authority is, accordingly, positively associated with the ratio of disputes ($t = .39$), although it is inversely associated with the major incident ratio ($t = -.38$). (See Table 8-4.) Upon the introduction of other controls, it appears that both of these correlations are slightly more characteristic of less professional and less bureaucratic schools than of their counterparts.[14]

This pattern suggests that the contentions of Gamson and Coleman both may be correct in certain respects. On the one hand, the authority to make routine decisions offers subordinates more opportunity to express existing disagreement and provides more occasions for disputes to arise. But on the other hand, the very opportunity of teachers to participate in the decision-making process could prevent minor aggravations from accumulating and developing into major incidents.

Centralization of Policy Decisions

If the participation of employees in routine decisions is positively associated with organizational conflict, then it would seem reasonable to expect that the opposite characteristic—that is, the centralization of key policy decisions—will be inversely associated with conflict rates. However, although some of the correlations are in the expected direction, only a negative relationship between the centralization of nonprofessional policy decisions and the rate of severe conflict is statistically significant ($t = -.25$).[15] (See Table 8-4.) (Correlations involving the total rate of disagreement and disputes are in the same direction but they are not statistically significant.) Yet, there does at least seem to be less opportunity, and perhaps less reason, for severe disagreements in more centralized schools. And when the correlations were computed separately for the more and the less bureaucratic schools, there was an even more pronounced negative relationship with the total number of incidents as well as with the disagreement ratio.[16]

REGULATING PROCEDURES

Social organizations are curious. Like living creatures, they contain within themselves the seeds of their own growth and destruction. Ironically, the very characteristics that produce divisiveness provide the stimulus for still other procedures intended to control and regulate the tension. In the long run, then, the extent of change, growth, or decline in an organization depends upon the race between the divisive elements and the control mechanisms. Because the balance between these forces alternates erratically, it is extremely difficult to anticipate whether a particular form of control will be effective. One might perhaps expect that standardization and supervision, which are intended to narrow the discretion of subordinates and clarify situations, will normally help to reduce conflict rates. Kahn (1964), for example, thought that role conflict was highest where rules were not emphasized and where employees were not closely supervised. Yet, there are compelling reasons for the opposite conclusion. A group can fall back on rules to legitimate its position and for the support it needs in a conflict; rules are likely to be resented by some employees; and most important, standardization is likely to be implemented in settings where tension already exists.[17]

Hypothesis 10: Organizational tension and conflict are positively associated with the amount of emphasis on procedures used to regulate organizational conflict.

Three primary regulating procedures will be examined—standardization, emphasis on rules, and close and remote forms of supervision.

Standardization

Far from suppressing conflict, standardization is positively associated with it, especially with conflicts between teachers and administrators over authority issues. As standardization increases, there are significant increases in the total tension within schools ($t = .28$), in rates of severe disagreement ($t = .26$), in the total incident ratio ($t = .31$), and in the dispute ratio ($t = .31$). (See Table 8–5.) Probably what is even more significant, the authority structure is the less stable in schools that are most standardized; authority issues and incidents between teachers and administrators increase with level of standardization ($t = .32$ and $t = .53$).

These associations, especially with incidents between teachers and administrators and the total incident ratio, are especially pronounced in the highly professional schools (compared with low professional schools) and in the less bureaucratic schools (compared with more bureaucratic schools).

Moreover, although conflicts among teachers themselves show no increase in the total sample as a whole, in the 14 more professional schools there is a positive association ($t = .41$), whereas in the less professional

Table 8-5. Rank-order correlations between standardization, emphasis on rules, close supervision, and indices of interaction and indices of organizational tension and conflict

Indices of Organizational Tension and Conflict	Standardization Index (N = 21)	Emphasis on Rules (N = 28)	Close Supervision (N = 28)	Proportion of Faculty Lunching Very Frequently (N = 28)	Proportion of Faculty Seeing Each Other Socially Very Frequently (N = 28)
Avg. total tension bet. all roles (reported by faculty members)	.28*	.10	−.04	.09	.26*
Rates of Disagreement					
Total no. of disagreements per faculty member	.20	.24*	.13	−.03	.15
No. of severe disagreements per faculty member	.26*	.06	.12	.15	.29*
No. of incidents reported per interview					
Total no. of all types of incidents (gross incident ratio)	.31*	.22*	.13	.11	.43†
Disputes	.31*	.21*	.28*	.21*	.21*
Heated discussion	.17	.27*	.02	.38[a],*	.47†
Major incidents	.21	.13	−.14	−.13	.25[b],†
No. of incidents per interview involving the following partners					
Teacher(s) vs. administrator(s)	.53†	.11	.03	.12	.30*
Teacher(s) vs. Teacher(s)	.03	.12	.15	.00	.32†
No. of incidents involving authority problems (reported per interview)	.32*	−.10	−.11	.10	.42†

*Rank-order correlation significant at $p \leq .05$.
†Rank-order correlation significant at $p \leq .01$.

Key:
[a]Size of school.
[b]Professional orientation.

schools the relationship is negative ($t = -.41$). Standardization, then, appears to arrest conflict among subordinates in less professional climates and provoke it in more professional climates. In other words, standardization becomes a source of tension, in situations where it is least compatible with the organizational tradition and with the desire for self-direction—that is, in the less bureaucratic and more professionally oriented schools.

Emphasis on Rules

The rates of total disagreement, the total incident ratio, and ratio of disputes and heated discussions also increase with emphasis on rules ($t = .21-.27$). (See Table 8–5.) These correlations, however, are affected by the number of staff additions (except for heated discussion), tending to drop when that element is controlled. Neither conflict over authority issues nor teacher-administrator conflict, however, are characteristic of schools where there is more emphasis on rules.

As in the case of standardization, the correlation between total disagreement rate and emphasis on rules is found primarily in the more professional ($t = .32$) and less bureaucratic schools ($t = .33$). The correlation between rules and major incidents also approaches statistical significance in the more professional schools ($t = .30$ ns); whereas in the more bureaucratic schools rules are actually accompanied by reductions in authority problems ($t = -.36$). Rules do not appear to be an effective means of controlling conflict in tension-ridden professional schools where controls can interfere with professional autonomy and are likely to be resented for that reason. In the less bureaucratic schools attempts to impose rules probably violate the more informal tradition; also, such schools probably have fewer control measures of other kinds which reinforce rules. It is reasonable that rules can actually stabilize relationships among subordinates in less professional and already bureaucratized schools even while serving as sources of irritation in these other settings.

Teachers in schools where rules are emphasized also report a high degree of tension between themselves and students ($t = .38$). Rules may be invoked in schools where tensions already exist, but it is also possible that rules interfere with the teacher-student relationship by reducing the teachers' flexibility to cope with students. Rules can aggravate the inherent conflict in schools between the tendency of students to request specific treatment on the basis of their personal relationship with teachers, and the pressures on teachers to judge their students impersonally on the basis of their accomplishments without regard to their informal status (Gordon, 1957). Of course, to answer these questions it would be necessary to examine the specific rules involved.

Close Supervision

On the one hand, close supervision may keep channels between employees and supervisors open, helping to prevent the accumulation of unresolved problems. However, it is also true that close supervision is a precarious relationship at best and is quite likely to be especially irritating to professional employees.[18] There is some support for the latter viewpoint, but the relationships with some of the conflict measures, though in the positive direction, are very low; only the number of disputes reported per interview is statistically significant ($t = .28$), and it remains significant after school size has been controlled. (See Table 8-5.)

It is possible that under some conditions close supervision provides an opportunity for subordinates to discuss their problems openly with supervisors; though not statistically significant, the low negative association between close supervision and the ratio of major incidents ($t = -.14$ ns) is revealing from this perspective. But the general conclusion is that the same supervisory practice proven effective in curbing major incidents in less professional and less bureaucratic organizations can fail in the more professional and more bureaucratic ones.

REFERENCE GROUP CLIMATES

The value climate of an organization is revealed in the way its members identify with different reference groups with whom they associate— that is, their clients and colleagues and the administrators. This climate will, in turn, determine the prevalence of conflict with each of these groups. The emphasis teachers in the sample give to various components of the professional and employee role orientations is one way of looking at the value climate.

Hypothesis 11: (a) Authority problems and problems with administrators increase with the priority teachers attach to decision-making authority and knowledge and decrease with their loyalty to the organization and to the administration; (b) problems with colleagues increase with colleague orientation; and (c) conflict with both colleagues and administrators increases with teacher's orientation to clients.[19]

As expected, incidents between teachers and administrators and the number of authority issues both are associated with a faculty's emphasis on knowledge ($t = .22$ in both cases) and its desire for decision-making authority ($t = .25$ and $t = .13$ ns; *not* reported in the tables). Also, incidents arising among the teachers themselves can be explained partly in terms of the strength of their orientation to their colleagues ($t = -.30$); the stronger their commitment to colleagues, the less conflict that takes place among them. However, strong commitment to client welfare apparently does not influence militancy to the same extent that commitment to authority and concern for reputation among colleagues does.[20] The client-orientation measure increases positively with only one of the conflict measures (authority, $t = .23$). In short, the emphasis teachers place on knowledge and their quest for decision-making authority seem to aggravate conflict with administrators, while desire for a favorable reputation among colleagues suppresses peer-group conflict (or solidarity increases in the absence of conflict). These points of reference have more bearing on teacher militancy than commitment to student welfare.

Role Consensus Between Principal and Faculty

It seems likely that the amount of conflict in an organization will be affected by differences between role conceptions of chief administrator and subordinates. Schools were ranked on the basis of the magnitude of difference between each principal's role conception and the average (mean) role conception of his faculty. It was expected that the amount of conflict in a school would tend to increase with the amount of dissention.

There appear to be relationships with conflict measures. The difference between a principal's and a faculty's professional orientation is positively associated with the major incident ratio ($t = .21$) and with the severe disagreement rate ($t = .21$). Also, the difference in employee orientation is positively associated with severe disagreement rate ($t = .25$). These relationships hold after controlling for the principal's professional and employee orientation.

FACILITATING CHANNELS

Regardless of the number of potentially tension-ridden conditions which may exist, overt incidents are unlikely to materialize unless people have the occasion, as well as the desire, to express themselves. Participation in decision making provides one such occasion, but informal channels of communication provide many other occasions. Of course, peer-group solidarity can suppress conflict, too, but if underlying tensions exist, it is more likely that they will materialize when contenders interact with one another (Gamson, 1966).

The general working hypothesis is that

Hypothesis 12: Organizational tension and conflict are positively associated with the rate of informal interaction among a faculty and between a faculty and its administration, and with their participation in employee associations.

Two types of facilitating interaction channels will be considered:

1. Informal interaction patterns among peers
   (a) The proportion of faculty who lunch together
   (b) The proportion of the faculty who see each other socially
2. Employee associations
   (a) The proportion of faculty belonging to a teacher's union
   (b) The proportion of faculty not active in professional associations

Lunching Patterns

There is some support for the proposition that more conflict materializes where teachers are more sociable over lunch, but it is not consistent. Only two of the conflict measures are statistically correlated to the index; the proportion of the faculty who eat together very frequently is statistically associated with the number of disputes reported per interview ($t = .21$), and controlling for the size of the school, the heated discussion ratio also becomes significant. (See Table 8–5.) This latter relationship, however, holds up only in the less professional schools ($t = .47$ vs. $t = -.12$); and the former relationship is more typical of the less professional and of the less bureaucratic schools than of their counterparts.

The meaning of lunching behavior is altered by a faculty's shared experience. It is in the older faculties that frequent lunching most often leads to conflict.[21] Schools were classified by dividing them at the median, both on average age of the faculty and proportion of faculty employed in the school for more than four years. In both cases the correlations between lunching frequency and each measure of conflict (except major incidents) hold only for the older faculties; in younger faculties, most of the conflict indices decline with interaction (again with the exception of major incidents).

Social Occasions

The facilitating effects of interaction can be seen more clearly when the proportion of a faculty who very frequently see one another socially outside of school is used.[22] (See Table 8–5.) That measure is positively associated with nine of the ten conflict indices, with correlations ranging from $t = .21$ in the case of disputes to $t = .47$ in the case of heated discussions. (Though both social interaction and conflict are associated with organizational size, the relationship between them stands up independently of size.)

Membership in Employee Associations

More formal settings can also provide the communication channels that can facilitate the expression of disagreement. While professional associations and teachers unions provide teachers with access to the administration, their willingness to support an association reflects a kind of employee solidarity which can serve as a basis for opposing the administration. At the same time, the existence of competing associations and the reluctance of some employees to join at least one of them can be indicative of conflict among the employees themselves.

Union membership

However, the rank of schools on the proportion of faculty belonging to a union is not associated with most of the conflict measures, except for the ratio of heated discussions reported per interview ($t = .21$), and even this figure diminishes when school size is controlled. While schools in which faculties are predisposed toward unionization are perhaps more prone toward heated discussions, there are fewer, rather than more, open conflicts with the administration ($t = -.21$). Nor is the proportion of union members in a school associated with conflicts over authority.

It should be noted that many of the union members in the study are in the conservative segment of the AFT and located in nonunionized schools. But also, it is quite possible that these primitive forms of unionization act as mechanisms which reduce the need for more overt incidents, especially because administrators, under the threat of impending unionism, may be sensitive to the opinions of the faculty and make necessary concessions in order to forestall more widespread discontent.

Nonmembership in professional associations

Because administrators are permitted to join classroom teachers' professional organizations and probably dominate them in some respects, the refusal of teachers to join these organizations could reflect a belligerent posture toward the administration.[23] In fact, even their colleagues would probably have some difficulty in controlling teachers who are not members of classroom teachers' organizations. Accordingly, both the severe disagreement rate and the ratio of major incidents increase with the proportion of teachers refusing to join professional associations ($t = .25$ and $t = .21$, respectively). More important, the ratio of conflicts between teachers and administrators increases ($t = .27$) as does the rate of authority issues ($t = .21$).

Contrary to the original expectations, then, the formal associations of employees do not facilitate conflict in the same way as informal relationships do. Militancy, in fact, is greater where employees boycott their professional association. Perhaps one reason is that two of the conditions that logically should be present in order for employee associations to facilitate conflict are not simultaneously present in most schools in this sample: (1) exclusion of administrators from membership and (2) an officially recognized right of the organization to represent all of the employees.

VULNERABILITY AND STABILITY

The stability of an organization and its vulnerability to outside influences both depend upon the way it is linked to the external environment. Recruiting practices are critical as points of linkage because they determine what kinds of "latent roles" will become a part of the organization. "People carry culture with them" (Becker and Geer, 1960, p. 305); this includes conflicts in the general culture based on differences in training, age, religion, sex, and ethnic backgrounds. But Becker and Geer point out that if latent culture can influence an organization's procedures, the organizational structure can, in turn, be used to restrict the influence of latent culture. Therefore, one might expect that heterogeneous backgrounds are more likely to be a source of conflict in the less standardized organizations by comparison to those which are more formalized.

We shall look at the latent culture from the standpoint of the heterogeneity in the backgrounds of school teachers and the number of staff additions.

Hypothesis 13: Organizational tension and conflict are positively associated with the diversity of latent values represented in an organization and with the disruption that usually accompanies staff additions.[24]

As expected, heterogeneity is positively associated with at least three measures of conflict: among teachers ($t = .36$); and, when organizational size is controlled, the gross incident ratio ($t_p = .25$) and the dispute ratio ($t_p = .21$). (See Table 8–6.) However, in opposition to the hypothesis, there is also a negative association with the major incident ratio ($t =$

Table 8-6. Rank-order correlations between heterogeneity of personal background and staff additions and indices of organizational tension and conflict (Taus)

Indices of Organziational Tension and Conflict	Hetero-geneity ($N = 28$)	No. of Faculty Hired During 5 Years	Mean Tenure of Faculty	Morale: Satisfaction with	
				Job	Career
Avg. total tension bet. all roles (reported by faculty members)	.03	.34†	−.26*	.39†	.21*
Rates of Disagreement					
Total no. of disagreements per faculty member	−.08	.30*	.06	.29*	.15
No. of severe disagreements per faculty member	.10	.37†	−.40†	.25*	−.10
No. of incidents reported per interview					
Total no. of all types of incidents (gross incident ratio)‡	.18; .25[a],*	.58†	−.24*	.26*	−.01
Disputes	.16; .21[a],*	.41†	−.23*	.03	.14
Heated discussion	.08	.39	−.26*	.15	−.12
Major incidents	−.21	−.13; −.21[a]	.12	.05	−.34†
No. of incidents per interview involving the following role partners:					
Teacher(s) vs. administrator(s)	.03	.47†	−.19	.32†	.03
Teacher(s) vs. teacher(s)	.36†	.09	−.21*	.29*	−.07
No. of incidents involving authority problems (reported per interview)	.14	.31*	−.25*	.44*	−.16

*Rank-order correlation significant at $p \leqslant .05$.
†Rank-order correlation significant at $p \leqslant .01$.
‡Complaints are not included in "Total no. of incidents reported."
Key:
[a]Organization size.

—.21). It is not immediately clear why, but it may be related to the fact that heterogeneity is associated with close supervision and with the proportion of faculty seeing each other socially, both of which tend to be inversely related to the appearance of major incidents.

Staff Additions

Additions of new staff members, even ones with relatively homogeneous backgrounds, in itself is likely to produce tension. This is not only because of the interruptions and the readjustment problems associated with incorporating new members, but also, because the processes of turnover and/or adding new members could itself reflect the existence of other problems. Turnover among the leadership, in particular, seems to be associated with dissatisfaction in organizations (Levenson, 1961; Carlson, 1963).

As expected, all but one or two of the conflict measures (conflict among teachers and the occurrence of major incidents) are associated with the number of staff members added to a school during the preceding five years.[25] (See Table 8–6.) It appears to be even more difficult to integrate new members into the administrative system than into the peer-group system in that peer-group conflict does not increase with the number of staff additions. Both the total incident ratio and heated discussions specifically between teacher and administrators are relatively highly correlated with staff additions ($t = .58$ and $t = .47$) and remain significant after controlling school size. But it should be pointed out that both of these relationships are higher in the less bureaucratic schools than in those that are more bureaucratized ($t = .71$ vs. $t = .13$). Bureaucratization, in other words, can minimize the effects of turnover and expansion, which is, of course, a primary reason for bureaucratizing. So, if bureaucratization creates or aggravates some problems, it minimizes others.

However, the negative association between turnover and major incidents is contrary to the dominant pattern ($t_p = -.21$; controlling for school size). Perhaps high rates of staff replacements reflect a tendency for the more discontented faculty members to be siphoned off, preventing conflicts from developing into major incidents.

Local and Cosmopolitan Principals

Because one might expect outsiders to have new ideas and even to be sought out for their creativity, we expected, in accordance with Carlson's (1963) findings, that outside administrators would be more likely to be hired when the school board is not satisfied with the present system.

Table 8-7. Schools with principals from inside and outside the system and indices of organizational tension and conflict

	Principal Hired from:				
	Inside the System (N = 18)		Outside the System (N = 10)		
Indices of Organizational Tension and Conflict	Less Than 3 Years (Mean)	Total (Mean)	Less Than 3 Years (Mean)	Total (Mean)	Total
Avg. Total Tension bet. All Roles (Reported by Faculty Members)	7.13	7.72	8.29	7.79	7.74
Rates of disagreement					
Total no. disagreements per faculty member	2.26	2.18	2.99	2.36	2.23
No. of severe disagreements per faculty member	0.69	0.35	0.40	0.20	0.31
No. incidents reported per interview					
Total no. of all types of incidents (gross incident ratio)[a]	1.79	2.05	1.17	1.49	1.85
Disputes	0.62	0.71	0.32	0.31	0.57
Major incidents	0.32	0.55	0.09	0.12	0.40
No. incidents per interview involving					
Teacher(s) vs. administrator(s)	1.41	1.57	0.80	1.31	1.48
No. incidents involving authority problems (reported per interview)	1.39	1.48	0.70	1.13	1.35

[a]Complaints are not included in "Total no. of incidents reported."

Because of numerous job opportunities, career-bound administrators are in a strong bargaining position with respect to the board and are likely to be given broad mandates to change the system. We expected that at least some of these changes would be resisted by teaching faculties, and therefore that the appointment of an outside principal would be a source of tension.

Instead, we found that it is schools with principals from inside the system that have higher conflict rates (on six of the eight measures considered). In schools with inside principals the major incident ratio and the dispute ratio are at least double those of schools with principals from outside, and the total incident ratio is one third higher.[26] (See Table 8–7.)

The pattern seems to vary with the length of time a principal has been in office, however. Although there is not a simple linear trend, the fewest overt incidents seem to occur in schools where principals have come from outside fairly recently. The major incident ratio, total incident ratio, teacher-administrator ratio, and ratio of authority conflicts are all low in these schools compared with schools whose principals have come from the outside within the last three years. (See Table 8–7.)

Longevity

March and Simon's (1958) hypothesis that the more experience that all parties have had with a situation the less probability that intra-individual conflict will arise served as a guide for the next hypothesis:

Hypothesis 14: Conflict and organizational tension are inversely associated with a faculty's length of tenure.

As expected, as the length of tenure increases the incidence of conflict declines on seven of the ten measures considered. (See Table 8–6.) Only the major incident ratio shows a slight (though not statistically significant) tendency to increase with average age. Most of these relationships remain after complexity and the number of staff additions have been accounted for, although the fact that the latter control lowers the relationship with the total incident and dispute ratios would indicate that the relationship with longevity is influenced by other factors.

GOALS[27]

Each respondent was asked to rank the importance of six basic goals of education. The schools were ranked on the basis of the proportion of members considering each goal to be of primary importance. The rank-order correlations of these measures with the conflict measures, although not entirely consistent, at least suggest certain patterns. For example, the total incident ratio increases with emphasis on critical thinking and character training and diminishes with emphasis on vocational training and knowledge of subject matter. The ratio of incidents involving authority increases with emphasis on critical thinking and diminishes with emphasis on vocational training. Total tension, heated discussions, and disputes all become more frequent with a school's emphasis on character training and socialization (that is, ironically, the ability to get along with others). Teacher-teacher conflict diminishes with emphasis on subject matter and increases with emphasis on character training, while teacher-administrator conflicts diminish with emphasis on vocational training.

SOME CONSEQUENCES

While the primary aim of this analysis has been to explore the organizational characteristics conducive to conflict, it will be worthwhile to consider for a moment some of the possible consequences that conflict might have on employee morale and on the quality of an organization's product.

Conflict seems to resemble committee work. While particular conflicts may be dissatisfying to the parties involved during their duration, an environment full of conflict, contrary to common impression, can be satisfying to the extent that it provides groups with the means to express themselves, advance their interests, and defend their principles. Tension probably develops because a faculty is committed and concerned about improving conditions. And above all, tension-ridden situations represent an atmosphere where change and flexibility are possible. Therefore, taking the average job satisfaction of a faculty as one indication of its morale, we propose:

Hypothesis 15: Organizational tension and conflict are positively associated with job satisfaction and satisfaction with the teaching career.

Job Satisfaction and Work Satisfaction

The average job satisfaction of a faculty is positively associated with seven of the ten measures of conflict. It is especially noteworthy that job satisfaction increases with conflict between teachers and administrators ($t = .32$) and with the ratio of authority issues ($t = .44$). (See Table 8–6.) Perhaps even more important, however, is the fact that satisfaction with the job does not increase with the ratio of major incidents, and career satisfaction actually declines with involvement in major incidents. These teachers do not seem to like the really fierce conflicts, perhaps because of the animosity that lingers, but perhaps, too, because major incidents do not develop unless teachers have not been able to exert their influence in any other way and also because they probably are less likely to win them. Conflict has less relevance to the level of a faculty's career satisfaction. Only the positive relation with total tension and a negative relationship with major incidents are statistically significant ($t = -.34$).

Although the associations of job satisfaction with conflict are due possibly to other factors and could exist despite the existence of conflict, at least the minor forms of conflict do not seem to undermine morale.

Quality of Product

As a final consideration, we considered the possible effects of conflict on learning outcomes—that is, the proportion of students in a school who drop out before graduation and the proportion of students attending college in relation to conflict. There appears to be little relationship between the dropout rate and conflict indices, except that there seems to be more competition in schools with lower dropout rates ($t = -.22$). The proportion of high-school graduates attending college actually increases with the rate of severe disagreements ($t = .30$) and the total incident ratio ($t = .25$).

Perhaps the most that can be said is that conflict has no visibly detrimental effect on learning outcomes, and that it may have some beneficial outcomes, at least in the sense that more effective schools may simply have to tolerate militant faculties.

SUMMARY

To conclude this chapter we shall attempt to present a composite picture of the more discordant or the more tranquil organizations in the sample. Three of the four schools that were highest on five separate measures of conflict were compared with three schools ranking among the lowest on these conflict measures. A profile of the characteristics differentiating the two organizations was constructed from all available relevant information.

Compared with the tranquil schools, we find that discordant schools have younger faculties which have been in the system for a shorter period of time; they have more professional faculties (with the exceptions that they have lower client orientations and slightly smaller proportions inactive in professional organizations). They are more gregarious, but they talk less frequently with the principal and are more negative toward the principal. They have higher job satisfaction but lower career satisfaction.

The discordant schools are larger, more bureaucratic, more heterogeneous and have higher rates of staff turnover and expansion, but they permit teachers to assume more routine decision-making authority, are less complex, rely less on rules, and are less closely supervised; they also have a lower total tax base. They place more emphasis on character training and critical thinking and put comparatively less emphasis on subject matter and vocational training. They also have a higher proportions of students attending college.

NOTES: Chapter 8

[1] For convenience, the measures of conflict incidents derived from the interviews will be referred to as "ratios"—that is, the number of each type of conflict reported per interview conducted in the school. Unless otherwise indicated, complaints are excluded from the "total incident ratio" which refers to the total number of incidents of all types reported in a school.

[2] Compared to 11 percent of the teacher-administrator conflicts specifically involving control over the classroom, curriculum, or school policy, only 2 percent of the teacher-teacher conflicts involved these types of authority issues. Complaints were more typical of incidents between teachers and administrators than among teachers (37 vs. 25 percent). Nineteen percent of all incidents among teachers involved competition for official status or prestige; by comparison, only 5 percent of the teacher-administrator incidents were of this type.

[3] The relative prestige of each department was estimated as the difference between (a) the proportion of teachers advocating that a department's courses should be the last to be eliminated if the curriculum has to be curtailed and (b) the proportion of teachers advocating that they (the courses) should be the first to be eliminated. This constitutes a measure of the department's functional importance and is not an evaluation of its particular members.

[4] The tau is used as a measure of rank order correlation. The levels of significance for taus of different sample size used in the study are as follows:

Level of Significance

N	.05	.01
28	$t = .21$	$t = .32$
21	$t = .25$	$t = .37$
14	$t = .33$	$t = .47$
11	$t = .39$	$t = .55$
10	$t = .41$	$t = .58$

Each rank order correlation was computed several times, controlling for the variables already found to be associated with either the dependent or independent variable. Also, many of the correlations were computed separately for schools above and below the median of schools': (a) professional orientation scores and (b) total bureaucratization scores. Because of the difficulty in attempting to report all of these detailed tests, they will be referred to only where they alter the general conclusions.

[5] The lack of correlation between professionalism and conflict at the departmental level raises a question about whether something happens to professional orientations in particular contexts. The traditions of some disciplines may counteract the professional values of their members. However, because the professional behavior index is associated with conflict, it is also possible that the lack of association with orientation is a fluke of the small sample size and limited variability in orientations. An analysis of departments ranked according to the proportion of their members who simultaneously held high professional and low employee expectations was more consistent with the expectation on 11 measures of conflict, but only two were statistically significant for a sample of this size.

[6] When counselors and administrators were omitted from the analysis, differences between several of the comparisons were reduced, but their patterns remained basically unchanged.

[7] Although linkages will not be specifically identified as such in the following data, the concept of linkage may help the reader better to appreciate the significance of the indicators that we use.

If a system is incompletely linked together, inconsistencies in the practices and role conceptions of separate units are likely to develop. For this reason, complex linkage systems tend to contribute to a general sense of uncertainty, which White (1961), Crozier (1964), March and Simon (1958), and others insist is a major source of conflict. We prefer, however, to describe the problem in terms of the structural conditions that create uncertainty rather than emphasize the mental state of organizational members.

For the present purposes it will be assumed that the number of linkages roughly increases with the number of subdivisions in an organization. Ideally, of course, linkages should be explicitly identified by separate measures of the number of distinct connections between each autonomous part; patterns of linkage may have an even more important influence on system stability (Dubin, 1959).

[8] Also, in a study of friction incidents within work groups in two hospitals, Haas (1963) found a direct rank order correlation between the number of incidents observed and the size of work groups. Also, the clarity of certain subdivisions of labor was found by Ford and Stephenson (1954) to be inversely related to the size of the hospitals they studied and directly related to the degree of tension among workers.

[9] Namely, rates of total tension ($t = .22$), rate of severe disagreement ($t = .35$), total incident ratio ($t = .38$), ratio of disputes ($t = .27$), and heated discussion ratio ($t = .37$) are all associated with size. The pattern is similar for the number of teachers in the system. Also, in another analysis it was found that the ratio of major incidents and heated discussions specifically between teachers and administrators all are associated with school size ($t = .29$, $t = .34$, and $t = .48$, respectively). Size, however, does not appear to be statistically associated with the number of major incidents reported per interview.

However, in the 14 less professional schools and in the 14 more bureaucratized schools, conflicts among teachers actually seem to decline with size ($t = -.30$ and $t = -.35$). Size also seems to make more difference with less bureaucratized schools in respect to incidents pertaining to authority issues and total rates of disagreement ($t = .36$ and $t = .38$, respectively vs. $t = .07$ and $t = -.02$ in the more bureaucratized schools). After a certain level of bureaucratization further increases do not seem to be associated with conflict (with the exception of severe disagreements). Severe disagreements, on the other hand, are more likely to increase with size in highly bureaucratized organizations than in less bureaucratic ones ($t = .57$)—severe disagreement rate ($t = .12$).

[10] Namely, rates of total tension ($t = .30$), severe disagreement rate ($t = .37$), total incident ratio ($t = .48$), dispute ratio ($t = .32$), and heated discussion ratio ($t = .39$) all increase with the number of levels of authority.

[11] For example, under a condition of low bureaucracy, the correlation between the number of levels of authority and incidents involving authority issues is $t = .60$, and with teacher-administrator incidents it is $t = .78$; by comparison, in highly bureaucratized schools the corresponding correlations are low and not statistically significant. The same pattern exists with respect to disputes ($t = .69$ vs. $t = .07$ in bureaucratic schools) and total disagreements ($t = .33$ vs. $t = .04$). The level of professionalism also makes a difference. The relationship between hierarchical control and authority issues and the teacher-administrator incidents is found primarily in the more professional schools ($t = .60$ and $t = .53$ vs. $t = .07$ and $t = .20$ in the less professional schools).

[12] Teachers in each school were asked to estimate how frequently they received inconsistent instructions from different supervisors (on a five-point scale ranging from frequently to never). This measure is the mean of the responses for each school.

[13] The relationship between disputes and the proportion of faculty assigned outside their majors and minors persists in both the more and less bureaucratized schools; but controlling for levels of bureaucratization illuminates certain other relationships concerning specialization which otherwise are scarcely discernible. The relationship with the total disagreement rate, rate of severe disagreement, and teacher-teacher conflict are significant only in more bureaucratic organizations. Controlling for a faculty's level of professional orientation also alters the association with disputes; low

professionalization is associated with disputes only in the more professional school ($t = -.44$ vs. $t = .03$).

[14] The more bureaucratic schools are likely to have other means of controlling subordinates. This fact could counteract the problems that develop with centralization. Similarly, in less professional schools professional peer-group controls might not be so effective in controlling individualistic sources of conflict; in highly professional schools the incidents involving authority show a slight tendency to diminish with decision-making authority ($t = -.29$ ns).

[15] There is some evidence that teachers are not as dissatisfied with their role in the more basic policy areas, even if they would like more authority over routine decisions. Even so, an average of one fourth of the sample registered some discrepancy between the actual and preferred level at which selected policy decisions are made, the discrepancy being somewhat larger for certain types of decisions—namely, formulating instructional policy, granting permission for outside groups to speak, hiring new teachers, adding or dropping courses, determining required courses, selecting required textbooks, determining whether a required textbook should be used, teaching assignments, and determining qualifications of teachers to teach. The sorest point occurred on the few occasions when school boards made decisions teachers considered to be outside the board's sphere of authority; decisions centralized at the level of the principal and the failure of the principal to consult teachers ranked second and third, respectively, as contributors to discontent with the decision-making process.

[16] In the more bureaucratic schools both the total rate of disagreement and the total incident ratio diminish with this measure of centralization ($t = -.34$ and $t = -.34$). The absence of severe disagreement from centralized schools is especially characteristic of the more professional schools ($t = -.32$) and of the more bureaucratic schools ($t = -.50$) compared with their counterparts.

[17] There are several reasons why emphasis on standardized control procedures might be associated with conflict. First, standardization provides rationality and a sense of support which are conducive to conflict. The very rules that limit the discretion of some groups protect others and give them a sense of independence (Gouldner, 1959). In fact, the protective function makes rules useful as implements of conflict. Each group in conflict, says Crozier, supports the rules, pressuring others to obey them while at the same time fighting to preserve its own area of freedom. Referring to rules, he continues (1964, p. 189):

Every member of the organization, therefore, is protected both from his superiors and from his subordinates. He is, on the one hand, totally deprived of initiative and completely controlled by rules imposed on him from the outside. On the other hand, he is completely free from personal interference by any other individual—as independent, in a sense, as if he were a nonsalaried worker.

A study of teachers' sense of power suggests that, although different school systems probably select out teachers having a different sense of power, certain bureaucratic characteristics of school systems themselves always will reinforce this. Teachers in more bureaucratic systems expressed a significantly higher sense of power than did those in less fully bureaucratized systems, where particularism and lack of policy are more typical (Moeller and Charters, 1966). An orderly, understandable, and predictable organization helps individuals to anticipate and influence possible consequences of their actions.

Second, control procedures will be a special source of contention to those professionals who are seeking self-determination. Compared with factories, for example, schools appear to have fewer completely routine tasks, and their members have more desire to achieve professional status. This is an age of experimentation in education. It is likely to be more difficult to control the nonroutine work of status-conscious groups than to control more routinized situations where rules are more appropriate (Litwak, 1961). Tension is the product of efforts to maintain the tradition of controlling public schools from above (as some evidence in the preceding chapter suggests that it does) in a setting that is otherwise becoming highly complex and variable.

Third, regulatory procedures are likely to be introduced into precisely the situations that are already troubled and where there is preexisting tension. Rushing (1966), for example, maintains that emphasis on rules will be greater during periods of conflict than during periods of harmony in order to protect threatened groups. Hence, rules will be made by administrators to obtain compliance when compliance cannot be assured by other means and where some autonomous groups are already getting out of hand.

Finally, the broader social trends within the society are probably relevant in this connection. The direction of societal change generally favors relaxation of control. The trend in public schools is currently toward decentralization, specialization, departmentalization, experimentation, and professionalization (rather than closer control), and the current emphasis is on improving the quality of education, not on the efficaciousness an efficiency-conscious society was demanding three or four decades ago.

[18] Gamson (1966) proposes that rules are more likely than close supervision to be used in conflictful situations because it is difficult to maintain interpersonal relations in such situations.

[19] This hypothesis will be examined by analyzing the component subscales of the faculties' professional and employee orientation scale scores, and the modal way in which each faculty organizes its professional and employee roles.

[20] This need not mean, however, that professional militancy is detrimental to client welfare. It is possible that in the long run increased decision-making authority for teachers will be as beneficial as a more personalized, direct commitment to students.

[21] Lunching is associated with years with the system ($t = .45$).

[22] The proportion of a faculty who see one another socially very frequently is positively associated with the amount of tension ($t = .26$), rate of severe disagreements ($t = .29$), total incident ratio ($t = .43$), dispute ratio ($t = .21$), heated-discussion ratio ($t = .47$), conflict between teachers and administrator ($t = .30$) and among teachers ($t = .32$), and number of conflicts involving authority issues ($t = .16$), and reaches statistical significance when the faculty's professional orientation is controlled ($t_p = .25$).

[23] Also, because most teachers are members of professional associations, it seemed more important to concentrate on the small minority in most schools who are not members. The fact that professional teachers' associations—the NEA affiliates—not only admit administrators into their membership but also rely on administrators for leadership is likely to reduce their militancy. The unions, on the other hand, exclude administrators and supposedly have a clearer view of the conflict of interest between the administrators and classroom teachers. The fact that there are only four schools in the study with recognized unions probably reduces the opportunity of union members to express their grievances. Most of the nonunion schools, however, include at least a small percentage of teachers who are union members.

[24] Argyris (1954) emphasizes the importance of the dominate-personality-types in organizations, such as the "complaint" employees selected by a bank he studied. However, of equal importance is the variety of social types recruited to an organization, which is tied to broader, institutional conflicts and changes in the society.

[25] As staff additions increase, so do total incident ratio ($t = .58$), open dispute ratio ($t = .41$), heated discussion ratio ($t = .39$), total tension ($t = .34$), total disagreement rate ($t = .30$), and severe disagreement rate ($t = .37$). The ratio of conflict involving authority issues also increases with this measure ($t = .47$); this relationship, however, is more typical of the 14 less bureaucratic schools than of more bureaucratic ones ($t = .04$ in the more bureaucratic schools). These measures, moreover, remain significant after organizational size has been controlled.

[26] Because statistical tests were not computed for these comparisons, they must be interpreted cautiously.

[27] A few relationships were also found between the economic variables and

conflict. A positive association was found between a system's total receipts and a school's major incident ratio ($t = .31$). This relationship holds after controlling for school size, complexity, professional orientation, and staff additions. But also controlling for school size, the total receipts of a system seem to be negatively associated with more minor forms of conflict—that is, total disagreements ($t_p = -.21$) and the total dispute ratio ($t_p = -.21$). There may be some tendency for conflict to increase with level of economic support per pupil in the system, but only two of these relationships are statistically significant, and even these are not significant when school size and complexity have been controlled. No significant relationship or pattern of relationships was found between the average salary level of a faculty and the measures of conflict being considered here.

REFERENCES: Chapter 8

Argyris, Chris. Human relations in a bank. *Harvard Business Review*, 1954, 32, 63–72.
Becker, Howard S., and Geer, Blanche. Latent culture: A research note. *Administrative Science Quarterly*, September, 1960, 5, 304–313.
Carlson, Richard O. *Executive succession and organizational change: Placebound and career-bound superintendents of schools.* Chicago: Midwest Administration Center, The University of Chicago, 1963. Pp. 30–35.
Clark, Burton R. Organizational adaptation to professionals. In Howard L. Vollmer and Donald L. Mills (Eds.), *Professionalization*. Englewood Cliffs, N.J.: Prentice-Hall, 1966. Pp. 282–291.
Coleman, James S. *Community conflict*. New York: Free Press, 1957.
Colombotos, John L. *Sources of professionalism: A study of high school teachers.* U.S. Office of Education, Cooperative Research Project No. 330. Ann Arbor: Department of Sociology, University of Michigan, 1962.
Crozier, Michel. *The bureaucratic phenomenon*. Chicago: The University of Chicago Press, 1964.
Dahrendorf, Ralf. Toward a theory of social conflict. *Journal of Conflict Resolution*, June, 1958, 7, 170–183.
Dubin, Robert. Stability of human organization. In Maison Haire (Ed.). *Modern organizational theory*. New York: Wiley, 1959. Pp. 218–251.
Ford, Thomas R., and Stephenson, Diane D. *Institutional nurses: Role relationships and attitudes in three Alabama hospitals*. University, Ala.: University of Alabama Press, 1954.
Gamson, William A. Rancorous conflict in community politics. *American Journal of Sociology*, 1966, 31, 71.
Gordon, Wayne. *The social system of the high school*. New York: Free Press, 1957.
Gouldner, Alvin W. Organizational tensions. In Robert K. Merton, Leonard Broom, and Leonard S. Cottrell, Jr. (Eds.). *Sociology today*. New York: Basic Books, 1959. Pp. 400–428.
Haas, J. Eugene. *Role conception and group consensus*. Research Monograph No. 117. Columbus: Bureau of Business Research, The Ohio State University, 1963.
Henry, Jules. The formal structure of a psychiatric hospital. *Psychiatry*, May, 1954, 17, 139–151.
Homans, George. *Social behavior*. New York: Harcourt, Brace and World, 1961.
Kahn, Robert L. Field studies of power in organization. In Robert L. Kahn and Elise Boulding (Eds.). *Power and conflict in organizations*. New York: Basic Books, 1964. Pp. 52–66.
Katz, Fred E. The school as a complex organization. *Harvard Educational Review*, Summer, 1964, 34, 428–455.

Landsberger, Henry A. The horizontal dimension in bureaucracy. *Administrative Science Quarterly*, December, 1961, 299–332.

Levenson, Bernard. Bureaucratic succession. In Amitai Etzioni (Ed.). *Complex organizations: A sociological reader*. New York: Holt, Rinehart & Winston, 1961. Pp. 262–275.

Litwak, Eugene. Models of bureaucracy which permit conflict. *American Journal of Sociology*, September, 1961, 177–185.

March, James, and Simon, Herbert. *Organizations*. New York: Wiley, 1958.

Moeller, Gerald H., and Charters, W. W. Relation of bureaucratization to sense of power among teachers. *Administrative Science Quarterly*, March, 1966, **10**, 444–465.

Rushing, William A. Organizational rules and surveillance: Propositions in comparative organizational analysis. *Administrative Science Quarterly*, March, 1966, **10**, 423–443.

Smith, Clagget, and Ari, Aguz N. Organizational control structure and member consensus. *American Journal of Sociology*, 1964, **69**, 623–638.

Thompson, James D. Organizational management of conflict. *Administrative Science Quarterly*, March, 1960, **4**, 389–409.

Thompson, Victor A. Hierarchy, specialization and organizational conflict. *Administrative Science Quarterly*, 1961, **5**, 485–521.

White, Harrison. Management conflict and sociometric structure. *American Journal of Sociology*, September, 1961, **67**, 185–199.

Wilson, James Q. Innovation in organization: Notes toward a theory. In James D. Thompson (Ed.). *Approaches to Organizational Design*. Pittsburgh: University of Pittsburgh Press, 1966.

FROM TALKS WITH TEACHERS more on community relations

I THINK *one phone call can make quite a few changes around this school; one complaint. I tend to have the feeling that, after six years of observation, teachers' complaints or recommendations are rarely considered. For example, I could make some recommendations in my own subject area and they wouldn't be taken very seriously. This is a system where if it was taught this way ten years ago, it will be taught this way now.—a teacher*

WELL, WE *have no PTA. And thank God!—and use four or five exclamation points after it! And I don't think we'll ever have one because there are too many of us that feel that PTA is a waste of time. The ones that come to PTA, as a rule, come to have a chance to take a bite out of the teacher.—a teacher*

I HAVE *taken the stand, for better or worse, that the community will get what it wants. Out of hundreds of thousands of books that are in print, I do not believe that it is worthwhile having a tempest in a teapot over one particular book. I think a satisfactory substitute can be found without upsetting the whole curriculum. We have attempted, in establishing the curriculum, to use books which are not going to raise controversy. If there is something that I feel strongly about, it is there anyway. Usually, if the reasons are sound, the administration will stand back of it.*
—*a teacher*

I THINK *they [parents] want the prestige of a fancy school system, but they don't understand what it means to implement the school system and implement the programs. . . . The parents seem to want to have the prestige of courses, of an elaborate curriculum, and the prestige of A's. But they do not want to make the sacrifices, and the students do not want to do the work and [make] sacrifices, too. I do not feel that teachers as a group receive enough respect from the population as a general thing. I noticed this particularly because of the community in which I previously worked. I worked in an industrial community where teachers were among the higher echelon of people and were therefore on a higher plane. Here, we are the lower economic level and are in general looked down upon, and the switch is noticeable.—a teacher*

9. Profession and bureaucracy in process

> *It appears that not only in social life, but wherever there is life, there is conflict. May we perhaps go so far as to say that conflict is a condition necessary for life to be possible at all?—Dahrendorf, 1959, p. 208.*

Mr. Sears witnesses disputes one at a time, as incidental interruptions of his work routine. From where he sits, each conflict is unique and only a part of the thousand random events that form his daily life. So almost certainly, unless he watches carefully, he will not notice the general patterns that lie behind the individual incidents. What Mr. Sears is not likely to have, and what we need, are distinctive concepts through which we can translate personal events into their implications for organization. This chapter considers some of the concepts that might provide a more coherent framework for the variables already introduced and then reports tests of a series of propositions which have the potential of becoming the basis of a primitive theory of organizational conflict.

We have observed elsewhere in this discussion that understanding the conditions responsible for disorganization may be less important than the conditions responsible for the emergence of organization. In this chapter that theme will be examined further. The way concepts of organization and disorganization, or conflict, are handled depends upon the model of organization that is used. These issues are of utmost importance at the present stage of organizational theory, especially because writers often fail to make explicit the underlying model being used and generally do not systematically consider the implications that studies of organization and disorganization might have for one another.

Of course, a number of writers have been fully aware of these issues for some time—Coser, Dahrendorf, and Litwak, among others. The interdependence of one upon the other has been noted by Moore, who observed that the indices of organization increase with indices of disorganization. And Blau and Scott's statement (1962, p.7) suggests that organization may be a direct response to disruption: "... the larger the group and the more complex the task it seeks to accomplish, the greater are the pressures to become explicitly organized." In other words, it is plausible that organizations develop in response to disrupting circumstances—that is, the threat of disorganization.

As explained in Chapter 7, there appear to be at least three alternatives available to organizations threatened with the instability that accompanies large size, complexity, heterogeneity of staff, staff turnover and expansion, and professionalism and the lack of compliance among employees. Each alternative will be briefly reviewed here. First, a few controls can be applied in a stringent way. That is, when disruption threatens to reduce the organization's continuity or administrative control, some forms of control will be increased, but this will be done selectively, with one substituting for another. For example, control can be achieved either by close supervision or by a well-enforced system of explicit rules. Many of the available controls will not necessarily be brought to bear, and in fact there may be a state of tension between the alternate mechanisms available, in such a way that when one is applied others are relaxed—for example, when rules are emphasized, close supervision will be relaxed. This was referred to as the compensatory model of organization. In other words, one interchangeable form of control is emphasized to compensate for the relative absence of other forms of control.

A second alternative is that several forms of control will be brought to bear at once in mutual support of one another. It is even possible that some bureaucratic controls depend upon other controls and cannot function adequately without them—for example, centralized organizations may not function adequately in the absence of well-defined rules regulating the jobs of employees. This was referred to as the reinforcement model. That is, alternate mechanisms of organization increase simultaneously and seem to reinforce one another.

Of course, the third alternative is that the various dimensions of control function independently, in such a way that increases in one form of control says nothing about other forms of control. This was referred to as the independence model.

These models are not necessarily unrelated, and in fact they can be placed along a continuum based on the degree of consistency among the various dimensions of bureaucracy. In the independence model the dimensions are randomly inconsistent, in the compensatory model the various dimensions are systematically but inversely related, and in the reinforcement model they are entirely consistent.

This chapter will explore the general assumption that bureaucracy grows in response to conflict in the organizational environment and in turn provides a setting in which conflict is more easily sustained. One underlying premise is that bureaucratic controls will not be invoked without provocation. There are several arguments in support of this premise. Foremost is the fact that there are constraints on the amount of resources that can be allocated for the purpose of control. All controls require some expenditures of time, energy, and other scarce resources. Once resources have been allocated in a particular way (such as to assure close supervision), there will be fewer resources available for other alternatives. Given this constraint, it can be expected that organizations can manage with a minimum amount of control primarily in the more peaceful settings, but that as the situation becomes more tension ridden, more forms of control will be utilized, the less effective controls being combined in order to reinforce one another. A consistently reinforced control system is not likely to be used until the degree of threat becomes especially great or until those employees who are to be controlled become insufficiently responsive to minor degrees of control. In other words, the reinforcement pattern will take precedence over the compensatory pattern in the most tension-ridden situations where no one form of control is likely to be effective in itself. And the presence of controls can make the conflict more tolerable.

However, the effectiveness of bureaucratic controls depends upon whether they are accepted as legitimate. Attempts to apply bureaucratic principles to incompatible situations can simply aggravate already existing problems. A professional climate may represent one such incompatible situation. Bureaucratic principles are at least in some respects incompatible with professional principles of organization.

Furthermore, there is evidence that professionalization itself is a militant process, and hence an independent source of disruption which makes professional faculties subject to further bureaucratic controls. If bureaucracy is incompatible with professionalism, then conflict should be most prevalent when professional and bureaucratic principles are simultaneously emphasized—that is, as professional schools are bureaucratized and as bureaucratic schools are professionalized.

CONCEPTS AND PROCEDURES

As a means of bringing into focus several critical but neglected features of organizations, three additional concepts will be introduced: total bureaucratization, structural crystallization, and bureaucratic pattern. Together with professionalism these concepts will form the nucleus of the theoretical framework.[1]

Total Bureaucratization

Although the components of a bureaucracy (such as standardization, centralization, interchangeability, and the like) can function somewhat independently, in reality they tend to exist together, sometimes in close association. Combinations of the variables are likely to have a cumulative impact on conflict different from that of any variable taken by itself.

The term "total bureaucratization" will be used to refer to the combined index of the bureaucratic components. As a crude measure, the ranks of a school on each of the following variables were totaled: (1) close supervision, (2) emphasis on rules, and (3) centralization of (a) professional policy decisions, (b) nonprofessional policy decisions, and (c) routine decisions.[2] A school's total bureaucratization score represents the sum of its ranks on these five variables.

Structural Crystallization

Whereas the total bureaucratization score reflects the cumulative force of bureaucracy, there also is an element of consistency and inconsistency to be taken into account. The consistency of a school's rankings on organizational measures will be called "structural crystallization."[3] The degree of crystallization within each school was computed as the sum of the combined differences between its ranks on the five variables used in the total bureaucratic index. Lower total scores signify smaller differences between a school's separate rankings, and hence greater crystallization of the separate structures.

The concept "structural crystallization" permits patterns of organization to be classified independently of their levels of bureaucratization. The concept is significant because it is relevant to the reinforcement and compensatory models. In crystallized organizations bureaucratic practices are used with consistently uniform emphasis and hence reinforce each other; in uncrystallized organizations one or two practices are disproportionately stressed in accordance with the compensatory model.

The Bureaucratic Pattern

The relative priority given to various processes, such as standardization and centralization, could have as much bearing on conflict rates as the over-all magnitude and consistency of these two dimensions. Therefore the patterns of combination among the set of variables will be considered as well.

Professiónalism

Finally, the average professional and employee orientations of each faculty (as well as indices of their professional behavior) will be considered, using the measures described in Chapter 4. Like organizational complexity, staff expansion, and turnover, professionalism can pose a prominent threat to the maintenance of control in school systems.

ASSUMPTIONS AND HYPOTHESES

The hypotheses will be stated before presenting an overview of the findings and the details. The question of first priority concerns the relationship of teachers' professionalism to their militancy.

The growth of systematic knowledge about the teaching process, specialized training programs, and career patterns, plus some signs of concern among teachers for students' welfare, all support their claims to the right to control certain aspects of teaching. Furthermore, professionalization represents a "drive for status," which signifies the efforts of a vocation to gain more control of its work. Professional associations generally were originally formed to free vocations from lay control, and the efforts of teachers to professionalize are no exception. There is already a certain amount of empirical support for the proposition that professionalism is a militant process. We have already seen evidence (in Chapter 5) that individuals with exceptionally strong commitments to their professional roles are conflict prone, and a pilot study of seven schools in this sample indicated that the professionalism of a faculty is directly associated with organizational tension and conflict. In short, professionalizing a publicly supported vocation having a strong tradition of administrative control is likely to provoke some militancy. For these reasons, it is hypothesized that

Hypothesis 1: Organizational tension and conflict are positively associated with professionalism.

In contrast to professionalism, bureaucracy is a form of administrative control and a means of controlling subordinates which is, in part at least, designed to regulate and suppress conflict in the interest of predictability.[4] Assuming that efforts to control are effective, conflict can be expected to diminish with bureaucratization. Therefore, as a first approximation, it is expected that

Hypothesis 2: Organizational tension and conflict are negatively associated with bureaucratization.

However, it cannot be assumed that bureaucracy is uniformly effective. Its effectiveness will depend upon (a) the amount of preexisting conflict to be overcome, (b) the degree to which controls reinforce one another, and (c) the amount of conflict provoked by the structure itself. In fact, it is equally plausible that organizations evolve in response to problems and to some extent generate their own problems; and, hence, it can be expected that under some conditions the rate of conflict will increase rather than diminish with degree of organization. Organizations do not necessarily have a life of their own with an internal force driving them to maximize control. Rather, fully consistent bureaucracies seem most likely to evolve in response to conflict-ridden situations. Conversely, an organization is unlikely to become fully crystallized in the absence of conflict. In other words, it is expected that structural crystallization will be found in tension-producing situations and that uncrystallized organizations will be found in more peaceful situations.

For these reasons, it is expected that

Hypothesis 3: Organizational tension and conflict are positively associated with structural crystallization and negatively associated with lack of crystallization.[5]

However, the data will not permit a conclusive test of the assumptions behind the hypothesis; they could be right for the wrong reasons. It is still possible, for example, that the expected relationships between conflict and crystallization, and between the lack of crystallization and the lack of conflict, reflect the relative effectiveness of these two types of organizations—that is, that less crystallized organizations could be simply more effective in controlling conflict.

Corollaries

Several corollaries also can be derived from the above hypotheses. First, if organizational conflict is positively associated with professionalism and negatively associated with bureaucratization, then it can be expected that

Hypothesis 1-A: Professionalism is inversely associated with bureaucratization.[6]

This hypothesis has been advocated by several writers who believe that bureaucratic forms of organization are being modified under the thrust of professionalization—that is, accommodating to professional expectations.

If conflict is inversely associated with bureaucratization and positively associated with structural crystallization, then it can be expected that

Hypothesis 1-B: Bureaucratization and structural crystallization are inversely associated.

If bureaucratization and professionalization are working at cross-purposes, still another corollary can be derived. If professionals are attempting to increase their autonomy, and if administrators use bureaucratic practices to control professional subordinates, then situations in which these principles are simultaneously emphasized will be especially tension ridden. The clash between these two types of principles will provoke disagreement not only between subordinates and the administration, but also among the subordinates who are likely to differ in the degree to which they subscribe to professional and bureaucratic principles (Bucher and Strauss, 1961). Therefore, it is expected that

Hypothesis 2–A: Bureaucratization of the more professional organizations is positively associated with organizational tension and conflict.

A third set of corollaries also can be derived from the major propositions. If conflict increases with structural crystallization and declines with the level of bureaucratization, then it will be difficult to predict the level of conflict in organizations that are simultaneously highly bureaucratized and crystallized. However, where crystallization is low and bureaucratization is high, it can be expected that

Hypothesis 3–A: In the less crystallized organizations rates of organizational tension and conflict will DECLINE with bureaucratization.

(However, the relationship of conflict to bureaucratization in crystallized organizations will be indeterminant, because it is supposed that conflict is negatively associated with the former variable and positively associated with the latter one.)

Finally, because tension-producing patterns are probably inherent in the structure of an organization itself, it is expected that specific patterns of relationships among the structural variables will be associated with conflict in different ways. Perhaps certain types of structural patterns can be identified which contribute to conflict independently of either their degree of inconsistency or the existing threat to control.

OVERVIEW OF FINDINGS

Perhaps the most important result of the analysis was the finding that (except for an inverse relationship with major incidents), most measures of staff conflict increase with the average professional orientation of a faculty, as hypothesized. However, there is an important exception: The major incidents become less frequent as a faculty's professionalism increases. This fact may indicate that more professionally oriented teachers police themselves, preventing conflict from getting out of bounds, or it may indicate that professionally oriented teachers accomplish what they want without needing to resort to major incidents. Whatever the reasons, "militant professionals" themselves are more successful in resolving conflict in other ways or do not necessarily lead the most dramatic and belligerent forms of conflict currently associated with the teaching movement, except in the most bureaucratized schools (where it appears that professionalism may help to provoke major incidents).

Although the average age of the faculty accounts for some of these relationships, they nevertheless persist at all age levels. But the association between professionalism and conflict rates is characteristic primarily of those schools where faculties do not frequently associate over lunch. And they were found more typical of the less professional schools than of the more professional ones. Apparently, once a plateau has been reached, further professionalism does not necessarily lead to more militancy, perhaps indicating that it is not the process of change, but the process of professionalization itself, which is most important. Similarly, the positive correlation between professional orientation and disagreement rates, and the negative association with major incidents, are both more characteristic of the more bureaucratic schools than the less bureaucratic ones; the association with incidents between teachers and administrators is slightly more typical of less bureaucratized organizations. The professional behavior index reaffirmed the conclusions derived from the professional orientation scale, though not as consistently.

Also, looking at the problem in a slightly different way, faculties in the top seven professional schools rank significantly higher on most of the conflict measures than those in the lowest seven schools. The total number of disagreements and the number of severe and moderate disagreements, plus the number of disputes reported per interview, are all approximately twice as high in the top professional schools as in the lowest group. However, again, major incidents are found primarily in the least professional setting; this measure is four times higher in the least professional group of schools. When faculties are classified on the basis of their predominant style of role organization, schools with the highest proportions of the faculty holding simultaneously high professional and low employee orientations have more conflict on 10 of 13 measures than schools that place the reverse priorities on these two roles.

Most of the associations between a faculty's employee orientation and its conflict rates are not significant, although all of the correlations indicate an inverse relationship; these relationships are accentuated in the more professional schools. The faculty's average employee behavior scores reinforce these trends.

Turning from professionalism to bureaucratization, it was found that, first, using a correlational analysis, in the more professional schools both total rate of disagreement and incidents between teachers and the administration increase directly with bureaucratization. Next, still considering only the 14 most professionally oriented faculties, the mean scores on all measures of conflict (except severe disagreements) are higher in the more bureaucratized schools than in those less bureaucratized; whereas, among the 14 least professionally oriented faculties, most of the measures of conflict are lower in the more bureaucratized than in the less bureaucratized schools. This suggests that bureaucratization may be an effective means of control under some conditions (that is, in the absence of a professional climate), and that professionalization is most likely to provoke conflict when it is in a bureaucratic context.

When schools are ranked according to their structural crystallization, that variable is positively associated with several measures of conflict. Also, when classified by level of structural crystallization, the most crystallized schools have uniformly higher conflict rates than the less consistent ones (except for major incidents). Moreover, less crystallized schools have lower conflict rates if they are more bureaucratized; whereas most types of milder friction occur relatively frequently in schools which are simultaneously bureaucratized and crystallized. But schools with high rates of intense conflict (that is, severe disagreement and major incidents) again have the opposite pattern.

Looking more closely at the patterns of bureaucracy, conflict rates are high in schools that emphasize rules while deemphasizing close supervision. Second, compared to schools in which decision making is centralized and rules and close supervision are deemphasized, schools with the opposite priorities (that is, that emphasize rules and close supervision while simultaneously decentralizing the decision-making process) have higher rates of all types of conflict, again with the exception of major incidents. Again, it is significant that the difference is reversed for major incidents; they occur most frequently in centralized schools which fail to emphasize rules and close supervision.

We can conclude, then, that professionalization is, generally speaking, a militant process. However, this simple statement of the situation now can be qualified in several ways, on the basis of these data at least.

First, it is clear that the organizational context makes a substantial difference. Increases in professionalism are less likely to lead to conflict in the less bureaucratized schools and in those that have achieved a relatively high degree of professionalism. Moreover, as the less professional organizations become bureaucratized, most forms of conflict diminish. The latter finding indicates that bureaucratization is not necessarily ineffective, but the first finding indicates that it may be ineffective in some settings and warns against attempting to apply a single form of organization uniformly to all settings.

Second, professionalism is not likely to be associated with the occurrence of major incidents, except in the most bureaucratized schools.

Third, the association between professionalism and conflict rates is characteristic only of those schools where faculties do not frequently associate over lunch.

Because bureaucratization and structural crystallization seem to evolve as direct responses to conflict, it is plausible that bureaucratization represents a response to other tension-producing conditions—such as professionalism, organizational complexity, and staff turnover—which, in turn, are themselves more directly associated with conflict. Highly organized systems should be viewed as problematic, developing only under special circumstances, rather than as a natural development. Conflict, therefore, not only represents the breakdown of organization, but also can be a *cause* of organization. In particular, where there is relatively little conflict, schools have not become as crystallized; crystallization, however, seems to have evolved in either the conflictful or in less conflictful environments—depending upon how bureaucratic the school is.

ANALYSIS

1. *The professionalism of a school is positively associated with its rates of organizational tension and conflict.*[7] *(See Table 9–1.)*

This finding supports the first hypothesis. The data will be discussed separately for professional orientation and behavior and for employee orientation and behavior.

Professional Orientation

Rank-order correlations

The number of conflicts reported per interview among a faculty increases with its average professional orientation. As professional orientation increases, all but two of the 12 indices of conflict increase (that is, tension between teachers and principal and major incidents); of the remainder, only the correlation with "heated discussions" is not statistically significant, and even this measure reaches statistical significance when other relevant factors have been controlled. (See Table 9–1, col. 1.) It is noteworthy that incidents among teachers increase ($t = .24$) as well as incidents between teachers and administrators ($t = .22$) and incidents involving authority ($t = .27$); as indicated previously, the most profes-

Table 9-1. Rank-order correlations between a faculty's professional and employee role orientation and indices of organizational tension and conflict ($N = 28$ schools)

Indices of Organizational Tension and Conflict	Professional Orientation	Professional Behavior	Employee Orientation	Employee Behavior	Total Bureaucratization	Structural Crystallization
Avg. total tension bet. all roles (reported by faculty members)	.40a	.27	.04	−.02	.02	.22a
Avg. tension bet. teachers and principal	−.01	.29a	−.09	−.43b	—	—
Avg. tension bet. teachers and students	.49b	.07	.06	−.04	—	—
Rates of Disagreement						
Total no. of disagreements per faculty member	.26a	−.16	−.03	−.07	.02	.14
No. of severe disagreements per faculty member	.34b	−.07	−.16	−.19	−.03	.16
No. of incidents reported per interview						
Total no. of all types of incidents (gross incident ratio)c	.26a	−.16	−.11	−.08	.03	.04
Disputes	.28a	.28a	−.15	−.02	.07	.26a
Heated discussion	.11	−.18	−.19	−.09	.22	−.15
Major incidents	−.21a	−.26a	−.21a	−.29a	.26	−.44b
No. of incidents per interview involving the following role partners						
Teacher(s) vs. administrator(s)	.22a	−.08	−.08	−.31a	.09	−.06
Teacher(s) vs. teacher(s)	.24a	−.08	.07	.01	.02	−.03
No. of incidents involving authority problems (reported per interview)	.27a	.29a	.02	−.35b	−.04	−.05

aRank-order correlation significant at $p \leq .05$.
bRank-order correlation significant at $p \leq .01$.
cComplaints are not included in "Total no. of incidents reported."

sionally oriented segment of teachers alienates itself from the majority whose accommodation to the existing system is threatened by militancy.[8]

The fact that major incidents, in contrast to other forms of conflict, decline with professionalism ($t = -.21$) may provide clues to some important features of professional militancy. While professional norms may encourage professionals to stand up for themselves in disputes, the same norms seem to have made the more violent means inappropriate and, perhaps under some circumstances, unnecessary. Major incidents disrupt an entire organization, divert the energy of its faculty from the more immediate objectives, and leave scars which discourage compromise. And it is possible that professionally oriented faculties are able to secure enough of their demands through more limited forms of militancy so that they do not have to resort to more extreme measures.

The association between professionalism and conflict is especially prominent in schools where teachers do not frequently eat lunch together; every correlation except the one with major incidents holds only in schools where lunching is less frequent. (Schools were divided at the median on this variable.) At first glance, this might be interpreted to mean that militancy is more likely to materialize in an impersonal setting than in one where people feel constrained by close interpersonal relationships. But this interpretation is not consistent with two findings reported in a previous chapter, namely that sociability is sometimes conducive to conflict and that it is only in the least professional schools that increases in the frequency of lunching are accompanied by more conflict. Rather, it appears that both professionalism and sociability contribute independently to conflict. The relationship of either variable becomes apparent when the other is (relatively speaking) absent; but when both are simultaneously present, they contaminate the relationship of one another in relation to conflict, so that slight increases in one do not further alter the existing high level of conflict. (As a result, it is not surprising that a separate analysis revealed that conflict rates are exceptionally high in a few schools which have simultaneously high scores on professionalism and lunching frequency.)

Also, older faculties appear to be less militant, but perhaps partially because they are also less professionally oriented. The rank-order correlation between a faculty's mean age and its professional orientation is $t = .36$; the correlation of age with severe disagreement is $t = -.40$. When faculty age is "partialled out," consequently, the associations of professionalism with the various measures of conflict drop slightly, although they do remain statistically significant in all cases.[9]

The associations between professionalism and militancy are much more characteristic of the less professional schools than of the more professional ones (See Table 9–2.) The 28 schools were divided at the mid-

Table 9-2. Rank-order correlations between (a) a faculty's endorsement of professional roles and (b) total bureaucratization[a] with selected indices of organizational tension and conflict, controlling for levels of bureaucratization and professionalism

Indices of Organizational Tension and Conflict	Mean Level of Professional Orientation				Mean Level of Bureaucratization			
	High (N = 14)		Low (N = 14)		High (N = 14)		Low (N = 14)	
	(a)	(b)	(a)	(b)	(a)	(b)	(a)	(b)
Rates of Disagreement								
Total no. of disagreements per faculty member	−.46[c]	.29	.43[c]	−.01	.55[c]	−.05	.03	−.06
No. of severe disagreements per faculty member	.02	.13	.39[b]	−.08	.45[b]	−.09	.17	.03
No. of Incidents Reported Per Interview								
Total no. of all types of incidents (gross incident ratio)[d]	−.07	.15	.16	.08	.18	−.27	.23	.19
Disputes	−.22	.00	.25	−.35[b]	.29	−.14	.19	−.01
Heated Discussion	.13	.18	−.08	.21	.07	−.16	.14	.10
Major Incidents	.04	.32	.14	−.03	.37[b]	.36[b]	−.05	.10
No. of incidents per interview involving the following role partners								
Teacher(s) vs. administrator(s)	.07	.21	.45[c]	.17	.18	−.16	.34[b]	−.01
Teacher(s) vs. teacher(s)	−.07	−.04	.19	.17	.20	−.05	.19	.14
No. of incidents involving authority problems (reported per interview)	.02	.09	.60[c]	−.03	.33[b]	−.52[c]	.23	.06

[a] Correlations with total bureaucratization are recorded in column (b); correlations with professionalism are in column (a).
[b] Rank-order correlation significant at $p \leq .05$.
[c] Rank-order correlation significant at $p \leq .01$.
[d] Complaints are not included in the "Total no. of incidents reported."

point on their mean professional orientation. In the more professionally oriented schools most of the correlations are positive, but none is statistically significant, and the total disagreement rate is negatively correlated. But in the less professionally oriented schools professional orientation is positively associated with two disagreement measures and with the authority-incident ratio. This suggests that once a faculty reaches a certain plateau of professionalism further increases in their professional orientation do not contribute to further conflict. Perhaps this is partially because in such schools professional expectations have already been implemented.

But the latter stages of professionalism may, nevertheless, be more difficult. In the more professional schools major incidents seem to increase with further increases of professionalism (although the association is not statistically significant), indicating that as these faculties become further professionalized, the conflict takes more violent forms.

Level of bureaucratization also makes a difference. Professional militancy seems to be provoked primarily in the more bureaucratic situations. The schools were divided at the midpoint on total bureaucratization scores, and the correlations were recomputed for each group. (See Table 9–2.) The positive correlations between professionalism and the total and severe disagreement rates hold only in the more bureaucratic schools. The association with incidents between teachers and administrators holds in the less bureaucratic schools but not as in the more bureaucratic ones.[10] At the same time, it is important to note that in the more bureaucratic schools, as professional orientation increases, the frequency of major incidents also increases ($t = .37$). In other words, when professionalization takes place in a relatively bureaucratized context, there is likely to be an outbreak of major conflicts. These findings lend further support to the thesis that bureaucratization is incompatible with professionalization.

Professional Behavior

The professional behavior index supports the conclusions derived from the professional orientation scale (Table 9–1, Col. 2). The more professional a faculty's conduct, the more authority incidents and disputes per interview ($t = .29$ and $t = .28$) and the more tension reported between the faculty and the principal ($t = .29$).[11] In view of the fact this behavioral measure taps a different dimension of professionalism, professional militancy does not seem to be solely a function of the particular items that make up the scales nor solely a reflection of the value system.

Employee Orientation

The over-all associations between a faculty's employee orientation and its rates of conflict are not clear cut. Most of the correlations are in the negative direction, but only the association with major incidents is statistically significant ($t = -.21$). (See Table 9–1, col. 3.) However, when the correlations are computed separately for schools above and below the median of professionalism scores, the relationships become clearer (not reported in tables). In the more professional schools employee orientation is negatively associated with the gross incident ratio, heated discussion, incidents between teachers and administrators and among teachers, and authority incidents. A strong employee orientation, in other words, seems to have more effect on the reduction of conflict in precisely the schools that otherwise are the most militant—that is, the professionally oriented schools.

Employee Behavior

The average employee behavior scores of a faculty support the proposition that "good" employees do not become involved in conflicts. (See Table 9–1, col. 4.) The employee behavior index is inversely associated with the major incident ratio ($t = -.29$), teacher-administrator conflict ($t = -.31$) and tension ($t = -.43$), and the ratio of conflicts involving authority ($t = -.35$). The correlations are not altered appreciably by controlling for number of staff additions, frequency of contact with the principal, or routine decision-making authority of the faculty.

Comparison Between the Extremes

When schools in the extreme upper and lower quartiles of professionalism (and of employee orientation) are compared, the relationships become even clearer. On most of the measures the highly professional schools have conflict rates that rank them twice as high as the least professional ones. (See Table 9–3.) The total number of disagreements, the number of severe and moderate disagreements, and the number of disputes reported per interview are all approximately twice as high in the top professional schools as in the lowest ones. All of these differences are in the expected direction. However, again, the ratio of major incidents is four times higher in the extreme lowest professional category. With the exception of the major incident and teacher-teacher ratios, the differences are statistically significant at least at the $p \leq .08$ level (and nine of the 13 comparisons are significant at $p \leq .05$ level or above).[12] (A similar comparison was made for schools in the extreme quartiles on the professional behavior index. Most of the differences conform to the same pattern.) (See Table 9–3.)

Similar comparisons of extreme quartiles of employee orientation are

Table 9-3. Comparisons between schools with extreme professional and employee role orientations on indices of organizational tension and conflict ($N = 14$)

	Schools in Extreme Quartiles of											
	Professional Orientation				Professional Behavior				Employee Orientation			
	High Q		Low Q		High Q		Low Q		High Q		Low Q	
Indices of Organizational Tension and Conflict	$\bar{X}$	Avg. Rank	$\bar{X}$	Avg. Rank	$\bar{X}$	Avg. Rank	$\bar{X}$	Avg. Rank	$\bar{X}$	Avg. Rank	$\bar{X}$	Avg. Rank
Degrees of tension bet.:												
Students and teachers	1.06	10.7 $U = 2^c$	.84	4.1	1.0	8.7 $U = 16$	.89	6.1	1.0	8.7 $U = 16$	.90	6.3
Teachers and principals	.89	9.1 $U = 13^a$	.84	7.0	.92	8.1 $U = 20$	.82	6.8	.70	3.4 $U = 3^c$	1.1	10.6
Total tension	6.2	10.6	6.3	4.3	8.8	9.6	6.2	5.2	7.3	12.4	7.5	13.1
Rates of disagreement												
Total no. of disagreements per faculty member	2.5	9.6 $U = 10^b$	1.6	5.4	3.0	9.7 $U = 9^b$	1.3	5.1	2.1	8.3 $U = 19$	2.2	6.7
No. of severe disagreements per faculty member	.31	9.6 $U = 10^b$	.08	5.1	.12	7.4 $U = 25$	.29	7.4	.25	6.6 $U = 19$	.14	8.3
No. of incidents reported per interview												
Total no. of all types of incidents (gross incident ratio)	22.2	9.9 $U = 8^b$	14.8	5.1	20.5	9.1 $U = 13^a$	14.6	5.6	19.7	8.0 $U = 21$	17.7	7.0
Disputes	.64	9.6 $U = 10^b$	.39	5.3	.74	9.3 $U = 12^a$	.43	5.8	4.5	5.4 $U = 10^b$	6.4	9.4
Heated discussion	6.25	10.1 $U = 6^c$	2.6	4.9	3.7	9.0 $U = 14$	2.9	6.0	4.5	9.6 $U = 10^b$	2.3	5.4
Major incidents	.64	6.4 $U = 18$	2.6	8.4	1.4	5.3 $U = 10^b$	3.8	9.6	6.0	9.0 $U = 14$	2.2	6.0
No. of incidents per interview involving the following role partners												
Teacher(s) vs. Administrator(s)	16.8	9.1 $U = 13^a$	11.9	5.7	16.2	8.1 $U = 20$	13.6	6.9	14.4	7.6 $U = 24$	15.3	7.0
Teacher(s) vs. Teacher(s)	12.1	7.9 $U = 22$	8.9	5.7	1.1	8.4 $U = 18$	9.4	6.6	12.1	8.0 $U = 20$	10.5	8.0
No. of incidents involving authority problems (reported per interview)	15.7	9.9 $U = 8^b$	11.2	6.3	15.4	7.7 $U = 23$	15.3	7.1	18.0	8.6 $U = 17$	13.3	6.0

[a] U significant at $p \leq .08$.
[b] U significant at $p \leq .05$.
[c] U significant at $p \leq .01$.

less conclusive. However, the evidence seems to indicate that schools that give the most support to the employee orientation have significantly fewer disputes and less tension between teachers and the principal. Interestingly, in contrast to the general pattern, the most employee-oriented faculty becomes involved in twice as many heated discussions. (See Table 9–3.)

Parallel comparisons of extreme quartiles on employee behavior also confirm the general conclusion that the most loyal employees are not very militant, at least in some respects. The group exhibiting the lowest employee behavior has significantly fewer major incidents, teacher-administrator conflicts, and incidents involving authority, and less tension between teachers and the principal (not reported in the tables).

Role Organization

Faculties were also classified on the basis of four predominate (modal) styles of role organization. (See Table 9–4.) The differences on the 10 of the 13 conflict indices are statistically significant (as tested by the Mann-Whitney analysis of variance between ranks).[13] Schools with the highest proportions of faculty having simultaneously high professional and low employee orientations generally rank statistically higher than the other three types on most of the measures (all except total tension, the major incident ratio, and tension between teachers and principals); in the latter two cases, their rates are lowest. However, the reverse is not necessarily true. That is, schools in which the low professional-high employee pattern dominates do not always have lower conflict rates (although they have lower rates of moderate and severe disagreements, heated discussions, teacher-teacher conflicts, authority incidents, and perhaps gross incidents). Schools in which faculties characteristically subscribe strongly to neither conception have erratic conflict patterns. Tension between teachers and students is lowest in these schools whereas it is the highest beween teachers and the principal; the dispute ratio is the lowest and the major incident ratio the highest.

It has been shown, then, that there is a crude positive relationship between professional orientation and various measures of organizational tension and conflict, that extremely professional faculties have higher rates of conflict than the less professional extreme, and that the faculties that combine a high professional orientation with a low employee orientation are more conflict prone than faculties which organize their roles in other ways.

1–A. *The association betweeen bureaucratization and professionalism is in the expected direction but it is not statistically significant ($t =$*

Table 9-4. Comparisons between four modal types of professional-employee role organization of 28 faculties on indices of organizational tension and conflict (N = 31)[a]

Schools Classified by Modal Role Organization[b]	Number of Disagreements Among Teachers						Organizational Tension Between					
	Total Number		Severe Disagreements		Moderate Disagreements		Teacher vs. Student		Teacher vs. Principal		Total Tension	
	Average Rank	$\bar{X}$	Average Rank	$\bar{X}$	Average Rank	$\bar{X}$	Average Rank	$\bar{X}$	Average Rank	$\bar{X}$	Average Rank	$\bar{X}$
High professional-high employee (N = 9)	12.5	2.01	14.8	.27	13.4	.41	16.9	1.09	14.1	0.79	18.5	8.04
High professional-low employee (N = 5)	19.8	2.93	21.8	.58	21.2	.65	19.2	1.07	13.2	0.84	19.8	8.37
Low professional-high employee (N = 9)	13.6	2.07	11.8	.08	11.7	.33	13.0	1.00	15.6	0.78	13.0	7.14
Low professional-low employee (N = 8)	12.3	2.13	14.5	.24	12.8	.37	10.8	0.95	18.9	1.00	12.3	7.36
	H = 21.17[e]		H = 8.74[d]		H = 19.21[e]		H = 13.73[e]		H = 15.42[e]		H = .71	

[a] N = 31. Schools were classified on the basis of style of role organization of the modal proportion of faculty. Three schools where two styles were exhibited by an equally high proportion of faculty were included under two headings, which inflates the N by 3.
[b] Based on the modal proportion of faculty members in a school who simultaneously hold each combination of status orientations.
[c] All $\bar{X}$ Ratios refer to the number of incidents reported per interview.
[d] Statistically significant at $p \leqslant .05$.
[e] Statistically significant at $p \leqslant .01$.

— .18 ns); controlling for the mean age of the faculty does not alter the relationship. Also, it will be recalled that another analysis (reported in the preceding chapter) indicated a positive relationship between the decision-making authority of teachers and their level of professionalism. This is perhaps the one respect in which schools are most clearly accommodating to professionalism. Therefore, there is at least some meager support for Hypothesis I–A. But this tendency for bureaucratic organizations to adapt to professional roles or selectively to recruit less professional teachers is not yet impressive. At the same time a positive association between employee orientation and bureaucratization is statistically significant ($t = .24$), which indicates that bureaucratic organizations selectively give support to the employee role conception. This pattern of recruitment and accommodation probably serves to minimize the potential level of conflict.

1–B. *Total bureaucratization is not linearly associated with structural crystallization* ($t = -.04$). Hypothesis 1-B, therefore, is not supported by the rank-order correlation. The lack of conformation on this point will require subsequent modifications in the theory.

2. *Total bureaucratization is not associated with most of the measures of conflict in any simple way.* (See Table 9–1, col. 5.) The lack of a clear negative association between bureaucratization and conflict may be due to the contradictory effects of bureaucracy itself operating under different conditions. As already pointed out, while bureaucratic control may be easily achieved if there is little resistance, attempts to use bureaucratic practices in inappropriate situations may simply provoke more problems. Perhaps this explains why bureaucratization is positively correlated with major conflicts and heated discussions (both of which become statistically significant when relevant variables are controlled).[14] (See Table 9–1.)

In the 14 most bureaucratic schools, however, further bureaucratization does seem to be accompanied by a reduction in authority problems ($t = -.52$), even though there is an increase in the outbreak of major incidents in these schools ($t = .36$). (See Table 9–2.) It appears that only after a school has been relatively bureaucratized does further bureaucratization begin to contain authority problems, and even then there is an increase in the more severe problems. This latter finding seems to reaffirm the "escape valve" function of routine conflict as a means of releasing pressure which was discussed in Chapter 8: When there is a lack of opportunity to discuss minor disputes in highly bureaucratic organizations, tension appears to build up, with conflict taking the form of major incidents when it does materialize.

The hypothesis, then, must be modified to take into account the level of professionalism and bureaucratization an organization has achieved. Interpreting these patterns loosely, it would appear that in the more

Table 9-5. Comparisons among levels of total bureaucratization of 28 schools on indices of organizational tension and conflict, by level of professional orientation

Indices of Organizational Tension and Conflict	High Professionalism				Low Professionalism				High vs. Low Professionalism (t-Tests Totals Only)
	Level of Bureaucratization (N = 14)				Level of Bureaucratization (N = 14)				
	High (N = 3)	Average (N = 6)	Low (N = 5)	Total (N = 14)	High (N = 5)	Average (N = 5)	Low (N = 4)	Total (N = 14)	
Avg. total tension bet. all roles	8.57	8.70	7.61	8.28	6.15	7.28	7.17	6.84	46.67[b]
Total no. of disagreements per faculty member	4.32	2.48	2.56	2.90	1.62	1.64	2.24	1.80	28.87[b]
No. of severe disagreements per faculty member	0.26	0.49	0.56	0.43	0.05	0.09	0.13	0.09	2.14[b]
No. of major incidents reported per interview	0.22	0.24	0.11	0.19	0.30	0.16	0.73	0.38	1.90[a]
No. of disputes reported per interview	0.91	0.67	0.73	0.74	0.61	0.47	0.45	0.51	0.33
Total no. of incidents reported per interview	2.25	2.30	2.05	2.20	1.76	1.58	1.88	1.73	2.81[b]

[a] Statistically Significant, one tail test, $p \leq .05$.
[b] Statistically Significant, one tail test, $p \leq .01$.

bureaucratic organizations an increase in bureaucratization does appear to reduce authority problems and routine organizational tensions, but even here bureaucratization is not effective in controlling the major incidents, and it may even contribute to the more basic problems.

Returning to the problem of professionalization, it is significant that bureaucratization does not seem to reduce conflict in the more professional organizations. Indeed, although the correlations do not reach statistical significance, it can be noted that in the more professional schools several types of conflict show signs of increasing with bureaucratization (that is, the total disagreement rate and major incidents and the frequency of incidents between teachers and the administration). (See Table 9–2.) In fact, of the 14 most professional schools the three that are most highly bureaucratized have higher rates of conflict on all the measures (except severe disagreements) than the five least bureaucratized schools. (See Table 9–5.) In these highly bureaucratized professional schools there is a high rate of conflict, which typically takes the form of disputes and/or major incidents; this also may have something to do with the decline in severe disagreements, in the sense that open disputes will either provide opportunity to resolve the more severe differences or materialize into full-scale major incidents.

On the other hand, compared with the more professional schools, in the less professional ones most forms of conflict appear to decline with bureaucratization. Among the 14 least professional schools those that are most bureaucratized have lower rates of total disagreement, total tension, severe disagreement, major incidents, and gross incident ratios than the least bureaucratized.[15] (See Table 9–5.)

Again, these findings provide a further indication that bureaucratization is incompatible with professionalization. While bureaucratization may help suppress conflict in the less militant professional schools, it seems only to aggravate it in professionally oriented organizations.

To this point, though the theory requires some modification, most of the hypotheses have been supported. Now, turning to the concept of structural crystallization, more complications will develop.

3. *There are statistically significant positive associations between structural crystallization and total tension* (t = .22) *and the ratio of disputes* (t = .26); *there is a negative association with the ratio of major incidents* (t = −.44). (See Table 9–1, col. 6, and Table 9–6.) The associations with severe and total disagreement rates are positive also, though they are not statistically significant. These findings provide some support for Hypothesis 3, then, and in further support of the hypothesis the nine most structurally consistent schools were found to have uniformly higher rates of tension, disputes, and major incidents than the nine least crystallized schools.[16] (See Table 9–6.)

However, the fact that at least the frequency of major incidents

Table 9-6. Comparisons among levels of structural crystallization of 28 schools on indices of organizational tension and conflict

	Level of Structural Crystallization				
Indices of Organizational Tension and Conflict	High (N = 9) $\bar{X}$	Average (N = 10) $\bar{X}$	Low (N = 9) $\bar{X}$	t-Test High vs. Low	Total $\bar{X}$
Avg. Total Tension Between All Roles	8.09	7.63	6.69	2.86[a]	7.74
Total no. of disagreements per faculty member	2.95	2.09	2.05	1.41	2.35
No. of severe disagreements per faculty member	0.40	0.12	0.32	0.31	0.31
No. of major incidents reported per interview	0.11	0.22	0.54	2.87[a]	0.23
No. of disputes reported per interview	0.77	0.61	0.51	2.60[a]	0.68
Total no. of incidents called Type I reported per interview	1.94	2.07	1.85	0.32	2.02

[a] Statistically significant, one-tail test, $p \leq .01$.

declines as schools become more structurally consistent ($t = -.44$) indicates that using several bureaucratic procedures simultaneously might effectively reduce the major violent forms of conflict, even if they do not appear to be effective with the milder forms of conflict.

Finally, when the level of bureaucratization and of structural crystallization are considered jointly, it is possible to distinguish organizations that are consistently highly bureaucratic from those that are consistently less bureaucratic. It was felt that the interaction effect would alter the association of either variable taken by itself, and this tends to be the case. (See Table 9–7.) The bureaucratization of less crystallized organizations is associated with reductions in every measure of conflict, while the bureaucratization of the most crystallized organizations is accompanied by increased conflict on four of the six measures. Of course, because the cell sizes are extremely small the data can be considered only as suggestive.

3–A. *Considering only the least crystallized schools, the two that are also most bureaucratic have lower conflict rates than the five least bureaucratized schools.* (See Table 9–7.) Again, the cell sizes are small, but for the cases at hand uncrystallized, highly bureaucratized organiza-

Table 9-7. Comparisons among levels of bureaucratization of 28 schools on rates of disagreement and organizational tension, by level of structural crystallization

Indices of Organizational Tension and Conflict	High Crystallization			Average Crystallization			Low Crystallization		
	Bureaucratization			Bureaucratization			Bureaucratization		
	High (N = 2)	Average (N = 3)	Low (N = 4)	High (N = 4)	Average (N = 6)	Low (N = 0)	High (N = 2)	Average (N = 2)	Low (N = 5)
Avg. total tension bet. all roles	8.48	8.53	8.00	7.42	8.11	—	5.97	7.81	7.43
Total no. of disagreements per faculty member	4.45	1.98	2.59	1.85	2.47	—	1.31	2.03	2.44
No. of severe disagreements per faculty member	.09	.27	.94	.17	.13	—	.09	1.54	.23
No. of major incidents reported per interview	.10	.11	.17	.26	.20	—	.34	.42	.44
No. of disputes reported per interview	1.03	.63	.79	.66	.58	—	.55	.63	.61
Total no. of incidents reported per interview	1.97	2.17	1.91	2.24	1.97	—	1.36	1.81	2.21

tions have the lowest rates of conflict in the entire sample on every measure except major incidents. On the other hand, considering only the crystallized schools, the two that are most bureaucratic have higher total tension, disagreement rates, and dispute ratios than the four least bureaucratic schools. (See Table 9–7.) The sample again is too small for other than suggestive purposes, and some of the differences are slight and nonuniform. But they do suggest the beginning of a pattern. In the most crystallized schools the total disagreement rate doubles if they are highly bureaucratized. However, severe disagreements and major incidents have a reverse pattern; the former are several times higher in less bureaucratic, crystallized organizations.[17]

Again, we find that attempts to bureaucratize already conflictful organizations, in this case structurally consistent ones, seem merely to aggravate certain types of problems; it is the less consistent organizations that are less tension-ridden and in which bureaucracy seems to be most effective. Yet, we must admit that it is still plausible that structurally consistent bureaucracies simply are less effective than those that use the reinforcement approach by emphasizing one or two controls to the exclusion of the rest.

The over-all pattern of data suggests that it is worth looking more extensively into the relationship of bureaucratization and crystallization to conflict. Therefore, we shall turn our attention to a still more detailed case analysis.

Patterns of Bureaucracy

But if patterns of bureaucracy tend to evolve as responses to existing tension, they cannot be viewed exclusively in these terms. Once established, certain patterns of consistency and inconsistency, in turn, probably independently, aggravate conflict. In view of the sample size the findings again must be considered as only illustrative, but the following breakdown illustrates how conflict fluctuates with the pattern of priorities given to the various procedures.

The schools were classified as follows (according to the practices that are simultaneously most emphasized and deemphasized):

Type I Schools
    Standardization emphasized (that is, emphasis either on rules or on close supervision)
    And decentralization of either
      (a) professional policy decisions
      (b) nonprofessional policy decisions
      (c) routine decisions

Type II Schools
    Centralization of either
      (a) professional policy decisions
      (b) nonprofessional policy decisions
      (c) routine decisions
    And deemphasis of either
      (a) rules
      (b) close supervision

Type III Schools
    All "other" combinations

It was found that schools with Type I pattern, which stress standardization and decentralization of decision making, generally have higher rates of conflict and tension than those in Type II, which are centralized

Table 9-8. Types of high-low structural patterns and indices of organizational tension and conflict

Selected Measures of Organizational Tension and Conflict	Types of High-Low Structural Patterns		
	Type I[a] (N = 10)	Type II[b] (N = 7)	All Other (N = 11)
Avg. total tension bet. all roles (reported by faculty members)	7.94	6.92	7.94
Rates of Disagreement			
Total no. of disagreements per faculty member	2.73	1.46	2.41
No. of severe disagreements per faculty member	0.56	0.10	0.13
No. of incidents reported per interview			
Total no. of all types of incidents (gross incident ratio)	2.27	1.66	1.86
Disputes	0.80	0.46	0.58
Major Incidents	0.19	0.38	0.32
No. of incidents per interview involving the following role partners			
Teacher(s) vs. administrator(s)	1.65	1.60	1.47
Mean professional orientation	58.59	57.29	57.68

[a]Type I: Emphasis on either rules or close supervision, and decentralization of professional or nonprofessional policy decisions on routine decision.
[b]Type II: Centralization of professional and nonprofessional policy decision on routine decisions, and deemphasis of either rules or close supervision.

but deemphasize either rules or close supervision; this is true in every case except major incidents—where the difference is reversed.[18] (See Table 9–8.) However, there is one important exception. The highest tension and disagreement rates in the sample occur in schools where rules are emphasized and supervision deemphasized (which is one of the patterns in the "other" category).

IMPLICATIONS

Conclusions based on a few cases obviously must be regarded as only suggestive, but when organizations are the sampling unit it is difficult to accumulate a larger sample. It is revealing that even in this small sample linear relationships were consistently found between a faculty's professional orientation and various measures of organizational tension and conflict, especially at certain levels of professionalism. Administrators who want to support professional faculties may also have to put up with some problems. Extremely professional faculties have higher rates of conflict than the less professional extremes, and the relationship is even more prominent in faculties that combine high professional orientations with low employee orientations. But it is essential to recognize the distinction between major incidents and other forms of conflict. In almost every type of analysis, except in the most bureaucratic of schools, major incidents seemed to decline with professionalism. It is possible that major incidents could be reduced more effectively by supporting the efforts of teachers to professionalize than by trying to impose more control on professionally oriented faculties.

The findings about bureaucratization indicate that it is frequently employed as a means of keeping situations from getting out of control. Undoubtedly, many administrators react to professional militancy by attempting further to bureaucratize the school in an effort to keep control over the situation. However, because bureaucratic principles are not always compatible with a professional orientation to teaching, they may simply aggravate the problem. Accordingly, in schools already highly bureaucratized, authority problems decline with further bureaucratization, but major incidents increase: Bureaucratization itself does not necessarily contain conflict.

Two types of situations were considered, the bureaucratization of less professional schools and the professionalization of more bureaucratic schools. Regarding the first, there are indications that bureaucratization may help contain conflict in the less professional schools. Although perhaps they are already more peaceful; the number of disputes, in particular, is inversely related to the bureaucratization of the least professional schools, and several other forms of conflict are lower in the few less professional schools, which are relatively bureaucratized. But in the most professional schools, conflict increases as they become bureaucratized; this includes the more severe forms of major incidents as well. There is a corresponding tendency for bureaucratization of the highly professional schools simply to aggravate conflict. Militant prefessionalism, then, is primarily characteristic of the most bureaucratic schools.

Major incidents might be more effectively curbed if the efforts of teachers to professionalize were supported than by trying to impose more bureaucratic controls on already militant professional teachers.

Indeed, as schools become more consistently bureaucratic, certain forms of conflict show an especially marked tendency to increase, whereas uncrystallized schools are more peaceful. This could be the result of a combination of two tendencies—uniformity of bureaucratic control evolves in response to preexisting conflict, and uniform, across-the-board bureaucratization itself provokes resistance and conflict. While the former may be of more importance, the latter cannot be minimized. But the fact that the frequency of major incidents declines in more structurally consistent schools suggests that the crystallization, unlike the total amount of bureaucratization, can help to minimize some of the more severe forms of conflict.

Conflict appears to be especially prevalent in highly bureaucratic schools that are also highly crystallized, whereas it is less frequent in less crystallized schools, whether bureaucratized or not. Major incidents are the important exception, for they appear to be lower in crystallized organizations. It is possible that crystallization, rather than suppressing underlying conflict, simply clarifies the structure sufficiently so that there is less reason for major incidents to develop.

NOTES: Chapter 9

[1] As used in this context, the term "empirical theory" refers to a logically coherent body of confirmed generalizations which have in common certain assumptions and concepts, the relationships of which can be specified with known precision (Broadbeck, 1959). The theory to be explored consists of the four concepts mentioned plus certain assumptions and derivative hypotheses and their corollaries. The system is reasonably coherent and has a limited amount of empirical support.

There is no formula for developing a theory other than to say that theory develops as a result of attempts to think through problems in conjunction with rather close and systematic observation. Data from limited, exploratory studies seldom permit confirmation of interpretations, and in this case the problem is particularly acute because in its present state the theory neither clearly specifies the cause of conflict nor accounts for its intensity. Moreover, it is seldom possible directly to confirm causal relations with survey data, though such theories usually assume causality (that is, a time sequence). The sample used to explore the theory suffers from the additional handicap that it is for many purposes too small for statistically reliable conclusions; the analysis should be regarded as a multiple case study.

[2] The standardization index was not included in this measure because data were unavailable for seven of the 28 schools.

[3] This concept parallels what Lenski refers to as (in another context) as status crystallization. Some evidence has accumulated showing that the consistency of a person's separate statuses is at least as important in explaining his preference for change and his political liberalism as his rank on any one status (Lenski, 1954; Goffman, 1957; Jackson, 1962). But the equally important sociological problem of consistency among an organization's structural positions has been relatively neglected, Landecker's (1960) and Hodge's (1962) studies being notable exceptions. The concept "structural crystallization" provides a way of classifying organizations according to their structural configurations, independently of their levels of bureaucratization. This concept is also relevant to the reinforcement and compensatory bureaucratic models. In crystallized organizations bureaucratic practices are used with consistently uniform emphasis and in that sense may be said to reinforce each other; in uncrystallized organizations one or two practices are disproportionately expressed, which is similar to the pattern portrayed in the compensatory model.

[4] Other studies report that teachers want more decision-making authority than they have at present (Sharma, 1955). From a study of 20 former teachers, Washburn (1957) concluded that there is a pervasive conflict in schools between the professional status of teachers and the fact of their subordination. While teachers had thought of themselves as professionals who, by rights, should have discretion over their work, they felt hampered and limited by administrators who specified both their goals and the appropriate procedures.

[5] The reinforcement model might lead to a different conclusion. If it were assumed that there is a natural drive within organizations to maximize control, and if consistency among bureaucratic dimensions were considered to be a normal state, then structural crystallization would represent a maximum degree of control, and conflict in such organizations would be minimal.

[6] The validity of this derivation is qualified by the fact that the "sign rule" applies only where the correlations among the premises are "high" (Costner and Leik, 1964).

[7] The number in the left-hand margin refers to the relevant hypothesis to the findings.

[8] Using the Pearsonian "r" to compute the linear correlations on school means does not substantially alter the conclusions reached by using the rank-order-correlation technique. Examples of the linear correlations are as follows:

	Professional (N = 28)		Employee (N = 28)	
Conflict Measures	Orientation	Behavior	Orientation	Behavior
Number of authority incidents per interview	.26	.16	−.28	−.38
Total number of incidents reported per interview	.18	.34	−.06	−.12

[9] For example, when a faculty's age is "partialled out," the correlation between professional orientation and severe disagreements is $t = .22$, and with total tension it is $t = .33$. It is worth noting, too, that tension (as distinguished from overt incidents) in professionally oriented schools is not primarily between principals and teachers, but between teachers and students. Conceivably, the fact that professionally oriented faculties feel more tension with their students arises because they place more emphasis on knowledge and expect more of their students in general. Students are probably less concerned about doing a "quality job" than about the pressures to achieve better grades. An analysis of the four subscales comprising the professional scale shows that tension between teachers and students increases significantly with teachers' emphasis on knowledge ($t = .43$), although it also increases with desire for decision-making authority ($t = .37$) and strength of colleague orientation ($t = .25$).

[10] It should be noted that professionals in the most bureaucratic organizations are not in a favorable position to express their annoyances directly to the administration.

[11] Also, schools at the top of the professional behavior distribution are statistically higher than those in the lowest quartile on the following measures (at $p \leq .08$): total disagreements, total tension, gross incident ratio, and dispute ratio. The top quartile also has a significantly lower major incident ratio.

[12] Finally, the schools were grouped into three levels, first on the basis of their mean professional orientations and then on the basis of their employee orientations. The analysis provided some indication about why the linear rank order correlation coefficients are not higher than they are. In most cases the relationship is slightly curvilinear, with the differences primarily due to the relatively low conflict rates of the low-ranking professional schools. (Six of the 10 comparisons of average ranks are statistically significant as tested by the Kruskal-Wallis analysis of variance method.) Only the relationship between levels of professional orientation and the average ranks on heated discussion and major incidents were completely linear.

[13] When the role organization of the 1,500 individuals in the sample was used as a basis of this correlation, the results were even more definitive than those computed on the basis of the modal type of faculty member in each of the 28 schools. The higher the proportion of faculty members who simultaneously support professional norms and reject the employee role, the higher their conflict rates on every measure but one (the major incident ratio). Correlations with both the gross incident ratio and with the number of authority issues reported per interview are relatively high ($t = .44$ and $t = .49$, respectively), and these correlations remain after controlling for both a faculty's sociability (that is, the proportion seeing each other socially very frequently) and its frequency of contact with the principal; however, two of the correlations (teacher-administrator incidents and dispute ratio) are reduced appreciably when the number of staff additions is "partialled out."

Conversely, the proportion of the faculty simultaneously upholding high employee and low professional orientations is negatively associated with all of the correlations; however, only the total incident ratio and the ratio of authority issues and the ratio of conflicts involving heated discussions were statistically significant—$t = -.22$, $t = -.22$, and $t = -.27$, respectively.

One of the few conditions found in this study to be conducive to major incidents is the lack of commitment of large proportions of teachers to either professional or employee role conceptions ($t = .32$). Again, it must be concluded that whereas conflict is characteristic of professionally oriented staffs, major incidents are not. Rather, they occur where neither professional nor employee norms dominate.

[14] Except for severe disagreements and major incidents the trends appear to be more dichotomous or curvilinear rather than linear, with schools of average bureaucratization hovering near one extreme or the other.

[15] Also, schools were dichotomized on each conflict measure (on the basis of the sample mean). The conflict frequency distributions of the high and low professional schools within the highly bureaucratic category were compared. All three of the highly professional schools exhibited a high level of total tension and all five of the least professional schools had a low level of tension. Most of the comparisons showed a similar pattern with only one or two deviations; however, there was not a similar pattern within the less bureaucratic group of schools.

[16] Uncrystallized organizations seem to evolve only where there is relatively little conflict. But the case of structural crystallization is more complicated. While crystallization seems to be associated with tension-producing situations, this does not mean that it is necessarily a direct response to conflict; it may, instead, be a response to other tension-producing, threatening conditions which themselves are associated with conflict, such as professionalism, organizational complexity, and staff turnover and expansion. For example, the fact that the most structurally consistent schools also have the most professionally oriented faculties ($X = 59.2$) suggests that structurally consistent organizations might have evolved partly as a response to professional militancy and related conditions, and that militancy in turn may be aggravated in the context of such organizations.

[17] Table 9–7 shows that conflict increases as crystallized organizations become more bureaucratic. It is also true that conflict increases as bureaucratic organizations become more crystallized. Among the most bureaucratic organizations those that are highly crystallized have higher conflict rates than those that are less crystallized, except for severe disagreements and major incidents, where the pattern is reversed; they are least prevalent in organizations that are simultaneously highly bureaucratic and crystallized. Crystallization, in other words, seems to be ineffective with milder forms of incidents, but apparently it can be successful in retaining the more intense forms of conflict.

[18] For example, four of the five schools having the lowest rates of total disagreement have a Type II pattern. The mean total disagreement rates of schools with the Type I pattern are uniformly higher than those of the Type II pattern. However, in view of the fact that the conflict rates associated with these structural patterns have correspondingly high and low professional orientations, one should not conclude prematurely that the pattern itself is responsible for the conflict; it is possible that certain types of structural arrangements simply reinforce professionalism or other disruptive features, which in turn are responsible for the conflict.

REFERENCES: Chapter 9

Blau, Peter, and Scott, W. Richard. *Formal organization.* San Francisco: Chandler, 1962.

Broadbeck, May. Model meanings and theories. In *Symposium on Sociological Theory.* Llewellyn Gross Edition. New York: Row, Peterson, 1959. Pp. 373–403.

Bucher, Rue, and Strauss, Aselm. Professions in process. *The American Journal of Sociology,* 1961, 66,

Costner, Herbert L., and Leik, Robert K. Deductions from "axiomatic theory." *American Sociological Review,* December, 1964, 29, 819–835.

Dahrendorf, Ralf. *Class and class conflict in industrial society.* Stanford, Cal.: Stanford University Press, 1959. P. 208.

Goffman, Irwin W. Status consistency and preference for change in power distribution. *American Sociological Review,* June, 1957, 22, 275–281.

Hodge, Robert W. The status consistency of occupational groups. *American Sociological Review,* June, 1962, 27, 336–343.

Jackson, Elton F. Status consistency and symptoms of stress. *American Sociological Review,* August, 1962, 27, 469–480.

Landecker, Werner S. Class boundaries. *American Sociological Review,* December, 1960, 25, 868–877.

Lenski, Gerhard. Status crystallization: A non-vertical dimension of social status. *American Sociological Review,* 1964, 19, 405–413.

Sharma, C. L. Who should make decisions? *Administrators' Notebook,* April, 1955, 3, 1–4.

Washburn, C. The teacher and the authority system. *Journal of Educational Sociology,* 1957, 30, 390–394.

part IV. Aftermath

FROM TALKS WITH TEACHERS *more on students*

I FEEL *there is a closer relationship with students now than formerly. You can be friends with your teacher, and the teacher can speak to you in an informal way, which is very nice. But, I also think the teachers don't have enough authority over the students, and when they want to turn this informal thing off, there's trouble.—a teacher*

I AM *thinking of one teacher in particular. He is a very good mathematician, I have no doubt. He probably has a very good mind when it comes to math. But when it comes to teaching, I don't think he has a place in it because of his attitude toward the kids. He is not flexible; he doesn't take into consideration individual differences, from what I have observed. He goes into the class and teaches on his high plane, and they either understand or they don't. If they don't, "Who cares?" He has been called down for the number of F's he was giving. All he did was lower the distribution—he didn't want to get into trouble. But he hasn't changed his teaching in any way. A lot of the boys think he is picking on them. . . . But there are a few in his classes that really like him. He is teaching to the upper level students, and the other students are struggling along, just trying.—a math teacher*

10. The anatomy of militant professionalism

> *In dealing with the strategy and tactics of conflict resolution in organizations, it is well to bear in mind that much organizational conflict is built in by the very nature of a complex system.*—Katz, 1964.

Teacher militancy clearly is not the reaction of downtrodden groups to despair; rather, it reflects the hope of an increasingly important segment of the society. Several now familiar forces in our society, some within the schools themselves, have contributed to this tidal wave of hope. It would be useful to review these, and in the process to add some qualifications which often have been overlooked in the heat of controversy over this perplexing development.

INSTITUTIONAL DEVELOPMENTS

Teacher militancy is, in part at least, a product of a number of institutional changes.

National Relevance of Education

First, there is the now familiar "revolution" in technology which has thrust institutions of formal education into unprecedented positions of national relevance. However, this relevance has been extracted at a price, because it has meant that the limited resources of schools have been strained in attempting to assume increasing responsibility for a diverse set of demands provoked by an emergent urban society. In particular, as a result of the fact that less well-educated persons have been excluded from the labor market, schools are being transformed into welfare agencies. But the transition has been painful and erratic. New demands create the need for new teaching specialties. Yet teacher training institutions have been slow to respond to this particular need. The consequence is that teachers are relatively well trained, but they have not been prepared to cope with many of the problems for which they are being held responsible. But clearly, too, the new demands will require more than new and novel ways of training teachers; new concepts of administration and of school organization itself will be required. Teachers are beginning to demand it.

Affluence

These new responsibilities are being assumed in an affluent society, which is, to many people at least, evidence that this nation has the way, if not the will, to pay for the requested reforms. Expensive modifications demanded by teachers make sense only within the context of a revolution in expectation which has fed upon our national wealth. But, in practice, the Vietnam war has drastically altered expected resource allocations, and the ability of local communities to compete for national resources varies, while the demands of teachers—benefiting from national networks of communication— are more uniform. And in practice, too, teachers have been forced to compete for resources with even better organized local employees, such as nurses, policemen, and transit workers.

Involvement in Politics

This competition for vast amounts of resources inevitably has thrust educators squarely into the political arena. In particular, teachers seem to have adopted some of the tools of protest which have worked for the civil rights movement and are so well adapted to this age of existentialism, with its doctrine of personal commitment and decisive action. This is a generation, after all, that blames much of its plight on a self-conscious sense of alienation and loss of control, the source of which springs from the failures within existing organizations; to such people collective action can be an attractive recourse.

CHANGES IN SCHOOL SYSTEMS

These developments in the national level are paralleled by pressures on schools to develop new points of departure.

The Climate of Innovation

Under recent criticism schools have become enveloped in a climate of innovation. They are in the process of reorienting themselves from reliance on routines to more problem-centered approaches to education. Of course, change is not new to schools, but innovation now has been elevated to the level of a principle. Not only has the pace been stepped up, but also the scope of some of the changes proposed promises to be more sweeping than usual, encompassing entire systems and regions rather than individual classrooms. If, as some critics charge, there has been little evidence of change from all of this innovation, the problems are only aggravated.

Teacher Power

In this time of change and experimentation it is perhaps natural that teachers are becoming more powerful. For this is, by definition, a time when no particular group has a monopoly on the answers. And in practice it has become necessary to delegate decisions, implicitly if not officially, because administrators cannot maintain firm centralized control over a system that does not work effectively. The failures of the system cannot help but reflect on the authority of those who run it, and teachers are not likely to submit enthusiastically to the authority of an administrative system that has failed to come to grips with their occupation's problems.

Added to this general situation is the fact that in this era of job opportunity and a supply-demand ratio favorable to teachers, the proportion of teachers in the work force is also expanding at a rate four times faster than the general population explosion. The projected growth, together with the continuing trend toward concentration in metropolitan areas, is likely to serve only to strengthen their influence.

But probably the most important basis of the teacher's sense of power is the growth of specialization within teaching. Not only has a segment of teachers made a substantial gain in their educational level, but also, there is likely to be marked increase in the specialized use of teaching techniques for distinct populations, and perhaps separate career lines for teaching various classes and types of students are beginning to appear as well. All of this gives teachers leverage in knowledge and skill over the administrators, who nevertheless are still responsible for evaluating them. The time may be rapidly approaching when it will be difficult, if not impossible, for administrators to assume the exclusive responsibility for evaluating teachers.

And if teachers have gained more access to power, they also have found more reasons for exercising it. Disproportionate numbers of lower-class people are being attracted to the profession precisely as a way to improve their social status, and they are finding that their own positions depend as much on the fortunes of their occupation as a whole as upon their individual efforts: the relative lack of opportunity for individual mobility within the occupation only encourages their efforts to achieve collective mobility.

It is important, too, that at a time when teachers are beginning to develop a sense of competence which would justify greater control over some decisions, they are bearing the brunt of much criticism for poor quality education, particularly in the inner-city schools, for which many of them feel they really are not responsible. The fact that many of the changes being proposed are aimed at altering the teachers' classroom behavior seems to suggest that they somehow are responsible for the problems; and many of them seem to be saying that if they are to be held responsible, they have the right to exercise more control over the situation.

But a number of crucial questions remain unanswered here. For example, does the reading achievement of students reflect the quality of classroom teaching, or does it more accurately reflect the quality of the administration responsible for deploying adequate resources and making the necessary adjustments in procedure? Or perhaps it reflects the unrealistic goals and inadequate procedures of the system itself. A persistent problem is that though the system of organization may be at fault, it is unlikely that teachers and administrators who benefit from the system will be willing to change their own roles—and often these are precisely the roles that need to be changed.

Erosion of Traditional Modes of Administration

The corollary of teacher power is the impending change in the roles of administrators. Their traditional jurisdictions, which already are being undermined by the growing influence of the federal government and of local militant groups, are being challenged by the demands of teachers as well. Just as it is now recognized that the logical distinction between "policy decisions" and "administrative decisions" has not really provided an effective division of labor between administrators and school boards, so the presumed division between "administrative" and "teaching" responsibilities will be no real barrier against the encroachment of teachers on traditional administrative prerogatives. It is probably significant in this connection that this study of staff conflicts has demonstrated that the most frequent type of dispute in public schools—one in every four—concerned authority problems between teachers and administrators. Teachers are demanding a greater role in the decision-making process.

The tension between teachers and administrators is also accentuated by the fact that they are often separated by more than a generation of experience. Most administrators were trained during an era when the problems of classroom teaching could be reduced (or so it was thought) to the psychology of individuals, and when the central administrative problems seemed to revolve around efficient internal management. The current generation of teachers, by contrast, has been reared in a sociological era characterized by rapid social change and group conflict, and during which administration has become largely a matter of managing increasingly complex balances of forces from both outside and inside the schools.

But in final analysis the professional status teachers are demanding is in many crucial respects incompatible with traditional principles of administration—principles originally fashioned in a unified, small-town America, premised on teacher compliance and justified by the legal fact and fiction that administrators are, and can be, responsible for literally every facet of what is sometimes referred to as "their" system. Centralized authority and system-wide uniformity are difficult to reconcile with decentralized decision-making authority—the central component of professionalism. If classroom teachers are to professionalize, therefore, they must gain more control, perhaps the primary control, over key matters.

Limited evidence that professionalization is a militant process came from this study; the incidence of most types of conflict in a school (with one important exception which will be noted) increased with the faculty's average level of what we took to be indicators of their professionalism. But what is perhaps even more important is the fact that this association was most prominent in the more bureaucratized schools (compared with the least bureaucratic). In other words, it is in precisely the most highly organized schools that support for professional concepts seems most likely to produce conflict. But these general propositions now need to be qualified in light of the evidence.

SOME QUALIFICATIONS

Despite all of the discussion about teacher militancy, probably only a minority of teachers are militant, and an even smaller minority are what might be termed militant professionals. However, it is equally apparent that, given the growing concentration of the population, small proportions can be numerically large enough to be important. The numerical minority of militant professionals identified in most of the schools in this study is far from being a marginal group. On the contrary, they constitute a core of the leadership and have the backing of the majority of teachers. Compared to their colleagues they are better educated and more respected and better integrated into their peer groups, and they have more support from their peers. Also, although it is often thought that the youngest, least "mature" teachers are the ringleaders, it is the middle-aged, well-established men in this sample who most frequently actually become involved in conflict (even though it is true that the youngest teachers express the most belligerent attitudes). This seems to indicate that opposition to professionalization, in effect, means opposing the most influential segment of teachers.

In this connection, the evidence also suggests that there are no clear answers to the great debate over the relative degree of militancy of the AFT and the NEA. The AFT officers in this sample are more professionally oriented and express more militant attitudes in some respects, and they become involved in more disputes over authority. But over all, the NEA officers have become involved in more of almost every other type of conflict (although this sample was from the Mid-West, which does not necessarily include the most militant AFT chapters). What is more important than this debate is the fact that there seems to be a group of informal leaders who have not been officers in either organization, but who are by far more militant than either group's official leaders. In sum, militancy is spearheaded by a small group of largely unidentified but influential teachers.

There is a second point that sometimes remains obscure in these discussions: The issue of whether teaching is in fact a "profession" (in some ultimate sense of that term) is in many respects less important than the fact that a large proportion of teachers believe that they are entitled to more authority than they now have; for example, 70 percent of the sample agree with the statement that they should have "the ultimate authority over major educational decisions."

Participating in militant causes may restore some of the sense of influence not provided within the system itself. It is in this connection that one finding from the study has its real significance: Both job satisfaction of individual teachers and morale of school faculties increase with rates of conflict within the staff.

However, as another qualification one must add that it would be a mistake to assume that militancy comes about as a reaction to any presumed loss of control on the part of teachers. It is sometimes assumed that they have lost influence as schools have become less personal and more bureaucratized. Perhaps there are elements of this, but the data suggest that teachers in the larger, more hierarchical schools actually have more decision-making authority over their classrooms than teachers in less bureaucratic schools. And these are also the schools where the most conflict occurs.

The preceding comments suggest still another qualification which will be of interest to those who hope to pacify teachers' desires for authority by giving them only minor concessions. Increases in teachers' decision-making authority seem to lead to more rather than to less conflict. Apparently, a little authority does not "go a long way" toward pacifying professional employees. On the contrary, expectations in this area seem to be increasing faster than achievements. Success feeds aspiration; and involvement in the decision-making process, even in a minor way, can involve teachers in a wider range of issues than would otherwise have been the case. Some possible reasons will be explored later in this discussion.

But this statement is, in turn, qualified further by still other evidence. For it is true that some of the most severe conflicts in the study occur less frequently in schools where teachers report having more authority. In other words, an opportunity to participate in decision making seems to be more conducive to disputing in general, but it may prevent grievances from accumulating and erupting into major outbreaks. The establishment of regularized communication procedures could have the same effect.

Also, an earlier generalization must be qualified in that professionalization does not necessarily lead to conflict—if the environment is already compatible or if accommodations have been made. Professionalization, for example, is not necessarily associated with conflict in the less bureaucratic schools, and there are some signs that schools are making at least some minor adaptations to professionalization. The more professionally oriented faculties in the sample report having more decision-making authority over classroom matters even though, in other respects, the schools are not adjusting to professionalism as rapidly as might have been expected.* Also, the data suggest that even more conflict might have been found were it not for the fact that the most professionally oriented teachers are randomly distributed among schools instead of being concentrated in a few, whereas the most employee-oriented people are concentrated in the most bureaucratic schools to which they are most compatible.

The corollary to the previous point, of course, is that bureaucratization in itself does not necessarily lead to conflict either. The problem occurs when there are attempts to apply mechanisms such as close supervision, standardization, special rules, and centralized decision making to faculties intent upon increasing their professional status. It was found that in the least professionally oriented faculties the rates of conflict were lower when they were more bureaucratized. The effectiveness of administrative practices, therefore, obviously is not inherent in the practices themselves, but depends largely on the setting to which they are applied. While this point is perhaps obvious, it seems safe to assume that most administrators probably have not systematically tailored their practices to the changing conceptions of their faculties.

* The over-all index of bureaucratization is not negatively related in any significant way to the degree of support given for professional roles, as might have been expected if bureaucratic schools were debureaucratizing to any appreciable extent.

As still a further reservation, it should be recognized that professionalization produces not only conflict with the administration but also conflict and segmentation among the teachers themselves. Tension rises between the militant teachers who are professionally motivated and those who are militant for other reasons. It is essential to keep this distinction in mind when interpreting the meaning of militancy. While the most professionally oriented faculties in the sample have higher conflict rates than those which are less professional, the reverse is not necessarily true—that is, the most conflictful faculties do not necessarily strongly subscribe to professional principles. Other sources of tension include the organization itself (that is, complexity in the authority structure), general conditions within the society (such as the adolescent revolt and variations in militancy based on differences between the sexes), and the civil rights movement in the big cities. The civil rights movement in particular seems to be on a collision course with teacher militancy. Questions can be raised about the degree of support that teacher organizations have given desegregation plans and experimental projects leading to more community control and about what this means for the prospects of professionalization.

This leads to still another qualification which, while obvious, nevertheless sometimes eludes the discussion. Militancy can take a variety of forms and degrees of intensity. While the term is most frequently used in connection with work stoppages, strikes represent only the most visible signs of a much more prevalent phenomenon—a posture of challenge to authority. Authority can be challenged in a variety of ways. In particular, the most professionally oriented militants in the sample are involved in very different forms of conflict than their less professional counterparts who also become involved in disputes. With one exception, they did shy away from what were labeled here as the "major incidents"—that is, the sustained, heated conflicts involving large numbers of persons. This might at first seem to suggest that the more professionally oriented teachers are not the ones actively leading the recent rash of strikes, except that the data do not warrant such a conclusion. It seems more reasonable to assume that the role that professionally oriented teachers play in strikes will depend heavily on the circumstances. For, in contrast to the general pattern, in the most bureaucratic schools professionalization is associated with even the frequency of major incidents.

Perhaps the lesson here is that administrators will have to put up with many forms of friction if they want to maintain professional faculties; but supporting the professionally oriented teachers may be a more effective way of controlling the outbreak of at least the major incidents than attempting to suppress them by imposing more bureaucratic controls—which is probably a more typical reaction.

In any event, the behavior of teachers can be explained better in terms of principles of social power than exclusively in terms of either idealism or economic considerations. For one thing, teachers no longer have to rely exclusively on cultivating the public's benevolence. Many people believe this to be unfortunate, and perhaps it is only natural to formulate the philosophical questions about whether this or that practice is "right" or "wrong," according to one's personal values (and, of course, his own personal interests), but the questions that need answers right now concern what is going to happen.

Perhaps at this point it is too early to expect teachers to be concerned about justifying their every move or staying within the limits of legitimate behavior; given the fact that they are challenging the legitimacy of the present system, and must act defensively against it, one could hardly expect them to stay within the bounds of propriety. Within all professions (and not just teaching) there is a generic tension between idealism and self-interest. Professionalization is motivated partly by material gain as critics frequently claim, but what is distinctive about professionalization is that it represents a shift from self-interest, or what Hofstadter (1964) calls "interest politics," toward the "politics of status."

But if the immediate objective of teachers is power, they eventually must return to the question of how to legitimate that power once it has been achieved. And in order to legitimate professional status, the occupation eventually must demonstrate its ability to protect its clients' welfare. Therefore, it is obviously to the profession's advantage to combine self-interest with idealism. Teachers, for example, maintain that they cannot do their best for students under poor working conditions and without sufficient authority, and that high salaries are needed to attract qualified people. It is no accident that these assertions are difficult to prove or disprove and that there is no clear-cut answer to the question of the "real" motives of teachers. But, of course, all professions seek to use ideals in the service of self-interest, and to mobilize self-interest so that it better serves professional ideals. Physicians do not often strike, for example, but they restrict the number of people who can enter the profession and restrain economic competition among themselves. The situation is not unique to teachers.

The evidence on this point is not very convincing, but it appears that among the most militant teachers those who are most professionally oriented are at least more concerned about the welfare of their students than their less professionally oriented, but equally militant, colleagues. At the same time, it appears that teachers are more ready than administrators to define certain children as being unable to learn.

It also should be noted in this connection that professionals obviously are not the only ones who have ideologies. There are competing contentions advanced by administrators and laymen which are equally difficult to prove, such as the notions that "employees must be supervised," that there is a special class of "decision makers" in schools, and that school boards' sovereignty must remain inviolable in a democracy. In these ideological disputes, of course, each side seeks to define the public interest to suit its own purpose.

THEORETICAL PERSPECTIVES*

Some of these propositions can be further amplified by weighing several competing theoretical perspectives. Most people probably would be inclined to start explaining conflict from the assumption that it simply represents another phase of the Hobbesian war of "all against all," especially among certain belligerent types of people having deviant personality traits—that is, abnormal degrees of vanity, drive for recognition, inability to adjust to others, emotional instability, and so forth. Without denying the relevance of such factors, it seems much more important to recognize that certain situations apparently produce tensions which are easily kindled almost independently of the particular people who happen to be part of the situations. In nearly every school interviewed, for example, teachers in academic subjects have some complaint against teachers in the extracurricular programs because of the class disruptions created by activity practices and special events. Similarly, vocational teachers often express antagonism toward academic teachers and counselors who monopolize the good students and send them the castoffs. And schools with high rates of faculty turnover are simply more conflict prone than more stable schools. Even so important a characteristic as a person's age does not completely account for his conflict rate; the correlation between professional orientation and conflict rate held for all age categories tested. Moreover, as already mentioned, the most belligerent professionally oriented teachers, far from being marginally "deviant" people, were better integrated into their peer groups, better educated, and more respected and had more group support from their colleagues. While teachers who are both professional and militant are only a small portion of all teachers, they are a group with backing from a broad base of teachers. What is important to note here, however, is that whereas administrative personnel policies traditionally have been based on assumptions about individual psychology, in fact personnel problems in the public schools today seem to be basically sociological in nature.

The personality deviance hypothesis also underlies several variants on the frustration-aggression theme. But in this case, conflict is portrayed as a generic human response to social constraints rather than being the

* Parts of this section are adapted from Ronald G. Corwin, "Teacher Militancy in the United States; Reflections on Its Sources and Prospects," *Theory into Practice* (Vol. VIII, No. 2), by permission of the College of Education, The Ohio State University.

product of unique personality traits. From this perspective, teachers appear to have become belligerent because they have been prevented from obtaining their objectives. While in a sense this may be true, such an interpretation is rather mechanistic, because in itself it accounts for neither the origin of the objectives frustrated nor the sources of frustration.

The alienation thesis, which has become so popular in some ways amounts to a more elaborate frustration-aggression hypothesis. But in this case the sources of frustration usually are traced to social roots, such as disenfranchisement, marginality, and powerlessness; and the objective usually can be more explicitly indentified as the search for identity and control over one's destiny, which means more meaningful participation in life. It is possible that engaging in conflict provides some people with a sense of meaningful participation in their society. The findings that both the personal job satisfaction of teachers and the over-all faculty morale increase with individual and faculty conflict rates would support this thesis.

The alienation thesis would suggest that the militant leadership in teaching is coming from its youngest members who are closest to the current generation of alienated youth. However, the backgrounds of the most belligerent professional teachers in the sample indicate that while it is true that the young males do not seem to be among the most loyal of employees, it is the middle-aged men who most frequently become involved in conflict; apparently, it takes time for even the militantly inclined to develop the respect, group support, and margin of security necessary to nurture the capacity for militant leadership.

The alienation theme, moreover, seems to focus on only the negative side of a larger equation. For, while alienated people are in some sense in a state of rebellion against something, at least some of them also seem to be positively identifying with alternative standards, in this case professional standards. It is difficult to believe that teachers who are well integrated into their professional groups are entirely alienated. Nor is it entirely accurate to say that these teachers are simply opposed to "the system." It seems more accurate to say that they are caught between competing parts of the system and forced to choose between divergent standards.

Once the dynamics of the interplay among competing alternatives have been introduced, the full complexity of the situation comes into better focus. Some of this complexity is faintly captured in the notions of relative deprivation and reference group theory. The former concept alludes to the differences between a person's present situation and some outside standard, often either a former state of his own being or the achievements of his contemporaries. The latter concept capitalizes exclusively on the social basis of standards by which one compares himself, indicating that they are usually advocated by, or exemplified in, some social group with which he identifies. Teachers, then, compare their situation in life with that of people having equivalent education or income or with people doing similar work. They are likely to expect rewards at least equivalent to those obtained by people with similar levels of education.

Moreover, even when they are making progress, they may become discontented if they are not progressing as rapidly as the groups with which they compare themselves. Hence, although in recent years teachers' average income has increased faster than that of industrial workers (there has been over a 20 percent increase during the last five years alone), they still lag behind other professional groups. Similarly, although there has been a substantial reduction in the proportion of teachers without the B.A. and more than half of the high school teachers now have more than five years of education, even with this educational progress they have barely kept pace with the general society, while still lagging far behind other professional groups; and the proportion of all teachers with the master's degree has not increased during the past decade, perhaps partly because of the influx of new teachers (NEA *Research Bulletin*, 1967).

There is still another comparative dimension of status which is not explicit in any of the foregoing concepts, but which is essential for understanding the set of forces behind teacher incentive. It is important to recognize that there are several dimensions of teacher status, each of which may change at variable rates. The status congruency framework explicitly focuses on this element of convergence and divergence among a person's present statuses. Incongruence among statuses has become a critical feature of our society, where there is no longer a close connection between various dimensions of status, such as salary, authority, and level of education; winning salary increments, for example, does not in itself provide access to power. It can be assumed then, that a group compares its achievements in one area not only with those of other people, but also with its own achievements in other areas. Hence, teachers are likely to consider their standing in education relative to their salary, occupational prestige, and authority. The consistency of expectations other people have about them, and the demands they in turn can make of them, each depends upon the consistency of their ranking on the various dimensions of status. Congruent statuses mutually reinforce their position, whereas incongruent ones are likely to lead to confusion and precariousness of status; lower statuses detract from achievements. Therefore, we can expect that people with incongruent statuses will be prompted to increase their respectability in those areas in which they have not yet become respectable enough. A significant advance in one form of status merely illuminates the disparities in the over-all status pattern. Consequently, progress in one respect, far from satiating the status quest, can in itself encourage a group to increase its efforts to improve in other respects as well.

One gets the impression that any increases teachers may have made in their authority have not kept pace with their advances in salary and education in recent years. Such a discrepancy could be an important incentive behind their recent efforts to achieve new levels of authority. It is significant that in this connection Goffman (1957) found that for people occupying middle-class and upper-middle-class positions there was an inverse relationship between consistency of their statuses and preference for extensive change in the distribution of power in the society.

The equilibration of a total system is a product of the mutual congruencies among interdependent positions. Conversely, advances in any one position may threaten counterpositions. In public education, for example, the changing relationships of teachers to administrators, parents, and students have played a part in producing the current state of tension. Administrators, for example, have some reason to be defensive toward teachers. The subordination of teachers developed during an era when they were poorly trained and when administrators had already taken significant steps toward professionalization. But since that time, while teachers have become better trained and the supply-demand ratio for trained teachers has become more favorable to them, consolidation has reduced the demand for administrators at the highest levels, and the larger role of technical decision and the increasing magnitude of public school systems have inevitably made administrators more dependent upon the judgments of teachers.

At the same time, teachers, too, have reason to be defensive about the recent efforts of laymen from all strata to reassert their authority in the wake of the crisis in education. For a time it seemed, especially in the big cities, that administrators had gained the upper hand and communities were content to let the professional administrators run things. However, middle-class parents appear to be more anxious than ever before about their children's educational achievement, while the civil rights movement has mobilized previously lethargic lower-class parents, who are demanding a greater voice in the schooling of their children. Plans to decentralize the inner-city schools, such as those prepared for New York City, will bypass teachers and increase the authority of laymen at precisely a time when teachers want more authority for themselves.

Finally, the adolescent revolt, reflecting a new level of power for children, poses another threat to teachers. Children have gained leverage through a variety of devices ranging from innocuous forms of intimidation via their parents to walkouts, slowdowns, and outright violence against teachers. In most schools teachers complain about discipline problems, often casting some of the blame on what they believe to be feeble administration.

Given the quest of teachers for power and the mutual defensiveness of teachers and administrators, their relationship assumes more of the character of naked bargaining than clear-cut subordination. Exchange theory provides one way to systematically analyze bargaining relationships. From the perspective of this theory, it would appear that as an occupational group approaches the upper occupational bracket, it develops a margin of security which in turn alters its ratio of investment to reward. The extended period of training of teachers and the current affluence of this country increase the teachers' career alternatives and reduce the risk in losing. As teachers achieve their own leverage, they can afford to rely less on administrators to do their bargaining for them—especially because the latter are likely to bargain low, operating as they do under different constraints.

Administrators probably are accustomed to thinking in terms of the bargaining model. Therefore, it is important to note that the exchange and congruence models give different answers to a crucial question. From a strictly bargaining point of view, for example, one might have expected that teachers would feel compensated for their low authority and prestige by their recent salary increments, whereas we have seen that within the congruence framework, a salary increase may simply whet the ambitions of employees to achieve other forms of advancement. The shortcoming of the bargaining model is that in itself, it does not indicate what a group will and will not be willing to bargain away. Apparently, that depends on the particular combination of their statuses; less well-educated groups seem more willing to settle for salary as a compensation for their lack of authority, while better educated groups appear to be less willing to tolerate extreme discrepancies between income and authority. The bargaining model, then, must be interpreted against the background of status congruency.

CONCLUSION

Often, the existence of organizational conflict simply reflects the fact that there already have been changes in social functions which have not as yet been recognized and incorporated into the ongoing social organization. The situation is well beyond the point where school policy can be equated to the proclamations made by administrators; and yet that is the myth this nation is trying to live with. School systems have become so complex and must adapt to so wide a range of circumstances that administrators can no longer maintain centralized control over educational practice, even though they may feel obliged to do so because of tradition and their legal responsibility. That is the administrative role conflict. This persistent effort, on the part of the teachers as well as administrators, to maintain customary routines and traditional evaluation standards in a climate of relative failure has only served to aggravate the tension.

Alternatives, then, are needed to the industrial-military models of organization with their chain of command, system-wide uniformity, and universal evaluation standards. It is now clear that in practice bureaucratization has not meant more centralized control, but that, on the contrary, it has meant more autonomy among groups within the system. The immediate problem, then, is not just how to preserve central control, but how to harness the potential of that autonomy. There are probably more effective ways for teachers to participate in schools, and more effective participation will mean more than annual confrontations at the negotiation table.

One possible development is that teachers will evolve their own line of authority and communication within each school and school system. The dual lines of administrative and professional authority found in some hospitals provide one model, though not necessarily the only one.

Perhaps of even greater moment is the now realistic possibility that if teachers pursue state-wide negotiations, they eventually will gain control over the certification and accreditation standards, which will necessarily mean much greater control over the entire occupation. If that should happen, there certainly will be substantial changes in the authority roles of teachers.

Ultimately, these or similar changes will mean that administrators will have to find some new roles as teachers assume some of their traditional functions. Possibly administrators will turn more of the internal matters over to teachers and become more concerned about managing the sociological problems inherent in schools' relationships with their communities and governments. The present crisis faced by the public schools has occurred partly because the external sociological problems have been for so long neglected.

It may be that in order to achieve stability the growing power of teachers will have to be recognized by including them more centrally in the decision-making process within school systems themselves. Historically, in this country we have had to learn either to include the excluded or to live with strife. Until teachers create a more central place within the system for themselves, we can expect that they will continue to go around it.

REFERENCES: Chapter 10

Corwin, Ronald G. Teacher militancy in the United States: Reflections on its sources and prospects. *Theory into Practice,* April, 1968, I, 96–102.

Goffman, Irwin W. Status consistency and preference for change in power distribution. *American Sociological Review,* June, 1957, **22**, 275–280.

Hofstadter, Richard. The pseudo-conservative revolt. In Daniel Bell (Ed.). *The radical right.* Garden City, N.Y.: Doubleday, 1964. Pp. 75–96.

Katz, Daniel. Approach to managing conflict. In *Robert L. Kahn and Elise Boulding* (Eds.). *Power and conflict in organizations.* New York: Basic Books, 1964. P. 105.

National Education Association. *NEA Research Bulletin,* October, 1967, **45**.

11. Teacher militancy: Reflections

> *According to my lights, a last chapter should resemble a primitive orgy after harvest. The work may have come to an end, but the worker cannot let go all at once. . . . Accordingly he is allowed a time of license . . . when he is no longer bound by logic and evidence but free to speculate about what he has done.—Homans, 1961, p. 378.*

In this last chapter, we shall return to the questions posed in the first. It must be remembered that only tentative answers can be inferred from the gross indices that were available; but the data begin to provide part of the picture.

The average professional and employee orientations of a school's faculty members were estimated from a series of questionnaires and interviews designed to elicit their beliefs about their rights and obligations to students, colleagues, the administration and administrative procedure, and the public. A school's conflict rate was estimated from the number of incidents reported (per interview) by a smaller sample of teachers. The degree of a school's bureaucratization was estimated from indices and scales based on the reports of faculty members about their schools' operation—that is, the way decisions are made, supervisory practices, the uniformity of procedure, and so forth.

CHARACTERISTICS OF MILITANCY

Is Professionalization a Militant Process?

Probably the most important conclusion from the study is that faculties that seem to be more professionally oriented to their work (as measured by teachers' responses to a series of specially designed statements) are more tension ridden. Of course, conflict has many sources, and not all conflict is produced by professionalization, by any means. But, professionalization seems to entail a certain degree of conflict. In almost every test, as a faculty's average professionalism increases, its conflict rates increase accordingly. In fact, in the half dozen most professionally oriented schools, at least twice as many disagreements and disputes were reported (based on the average number reported per interview) as in the least professionally oriented schools.

Although gender and average age of faculty account for some of this militancy, the relationships between professionalism and conflict nevertheless persist in faculties having different terms of tenure.

Also, although it is not as definite, the same type of relationship seems to exist between an individual's professionalism and his frequency of involvement in various types of conflict. On the average, the 200 most professionally oriented teachers in the sample have higher rates of conflict than the typical teacher. The teacher with the strong professional orientation, for example, is involved in twice as many authority issues as his counterpart with a weaker orientation. But after close inspection it is apparent that the correlation is not linear. It is probably more accurate to say that teachers with the weakest professional orientations are likely to become involved in fewer incidents than those with either average or stronger orientations. The fact that the groups are reversed on their rates of involvement in major incidents parallels the pattern found for the average faculty orientation.

There is also a tendency for the most loyal employees to become involved in fewer conflicts. These negative associations are accentuated in the more professional schools, suggesting that when a more conservative person is in a liberal professional environment he has a greater tendency to withdraw than he has to become like that environment. Looking again at the individuals, there is a parallel tendency for teachers who are in most sympathy with their employee roles to become less militant. Accordingly, persons who have highly professional orientations but are simultaneously out of sympathy with their employee roles have disproportionately higher rates of involvement in conflict than individuals who have the reverse sympathies.

The general pattern is also qualified in several other important respects. First, by no means is there a one-to-one relationship between militancy and professional orientation. Even among the 200 select professionally oriented teachers, less than half have been involved in an overt incident. And, conversely, many of the most militant teachers are not especially professionally oriented.

Second, the relationship seems to be strongest among the least professionally oriented faculties. This would indicate that once a maximum has been reached, further increases in professionalization do not necessarily produce corresponding increases in conflict (insofar as can be determined by these crude measures and the small sample). Third, the relationship is not characteristic of the less highly bureaucratized schools. This fact can be explained by the theory, however, because in these schools professional-bureaucratic role conflicts are not likely to be salient. Fourth, the relationship does not appear to be strong where the faculty frequently associates over lunch; but there is no evidence as to whether these sociable settings in themselves discourage belligerency, or whether they reflect other conditions which indirectly reduce the need for conflict, such as differences in leadership practices. Finally, and probably most important, the relationship between a faculty's professional orientation and its conflict rate varies with the intensity of the incident involved. The number of "major incidents" (which refers to heated disputes involving several parties, usually including a substantial segment of the organization and/or community) declines with a faculty's professionalism; the ratio of major incidents reported per interview is four times higher in the least professional schools than in the most professional ones. This pattern of evidence seems to indicate that professionalism proscribes certain forms of militancy as well as influencing the frequency of other types of conflict.

How Militant Are Teachers?

Generally speaking, for the schools in this sample, at least, militancy cannot be regarded as a predominant feature of most high school teachers. Even the generally more aggressive men have been, on the average, involved in only one or two overt incidents. Rather, a small proportion have been involved in a large proportion of the incidents.

There is, in fact, some support for the traditional stereotype of teachers as compliant employees. By their own reports, the vast majority of the sample, for example, agree that teachers make it a practice to adjust their teaching to the administration's views and are obedient and loyal to the administration; at least one in every two teachers agrees that if his colleagues openly criticize the administration they should be encouraged to go elsewhere.

However, within this placid portrait are buried some of the seeds of militancy. Only one third of the sample, for example, would go so far as to say that they would deliberately try to keep out of "hot water" by following the wishes of the top administration, and at least half believe that their colleagues try to live up to what they consider to be the best standards of their profession even when the administration or community does not respect them for it.

What is more important than the majority of teachers, however, is the minority of teachers who are professionally oriented, because a high proportion of them are also militant. Although they are a minority, they have widespread support and respect. Compared with either the typical teacher in the sample or the professionally oriented teacher who has not become involved in conflict, the militant professionals have more support from their colleagues, are more respected, and have higher levels of education. The fact that, in almost every respect except one, the informal leaders are more militant than the officers of either the local NEA or AFT affiliates suggests that leadership for militant professionalism in education is coming from these behind-the-scenes informal leaders at least as frequently as it is coming from the more visible leaders.

Who Are the Militants?

Administrators, counselors, and teachers of social science are among the most militant people in the sample. Teachers of athletics and those working in the extracurricular areas also often get into disputes. On the other hand, teachers in the vocational program and in home economics have relatively low rates of conflict. Of the more militant disciplines only the social scientists have high professional orientations. Unlike schools as a whole, the militancy of a discipline is less closely associated with its professional orientation per se than with its level of prestige (which tends to be related to its professional orientation); the inconsistency between a department's prestige and its autonomy from the administration is also highly correlated to its militancy.

Also, men are definitely more militant than women, but on the whole they are only slightly more professionally oriented than women. It appears, however, that professional orientation is a much more important factor in the militancy of women than it is in men—that is, the correlation between militancy and professional orientation is higher for women. Women may need more moral justification for their militancy than men, which they might find in the professional role conception. This difference between the sexes with regard to militancy seems to parallel the double standard associated with other forms of deviant behavior, such as sexual relations, where women also are more likely to use a moral justification (such as love) for their acts.

Age is also a factor in militancy. However, while younger men are perhaps less loyal in their attitudes than older ones, the older ones, who also have shown more signs of professional behavior, are more likely to become involved in conflict than their juniors. The difference here may be related to the time that it takes to develop the group support and self-esteem necessary to challenge authority.

What Are the Issues?

An analysis of the key conflicts reveals that even on the most professional of faculties there appears to be a considerable amount of self-interest and petty, selfish in-fighting. Nevertheless, closer examination reveals that most conflicts in one way or another way reflect critical issues beneath the surface of the profession and inherent in the principles around which the schools have been organized. Nearly half of the conflicts could be classified as authority problems; an additional 20 percent involve scheduling and distribution problems. Half of all incidents occur between teachers and members of the administration, and half of these incidents, in turn, involve authority problems. Therefore, one out of every four incidents in the sample involves teachers and administrators in disputes over authority, which is the largest single category of conflict identified. By contrast, only 15 percent of the conflicts in the sample concern problems of authority among teachers themselves; over one in four incidents among teachers involves extracurricular activities. Scheduling and distribution problems also are more characteristic of problems between peers, whereas authority issues are more characteristic of disputes between teachers and administrators.

Few teachers are centrally involved in making policy decisions, and although many of them report having some control over the routine decisions that come up in the classroom, it is fair to say that the vast majority of teachers want more control over their work. The majority of teachers believe that they should exercise the ultimate authority over major educational decisions, and a handful are determined to increase their power, even at the risk of insubordination. On the other hand, many administrators do not subscribe to, nor even comprehend, the pretensions of teachers as specialists and authorities, and therefore do not envision teachers as anything other than employees owing obedience. Many teachers feel that their problems arise because they are inadequately protected by the administration from parents, school boards, and students.

Professionally oriented teachers become involved in systematically different types of conflict than the typical teacher. Among the most professionally oriented leaders those who are only "moderately" militant (that is, who have been involved in the less severe disputes) are more likely than the more belligerent professionals to concern themselves with scheduling and distribution problems and are readier to tangle with their own peers, especially those in vocational education. By comparison, the belligerents expent most of their energies on authority issues, many of them involving the administration. This difference in interest and definition among the more militant teachers indicates that there is segmentation and conflict among teachers, which is probably an inherent characteristic of professionalization.

Teachers insist upon having authority over students—over their academic performance and their personal lives as well. Desire to regulate student discipline is one side of the coin; a desire to obtain a fair share of able students is the other. In fact, the scarcest resource that teachers must share turns out to be students. Teachers are possessive and go to some lengths to assure that their colleagues do not violate the territorial claims they stake out over preferred students. From the viewpoint of teachers, there is an oversupply of unable delinquent types and a shortage of academically superior types. And teachers are not too hopeful about the unable ones. Administrators seem to be less willing than teachers to grant that some students are not capable of learning; teachers, their prestige weighing heavily on how their students perform, are more likely to believe that the kids just are not trying hard enough. The competition for students often spills over into extracurricular activities. The primary problem is that no one wants to specialize in working with undesirable students. So, some academic courses and vocational courses serve as "dumping grounds," and those who teach them lose prestige and resent that fact.

What Motivates Professional Militancy?

Because professionalism is a many-faceted concept, it by no means can be inferred that professional militancy is motivated exclusively, or even predominantly, out of teachers' dedication to their students. In fact, the degree of faculty devotion to students (or, in other words, their "client orientation") is associated with only one measure of conflict, albeit an important one—incidents that arise over authority issues. When the professionalism of individual teachers (as opposed to the average of the entire faculty) was examined, the more militant teachers appeared to be less oriented toward students and more concerned instead about their colleagues' opinions of them. This suggests that the quest for decision-making authority and a more favorable reputation are more important to even the professionally oriented teachers than is their commitment to students' welfare.

Nevertheless, one should not jump to the conclusion that professional militancy is detrimental to students; it depends on the standards endorsed by the professionals and their colleagues—that is, the connection between professional norms and ultimate student welfare. And there is a correlation, not only because client orientation and colleague orientation are correlated, but also because most professionally oriented teachers are, in fact, more concerned about the welfare of their students than are their adversaries. A select group of highly professionally oriented teachers who have become involved in major incidents seem to encounter hard-core resistance from people who show little concern for either professional norms in general or for students in particular. Hence, in the absence of the militant professionals the less professional adversaries could very well have dominated the schools in this sample.

There is also some evidence of in-fighting among the militant professionals themselves; some of the most belligerently militant teachers who become involved in major incidents seem to be held in check by the most professionally oriented of their peers. But, in general, the militancy of the professionally oriented leaders, and especially the most belligerent ones, was usually turned against either the administration or the rank-and-file teachers—that is, those who are less committed to professionalism. Perhaps these conflicts between the militant leaders and the rank and file are as important, then, as the conflicts that directly involve administration. For the militant professional leaders' relatively high client orientations tend to offset the exceptionally low client orientations of their colleagues who chronically oppose them.

What Is the Effect of Conflict on Morale?

Finally, looking at the human dimension, one may wonder about the price of organizational conflict for those involved—its effect on individual and group morale. Answers to this question can help determine if conflict is necessarily detrimental to the mental health of people involved. In view of the personal distaste many people have expressed toward conflict, it is important that no evidence was found that conflict is devastating for the morale of either organization or individuals. On the contrary, both an individual's personal satisfaction with his work and the faculty's average job satisfaction increase with the rate of conflict in a school, with the important exception of major incidents. One interpretation of this is that some forms of conflict may contribute to the morale of teachers, or at the very least that conflict is a product of high morale. Conflict may, in fact, provide a means by which a faculty can become personally engaged in and have influence over the development of public education. If so, conflict can provide an alternative to the alienation that is otherwise so symptomatic of a bureaucratic society.

Also, there was no evidence that militancy adversely affects school quality as it might be reflected in gross indices of the student drop-out rate and the rate of high school graduates' attendance at college.

Do Schools Have Characteristic Patterns of Organization?

Turning to the organizational dimension, the different characteristics of school organization seem to form certain patterns. For example, close supervision is more typical of smaller than of larger schools; standardization replaces close supervision as the dominant mechanism of control as schools become larger. However, although some social scientists have hypothesized that close supervision, is used as a substitute for rules, in this sample it seems, instead, to be associated with emphasis on rules.

The fact that standardization and emphasis on rules tend to be associated with many of the other bureaucratic characteristics—such as size, complexity, close supervision, specialization, and so forth—supports the reinforcement model of bureaucracy, a model that assumes that bureaucratic procedures consistently reinforce one another. However, many of the components of bureaucracy are negatively associated with one another. The compensatory model is more applicable to these cases; this model assumes that bureaucratic practices are interchangeable and partially inconsistent with one another. Finally, in many cases an independence model, which assumes that bureaucratic practices are simply independent of one another, must be used to account for the relatively low degree of correlations that occur among different bureaucratic characteristics in many cases.

In general, organizational controls seem to be used sparingly. There seems to be no natural tendency for organizations to become totally bureaucratized, unless otherwise provoked by threats of disruption and conflict.

Are Organizational Characteristics Associated with Conflict?

In general, mechanisms of control such as standardization and close supervision are associated with the more disruptive characteristics found in schools—such as staff turnover, organizational complexity, size, and so forth. While the over-all index of bureaucratization used here is not associated with conflict rates, several components of that index, and certain patterns among these components, are associated with specific types of conflict. Among the more important organizational components in this regard are standardization and emphasis on rules, school size, number of levels of authority in the system, number of departments and general complexity of the organization, specialization of teachers, decentralization of routine decisions, heterogeneity of staff background, rate of staff additions, emphasis the faculty places on critical thinking and character training, and informal and social interaction among faculty members. Also, schools with higher rates of disagreement are likely to emphasize either rules or close supervision and to have a decentralized decision-making process.

Informal interaction seems, in particular, to facilitate or to depress conflict, depending upon the circumstances. In general, the rate of conflict in a school declines with the frequency with which the faculty lunch together. However, it depends largely on faculty age, level of professional orientation, and type of incident involved. Lunching is most closely associated with lower rates of conflict in less bureaucratized schools and among less professionally oriented younger faculties. Conversely, professional orientation is most closely associated with conflict in schools where teachers frequently lunch together. Also, lunching is positively associated with conflict rates in schools having older faculties, although conflict typically declines with age of faculty members. However, even where lunching is inversely related to most types of conflict, it is postively associated with the rate of disputes. Finally, the more frequently faculty members saw one another socially outside of the school, the more conflict of all types was reported.

Ironically, it is in the smallest schools that decisions characteristically are made at higher rather than lower levels of authority. As decision-making responsibility is delegated downward, teachers seem to be more caught up in the issues, and the rate of nearly all forms of conflict increases. However, again there is an exception for major incidents, which decline with the authority of teachers to make routine decisions. One reason for this different pattern for major incidents may be that, generally speaking, participating in the decision-making structure opens channels and increases opportunities for teachers to express latent grievances, which therefore are not allowed to accumulate and erupt into more explosive situations.

The true significance of the role played by bureaucratization in the conflict process does not become fully evident until viewed simultaneously with professionalization. Bureaucratization, which in itself is designed to increase predictability and reduce conflict, succeeds in suppressing conflict only in the less professionally oriented schools. But by contrast, as the more professional schools become more bureaucratized, all forms of conflict appear to increase; in the more professional schools, in particular, incidents between teachers and administrators are associated with a degree of bureaucratization. One explanation is that professionals resent bureaucratic controls and are collectively in a better position to marshal resistance.

In view of the recent speculations about the way bureaucratic organizations in the society are being modified to account for emerging professional roles, it is significant that the over-all level of bureaucratization of the school does not decline significantly with the professional orientation of the faculty, as might have been expected if professionalization were making substantial inroads on traditional forms of school organization. However, the correlation is in a negative direction, and the facts that the faculty's decision-making authority increases directly with its level of professional orientation and that professionally oriented faculties are at least not any more closely controlled than less professional ones may all indicate that such accommodation is beginning to appear.

Another finding is that the extent to which a school is structurally "crystallized"—that is, has consistency of rankings on the different dimensions of bureaucracy—is positively associated with several measures of conflict. When schools are classified by level of structural crystallization, the most structurally consistent schools have uniformly higher conflict rates than those with lower consistency (again except for major incidents).

One way to interpret the evidence is that both bureaucratization and structural crystallization evolve as direct responses to conflict. A slightly different version is that bureaucratization is, in part, a direct response to other disruptive conditions—such as professionalism, organizational complexity, and staff turnover—which, in turn, are directly associated with conflict. Whatever the reason, it seems that organizations evolve more bureaucratic forms when provoked to do so; "organization" seems to be a response to the threat of conflict and in turn may provoke further conflict. From this viewpoint, conflict not only represents the breakdown of an organization, but also can be a cause of organization as well.

The same processes seem to be at work with respect to the evolution of structural crystallization. In other words, various characteristics of bureaucracy do not seem to crystallize in the absence of conflict. The crystallization of an organization, on the other hand, seems to occur in both conflictful and in less conflictful environments, depending upon whether the organization is highly bureaucratized.

Do Schools Form Characteristic Organizational Patterns?

Finally, bureaucratic components seem to form some uniform patterns. An inspection of the three most discordant and the three most tranquil schools in the sample illustrates some of this pattern. Tension-ridden schools in some sense seem to be "better" schools. Even though the discordant schools have fewer members active in a professional organization than tranquil schools, more persons in the discordant schools simultaneously emphasize their professional role and deemphasize their employee role; and average professional orientations and professional behavior scores of the faculties are also higher in the discordant schools. The members of such schools are more sociable, express more job satisfaction, and come from more heterogeneous backgrounds. These schools also have higher rates of additions to their staffs due to turnover and expansion. The discordant schools also place relatively more emphasis on character training and critical thinking, and more of their graduates go to college. Of course, these characteristics could be simply the by-products of other unknown variables also associated with conflict, and need not have been produced by the conflict environment itself. It is also possible that many of these qualities help produce conflict.

APPROACHES TO MINIMIZING CONFLICT

The inductive leaps from data to conclusions and again from conclusions to implications for action become tenuous at best. To arrive at some of our conclusions, we have been forced to make unsupported assumptions

Reflections

about the causes behind correlations reported here. What follows, therefore, must be viewed as a largely personal interpretation, albeit one that has slowly taken shape over the course of several years of fieldwork and data analysis.

Our premise is that although some relaxation of traditional forms of bureaucratic control has already taken place, the prevalence of conflict in some schools is evidence enough that the adaptations in school systems are not keeping pace with the demands of professional employees. If the sources of tension are structural, we have argued, then the potential solutions to organizational problems must be found at that level. Therefore, conflict analysis can help suggest some needed new approaches to organizing schools.

There is always a danger that concern over the problem of containing conflict will only obscure its more positive functions. However, conflict should not be romantically glorified either, and in any event answers to this question can reveal a great deal about the conflict process.

At least three approaches to reducing conflict can be inferred from conditions under which there was only a minimum of conflict in this study—recruitment procedures, manipulation of the informal structure, and structural changes.

Recruitment

The first recourse is through the recruiting process. Professionally oriented and employee oriented teachers already are distributed among the different schools in such a way as to reduce the amount of conflict below its full potential. Professionally oriented teachers were distributed randomly in different types of schools, rather than being concentrated in the more bureaucratic ones where the greatest incompatibility with the professional role exists, and the more employee-oriented teachers were found in the more bureaucratic schools, thus maximizing the compatibility between teachers who uphold this role and their context.

Administrators of the most bureaucratic schools might wish to increase the amount of match between role conception and school structure by hiring only employee-oriented teachers. The evidence suggests that even in generally professionally oriented schools the rate of conflict declines with the average employee orientation. However, because a person's employee orientation is not closely associated with his professional orientation (in fact tends to be negatively related), simply hiring people who are good employees provides no assurance that they will be of high professional caliber. To the extent that people who want more decision-making authority for themselves are excluded, it will also mean excluding the people who place most emphasis on knowledge and who are strongly oriented toward colleagues and to a lesser extent toward students. Also, because the more militant people are concentrated disproportionately in certain disciplines and are typically males rather than females, this tactic might soon become impractical.

Informal Structure

Administrators and teachers might be able jointly to arrange an informal interpersonal setting that would help minimize conflict. The data are not clear on this point, but it appears that professionally oriented faculties are more likely to become militant in schools where the faculty is less sociable (that is, does not frequently associate for lunch). However, obviously, there is no simple answer. In older faculties conflicts seem to increase with frequency of lunching, while in younger ones it seems to decline with lunching; and most conflict rates seem to increase in proportion to the frequency with which the faculty see one another socially outside of the school.

Structural Change

As a third approach, administrators and teachers might want to attempt to manipulate the way in which the school itself is organized. At present the almost universal administrative response to conflict seems to be to tighten bureaucratic controls. Yet, it appears that efforts to maintain close surveillance of employees in some types of organizations only aggravate conflict. In this sense, the efforts of administrators to control employees are as responsible for conflict as the actions of employees themselves.

There are at least three alternatives to tighter control—altering the authority system, establishing different evaluation standards, and experimenting with administrative style.

First, the process of decision making in public schools can be appreciably altered. This will probably happen anyway once the demands of teachers for more authority are officially recognized and accepted by the public. However, most forms of conflict will not automatically diminish as teachers gain more authority. On the contrary, our data suggest the opposite; most forms of conflict increase with a faculty's decision-making authority. Nevertheless, the fact that major incidents declined in direct proportion to a faculty's decision-making authority does suggest that participation in decision-making channels at least forestalls the more extreme forms of conflict.

Furthermore, were teachers given greater recognition, it would bring the lines of responsibility, power, and authority into closer harmony. In many instances teachers now have the power; the problem is that channels have not been provided for its exercise within the structure of the school system itself. And, while teachers do not necessarily have the answers, they share much of the responsibility for the present problems of education along with administrators and school boards. In a complex, technical society the best that can be expected is that mechanisms will be established for including the diverse viewpoints of many groups and for their compromise.

Of course, many school boards and administrators are now talking about "allowing teachers to participate more in the decision-making process." However, teachers undoubtedly want more than merely the opportunity to become involved with some stages of decision making at the discretion of the administration. They want final authority over certain types of decisions.

The problem with so-called "democratic administration" is that the participation of subordinates usually continues to be at the discretion of the administration. As an uncertain privilege, the opportunity to participate can be withdrawn or withheld in practice. Lefton, Dinitz, and their associates, for example, found that when wards in a hospital were operated according to so-called "democratic" principles of administration, the actual result was far from democratic; moreover, professionals working in this situation, where only an illusion of democracy was perpetuated, were more frustrated and negative than those working on boards that were admittedly less democratic [Corwin, 1964, p. 16].

Hence, to regard the problem simply as one of "creating good administration" is to ignore the very condition that professionalization is designed to remedy—that is, the fact that teachers' authority still depends on the discretion of the administration. When the problem is viewed as one of organization, it becomes apparent that the teacher's professional authority will continue to be in jeopardy until it is supported by the structure of the organization itself.

Yet the same authority structure that provides teachers with a measure of status will make them reluctant to accept the many changes proposed by the administration, just as administrators will be suspicious of teacher-initiated proposals for change. Conflict analysis can help to assess the relative investments of different groups in various aspects of the existing system and perhaps find acceptable status substitutes when a proposed change threatens someone's position.

The resolution of teacher-administrator conflicts strongly depends upon whether power in schools is necessarily a fixed commodity, in which case the expansion in the power of teachers would require a corresponding reduction in the power of administrators. It is possible, however, that it is not fixed but can be enlarged in such a way that both teachers and administrators can gain power concurrently. This, in turn, depends, in general, upon whether new divisions of labor emerge, especially new roles for administrators now threatened by the encroachment of teacher authority. Many of the problems persist because administrators continue to view themselves as curriculum and instructional leaders, which necessarily thrusts them into the teacher's classroom.

Other problems develop, on the other hand, because teachers are powerless to cope with community and national problems from their particular vantage point. If administrators shifted their attention from their traditional concerns with internal problems and attempted to provide more leadership in areas that involve the school with the community —problems involving race, poverty, and financial support—they could expand their sphere of influence even while teachers expand theirs.

If, on the other hand, administrators continue to react defensively to outside challenges, other agencies will capture, and indeed already have, the leadership over these problems. For example, school administrators have not as yet exercised substantial leadership with respect to the poverty program, the Job Corps, and even the Teacher Corps. It is significant that it was the Department of Defense that proposed a new exploratory program for educating the semiliterate people in this country. Until school administrators begin to exercise more leadership with respect to problems now being attacked by the Urban Coalition and the NAACP and other community organizations, they will not be able to stake out new areas of authority.

Second, evaluation standards can be manipulated in such a way that conflict will be channeled into more constructive directions. Certainly, as teachers assume more authority, the traditional standards and rewards are likely to become inappropriate. Many administrators now lack a coherent philosophy for evaluating professional employees and for guiding their own conduct with respect to conflicts that develop because of incompatibilities in professional and employee roles. The dilemma that has to be faced is that the teachers who are the most loyal employees, and the ones who make the administrator's job easier, are not necessarily the ones who will contribute the most to the long-range development of education, and certainly are not the only types worthy of support.

If recognition were provided for the more militant teachers in the system, it might provide for a system of checks and balances and prevent excesses of control or unwarranted dominance by specific groups and force compromises to be made. It does not seem likely that the militant professionals will receive much recognition under existing circumstances, while they endure much blame if they do take matters into their own hands when their professional standards are in jeopardy. What is to be the fate of a teacher guilty of "insubordination" while attempting to protect his students from a textbook or a curriculum guide he believes to be ineffective? And what should an administrator do with a teacher who rebels because his responsibilities exceed his authority? How is an otherwise competent teacher who leaves the building early to be treated?

At present, teachers are promoted or rewarded with salary increases largely on the basis of how long they have been in the system, how little trouble they have caused, and how closely they follow the curriculum guide and other directives. The person who attempts to defend his standards runs the risk of being penalized. Perhaps what is needed is a system that reverses this procedure—that is, a system in which the person who does not take risks is penalized and in which people are directly rewarded only for successfully participating in innovations. Also, perhaps it would help if evaluations were reviewed by groups outside the school system—for example, professional groups, universities, and regional committees, which have less vested interest in a particular school.

Third, more effort could be made to find more precise ways of combining administrative styles with appropriate organizational climates. Certainly bureaucratic procedures should not be entirely abandoned, or even indiscriminately modified. In some situations bureaucratic procedures might be used even more effectively than at present; and in some cases it might be sufficient simply to clarify existing communication and policy procedures and to give subordinates more access to them. Our data show that in the less professionally oriented schools conflict declines if there is tighter control. But different strategies are needed for more professionally oriented faculties.

What, then, are the alternatives to the hierarchical model? One alternative is a coalition form of government consisting of permanent steering committees composed of representatives of different types of teachers, the administration, and interested community groups. Teacher-school board negotiation teams represent the microcosm of such an arrangement. As teachers demonstrate that they are able to apply power upon a statewide and nationwide basis, they may achieve control over the certification and even the accreditation standards, and hence be in a better position to demand this form of participation. In some matters these committees would serve in an advisory capacity to the local school board, and in certain areas they might actually determine policy. Such committees would provide a stable system of checks and balances and channels for compromising competing vested interests. More important, they would institutionalize much of the concern and imagination now often dissipated on minor disputes and unexpressed frustrations.

Another alternative is a fully institutionalized dual system of administrative and professional authority based on a division of policy-making responsibility among teachers, administrators, and school board. For example, teachers might exercise final authority over textbook selection or the hiring of other teachers, while administrators would continue to control scheduling and salaries. As teachers make their demands felt to participate in the budget-making process, some such division of responsibility seems likely to develop. However, this division of labor would be more fruitful if ways could be devised to evaluate the long-range effectiveness of administrators and teachers. Evaluating teachers on the basis of changes they have brought about in students' achievement levels is at present not particularly relevant because teachers do not have the authority to change the system in such a way as to improve achievement levels. However, this standard might be more appropriate after teachers have achieved the necessary authority to experiment, alter the system, and make changes in resource allocation.

Perhaps it is remarkable that the principle of hierarchy has withstood so well the new complexities that have arisen and for which it was in no way designed. But, in practice, it *is* being modified by the intrusion of expertise and greater independence and greater lenience being shown by some administrators toward their subordinates. The hierarchy has imposed arbitrary limits on the amount of mutual exchange that can develop between the various levels. If the chain-of-command principles were modified, it would leave room for more open relationships between the echelons. If individual teachers or groups of teachers were able to approach relevant administrators at any level of hierarchy, and if they were brought into administrative decisions early in the process, they would be more likely to make contributions and to be more supportive of the decisions eventually made.

To summarize, then, conflict is not likely to be curbed simply by screening out belligerent people: its roots go deep into the organizational climate and structural variables. Conflict is so firmly implanted in complex organizations that, though it can be regulated, it seems futile to try to eradicate it. It may, in fact, not even be desirable to eliminate some forms of conflict which often perform important and beneficial functions. Therefore, because people can expect to live with conflict, we shall turn our speculations to ways of routinizing and coping with it.

INSTITUTIONALIZING CONFLICT

Procedures can be devised to institutionalize and routinize conflict in such a way as to minimize both the disruption and personal trauma that might otherwise be connected with it.

Routinizing Procedures

First, because much conflict seems to be a product of resistance to change, school systems could probably calculate the cost of innovation and change and incorporate it into their financial cost-accounting systems. That is, provision can be made for temporary salary increases to compensate people for the inconvenience and anxiety otherwise associated with changes in the system. Mistakes can be considered to be part of the cost of initiative and hence an operating cost that must be "cost accounted" into the scheme of things along with used pencils, teachers' salaries, and athletic programs. As a system grows in size, it can afford to absorb more risk in the same way that it is able to absorb other kinds of costs.

The appeal system is another procedure for routinizing conflict. Schools need a procedure to handle organization-based grievances—that is, problems that go beyond the individual's interests and personal problems. For, whereas people are normally inclined to defend their own interests (that is, to increase their salary), they need additional protection and incentive to raise questions about the underlying principles of the system itself; such questions are likely to threaten their colleagues and people in authority.

Grievance machinery, including provision for a hearing by impartial parties outside of a particular school, would provide some additional protection; special committees composed of administrators, teachers, and in some cases parents or students might be convened to hear special problems. The defender role also might be provided as part of the grievance machinery—that is, someone who functions as a defense lawyer to represent people in the system, and whose salary is paid from a non-local source such as the state or federal government.

Coping Mechanisms

In contrast to the routinizing procedures, which refer to procedures of organization, "coping" mechanisms refer to the personal reactions of people to a conflict situation. Two important coping mechanisms are "containment" and "reinterpretation." Containment refers to ways in which a person can psychologically keep his ideological differences from contaminating his personal relationships. For example, he can segmentalize his disagreements from the rest of his relationships. Or, he can practice avoidance—that is, simply avoid personal contacts with protagonists.

Reinterpretation of conflict involves placing it in another context. Sociological explanations of conflict do precisely this. If an individual's difficulties are considered to be part of a recurrent pattern, it suggests that certain situations are tension ridden, regardless of the people who may be involved. When people accept a sociological interpretation, they become less interested in blaming individuals and less likely to feel personal hostilities toward their opponents.

It follows that a person's ability to resolve these problems depends first upon his ability to perceive the situational sources of his problems, and then upon his ability to analyze the environment and to work for specific reforms in it.

Training programs could provide people with the kind of information that would help them cope more successfully. Educators need to be prepared to live in a dynamic world of tension. If even the most peaceable, reticent person will become militant when he is operating under certain pressures, then it is these pressures that school administrators and teachers need to understand.

Yet, the typical training program as presently structured seems to place nearly all of its emphasis on the transmission of technical information. The actual work situation tends to be portrayed in terms of static job description, and when the social context of the job is considered, emphasis is likely to be given to the need for cooperation between employees and their supervisors for work-group harmony.

The prospect of growing conflict among professionals within school systems means that specific job descriptions are likely to become outdated rapidly, and that emergent roles are likely to develop for teachers and administrators for which they have not been prepared in college. Increasingly, teachers will be in a position to define and defend teaching standards against opposition, and the administrators' job will be less one of directing the organization and more one of mediating between opposing groups. Hence, interpersonal relations, in which procedures for managing tension play a prominent part, should assume imposing proportions in training programs.

This means more than an occasional course in group dynamics, however. Indeed, if conflict is a routine and normal occurrence within an administration, then training programs should address themselves systematically to the proper role of conflict—its positive and negative functions. Administrative roles can be defined in terms of their conflict function. Finally, the boundaries in which conflict can fruitfully occur need to be more clearly indentified.

Research and Dissemination

Perhaps the most effective ways of coping with and routinizing conflict will be found only through further research. While it is, of course, convenient to recommend "further research" at the close of any research study, what is actually recommended is a more concentrated and systematic research effort aimed at a broad range of problems which promise to lend themselves to conflict theory. For, conflict theory could be very useful in explaining such diverse educational problems as dropouts, morale, and school support levels. Indeed, conflict theory could go a long way toward providing a basis for an organizational theory of learning—that is, a theory concerned with organizational structure. The premises of such a theory would be organizational principles rather than psychological ones. Among the relevant variables would be many of those already discussed.

Tension and conflict are an important part of educational practice. Personal conflict among teachers often directly involves the reshaping of curriculum and definitions of student welfare. Also, conflict with conservative elements in a school is probably a necessary part of improving teaching standards, programs, and services. Past theories of learning have been addressed to the characteristics of individuals—that is, stimulus-response reactions or reading readiness. The closest that learning theories approach a sociological theory is in the attention sometimes given to human relations in organizational settings, such as democratic versus autocratic teaching methods. But the consequences for learning of the settings themselves have, for the most part, been ignored.

Perhaps what is needed is a research and development center focused on developing the potential of conflict theory in educational settings. But the problem orientation around which most research and development centers have been organized has tended to cast theory in a secondary role. It is difficult to exploit the full potential of a theory when there are artificial limits on the kinds of problems to which it may be applied. Nor does the interdisciplinary composition of such centers help either, because the immature theories of a young discipline are too easily crowded out by the more advanced theories of other disciplines. Rather than being problem focused and interdisciplinary in character, the kind of center needed is one that would attempt to work out a coherent theoretical approach applicable to a variety of problems.

The findings of such a center should be continually consolidated and disseminated to practitioners through specially commissioned reports written by teams of researchers and practitioners, and which attempt to translate theory into its practical implications. If such a center accomplished no more than to make people more aware of the fact that many conflicts are products of certain situations, giant strides could be made toward making conflict more useful.

CONCLUSIONS

There is a curious impression circulating that men as workers have become "organization men," while at their play, they "express themselves." Relatively little tribute has been given to the serious play forms in the nation's work places. One meaning of "play" is to contend, or take part, in a game—hence, to gamble. Despair over the organization man and the bureaucratic personality has obscured the role of man the contender. Yet, if contenders are found within an organizational system that Willard Waller (1965, p. 10) at one time described as "despotic," then surely they will exist in other organizations.

However, the sources of belligerency will vary considerably among different types of organizations. One source of conflict resides in the personality and pits the individual against the organization (an explanation Argyris has developed, for example). However, in organizations with a substantial segment of professionally oriented employees, conflict is produced by the organization itself and involves one aspect of the organization against another: professional opposed to bureaucratic principles of organization. It seems unlikely that the cadres of militant leaders and their followers that emerge in support of opposing principles can be explained entirely in terms of personality needs, idiosyncratic maladjustment, and the like. They are fulfilling legitimate, if opposing, social roles. In that sense they are not only deviating from administrative principles, but also conforming to other principles of organization. Professional employees differ from other militant employees in that the cause they champion concerns more than the "rights of an individual"; their cause is a defense of the role of experts within complex organization.

The kinds of conflict that have captured the imaginations of social scientists tend to be the journalistic, large-scale problems that reach the newspapers. But it is in the daily round of routine friction that principles are defended or defeated. Inquiries into the conditions that precipitate belligerent action and produce routine organizational conflicts will expose the "sore spots" of organizations. Such investigation may also challenge presumptions that portray organizations as anything other than systems of checks and balances among temporary coalitions of contenders. In any event, the existence of routine conflicts demonstrates that the "bureaucratic personality" is not the only alternative for organization man. Conflicting principles of organization provide alternatives. These alternatives do not simply pit the individual against the organization; they align one group against another.

In the final analysis, although conflict may not be comforting to administrators, there is little evidence that most forms of conflict are detrimental either to schools or to a faculty's morale. Conflict can keep an organization honest and responsive to new circumstances. The first groups to feel the impact of a squeeze—due to a shortage of resources or new demands from the outside, for example—make known the organization's unresolved problems. Therefore, most organizations seem to depend on conflict, as a way both to maintain some balance between the need for initiative and control, and to bring problems into the open and to a head. Moreover, some groups tend to benefit from any particular conflict.

Indeed, the opportunity people in large-scale organizations have to fight about their beliefs, is perhaps a major compensation for many of the dehumanizing features of bureaucracy; perhaps, therefore, conflict should increase at least in proportion to the less humane aspects of such organizations. Conflict, then, is perhaps a small price to pay for modern organization, and probably one of its lesser costs.

Of course, all of the potential implications of this line of inquiry cannot be examined in one study, but some of the hypotheses explored here can be regarded as the initial necessary step in the direction of approaching these long-range problems.

What seems to be called for at this point is a model of organization in which power and conflict between groups can be analyzed more effectively as natural processes. It is hoped that this study has provided some insight into this problem.

REFERENCES: Chapter 11

Corwin, Ronald G. Professional persons in public organizations. *Educational Administration Quarterly,* Autumn, 1965, 1–22.

Homans, George. *Social behavior: Its elementary forms.* New York: Harcourt, Brace & World, 1961. P. 378.

Waller, Willard. *The Sociology of Teaching.* New York: Wiley, 1932. Reprinted (paper) (1965), p. 10.

Appendices

Appendix A (Part IV of Questionnaire) 29 Employee Orientation Scale Items ($r_n = .84$)[a]

Scale Items	Percentage of Total Sample Responding to Each Alternative ($N = 1,485$)					
	Strongly Agree	Agree	Undecided	Disagree	Strongly Disagree	No Response
Administrative Orientation ($r_n = .81$)						
1. Teachers *should* adjust their teaching to the administration's views of good educational practice.	10.8	57.1	15.1	13.0	3.0	1.0
A. At my school, typically, they *do* adjust their views.	5.8	55.6	20.8	12.3	2.4	3.0
2. The school administration *should* be better qualified than the teacher to judge what is best for education.	18.1	41.0	16.4	17.0	5.9	1.6
A. At my school the administration *is* generally better qualified.	7.2	41.1	27.5	16.8	5.2	2.23
3. Teachers *should* be obedient, respectful and loyal to the principal.	33.1	54.5	7.3	3.2	0.6	1.3
A. At my school the teachers *are*.	12.3	58.1	16.5	9.3	2.1	1.7
4. In case of a dispute in the community over whether a controversial textbook or controversial speaker should be permitted in the school, the teacher *should* look primarily to the judgement of the administration for guidance.	27.3	51.7	10.7	6.8	2.2	1.4

[a] r_n refers to the corrected split half reliability of the scale and subscale items.

Appendix A (cont'd.)

	Percentage of Total Sample Responding to Each Alternative ($N = 1,485$)					
Scale Items	Strongly Agree	Agree	Undecided	Disagree	Strongly Disagree	No Response
Administrative Orientation ($r_n = .81$) *cont'd.*						
5. Personnel who openly critize the administration *should* be encouraged to go elsewhere.	16.2	57.6	17.1	4.7	0.9	3.7
	19.4	32.7	19.2	20.8	6.6	1.4
A. At my school they *are*.	6.6	26.7	37.6	19.8	3.7	5.6
6. Teachers *should not* be influenced by the opinions of those teachers whose thinking does not reflect the thinking of the administration.	5.9	21.0	21.7	35.4	13.5	2.6
A. At my school, typically, they *are not*.	3.3	28.9	37.7	22.0	3.9	4.3
7. The only way a teacher can keep out of "hot water" is to follow the wishes of the top administration.	7.1	28.3	18.9	34.1	8.7	2.8
A. This *is* the case at my school.	6.7	29.6	25.0	28.8	6.4	3.9
Loyalty to the Organization ($r_n = .80$)						
8. What is best for the school is best for education.	4.7	19.0	26.2	32.1	12.3	5.7

A. At my school, teachers *do*. (row 4 — see note)

Percentage of Total Sample Responding to Each Alternative (N = 1,485)

Scale Items	Strongly Agree	Agree	Undecided	Disagree	Strongly Disagree	No Response
Loyalty to the Organization (r_n = .80) *cont'd.*						
9. A good teacher *should* put the interests of his school above everything else.	9.1	33.2	20.4	25.0	9.8	2.5
A. At my school the good teachers *do*.	4.7	31.5	31.1	24.4	4.6	3.7
10. In case of doubt about whether a particular practice is better than another, the primary test *should* be what seems best for the overall reputation of the school.	14.2	41.0	17.5	18.4	6.5	2.4
11. A good teacher *should* put the interests of his department above everything else.	4.4	17.8	18.4	43.9	12.7	2.7
A. At my school the good teachers *do*.	3.6	24.0	27.9	33.6	6.6	4.5
Experience Orientation (r_n = .21)						
12. Pay *should* be in relation to teacher experience.	18.0	45.2	15.4	16.0	3.6	2.0
A. This *is* the case at my school.	21.0	54.9	9.1	8.4	3.2	3.4
13. Often, classroom experience simply gives a teacher the opportunity to practice his mistakes.	6.7	35.6	18.3	25.5	9.0	4.9

Appendix A (cont'd.)

Scale Items	Percentage of Total Sample Responding to Each Alternative ($N = 1,485$)					
	Strongly Agree	Agree	Undecided	Disagree	Strongly Disagree	No Response
Standardization Orientation ($r_n = .70$)						
14. Teachers of the same subject throughout the system *should* follow the same kind of lesson plan.	3.9	19.6	13.7	38.9	22.1	1.9
A. This *is* the case in my system.	0.9	14.6	21.5	40.7	18.2	4.1
15. Teachers *should* teach their course in such a way that a substitute can take over at a moment's notice without serious interruption.	17.4	44.1	12.3	17.0	6.6	2.8
A. At my school teachers *do*.	3.5	29.9	31.3	24.9	5.7	4.7
16. The work of a course *should* be so planned that every child taking the same kind of course throughout the state eventually will cover the same material.	10.4	30.2	16.9	27.0	13.5	2.0
A. This *is* the case at my school.	3.3	23.6	26.1	32.0	10.6	4.5
17. A good teacher *should* be able to efficiently teach the children what they need to know in the limited time available.	15.1	47.6	14.3	15.3	4.0	3.6
A. This *is* the definition of a good teacher at my school.	7.2	37.3	26.3	19.3	4.4	5.5

	Percentage of Total Sample Responding to Each Alternative ($N = 1,485$)					
Scale Items	Strongly Agree	Agree	Undecided	Disagree	Strongly Disagree	No Response
Rules and Procedures Orientation ($r_n = .84$)						
18. Teachers *should* be completely familiar with the written descriptions of the rules, procedures, manuals and other standard operating procedures for running the classroom.	42.3	48.8	4.6	2.0	1.1	1.4
A. At my school, nearly all teachers *are*.	13.2	54.7	18.2	9.9	1.6	2.4
19. The school *should* have a manual of rules and regulations which are actually followed.	43.6	49.4	3.0	1.8	0.8	1.4
A. This *is* the case at my school.	23.3	53.4	10.1	9.1	1.9	2.2
20. Rules stating when the teachers should arrive and depart from the building *should* be strictly enforced.	18.8	44.4	13.1	17.0	5.0	1.8
A. This *is* the case at my school.	9.5	40.5	20.4	23.3	4.1	2.2
21. To prevent confusion and friction among the staff, there *should* be a rule covering almost every problem that might come up at the school.	7.5	26.2	20.0	31.9	12.2	2.2
A. This *is* the case at my school.	3.0	24.1	26.5	34.3	9.2	3.0

Appendix A (cont'd.)

Percentage of Total Sample
Responding to Each Alternative ($N = 1,485$)

Scale Items	Strongly Agree	Agree	Undecided	Disagree	Strongly Disagree	No Response
Rules and Procedures Orientation ($r_n = .84$) *cont'd.*						
22. There *should* be definite rules specifying the topics that are not appropriate for discussion in a classroom.	4.7	16.1	21.4	37.8	17.7	2.3
A. This *is* the case at my school.	1.7	11.4	27.7	41.5	13.7	3.9
23. When a controversy arises about the interpretation of school rules, a teacher *should not* "stick his neck out" by taking a definite position.	3.8	18.8	18.4	40.9	16.4	1.8
A. At my school, typically, they *do not*.	3.8	27.7	30.0	29.7	5.48	3.25
Orientation to the Public ($r_n = .84$)						
24. Teachers *should* take into account the opinions of their community in guiding what they say in class and in their choice of teaching materials.	9.4	48.4	22.9	13.7	3.8	1.9
A. At my school, typically, they *do*.	5.0	48.8	29.8	11.0	2.2	3.3
25. Teachers *should not* publicly advocate a position on the place of religion in the school which differs greatly from the majority opinion of the community.	17.4	40.8	18.2	15.6	4.5	3.6
A. At my school, typically they *do not*.	13.3	50.3	24.2	4.6	1.4	6.2

Percentage of Total Sample
Responding to Each Alternative ($N = 1,485$)

Scale Items	Strongly Agree	Agree	Undecided	Disagree	Strongly Disagree	No Response
Orientation to the Public ($r_n = .84$) *cont'd.*						
26. A good teacher is one who conforms, in general, to accepted standards in the community.	11.0	46.2	16.2	17.8	6.5	2.3
A. At my school, this is the definition of a good teacher.	7.7	41.4	25.2	17.2	4.1	4.4
27. The criterion of a good school *should* be one that serves the needs of the local community.	27.0	51.2	10.2	7.9	2.2	1.6
28. Teachers *should not* attempt to discuss any controversial issues (such as abolishing the House Un-American Activities Committee) which may jeopardize the school's public relations.	3.7	13.1	19.3	41.8	19.9	2.2
A. At my school teachers, typically, *do not*.	3.5	18.8	34.2	30.9	7.9	4.7
29. Local control over schools by school boards represents the most fundamental form of democracy in public education.	11.6	39.7	22.0	16.2	6.5	4.0

369

Appendix B. 16 Professional Orientation Scale Items ($r_n = .65$)

Scale Items	Percentage of Total Sample Responding to Each Alternative ($N = 1,482$)					
	Strongly Agree	Agree	Undecided	Disagree	Strongly Disagree	No Response

Client Orientation ($r = .54, .22, .50$)

1. It *should* be permissible for the teacher to violate a rule if he/she is sure that the best interests of the students will be served in doing so.

	13.0	47.0	22.6	12.6	2.1	2.8
A. At my school this *is* permissible.	3.2	30.9	38.4	20.2	2.6	4.7

2. Unless she is satisfied that it is best for the student, a teacher *should not* do what she is told to do.

	2.8	16.7	29.3	36.4	10.0	4.9
A. At my school, typically, teachers *do not* do what they are told unless they are convinced that it is best for the student.	2.1	16.4	34.4	32.0	8.1	7.0

3. A good teacher *should not* do anything that he believes may jeopardize the interests of his students regardless of who tells him to or what the rules state.

	4.0	19.6	29.8	34.6	7.2	5.0
A. At my school, good teachers *do not*.	2.8	27.5	42.9	16.4	2.9	7.5

Scale Items	Percentage of Total Sample Responding to Each Alternative ($N = 1,482$)					
	Strongly Agree	Agree	Undecided	Disagree	Strongly Disagree	No Response
Colleague Orientation ($r_n = .66$)						
4. Teachers *should* try to live up to what they think are the standards of their profession even if the administration or the community does not seem to respect them.	31.0	55.1	7.6	3.0	1.1	2.4
A. This *is* typically true of the teachers at my school.	7.1	44.7	27.7	13.6	2.3	4.6
5. One primary criterion of a good school *should* be the degree of respect that it commands from other teachers around the state.	14.4	51.8	18.0	10.2	1.9	3.6
6. A teacher *should* try to put his standards and ideals of good teaching into practice even if the rules or procedures of the school prohibit it.	7.5	35.2	29.0	20.2	2.5	5.6
A. At my school typically teachers *do* give priority to their professional ideals.	3.5	37.4	38.7	12.9	1.1	6.4

Appendix B (cont'd.)

		Percentage of Total Sample Responding to Each Alternative ($N = 1,482$)				
Scale Items	Strongly Agree	Agree	Undecided	Disagree	Strongly Disagree	No Response
Colleague Orientation ($r_n = .66$) *cont'd.*						
7. Teachers *should* subscribe to and diligently read the standard professional journals.	19.4	55.1	15.4	7.1	1.2	1.9
A. This *is* the case at my school.	3.4	29.0	41.6	18.9	2.5	4.5
8. Teachers should be active members of at least one professional teaching association, and attend most conferences and meetings of the association.	23.8	57.4	10.5	5.7	1.2	1.6
A. This *is* the case at my school.	6.0	36.1	27.9	22.3	4.1	3.7
9. A teacher *should* consistently practice his/her ideas of the best educational practices even though the administration prefers other views.	6.4	37.3	32.2	17.8	1.8	4.5
A. At my school, typically, teachers *do* give priority to their own ideas.	2.4	33.7	41.4	15.6	1.2	5.7

	Percentage of Total Sample Responding to Each Alternative ($N = 1,482$)					
Scale Items	Strongly Agree	Agree	Undecided	Disagree	Strongly Disagree	No Response
Monopoly of Knowledge (r = .18)						
10. A teacher's skill *should* be based primarily on his acquaintance with his subject matter.	9.2	39.4	18.4	26.2	4.3	2.5
A. This *is* the basis for judging teachers' skill at my school.	3.3	28.5	35.2	25.8	2.9	4.3
11. Teachers *should* be evaluated primarily on the basis of their knowledge of the subject that is to be taught, and their ability to communicate it.	33.3	47.3	7.8	8.0	1.6	2.2
A. This *is* how teachers are evaluated at my school.	8.9	38.4	25.9	19.2	3.1	4.4
12. Schools *should* hire no one to teach unless he holds at least a 4-year bachelors degree.	40.6	37.7	8.8	8.3	2.5	2.3
A. This *is* the case at my school.	23.6	36.5	13.3	17.2	5.4	3.9
13. In view of the teacher shortage, it *should* be permissible to hire teachers trained at non-accredited colleges.	4.2	14.4	16.7	33.1	28.5	3.1
A. My school *does* hire teachers from non-accredited colleges.	1.6	7.8	25.3	30.4	25.9	9.1

Appendix B (cont'd.)

	Percentage of Total Sample Responding to Each Alternative ($N = 1,482$)					
Scale Items	Strongly Agree	Agree	Undecided	Disagree	Strongly Disagree	No Response
Decision Making ($r = .90, .36, .40$)						
14. A teacher *should* be able to make his own decisions about problems that come up in the classroom.	31.1	59.9	5.6	1.2	0.4	1.8
A. At my school teachers *are* allowed to make these decisions.	18.1	53.7	9.1	13.9	2.6	2.6
15. Small matters *should not* have to be referred to someone higher up for final answer.	44.4	50.3	2.3	1.0	0.2	1.8
A. At my school small matters need *not* be referred to someone higher up.	27.3	45.2	7.6	13.3	4.1	2.6
16. The ultimate authority over the major educational decisions *should* be exercised by professional teachers.	25.4	45.4	16.3	8.4	1.3	3.2
A. This *is* the case at my school.	8.5	34.6	30.7	17.2	3.8	5.3

Appendix C. Items in the Centralization of Decision-Making Index Levels of Authority at Which Selected Types of Decisions Are Made and Levels at Which Respondent(s) Believe They Should Be Made

	Percent Indicating Final Authority to Approve or Veto ($N = 1,508$)							
	1 Individual Teacher Involved		2 Teaching Faculty		3 Principal with Teachers		4 Principal	
Type of Decision	Does	Should	Does	Should	Does	Should	Does	Should
I. Items in the Centralization of Professional Decision Making								
1. Selection of required textbooks	17.3	20.4	16.5	18.2	28.9	28.5	1.7	1.4
2. Selection of supplementary reading materials	48.3	47.6	13.6	15.4	14.8	14.4	2.7	0.9
3. Determining if faculty should have tenure	0.1	0.1	0.5	1.1	0.9	3.2	10.8	14.8
4. Giving permission to outside groups to speak to students	2.4	2.9	0.7	1.7	6.1	10.3	49.1	40.1
5. Formulating instructional policy	2.0	1.6	4.4	6.6	15.7	20.6	14.3	10.3
6. Establishing the essential minimum knowledge that students taking a particular course should derive in the course	35.5	30.1	12.7	15.0	20.9	21.3	5.8	3.8
7. Determining what concepts and values are to be taught in a particular course	36.3	31.4	17.1	18.0	22.4	22.5	4.0	2.9

Appendix C (cont'd.)

	Percent Indicating Final Authority to Approve or Veto ($N = 1,508$)							
	1 Individual Teacher Involved		2 Teaching Faculty		3 Principal with Teachers		4 Principal	
Type of Decision	Does	Should	Does	Should	Does	Should	Does	Should
I. *Items in the Centralization of Professional Decision Making (cont'd.)*								
8. The appropriate method for teaching particular courses	57.2	49.9	11.0	11.9	13.1	14.3	2.7	1.5
9. The appropriateness of lecture, discussion, term papers, types and frequency of tests for courses or for the school as a whole	41.4	34.8	16.2	16.7	17.1	19.8	8.0	5.2
10. The appropriate number of hours or homework to be expected of students in various programs	54.1	43.8	10.9	12.3	14.1	17.6	5.0	3.7
11. The appropriate grading curve; the percentage of students to be passed, failed, etc.	40.9	38.2	6.5	7.6	17.2	20.8	11.6	7.0
12. The departmental budget	2.8	3.4	4.2	6.4	16.5	21.7	16.2	13.4
13. What courses are to be taught	0.6	0.9	1.3	3.3	13.4	16.8	15.5	11.9
14. Whether a teacher needs to "tone down" her statements in the classroom	2.1	2.6	0.4	1.8	8.1	12.7	49.7	42.3
Subtotal of Differences		43.3		20.0		36.9		45.9

Percent Indicating Final Authority to Approve or Veto ($N = 1{,}508$)

Type of Decision	5 Superintendent		6 School Boards		7 State Department of Education		Total Diff. Does-Should
	Does	Should	Does	Should	Does	Should	
I. *Items in the Centralization of Professional Decision Making (cont'd.)*							
1. Selection of required textbooks	10.2	4.2	13.5	5.2	0.9	1.0	19.9
2. Selection of supplementary reading materials	5.0	2.1	3.6	1.6	0.2	0.2	9.6
3. Determining if faculty should have tenure	29.2	26.8	33.5	21.9	8.0	8.2	21.1
4. Giving permission to outside groups to speak to students	17.8	16.8	9.1	0.7	0.1	0.2	24.2
5. Formulating instructional policy	32.3	28.0	14.3	9.0	1.2	1.8	21.7
6. Establishing the essential minimum knowledge that students taking a particular course should derive in the course	3.9	2.7	1.7	0.7	3.1	4.3	13.5
7. Determining what concepts and values are to be taught in a particular course	3.4	2.2	1.7	0.9	1.7	2.2	9.5
8. The appropriate method for teaching particular courses	1.9	1.1	0.8	0.5	0.5	0.6	11.8

Appendix C (cont'd.)

Percent Indicating Final Authority to Approve or Veto ($N = 1,508$)

	5 Superintendent		6 School Boards		7 State Department of Education		Total Diff.
Type of Decision	Does	Should	Does	Should	Does	Should	Does-Should

I. *Items in the Centralization of Professional Decision Making (cont'd.)*

9. The appropriateness of lecture, discussion, term papers, types and frequency of tests for courses or for the school as a whole	2.8	1.5	0.9	0.7	0.1	0.2	14.2
10. The appropriate number of hours or homework to be expected of students in various programs	2.4	1.3	1.1	0.6	0.2	0.3	18.2
11. The appropriate grading curve; the percentage of students to be passed, failed, etc.	7.6	3.7	2.2	1.0	0.3	0.2	17.2
12. The departmental budget	25.0	18.6	16.5	11.3	0.3	0.4	22.5
13. What courses are to be taught	27.5	23.7	18.7	13.1	7.0	7.3	19.0
14. Whether a teacher needs to "tone down" her statements in the classroom	13.9	10.3	7.4	5.0	0.1	0.1	19.9
Subtotal of Differences		39.9		52.8		3.5	242.3

Percent Indicating Final Authority to Approve or Veto ($N = 1{,}508$)

Type of Tension	1 Individual Teacher Involved		2 Teaching Faculty		3 Principal with Teachers		4 Principal	
	Does	Should	Does	Should	Does	Should	Does	Should
II. *Nonprofessional Decision Making Index*								
1. Determining the required courses	1.1	1.2	1.9	3.8	12.9	16.5	8.7	6.6
2. Adding or dropping courses	0.7	1.4	2.3	4.4	19.3	27.0	23.6	17.4
3. Adding or dropping a program of courses	0.3	0.5	1.9	3.3	13.5	20.6	13.9	10.8
4. Hiring new teachers	0.1	0.1	0.0	0.2	0.2	1.0	5.4	9.0
5. Determining whether faculty members should be promoted to a higher position of authority	0.0	0.1	0.1	0.8	0.7	2.7	15.0	18.8
6. Deciding whether to renew a teacher's contract	0.0	0.0	0.1	0.2	0.3	1.7	12.9	15.1
7. Promoting a teacher to department head or other supervisory position	0.3	0.5	0.2	1.0	1.1	4.4	25.1	25.6
8. Deciding on the proper procedure of handling a student discipline problem	10.0	10.7	0.7	1.4	19.3	20.6	54.4	41.2
9. A teacher's competence to teach	0.5	0.5	0.3	1.9	3.3	7.1	43.2	39.2
10. Whether a controversial textbook should be used	1.6	2.9	2.3	4.5	9.8	17.1	6.5	4.5
Subtotal of Differences	3.3		11.7		38.3		40.7	

Appendix C (cont'd.)

	Percent Indicating Final Authority to Approve or Veto ($N = 1,508$)						
	5 Superintendent		6 School Boards		7 State Department of Education		Total Diff.
Type of Tension	Does	Should	Does	Should	Does	Should	Does-Should
II. *Nonprofessional Decision Making Index (cont'd.)*							
1. Determining the required courses	16.5	13.9	14.3	9.4	30.8	28.1	17.9
2. Adding or dropping courses	20.6	16.8	16.3	10.5	1.2	1.5	26.6
3. Adding or dropping a program of courses	25.6	22.6	23.2	16.3	2.9	2.3	22.3
4. Hiring new teachers	53.6	47.9	32.5	23.3	0.1	0.3	19.7
5. Determining whether faculty members should be promoted to a higher position of authority	44.5	40.8	24.2	14.5	0.3	0.6	20.3
6. Deciding whether to renew a teacher's contract	41.3	39.0	34.2	23.8	0.3	0.4	16.5
7. Promoting a teacher to department head or other supervisory position	38.4	34.0	18.2	11.1	0.2	0.3	16.4
8. Deciding on the proper procedure of handling a student discipline problem	4.3	2.9	2.7	1.6	0.0	0.0	18.4
9. A teacher's competence to teach	23.3	19.1	8.2	3.5	5.6	4.8	19.1
10. Whether a controversial textbook should be used	20.7	18.1	35.9	25.5	1.5	1.7	26.0
Subtotal of Differences		33.7		70.2		5.3	203.2

Percent Indicating Final Authority to Approve or Veto ($N = 1,508$)

Type of Decision	1 Individual Teacher Involved		2 Teaching Faculty		3 Principal with Teachers		4 Principal	
	Does	Should	Does	Should	Does	Should	Does	Should
III. *Items not Included in Indices*								
1. Dismissing present teachers	0.0	0.1	0.0	0.5	0.1	1.3	7.4	9.7
2. Ruling on teachers' grievances	0.2	0.3	2.5	4.1	5.2	10.7	19.7	16.0
3. Allowing outside groups to use school property	0.1	0.2	0.1	0.1	0.4	0.9	11.9	12.1
4. Who is to be assigned to teach each course	0.3	0.7	0.3	0.9	6.0	12.0	59.8	48.3
5. Who is qualified to teach each course	0.3	1.1	0.3	1.1	3.5	8.0	36.2	29.8
6. Whether or not a community needs a special school for the mentally gifted	0.1	0.1	0.6	1.7	0.9	2.7	1.1	1.1
7. The proportion of tax money to be allocated to slum schools within the city	0.1	0.1	0.1	0.0	0.1	0.1	0.1	0.2
8. Whether a controversial teacher should be re-hired	0.0	0.1	0.0	0.9	0.9	3.5	5.8	7.3
Subtotal of Differences		1.6		5.6		22.1		25.7
Grand Total		48.2		37.3		97.3		112.3

Appendix C (cont'd.)

Percent Indicating Final Authority to Approve or Veto ($N = 1,508$)

Type of Decision	5 Superintendent		6 School Boards		7 State Department of Education		Total Diff. Does-Should
	Does	Should	Does	Should	Does	Should	
III. *Items not Included in Indices (cont'd.)*							
1. Dismissing present teachers	42.1	38.5	39.5	29.2	0.2	0.7	18.5
2. Ruling on teachers' grievances	30.2	26.1	22.7	17.4	0.7	1.3	20.9
3. Allowing outside groups to use school property	29.2	26.6	45.5	38.9	0.4	0.7	10.3
4. Who is to be assigned to teach each course	18.6	14.8	2.8	2.3	0.5	0.3	23.0
5. Who is qualified to teach each course	29.8	24.1	4.2	2.6	13.1	12.3	20.6
6. Whether or not a community needs a special school for the mentally gifted	13.9	13.5	51.5	41.5	7.4	8.7	14.6
7. The proportion of tax money to be allocated to slum schools within the city	6.7	7.6	48.8	44.8	10.1	10.2	5.2
8. Whether a controversial teacher should be re-hired	30.9	28.6	45.8	35.3	0.9	0.9	17.9
Subtotal of Differences		23.4		48.8		3.8	131.0
Grand Total		97.0		171.8		12.6	576.5

Appendix D. Complexity Quasi-Scale:
Questions from Questionnaire for Guttman Scale

I. Questions Asked of Principals   Code

1. Suppose that a teacher would like to see a major change in his curriculum area. He goes to see the person immediately above him in the hierarchy; he sends the teacher to see the person above him, etc. What is the *maximum* number of such "levels of authority" (i.e., people above the teacher) that he might have to go through before he reaches the superintendent's office?   Enter actual number

2. How many weeks do you estimate that it might take before the teacher would learn whether or not his idea about the curriculum change has been accepted?   Enter actual number

3. Total number of staff in school system.   Enter actual number

4. Total number of staff in your school (including teachers, administrators, and nonteaching professional staff, such as school nurse).   Enter actual number

5. Total number of full-time teachers (include only personnel actually assigned to teaching duties).   Enter actual number

6. Total number of part-time teachers (include only personnel actually assigned to teaching duties).   Enter actual number

7. Total number of administrators in school system.   Enter actual percent

8. Total number of full-time "line" administrators (i.e., those who have the principal supervisory responsibilities).   Enter actual percent

9. Total number of full-time professional "staff" personnel engaged in nonteaching professional duties (such as school nurse, attendance officer, vocational guidance director, and finance officer) and not included above as an administrator.   Enter actual percent

10. Total number of full-time office, clerical personnel assigned to the school.   Enter actual percent

11. Total number of classes in which there is homogeneous ability grouping.   Enter actual number

Appendix D (con't.)

I. Questions Asked of Principals (cont'd.) — Code

12. Total number of separate vocational training programs (e.g., clerical, industrial, sales, etc.) —i.e., for which *separate* departments are responsible. — Enter actual number

13. Total number of part-time teachers advising extracurricular activities. — Enter actual percent

14. Total number of separate courses offered each year. — Enter actual number

15. Please estimate as accurately as possible the number of "separate levels of authority" (sometimes referred to as the "chain of command" or line of responsibility) in your school. — Enter actual number

16. Please estimate as accurately as possible the number of "separate levels of authority" (sometimes referred to as the "chain of command" or line of responsibility) in your school system. — Enter actual total

II. Questions Asked of Teachers

17. Suppose that a teacher would like to see a major change in his curriculum area. He goes to see the person immediately above him in the hierarchy; he sends the teacher to see the person above him, etc. What is the *maximum* number of such "levels of authority" (i.e., people above the teacher) that he might have to go through before he reaches the superintendent's office? — Enter actual number

Coefficient of reproducibility = .85.
Minimal-marginal reproducibility = .65.

This quasi-scale was ranked according to the Cornell Technique using 28 high schools and 17 variables. Respondent scale ranks were used in analyses with this particular scale.

Appendix E. Supervision Quasi-Scale: Questions from Questionnaire for Guttman Scale

I. Questions Asked Principals

1. What percentage of your teaching faculty do you observe each month?
   a. On the average, what is the length of time of a visitation?

Length	Code
40-60 minutes	0
20-40 minutes	1
10-20 minutes	2
Less than 10	3
Does not observe	4

2. Check the items that describe the type of follow-up experience that you provide after a visitation.
   _____ an evaluation report is filed in the superintendent's office
   _____ a conference is conducted with the teacher shortly after the visitation
   _____ no conference is held unless major difficulties are observed
   _____ a conference is held only when a teacher requests it
   _____ no follow-up experience is provided

Response	Code
Report filed	1
Conference	2
Conference only with difficulty	3
Conference only at teacher's request	4
No follow-up experience	5

3. Now, check the items that describe how you *do* conduct supervision.
   _____ I *do* spend most of my time in the office operating the school
   _____ Someone other than the principal in the school system *does* supervise teachers
   _____ I *am* careful not to neglect teacher supervision

Response	Code
Most of the time in the office	1
Someone else supervises	2
Principal does not neglect supervision	3

4. Now, check the items that describe how you ordinarily *do* conduct supervision.
   I *am* careful to observe that teachers do not violate the principles of learning in their classrooms.

Response	Code
Not checked	1
Checked yes	2

5. I *do not* offer specific advice to a teacher on how to conduct the classroom unless requested by him to do so.

Response	Code
Checked yes	1
Not checked	2

6. Are teachers required to get permission from you to discuss in class controversial topics such as politics, sex education, civil rights, etc.?

Response	Code
No	1
Yes	2

Appendix E (con't.)

Questions Asked Principals

7.	How frequently does the superintendent visit your school?	*Response* Rarely Occasionally Often Very frequently	*Code* 1 2 3 4
8.	In general, would you say that your school is "closely supervised" (in comparison to most schools with which you are familiar)?	*Response* No Yes	*Code* 1 2
9.	How many separate reports are you required to file with the superintendent's office? (enter number) ____daily ____weekly ____monthly ____annually	*Response* None 1-2 annually 3-5 annually 6-10 annually 1-2 monthly 3-4 monthly 1 or more weekly or 1 or more daily	*Code* 1 2 3 4 5 6 7
10.	What percentage of your teaching faculty do you observe each month?	*Percent* 0-9 10-19 20-29 30-39 40-49 50-79 80 and above	*Code* 1 2 3 4 5 6 7

II. Questions Asked Teachers

11.	Do you think that, generally, the administration's evaluations of you have been essentially *accurate* and *fair*?	*Percent of Respondents Who Said "No"* 0-2 3-4 5-6 7-8 9-10 11-12 13-18	*Code* 1 2 3 4 5 6 7
12.	How many times a year are you evaluated by the superintendent?	*Mean Response* 0-9	*Code* Enter actual number

II. Questions Asked Teachers (cont'd.)

13.	How many times a year are you evaluated by the principal?	*Mean Response* 0-9	*Code* Enter actual number
14.	How many times a year are you evaluated by department head?	*Mean Response* 0-9	*Code* Enter actual number

Coefficient of reproducibility = .85.
Minimal-marginal reproducibility = .71.

This quasi-scale was ranked according to the Cornell Technique using 28 high schools and 14 variables. Respondent scale ranks were used in analyses with this particular scale.

Appendix F. Standardization Index: Questions from Questionnaire for Guttman Scale

I. Questions Asked of Principal

1. Check the item that describes your school's policy concerning teachers' lesson plans (check only once except where otherwise indicated):

    1. Teachers have the choice whether or not to make lesson plans.

Response	Code
No	1
Yes	2

    If the response to item No. 1 was No, the respondent was asked to check one of the following:

    Check the item that describes your school's policy concerning teachers' lesson plans (check only once except where otherwise indicated):

2. Lesson plans are expected but there is no provision for reviewing them. (See 3a.)

    Teachers are required to make lesson plans covering
    (a) each day's work
    (b) each week's work
    (c) each unit's work
    (d) the period covered by the lesson plan is optional

Response	Code
	1 (expected only)
(d)	2 (yes; optional)
(c)	3 (yes; unit)
(b)	4 (yes; week)
(a)	5 (yes; day)

    If the response to item No. 1 was No and No. 2 does not apply, the respondent was asked to check one of the following:

    Check the item that describes your school's policy concerning teachers' lesson plans (check only once except where otherwise indicated):

3. Lesson plans are required and filed with the principal's office. (See 3a.)

    Teachers are required to make lesson plans covering
    (a) each day's work
    (b) each week's work
    (c) each unit's work
    (d) the period covered by the lesson plan is optional

Response	Code
	1 (required only)
(d)	2 (yes; optional)
(c)	3 (yes; unit)
(b)	4 (yes; week)
(a)	5 (yes; day)

I. *Questions Asked of Principal (cont'd.)*

If the response to item No. 1 was No and Nos. 2 and 3 did not apply, the respondent was asked to check one of the following:

Check the item that describes your school's policy concerning teachers' lesson plans (check only once except where otherwise indicated):

4. Lesson plans are required and conferences are held with teachers concerning them:
   a. conferences are held very frequently
   b. conferences are held frequently
   c. conferences are held occasionally

   Response
   (c)
   (b)
   (a)

   Code
   1 (required but no conference)
   2 (occasionally)
   3 (frequently)
   4 (very frequently)

Answer *either* Number 5 or 6:

5. Check the item that describes your school's policy concerning textbooks.

   A teacher is responsible to see that the content in textbook is completed in the course of a year.

   Response
   No
   Yes

   Code
   1
   2

6. Check the item that describes your school's policy concerning textbooks.

   Textbooks can be used as references or as guidelines for teachers rather than as material to be covered.

   Response
   No
   Yes

   Code
   1
   2

7. Is there a handbook or written description of your job? How specific is it?

   Response
   No
   Yes, very general
   Yes, general
   Yes, specific
   Yes, very specific

   Code
   1
   2
   3
   4
   5

8. Are you bothered by rules and regulations (or "red tape")?

   Response
   No
   Yes

   Code
   1
   2

Appendix F (cont'd.)

I. Questions Asked of Principal (cont'd.)

9.	What is the average class size in the English program?	*Number* 20-24 25 26-28 29-30 31-32	*Coded* 1 (very small) 2 (small) 3 (medium) 4 (large) 5 (very large)

II. Questions Asked Teachers

10.	Is there a standard lesson plan or curriculum guide for your principal course on file with the administration, which prescribes the course material to be covered and/or the preferred classroom procedures?	*Mean Response* Teacher prepared— no Teacher prepared— no to yes Teacher prepared— not followed Teacher prepared— seldom followed Teacher prepared— seldom to occasionally followed	*Code* 1 2 3 4 5
11.	If the answer to question 10 is yes, did *you* prepare the plan or guide?	*Percent Who Respond "No"* 0-15 16-22 23-29 30-36 37-43 44-50 51-72	*Code* 1 2 3 4 5 6 7
12.	Did you prepare the plan or guide?	*Percent Who Respond "Yes"* 9-14 15-19 20-24 25-29 30-34 35-39 40-49	*Code* 1 2 3 4 5 6 7

II. Questions Asked Teachers (cont'd.)

13. If the answer to question 10 is yes, how frequently do you actually follow it closely?

	Percent Who Respond Frequently or Very Frequently	Code
	0-2	1
	3-5	2
	6-8	3
	9-11	4
	12-14	5
	15-17	6
	18-26	7

Answer either 14 or 15:

14. How would you describe your authority over the tests which you administer examining the students over the content of their course work?

    Tests are given entirely at the teacher's option.

	Percent Who Respond "Yes"	Code
	1-15	1
	16-25	2
	26-35	3
	36-45	4
	46-55	5
	56-65	6
	66-100	7
	0	0

15. How would you describe your authority over the tests which you administer examining the students over the content of their course work?

    Tests are required, but they are designed by the individual classroom teacher.

	Percent Who Respond "Yes"	Code
	1-15	1
	16-25	2
	26-35	3
	36-45	4
	46-55	5
	56-100	6
	0	0

Coefficient of reproducibility = .84.
Minimal-marginal reproducibility = .74.

This quasi-scale was ranked according to the Cornell Technique using 21 high schools and 15 variables. Respondent scores, rather than scale ranks, were used in analysis with this particular index.

Appendix G. The Way You See It

Code Number _____

PART III.

Below is a list of incidents which have occurred in different schools throughout the country. We are interested in getting your reactions to these situations. There is no right or wrong answer. Just imagine yourself in each situation. Indicate (1) what *you would* do in each of these situations and (2) what is *likely* to happen when such a situation arises at your school.

1. The assistant principal told a teacher that he was too "outspoken" in criticizing certain policies of the school and that this was causing unrest among faculty members. The teacher continued to be critical of certain administrative policies.

    A. What would *you do* in the situation described above? (Check only one.)
    _____1. Comply with superior's request
    _____2. Try to compromise
    _____3. Seek support of colleagues
    _____4. Ask for an investigation by a professional organization
    _____5. Refuse to comply with request
    _____6. Quit the job

    B. What do you anticipate will happen to you if you do not comply with the above request? (Check only one.)
    _____1. No disapproval or mild disapproval from the administration
    _____2. Strong disapproval but no formal action from the administration
    _____3. Loss of reputation
    _____4. Loss of deserved promotion or deserved salary increase
    _____5. Transferred to less desirable position
    _____6. Dismissal from the school system

    C. Do you think it was *right* and *reasonable* for the assistant principal to make such a demand? _____No _____Yes

2. A mathematics teacher was told by the principal that he was not presenting his subject in the most effective way, and that he should revise his course content and the methods of teaching it. He refused to change his practices on the grounds that his professional society had recommended his procedures.

    A. What would *you do* in the situation described above? (Check only one.)
    _____1. Comply with superior's request
    _____2. Try to compromise
    _____3. Seek support of colleagues
    _____4. Ask for an investigation by a professional organization
    _____5. Refuse to comply with request
    _____6. Quit the job

B. What do you anticipate will happen if you do not comply with the above request? (Check only one.)

    _____1. No disapproval or mild disapproval from the principal
    _____2. Strong disapproval but no formal action from the principal
    _____3. Loss of reputation
    _____4. Loss of deserved promotion or deserved salary increase
    _____5. Transferred to less desirable position
    _____6. Dismissal from the school system

C. Do you think it was *right* and *reasonable* for the principal to make such a demand? _____No   _____Yes

3. The principal requested a teacher not to invite a well-known author to speak to his class because of the speaker's alleged "socialistic leanings." The teacher felt the allegations were unfounded, and that his students would benefit by hearing what he had to say. He proceeded to invite the speaker.

    A. What would *you do* in the situation described above? (Check only one.)

        _____1. Comply with superior's request
        _____2. Try to compromise
        _____3. Seek support of colleagues
        _____4. Ask for an investigation by a professional organization
        _____5. Refuse to comply with request
        _____6. Quit the job

    B. What do you anticipate will happen to you if you do not comply with the above request? (Check only one.)

        1. No disapproval or mild disapproval from the principal
        2. Strong disapproval but no formal action from the principal
        3. Loss of reputation
        4. Loss of deserved promotion or deserved salary increase
        5. Transferred to less desirable position
        6. Dismissal from the school system

    C. Do you think it was *right* and *reasonable* for the principal to make such a demand? _____No   _____Yes

4. The school board rules explicitly stated that teachers should not participate in the local school board elections. One teacher made a public statement that one of the present board members was a professional politician, and otherwise actively engaged in the campaign. He was told to desist.

    A. What would *you do* in the situation described above? (Check only one.)

        _____1. Comply with superior's request
        _____2. Try to compromise
        _____3. Seek support of colleagues
        _____4. Ask for an investigation by a professional organization
        _____5. Refuse to comply with request
        _____6. Quit the job

B. What do you anticipate will happen to you if you do not comply with the above request? (Check only one.)

_____1. No disapproval or mild disapproval from the school board
_____2. Strong disapproval but no formal action from the school board
_____3. Loss of reputation
_____4. Loss of deserved promotion or deserved salary increase
_____5. Transferred to less desirable position
_____6. Dismissal from the school system

C. Do you think it was *right* and *reasonable* for the school board to make such a demand? _____No _____Yes

5. A principal occasionally changed the grade given by one of his teachers if a student's complaint to him seemed to justify a higher grade. One teacher protested and was told by the principal that he had the final authority over whatever happened in his school, and he asked her to understand.

A. What would *you do* in the situation described above? (Check only one.)

_____1. Comply with superior's request
_____2. Try to compromise
_____3. Seek support of colleagues
_____4. Ask for an investigation by a professional organization
_____5. Refuse to comply with request
_____6. Quit the job

B. What do you anticipate will happen to you if you do not comply with the above request? (Check only one.)

_____1. No disapproval or mild disapproval from the principal
_____2. Strong disapproval but no formal action from the principal
_____3. Loss of reputation
_____4. Loss of deserved promotion or deserved salary increase
_____5. Transferred to less desirable position
_____6. Dismissal from the school system

C. Do you think it was *right* and *reasonable* for the principal to make such a demand? _____No _____Yes

6. The administration requested teachers not to use a standard textbook in American government because it was "socialistically" inclined. A history teacher felt that the book was the best available and proceeded to submit an order for it.

A. What would *you do* in the situation described above? (Check only one.)

_____1. Comply with superior's request
_____2. Try to compromise
_____3. Seek support of colleagues
_____4. Ask for an investigation by a professional organization
_____5. Refuse to comply with request
_____6. Quit the job

B. What do you anticipate will happen to you if you do not comply with the above request? (Check only one.)

_____ 1. No disapproval or mild disapproval from the administration
_____ 2. Strong disapproval but no formal action from the administration
_____ 3. Loss of reputation
_____ 4. Loss of deserved promotion or deserved salary increase
_____ 5. Transferred to less desirable position
_____ 6. Dismissal from the school system

C. Do you think it was *right* and *reasonable* for the administration to make such a demand? _____ No _____ Yes

7. The administration changed a course of study which included philosophy and music appreciation to one which was based strictly on the sciences and mathematics. A committee of teachers went to see the principal and voiced disapproval; they were told that the administration was in a better position to make the decision due to the complexity of the issue. One teacher complained to the school board.

A. What would *you do* in the situation described above? (Check only one.)

_____ 1. Comply with superior's request
_____ 2. Try to compromise
_____ 3. Seek support of colleagues
_____ 4. Ask for an investigation by a professional organization
_____ 5. Refuse to comply with request
_____ 6. Quit the job

B. What do you anticipate will happen to you if you do not comply with the above request? (Check only one.)

_____ 1. No disapproval or mild disapproval from the administration
_____ 2. Strong disapproval but no formal action from the administration
_____ 3. Loss of reputation
_____ 4. Loss of deserved promotion or deserved salary increase
_____ 5. Transferred to less desirable position
_____ 6. Dismissal from school system

C. Do you think it was *right* and *reasonable* for the administration to make such a demand? _____ No _____ Yes

8. A chemistry teacher took an active stand in favor of water fluoridation in a community that was divided on the issue. The superintendent requested him to avoid becoming further involved in the issue. He refused.

A. What would *you do* in the situation described above? (Check only one.)

_____ 1. Comply with superior's request
_____ 2. Try to compromise
_____ 3. Seek support of colleagues
_____ 4. Ask for an investigation by a professional organization
_____ 5. Refuse to comply with request
_____ 6. Quit the job

B. What do you anticipate will happen to you if you do not comply with the above request? (Check only one.)

_____1. No disapproval or mild disapproval from the superintendent
_____2. Strong disapproval but no formal action from the superintendent
_____3. Loss of reputation
_____4. Loss of deserved promotion or deserved salary increase
_____5. Transferred to less desirable position
_____6. Dismissal from the school system

C. Do you think it was *right* and *reasonable* for the superintendent to make such a demand? _____No _____Yes

9. The administration issued a directive that teachers should help to improve parent-teacher relations. A parent-teacher committee was established to select textbooks. One math teacher refused to participate, stating that the parents of such a committee are not qualified to select textbooks.

    A. What would *you do* in the situation described above? (Check only one.)

    _____1. Comply with superior's request
    _____2. Try to compromise
    _____3. Seek support of colleagues
    _____4. Ask for an investigation by a professional organization
    _____5. Refuse to comply with request
    _____6. Quit the job

    B. What do you anticipate will happen to you if you do not comply with the above request? (Check only one.)

    _____1. No disapproval or mild disapproval from the administration
    _____2. Strong disapproval but no formal action from the administration
    _____3. Loss of reputation
    _____4. Loss of deserved promotion or deserved salary increase
    _____5. Transferred to less desirable position
    _____6. Dismissal from school system

    C. Do you think it was *right* and *reasonable* for the administration to make such a demand? _____No _____Yes

10. One school system did not permit students to read several American literature classics by Faulkner, Hemingway, Steinbeck, and others. One teacher actively sought to have the policy repealed by soliciting the support of certain influential citizens in the community. The principal asked her to desist her campaign against the policy because she was stirring up trouble for the school. She refused saying that her action had the support of the National English Teacher's Association.

    A. What would *you do* in the situation described above? (Check only one.)

    _____1. Comply with superior's request
    _____2. Try to compromise
    _____3. Seek support of colleagues
    _____4. Ask for an investigation by a professional organization
    _____5. Refuse to comply with request
    _____6. Quit the job

B. What do you anticipate will happen to you if you do not comply with the above request? (Check only one.)

_____1. No disapproval or mild disapproval from the principal
_____2. Strong disapproval but no formal action from the principal
_____3. Loss of reputation
_____4. Loss of deserved promotion or deserved salary increase
_____5. Transferred to less desirable position
_____6. Dismissal from the school system

C. Do you think it was *right* and *reasonable* for the principal to make such a demand? _____No _____Yes

11. In one school, male teachers received preference in promotions. A group of women teachers at the school complained to the school board. They were told that the situation would be changed, but it was not. One female teacher who was passed over for a promotion wrote a letter to the NEA and State Department of Education. The principal ordered her to stop stirring up trouble.

    A. What would *you do* in the situation described above? (Check only one.)

    _____1. Comply with superior's request
    _____2. Try to compromise
    _____3. Seek support of colleagues
    _____4. Ask for an investigation by a professional organization
    _____5. Refuse to comply with request
    _____6. Quit the job

    B. What do you anticipate will happen to you if you do not comply with the above request? (Check only one.)

    _____1. No disapproval or mild disapproval from the principal
    _____2. Strong disapproval but no formal action from the principal
    _____3. Loss of reputation
    _____4. Loss of deserved promotion or deserved salary increase
    _____5. Transferred to less desirable position
    _____6. Dismissal from the school system

    C. Do you think it was *right* and *reasonable* for the principal to make such a demand? _____No _____Yes